De Gaulle *and the* Free French

in Bewdley
1942 - 1944

12 Nov 99
To Chris
from Nigel.

Nigel Knowles

This book is dedicated to Columb and Merryn Howell

STAR AND GARTER PUBLISHERS
18 WELCH GATE
BEWDLEY
WORCS. DY12 2AT
Tel: 01299 402343

Printed by Stargold Ltd., Kidderminster

British Library Cataloguing-in-Publication Data. A Catalogue record for this book is available.

October 1999 - Bewdley Festival

ISBN 0-9519130-9-3

STAR AND GARTER BOOKS

About The Author

Nigel Knowles was born in Worcester in 1946 and lived in Kidderminster until 1978 when he moved to Wood Green, London with his wife Jennifer, daughter Natasha and son Keiran. Nigel has pursued a number of occupations, including being a carpet weaver and a trade union education officer. He gained an Honours Degree in Politics and Certificate of Education. Nigel was five times a parliamentary candidate for the Labour Party and an elected Councillor in Haringey. He remains a Councillor in Bewdley and Kidderminster at Town, District and County level, and was recently Chairman of Wyre Forest District Council. This year Nigel is the Deputy Mayor of Kidderminster and Chairman of Worcestershire County Council.

In 1990, Nigel was one of the Heinemann New Writers, with his comedy, "The Tailors Dummy."

Family Knowles now has a vegetarian restaurant in Horsefair, Kidderminster - "Roots" (01562 751113) - Bon Appetit!

Photo by Natasha Knowles

Other books by Nigel Knowles, still available from 'Star and Garter,' are:

"Those in Favour." ISBN . 0. 9519130. 0.X. Price £5.00
"Observations Inside a Bewdley Ice-Cream Parlour."
ISBN.09519130.18. Price £4.00
"Identity Crisis." ISBN.0.9519130.2.6. Price £4.00
"Lord Lucan - The Letters of Sabrina."
ISBN.0.9519130.3.4. Price £5.00
"Politics, Sex and Garlic Mushrooms."
ISBN.0.9519130.4.2. Price £4.99
"Bewdley 1762 - The Diary of Jack Nowles"
ISBN.09519130.50. Price £4.00
"Bewdley Parish Magazine 1886"
ISBN.09519130.69. Price £6.99
"American Revolution 1776 - Letters from New York, Boston and London"
ISBN.09519130.77. Price £10.00
"Bewdley Parish Magazine 1878 - 1880"
ISBN.09519130.8.5. Price £10.00

De Gaulle *and the* Free French *in Bewdley* 1942 - 1944

Forward

This book is an attempt to record the history of De Gaulle and the Free French in Bewdley during World War Two. I do not for a moment consider myself to be the most apt person to try it. I do not know the French language. I do not have an academically thorough knowledge of either World War Two or indeed the Free French. But what I do have is enthusiasm for the subject and an appetite to get the issue down into a recordable form before it is too late - before a generation passes which was there, and lived with the French in Bewdley during the 1940's.

I have been extremely lucky to have met so many local people who were either around at the time of the Free French or like me, came after and had a genuine interest.

My family moved to Bewdley in 1988 but I have known Bewdley for all of my life. I was born in 1946, the year after the end of World War Two. Bewdley has not changed that much since then - it remains the gem of a Georgian town on the river Severn in Worcestershire.

I have written several books about Bewdley, but only quite recently decided to write this particular one. There is however another book begging to be written and really ought to be - The Americans in Bewdley during World War Two!

I was always interested in local, national and international history. The Free French idea had rumbled on with me since 1988. In the early summer of 1998 I decided to do something about it. I put a small advert in Bewdley library along the lines of - "De Gaulle and the Free French in Bewdley during World War Two (and the Americans). Do you remember them? Please contact Nigel Knowles etc, etc."

That advert did indeed generate a response from local people which I followed up and documented. Then a couple of months later I walked into the library and saw a wonderful exhibition to commemorate Bewdley's two Twin Towns - Fort Mahon Plage and Vellmar. And there it was! The display of photographs, artifacts and literature of the Free French and their time in Bewdley, in part presented and loaned by Columb and Merryn Howell.

My smouldering interest was ignited by that spark. Indeed, though I were not to have seen the exhibition, I would still have completed a brief history of the Free French in Bewdley. But it would have been tentative and incomplete. I telephoned Columb and Merryn. " I thought you might,' he suggested, then kindly invited me round to compare notes and have a chat. What a revelation! Firstly, the warmth of their welcome was wonderful. Secondly, the love they had for the Free French was apparent right away. I returned on two or three occasions and was permitted to photograph much of their Free French archive, with the help of John Pratt a professional photographer, my photographic attempts having previously proven insufficient. John had taken the photographs when Jennifer and I were married in 1970 and he had know Columb for about as long, so our photographic session together was an extra pleasure.

I wish to say in as plain language as possible that I dedicate this book to Columb and Merryn. The flame of the Free French burns clear and bright with them. I am sure that their stewardship and advocacy is recognised in the proper places - for me they are the most excellent and appropriate ambassadors.

The Howell family indeed bought Ribbesford House, home of the Free French Officer Cadets between 1942 and 1944, immediately after the War's cessation in 1947. Their interest and devotion therefore seem all the more worthy. What if Ribbesford House were to have been purchased by a leisure company or a self -made millionaire? That prospect seems awful.

Columb and Merryn continuing the family tradition are regular hosts to pilgrims who venture to Ribbesford House from France, England and many other countries. Their knowledge of the Free French in Bewdley is unique and unsurpassed. They have been of the greatest help to me and I thank them sincerely. I know it is their intention to publish their own history of Ribbesford House and Bewdley's Free French.

I mentioned earlier the logic of a history of the Americans in Bewdley during World War Two. Indeed the local people remember the Yanks as well as the French. But the reason why I might not be able to write, 'The Americans in Bewdley,' is the probable lack of photographic and documentary evidence - a great pity. But if the idea were to be extended to, 'The Americans in Bewdley, Kidderminster and Stourport on Severn during World War Two,' the project might yet get under way.

The Yanks were indeed in our three local towns in their thousands with their Jeeps, armoured cars and tanks, their food, their gum and their money. They were polite, kind and generous - all other stories of fighting, swearing and stealing the local women remain just that - stories!

However, the period of De Gaulle and the Free French in Bewdley needed to be placed in context.

In order to complete my study I employed several methods of investigation to provide evidence of the French presence. The methods were:

A The recollections of the local people

B Use of local and national newspapers

C The publication of Bewdley Town Council Minutes and Reports

D Photographic and Documentary evidence of the Free French in Ribbesford House and Bewdley.

The history of the Free French is a tribute to the values of freedom for which their men and women played a full part, as did the men and women of Bewdley - military and civilian - during the dark years of World War Two. Indeed, Ribbesford House and Bewdley were places where that freedom was nurtured and defended. About 70* of the 211 Free French Cadets who stayed at Ribbesford House died later in the battles of Europe and North Africa, as did many of our local troops from Bewdley, Kidderminster and Stourport. My own father, Arthur served as a sargeant with the Worcestershire Regiment and the Royal Electrical and Mechanical Engineers (17th Light Anti Aircraft Unit), in Tunisia, Libya, Egypt, Sicily, Italy and Austria, thankfully surviving.

The Wyre Forest area was a hive of activity during World War Two. Thousands of troops were based in the district - British, American, French - and thousands of civilians were involved in the war effort. The Kidderminster and Stourport carpet factories were quickly turned to war production after 1939.

The list below is not fully comprehensive but it is correct information, according to Tomkinson and contemporary local people, including my uncle, George Timmis, aged 89 years who worked at the engineering company Bradley and Turton in Kidderminster for over 40 years.

* (The figure of 70 Free French includes a number who were killed later in Indo-China)

The following armaments were made: shells, bullets, ammunition, guns and mountings, parachutes, engineering components, motor parts, aeroplane engines and spitfire cockpits, blankets etc.

Kidderminster Factories:

Imperial Chemical Industries made bullets, bombs and small arms under licence in the factories; **Naylors Ltd.** became a Royal Navy Stores; **Victoria Carpets** was the base of Shorts Aircraft design team; **Brintons** made aeroplane parts, tools, compasses, repaired Bren Gun carriers, made generating sets, Bailey Bridge parts, pumps etc; **Carpets Trades** produced cases and assembled munitions, Spitfire Cockpits under licence from Vickers; **Summerfield Factory** tested and filled explosives, made over six million rounds of ammunition; **Victoria Carpets** was home to Short Brothers aeroplane manufacturers; and **Pike Mills** for the Blackburn Aero Company; **Cooke Brothers** - Lockheed Brakes; **Adams** - BSA produced guns; **Carpet Manufacturing Company** used by Brook Tools; **SDF** - many forgings, engines, engineering components.

Other local companies: **Jellymans, Childema.**

Uncle George explained **Bradley** and **Turton** were engaged in making machines to produce gun shells from 1937; **Tomkinsons** produced - automatic components, blankets, webbing, ducking, tarpaulin, mortar bombs, aircraft parts, coolers for Lancaster Bombers, parachutes. My mother Florence worked there during the war.

At Oldington, between Kidderminster and Stourport was the 297th U.S. Military Hospital (partly underground) and at Wolverley the 52nd U.S. Army Field ~Hospital.

Drakelow - Underground factory with 9 miles of tunnels, made aeroplane engines from July 1941.

Bradley and **Turton** Engineers, made castings for Wickmans of Ham Lane, Coventry 4, 5 and six spindle lathe horizontal borers, to produce the shells for Bopha anti-aircraft guns, hydraulic

presses for Ministry of Supply (7 tons of metal).
In the surrounding countryside, men and women worked on the land to produce the food which was so vital (and rationed), during the War. Many women were enlisted into the Land Army and based in the area. The Home Guard were active and evacuees were placed here from Birmingham, London and even further afield.. Our local people, civilian and military, played a full part in the fight against the Nazis - we owe them a debt.

FOOTNOTE

On 26th June 1999, Monsieur Pierre Lefranc, President de L'amicale des Cadets de la France Libre, presented a ceremonial sword to the town of Bewdley in recognition of the association between the Ecole Militaire des Cadets, the Town of Bewdley and Ribbesford House. The ceremony took place at Bewdley Museum, part of the Guildhall, outside of which General de Gaulle took the salute some 57 years ago. The flame still burns brightly.

Nigel Knowles
'Star and Garter House'
18 Welch Gate
Bewdley
30th September 1999.

De Gaulle
and the
Free French
in Bewdley
1942 - 1944

Contents

Chapter One

1939
BRITAIN AT WAR

The Declaration of War at 11 am on 3rd September 1939 was the culmination of many years of economic and political crisis and military hostility in Europe, Africa and Asia. The Civil War in Spain 1936, the Italian invasion of Ethiopia in 1935 and Japanese occupation of Chinese Manchuria 1931 were terrible examples of the international crisis.

Europe had been unstable since the World War One Armistice in 1918. The collapse of Empires - Russian, Austro - Hungarian, Ottoman, German and the sweeping away of Monarchies had resulted in new nations being formed and new claims for territory, particularly by Germany.

The Democracies of Britain and France feared the new dictators - Stalin in Russia after 1924, Mussolini in Italy 1922,Franco in Spain 1936 and Hitler in Germany after 1933. Hitler occupied the de-militarised Rhineland on 7th March 1936, Austria 11th - 12th March 1938, Czechoslovakia 15th March 1939 and finally invaded Poland on Friday 1st September 1939. In the midst of Hitlers aggression, Mussolini invaded the Kingdom of Albania of Good Friday, 7th April 1939.

Britain and France had no choice but to declare War on Germany and the Axis Powers on 3rd September 1939. For the second time in the lives of my parents and millions of other people across the world, Britain and her Empire was at war with Germany. The following pages reflect the national and local situation at the time.

The Premier speaks to the nation 3 September, 1939

"BRITAIN IS AT WAR WITH GERMANY"

In a broadcast from Downing Street, at 11.15 a.m. on Sunday, 3 Sept., 1939, the Prime Minister said:—

"THIS morning the British Ambassador in Berlin handed the German Government a final Note stating that unless we heard from them by eleven o'clock that they were prepared at once to withdraw their troops from Poland a state of war would exist between us.

"I have to tell you now that no such undertaking has been received, and that consequently this country is at war with Germany.

"You can imagine what a bitter blow it is to me that all my long struggle to win peace has failed. Yet I cannot believe that there is anything more, or anything different that I could have done and that would have been more successful.

"Up to the very last it would have been quite possible to have arranged a peaceful and honourable settlement between Germany and Poland, but Hitler would not have it.

"He had evidently made up his mind to attack Poland whatever happened, and although he now says he put forward reasonable proposals which were rejected by the Poles, that is not a true statement.

"The proposals were never shown to the Poles, nor to us, and though they were announced in a German broadcast on Thursday night Hitler did not wait to hear comments on them, but ordered his troops to cross the Polish frontier. His action shows convincingly that there is no chance of expecting that this man will ever give up his practice of using force to gain his will. He can only be stopped by force.

"We and France are today, in fulfilment of our obligations, going to the aid of Poland, who is so bravely resisting this wicked and unprovoked attack on her people.

"We have a clear conscience. We have done all that any country could do to establish peace.

"The situation in which no word given by Germany's ruler could be trusted and no people or country could feel themselves safe has become intolerable.

"And now that we have resolved to finish it I know that you will all play your part with calmness and courage.

"At such a moment as this the assurances of support that we have received from the Empire are a source of profound encouragement to us.

"When I have finished speaking certain detailed announcements will be made on behalf of the Government. Give these your closest attention.

"The Government have made plans under which it will be possible to carry on the work of the nation in the days of stress and strain that may be ahead. But these plans need your help.

"You may be taking your part in the fighting services or as a volunteer in one of the branches of civil defence. If so, you will report for duty in accordance with the instructions you have received.

"You may be engaged in work essential to the prosecution of war, for the maintenance of the life of the people—in factories, in transport, in public utility concerns, or in the supply of other necessaries of life.

"If, so, it is of vital importance that you should carry on with your jobs.

"Now may God bless you all. May He defend the right. It is the evil things that we shall be fighting against—brute force, bad faith, injustice, oppression and persecution—and against them I am certain that the right will prevail."

BRITISH ULTIMATUM EXPIRES. The British ultimatum to Germany demanding the immediate withdrawal of her troops from Poland expired at 11 a.m. on Sunday morning, 3 September, 1939. The nation, still ignorant of the fatal hour, but knowing that only a miracle could avert the death-struggle between the forces of fear and of freedom, steeled itself for the ordeal that lay before it. To the democratic governments and peoples of Britain and France fell the awful responsibility of defending the freedom of the world against Nazi domination.

Man of the moment

3 September, 1939

WINSTON CHURCHILL AT THE ADMIRALTY. It was with an immense sense of relief that the British public learned on 3 September that Mr. Churchill had been appointed First Lord of the Admiralty. Twenty-five years earlier, in 1914, he had held the same post with outstanding success. Although Mr. Churchill had been virtually a political exile since 1929, he nevertheless had retained immense prestige with the British public. His repeated warnings of the ever-growing menace of Nazidom to the peace of Europe, had earned him the title of Nazi Enemy No. 1. Here he pauses on the steps of the Admiralty as he arrives to take up his new post.

HORRORS OF INVADED POLAND. The horrors of modern aerial warfare are forcefully illustrated by this picture of a little Warsaw boy squatting miserably among the wreckage of what was his home. Scenes such as this were common all over Poland where Goering's air force rained death and destruction on countless open towns and brought untold misery and hardship to Poland's civilian population. In spite of constant raids, however, and the indiscriminate damage they wrought, the morale of Poland's civilians remained unshaken to the end.

BOROUGH IS PREPARED

A.R.P. AND HOSPITAL SERVICES

RECEPTION OF EVACUEES

In addition to putting the finishing touches to Kidderminster's A.R.P. work, and bringing the borough's civil defence services up to the highest pitch of efficiency, Kidderminster is now carrying out plans for the reception of several thousands of evacuees from Birmingham and other crowded industrial areas. The local organisation had made complete preparations to deal with this large influx of "guests"—mainly schoolchildren, and the first contingent is due to arrive at Kidderminster to-day (Friday). Another contingent, including younger children, also blind persons and expectant mothers, will arrive in the town the next day.

Details of the plans made by various local organisations to meet the needs of the civil population in the event of war are given in this column.

Emphasis of some phases of the emergency work is necessary. In the first place, all A.R.P. personnel must report at once to the heads of their departments when an emergency is declared.

Lighting restrictions would immediately be put into force, and it will be the duty of all responsible persons to obscure a lights of business premises.

The Mayor (Alderman H. W. Cheshire) has made the excellent suggestion that the townspeople should do their shopping early, before lights are needed in the shops, and that would be a "safety first" as well as a fuel economy method.

AIR RAID WARNING

At the sounding of an air raid warning—five seconds blast repeated at

EMPLOYMENT EXCHANGE

The Ministry of Labour is working with a considerably augmented staff; all the members of the permanent staff having been kept in close touch with the premises throughout the week, subject to being called upon for duty at short notice.

The local arrangements to be carried out in conjunction with the Unemployment Assistance Board provide for payment of evacuees who require immediate assistance and reckoned in the following categories: Expectant mothers, mothers or persons acting as mothers with children under five years old, and others transferred under the scheme who are carrying with them an official transfer certificate.

Payment will be made at the following places on the days and times indicated:

Kidderminster (Arch Hill): First day after arrival, 9 a.m. to 7 p.m.

Bewdley (The Institute): Second day after arrival, 10 a.m. to 6 p.m.

Rock (Gorst Hill Village Hall): Second day after arrival, 10 a.m. to 3 p.m.

Shatterford Colliery Offices: Second day after arrival, 3.30 p.m. to 6.30 p.m.

Cookley Methodist School Room: Second day after arrival, 10 a.m. to 1 p.m.

Blakedown Re reation Room: Second day after arrival, 2.30 p.m. to 3.30 p.m.

Chaddesley Corbett Institute: Second day after arrival, 4 p.m. to 6.30 p.m.

Stourport Congregational Church: First day after arrival, 9 a.m. to 7 p.m.

Hundred House, Great Witley: Second day after arrival, 10 a.m. to 12 noon.

Little Witley Post Office: Second day after arrival, 12.30 to 1.30 p.m.

Astley Parish Room: Second day after arrival; 3 p.m. to 4.30 p.m.

Hartlebury (The Talbot): Second day after arrival, 5 to 6.30 p.m.

Clows Top (Crown Inn): Second day after arrival, 5.30 to 6.30 p.m.

Highley Working Men's Club: Second day after arrival, 2 to 6.30 p.m.

Milsom Post Office: Second day after arrival, 10 to 11.30 a.m.

Cleobury Mortimer (Ministry of Labour office): First day after arrival, 9 to 6.30 p.m.

All persons must bring billeting forms with them and be able to say how much

THE EVACUATION SCHEME

CHILDREN ARRIVE TO-DAY

As we go to Press, the first groups of children evacuees from the Smethwick area have arrived in Kidderminster.

They were met by Councillor O. W. Davies and Mr. A. J. Perrett, members of the Billetting Committee, and by helpers from the various districts under the scheme. The children were taken on foot to the High School and Lea Street School, given rations, and then taken by motor 'bus to schools in other parts of the town.

Afterwards, teachers and other helpers were busy conveying them to their temporary homes.

The Billetting Committee have been inundated by car drivers and others willing to help, and advantage is being taken of the offers. This morning a car with a loud-speaking equipment toured the streets of the town, giving information regarding the scheme which has been made complete in all its details.

Teachers from other areas not engaged in the scheme, are also helping with the work.

Mr. D. W. Handley, chief billetting officer, is installed at an office at Caldwall Hall, and enquiries regarding the scheme should be made to him (telephone 619).

The Borough Education Committee have given notice that borough elementary schools will not be opened on Monday, September 4th owing to the evacuation scheme being in operation.

Trains to-day were scheduled to arrive at 12.40, 1.57, and 3.52 p.m. To-morrow (Saturday), more groups consisting of expectant mothers, children under five, and their mothers and guardians, and a few blind and crippled persons will arrive by trains at 11.5, 11.30 a.m., 12.43 p.m., and 1.33 p.m.

IF WARNING COMES

Co-ordinating Officer's Instructions

The Borough Co-ordinating Officer, Captain G. Rainsford, O.B.E., seen in the control office, 16, Vicar Street (next to Town Hall) on Thursday night, said: "Immediately the warning comes to Kidderminster, the town can be put on a

EXAMINATIO RESULTS

AT KIDDERMI GRAMMAR SC

From the point of vie tions, the school year several respects the best H. S. Steward, who las well in the higher sch examination, broke a lar ground and has successf Intermediate Bachelor examination of London Economics.

In the higher sch examination of the No sities, G. N. Cald obtaine in physics and the high in pure mathematics, matics, and in the scholarship paper in ph

RINTON'S WEDDING

NY AT GLASGOW

ND BRIDEGROOM

Beck: Door stops.
Bate and family: Silver
ase dish in silver stand.
. H. Bean and the Misses
r.
Hugh Chance: Cut glass
broidered towel.
F. P. Evers: Travelling
ut glass dishes.
. V. Evers: Quilted case.
Mrs. Eddy: Silver Biscuit
moe: Lace mats.
ery: Decanter and glasses.
Cream and gold early tea
J. Howard and Miss
offee set.
orman Halbert: Fireproof
. L. Henderson: Swedish
Hutton: Shooting stick.
me: Cheque.
ooking glass.
Krause: Picture.
Ding: Glass vase.
vil Lloyd: Silver salver.
r Cheque.
Dudley Lambert, Miss
et.
ather file.
ad the Misses McClean:
and knife and travelling
L. C. Marks: Green and
: tea set.
eque.
smyth: Table cloth.
Handkerchief case.
e: Silver coasters.
C. Parsons: Glass vase.
Page: Silver tea strainer
Miss Boyds: Desk set.
Agate ash tray.
ling: Table mats.
ade: Enamel and silver
case and diamond and
ads: Thermos jug.
ck and inkpot on agate
. Odo Russell: Wooden
ward and family: Cheque.
Williams-Thomas: Glass
ht: Cocktail shaker.
desce: Silver muffin dish.
Harcourt Webb: Silver
Mrs. H. de Vere Watson
Table mats.
Webb: Three-tiered tea
on satin under glass.
er mug.
ry Chaplin: Silver Louis
: Address book.
ame: Painted glass mats.
Considine: Swedish glass
n tray to match.

Mr. and Mrs. J. Baker: Hand-painted tray.
Miss Betty Baron: Dresden china box.
Colonel Aubrey Maude: Silver mustard pot.
Major and the Misses Blew: Picnic case.
The Misses Mockett: Antique ormolu box with miniature in lid.
Mr. and Mrs. Austin Coley: Silver teaspoons.
Mr. and Mrs. H. Elliott and family: Brown glass vase.
Mrs. and the Misses Fearbye Evans: Early morning tea set and tray.
Mr. and Mrs. Alfred Eura and Miss Eura: Handbag.
Mr. and Mrs. R. Forrest: Green glass bowl.
Mr. and Mrs. O. Greenbrook: Cheque.
Miss Gibbons: Mother-o'-pearl box.
Mrs. T. Hanson: Cut glass dressing table set.
Captain and Mrs. and Miss Holder: Umbrella handle.
Mr. and Mrs. Howard Hatton: Cheque.
Miss Rachel Hatton: Address and telephone book.
Mr. and Mrs. Higgs Walker: Leather blotter.
Mr. and Mrs. Leonard Hillman: Large ornamental spoons.
Mr. and Mrs. G. C. Leslie: Lalique bowl.
Mr. and Mrs. Rupert Lee: Japanese knife.
Mr. Peter Montgomery: Silver double sauce boat.
Dr. and Mrs. Mackenzie: Ornamental tree.
Mr. and Mrs. Ivor Mills: Leather travelling clock.
Mrs. Kenneth Marsh: Cut glass bowl.
Miss Diana Myburgh: Handkerchiefs.
Mr. and Mrs. Pakenham: Irish lace gloves.
Dr. and Mrs. Drury Pennington: Cut glass vase.
Mr. and Mrs. G. N. Percival Humphries: Silver sauce boat.
Mrs. A. H. and Mr. R. Pearson: Lobster cutter and picks.
Mr. and Mrs. R. Bell: Dagger paper knife.
Miss Rutherford: Book.
Mr. and Mrs. Thorp: Brent spray and antique Bohemian glass bottle.
Mr. and Mrs. Geoffrey Tomkinson: cheque.
Mr. and Mrs. Gerald Tomkinson: Silver sweet dish.
Mr. and Mrs. Geoffrey Thomas: China box with ormolu mount and raised flowers on lid.
Lieut.-Col. and Mrs. Thornfield: Fountain pen.
Mrs. Nicholas Woodcock: Cut glass sherry glasses.
Mrs. H. Ebbsley Welch: Green car rug.
Mr. and Mrs. T. Ward: Silver napkin rings.
Mr. and Mrs. H. S. and Miss Williams-Thomas: Cut glass sugar bowls, dessert plates and dessert dish.
Mr. and Mrs. J. F. West: Silver photograph frame.
Brigadier-General and Mrs. G. R. Woodruffe: Three decanters on stand.
Miss Ida Weavers: Black lacquered tray.
Mr. and Mrs. Trygve Young: Blue enamel cigarette box.
Mr. Shoemonde: Jam jar.
Major and Mrs. Gordon Mockett: Baby travelling clock and chain.

OBITUARY

MRS. FLORENCE BEACH

The funeral took place at Cookley Church on Saturday, of Mrs. Florence Beach, of 9, Wolverhampton Road, Broadwaters, who passed away on August 31st, aged 74 years. The service was conducted by the Vicar, the Rev. W. L. Gutch.

Floral tributes were sent by her loving husband; Lizzie and Alice (daughters); Clara and Ewart; Iris and Basil; Martha and Beryl; Bill and Madge; Al, Edgar and Madge; Nellie; Alice and family, U.S.A.; Sid and family, West Bromwich; Maria, Albert and family; Nina and Fred; Gladys and Doris; Vera and George; Em and Reg; Mrs. G. Bennett and family; Mrs. Coats and family; Mrs. Baggott and family; all at Broadwaters Post Office; friends and neighbours, Broadwaters; Axminster department of Tomkinsons, Ltd.; sewing department of Brintons, Ltd.; the Childerma Carpet Co., Ltd.; Mrs. Crump; Edith and Gordon.

MRS. T. H. LURRING

The funeral took place at Kidderminster on Tuesday, of Mrs. Annie Lurring, aged 66, wife of Mr. Thomas Henry Lurring, of "Sunnyside," Franche.

The Rev. G. John, priest-in-charge of Franche Church, officiated.

Mrs. Lurring died on Saturday, at the residence of her son, Dr. R. F. Lurring, at 23 Church Street, where she had been staying. A native of County Wicklow, she lived in Dublin

METHODIST PLANS

In the Crisis

WELCOME TO NEW MINISTERS

On Wednesday the Kidderminster and Stourport Methodists decided after the end of summer time to hold evening services in the churches in the circuit from 3 to 4. This decision was reached at the quarterly meeting at Mill Street Methodist Church on Wednesday, presided over by the Rev. J. H. ......, supported by the Revs. A. Fenton, J. B. Dunkley, S. J. Bampton, Pastor Nell, and the circuit stewards (Mr. A. Edwards and Mr. A. Gaston).

Tea was served in the school room, provided by the Mill Street Society stewards and their wives, and at the close hearty thanks were tendered by Mr. W. H. Busby (Rock) and Mr. Parton (Lickhill), to which Mrs. E. J. Price replied.

At the business session a hearty welcome, brief but none the less sincere, was given to the new ministers (Rev. Alfred Fenton and Mrs. Fenton, Mill Street, and Pastor Nell, Birmingham Road. This was expressed by Mr. A. Edwards, Mr. E. J. Price and Mr. J. F. Woolley. The latter referred to the fact that in past days the circuit had provided four presidents of the Conference besides several chairmen of the district, so that these new pastors had something worthy to maintain. Happy replies were given by the Rev. A. Fenton and Pastor Nell, the former stating that he loved circuit work and looked upon chairmanships as a penance.

CONGRATULATIONS

Congratulations to Pastor Drake and Mr. R. W. Mumford were passed on their

KIDDERMINSTER HOSPITAL CARNIVAL, 1939

Street Collections

Groups

	£	s.	d.
Kidderminster Auxiliary Fire Service	20	11	8
Tomkinsons Limited:			
"British Isles" 5 7 1			
"Slaves of Khedda" 5 1 11			
"Gipsy Encampment" 1 19 7			
"Old Woman who lived in a Shoe" 1 11 1	13	19	9
Kidderminster Fire Brigade	11	8	9
Kidderminster Post Office	10	13	7
Stourport Fire Brigade	5	3	5
Bewdley Fire Brigade	6	2	7
Edwin Harris & Son	4	13	4
Kidderminster Silver Band	3	13	10
Kidderminster Shuttle Ltd.	2	6	2
Boy British (per Mrs. A. Tromans, 42 Queen Street)	2	8	1
HM Tap Charity Jazz Band	2	6	4
Individuals			
John Young, 13 Stretton Road	5	14	8
H. Shipton, 61 Bewdley Road, Stourport	3	19	6
Joan Ashley, "Wem," Northumberland Avenue	4	4	10
Sydney Taylor, 18 Lea Street	3	10	6
A. Strethen, "Northcliffe," Marlpool Lane	3	3	1
A. Turley, Cookes Road	3	16	10
Mrs. Clifford, "Brow," St. John's Avenue	3	14	9
R. Watkins, 38 Hurcott Road	3	13	1
Mrs. Pinkham, 64 Hurcott Road	3	8	10
Miss Violet North, c/o Kidder. Dis. General Hospital	3	3	9
S. Dunkin, 38 Dudley Street	3	1	10
Harper Bros., Mill Street	3	1	2
Roy Holland, 11 Dean Street	3	0	6

COUNTY PETTY SESSIONS

THURSDAY

HE JEWS

ALI

neither in this mountain nor in Jerusalem ye shall worship the Father." The Church was entering on a new course. In its new form the old sacred places would fall into disuse. Worship now was to be internal and spiritual; not external only: therefore worship in future would not be confined to any one place. It would be as our hymn declares:

ALOW

K-END HUTS

il were allowed it would air to the people with was in negotiation for the heir land as private open he public at large in the he countryside merely for an owner of one wooden

f an appeal in November, he Town and Country by Mr. Frank Sargent and lford, in connection with a similar wooden bunga-river-side at Hill Farm, Foreign, approximately 3 the present site, a site rd's farm was chosen and veek-end hut development s provided by Mr. Halford. nis agreement Mr. Halford move all the existing huts n-side to the land thus which was well screened r Severn valley and at reasonably accessible for of the huts. It was con-iable that Mr. Beesley red to remove his building r site to the one which . Halford and which had set aside for the purpose. Morris, assistant county ed that Mr. Beesley's erected without the con-hway Authority, and that to the Restriction of pment Committee at their ptember 13th, 1938, when l that notice be given to t unless the bungalow be 14 days, legal proceedings On December 13th, 1938, to the committee that the ndertaken to remove the March 31st, 1939, as it eat hardship to move the a fresh site had been resolved that this offer be January, 1939, Mr. Beesley, ated that he now under-a right of appeal to the ransport, but before doing be necessary to make a ition.

y 2nd, application forms l, and dated January 18th, from the Surveyor to the Rural District Council saying that the necessary would be forwarded in lo plans were forthcoming, utory period of two months apsed, the application was March 21st, 1939, on the insufficient details had d for dealing with the

ans were received by the yor on April 6th, 1939, and on was considered by the Ribbon Development Act, Committee at their meeting April, 1939. These were le recommendation of the eyor and the Planning

BRITAIN AT WAR

MEASURES TO MEET SITUATION

THE PREMIER'S BROADCAST

Britain knew that it was at war when the Prime Minister made an announcement over the wireless at 11.15 a.m. on Sunday.

His statement ran as follows:

I am speaking to you from 10, Downing Street.

This morning the British Ambassador in Berlin handed the German Government a final Note stating that unless the British Government heard from it by eleven o'clock that it was prepared at once to withdraw its troops from Poland, a state of war would exist between us.

I have to tell you now that no such undertaking has been received, and that consequently this country is at war with Germany.

You can imagine what a bitter blow it is to me that all my long struggle to win peace has failed.

Yet I cannot believe there is anything more or anything different that I could have done that would have been more successful.

Up to the very last it would have been quite possible to arrange a peaceful and honourable settlement between Germany and Poland. But Hitler would not have it. He had evidently made up his mind to attack Poland whatever happened and, although he now says he put forward reasonable proposals which were rejected by Poland, that is not a true statement.

The proposals were never shown to the Poles nor to us, and though they were announced in the German broadcast on Thursday night, Hitler did not wait to hear comments on them, but ordered his troops to cross the Polish frontier the next morning.

His action shows convincingly that there is no chance of expecting that this man would ever give up his practice of using force to gain his will.

He can only be stopped by force; and we and France are to-day, in fulfilment of our obligations, going to the aid of Poland, who is so bravely resisting this unprovoked attack upon her people.

"A CLEAR CONSCIENCE"

We have a clear conscience. We have done all any country could do

order—surnames beginning with A—H in the morning, the rest in the afternoon."

An order under the Imports, Exports, and Customs Powers (Defence) Act, prohibits imports of certain goods except under licence. The object of the Order is to limit imports of luxuries and goods of which there are sufficient home supplies, in order to conserve exchange for the additional purchases of other products required in war-time.

A wool control has been set up, with Sir Harry Shackleton as the Controller.

Under the Government's petrol rationing scheme, which will be introduced as from September 16th, it was announced earlier in the week that only one grade of motor spirit would be available to the public. It will be called "Pool" motor spirit, and will be on sale from pumps in England and Wales at 1s. 6d. a gallon. There are very substantial stocks of petrol in the country, but the best use must be made of them.

How the petrol rationing scheme, to be introduced as from September 16th, will work, was announced on Monday night. The following indicates the arrangements which will apply to private cars:

First issue of ration books will consist of two books, one covering the period of September 16th to October 15th, and the second October 16th to November 15th.

Number of coupons in each book will vary in relation to the horsepower of the car, in order to give as far as is practicable equality of mileage.

The coupons represent units of petrol. The unit for the present will be one gallon, but this is liable to modification from time to time.

To obtain ration books, owners of cars must apply at the Post Office or local taxation office from which they normally obtain their Road Fund licence, and must present their car registration book.

A warning notice to motorists issued by the Lord Privy Seal's Office states:

"The amount of light on the roads after sunset is still so great as to consitute a grave danger to public security."

The opening inside lamps must not exceed two inches in diameter, and this opening must be covered by two thicknesses of newspaper. Motorists will require also to blacken the reflectors inside.

Pending full instructions, the red glass of rear lamps should be covered with two thicknesses of newspaper. Headlight instructions, already made, must be strictly observed.

AIR RAID WARNINGS

In the event of threatened air raids, warnings will be given

guided to th vital

The Chief given permi ystwyth to constable in

The man area have have an o air raid w perfectly cl staff to en event of ar type indica and how t

Advice to templating in a Minis ment Th

"Many ordinary employmen ought to vo of nationa suited for wish to do such work, merce and leaving the

"The life it will mak bers of wom The woman volunteers time service doing her f

"Women industry co their neares is the best to find importance

The first the new lis the black-o Stipendiary were fined

WAR AR

It is stat continue un ex-Servicem orphans in on, take u families of held and requiring get into branch. been estab mond Hil House. E closed.

TH

(

Pu

FOOD CONTROL COMMITTEE

TOWN COUNCIL'S APPOINTMENTS

EVERY WARD REPRESENTED

Kidderminster Town Council, at a meeting in committee on Monday, appointed 15 members to constitute a Food Control Committee for the borough, with the Town Clerk as executive officer under the scheme, and the Borough Treasurer as his deputy. Ten members were nominated by the Council (including a representative of each of the six wards), and the remaining five by trade organisations in the town.

The full committee is the Mayor and Mayoress (Alderman and Mrs. H. W. Cheshire), Alderman W. T. Pearce, Councillors R. A. Dalley, G. N. Weston, J. Ferguson, L. Tolley and Miss E. C. Addenbrooke, Messrs. J. H. Broadley, G. N. Perry, L. W. Warder, T. Shingler, J. Allatt, J. P. Hough, and F. W. Tubb.

The Mayor (Alderman H. W. Cheshire) presided, and other members present were the Deputy Mayor (Alderman E. G. Eddy), Aldermen R. S. Brinton and W. T. Pearce, Councillors G. Anton, R. Tipler, A. W. Buckley, J. Ferguson, L. Tolley, O. W. Davies, J. Andrews, J. Wright, G. E. Lacy, J. E. Talbot, G. S. Chadwick, F. D. H. Burcher, G. N. Weston and J. Bristow, with the Town Clerk (Mr. J. H. Thursfield), Borough Treasurer (Mr. A. Shiner), and Baths Superintendent (Mr. J. E. Woodward).

SPECIAL BUSINESS

The Mayor said the business of that special meeting was to fix up the committee to deal with food control, to appoint a tribunal of appeal in connection with the Government evacuation scheme, and to consider the closing of the Castle Road Baths. They had gone into the first question, and had several suggested names for the Council's approval.

The Town Clerk explained that as food control would take effect in the event of war, the Council was asked to designate a Food Control Officer. They designated him, and he had received numerous circulars and instructions. The committee had to consist of 10 members selected so that all classes of consumers in the area were represented, including at least two women, and in addition five trade members—a retail grocer, a retail butcher, an officer of a retail Co-operative Society, and representatives of two other trades. Three suggested trade members were Mr. L. W. Warder (retail grocer), West End Stores; Mr. T. Shingler (retail butcher), [illegible]

The Town Clerk replied that the com[mittee] must be set up in accordance wi[th] instructions received six months ago.

The Mayoress was nominated as t[he] second woman member, and Mr. G. Perry completed the committee.

Mr. Thursfield said that was all t[he] Council had to do; the committee wou[ld] meet and appoint its chairman.

For the tribunal of appeal in conne[c]tion with the Government evacuati[on] scheme, the Education Committee s[ug]gested Mrs. Dauglish, Councillors Tol[ley] and Miss Addenbrooke, and the Coun[cil] agreed

Councillor Davies remarked: "I do[n't] think they will ever have to meet, becau[se] everything has gone so well."

Councillor Anton asked what were t[he] committee's duties.

Councillor Tolley: To force people [to] have evacuees if they refuse.

The Town Clerk: This tribunal de[als] with appeals by persons with wh[om] evacuees are billeted. People who may [be] so billeted include nurses brought into t[he] district, or other A.R.P. or civil defen[ce] workers brought into the town a[nd] billeted here.

FREE BATHS FOR "TERRIERS"

The Town Clerk reported that Maj. T. Guy Vale, in charge of the unit of 2[..] Territorials at Pike Mills, asked for t[he] use of the slipper baths for the men fro[m] 5 till 7 each evening, free of char[ge,] because they would bring their own tow[els] and soap.

"No charge for the hot wate[r,"] remarked the Mayor humorously, and [it] was agreed to allow the use of the bat[hs] free of charge.

In regard to the closing of the bat[hs] he said it would be better to keep t[he] swimming baths open in the day-ti[me] only, until such time as the A.R.P. Co[n]troller wanted the baths for other p[ur]poses (in connection with first aid).

This course was agreed to.

OBITUARY

MRS. ANNIE YATES

On Saturday, Mrs. Annie Yates, of Habberley Street, passed away after illness of five months, at the advan[ced] age of 76 years. The deceased l[ady,] who was the widow of Mr. John Ya[tes,] leaves three children—one daughter [in] Australia and the others in Kid[der]minster.

The funeral took place on Tues[day] afternoon at St. John's Churchyard, [the] family mourners being: Jack and F[...] (son and daughter), Annie and [...] (daughter-in-law and son-in-law), and Mrs. Jack Bird (nephew and nie[ce]), Mrs. R. Towers and Mrs. G. Humph[...], Mr. Jack Coates, Mrs. Bingham, [...] Guest (Smethwick), Mr. A. H. Ads[...].

Floral tributes were sent by: J[...] and Annie; Elsie and Ted; Edith [...] Sid (Australia); Betty and Babba; Je[...]

PUBLIC SHELTERS

AIR RAID PRECAUTIONS

The Borough Surveyor (Mr. Joseph [R]awcroft) states that strengthening [m]aterial has been provided for the [fo]llowing public shelters, near which are [n]otices directing people where to take [re]fuge if caught whilst in the shopping [ce]ntre during an air raid.

	Accommodation
Town Hall (basements)	100
Retail Market (basements)	200
Messrs. Radcliffe's Brewery, at Worcester Cross (in basement)	200
Mr. J. H. Smith, builder's yard, Station Hill	200
Caldwall Hall Crypt, Castle Road	50
Parker's Arms, Park Lane	50
Messrs. Wrenson's, Worcester Street	100
Wise Radio (basement in Worcester	

MINUTES OF THE PROCEEDINGS AT A SPECIAL MEETING OF THE COUNCIL FOR THIS BOROUGH DULY CONVENED AND HELD AT THE GUILDHALL ON WEDNESDAY, THE 6TH DAY OF SEPTEMBER, 1939 AT FIVE O'CLOCK IN THE AFTERNOON.

PRESENT

Councillor	Charles Rodman Pritchard (Mayor)
Alderman	Henry Neal Frost (Deputy Mayor)
"	Fergus Edward Mountford
"	Robert Bertie Jackson
Councillor	Gerald Mortimer Smith
"	William Harcourt Webb
"	Joseph Bates
"	Percival William Palmer
"	Frederick Reginald Welch

TMENT OF FOOD CONTROL COMMITTEE

52. Proposed by Councillor Welch seconded by the Mayor and RESOLVED That the following persons be nominated for membership of the Bewdley Food Control Committee

(i) Trade Members:-

(a) A retail Grocer or provision merchant - Mr: W. E. James

(b) A retail Butcher or flesher - Mr: T. F. Timmis

(c) An Officer of a retail Co-operative Society - The Manager for the time being of the Bewdley Branch of the Kidderminster Co-operative Society.,

ii) Two representatives of other retail food trades:-

(d) Mr: W. J. Godwin

(e) Mr: J. P. Thomas

iii) Women Members:-

(f) Mrs: J. Taylor

(g) Mrs: N. Palmer

iv) Eight other members representing all classes of consumers:-

(h) The Mayor (Councillor C. R. Pritchard)

(i) Alderman H. N. Frost

(j) Alderman F. E. Mountford

(k) Alderman R. B. Jackson

(l) Councillor Major W. Harcourt Webb

(m) Councillor J. Bates

(n) Councillor G. Mortimer Smith

Special Council Meeting 6th day of September, 1939

It was also RESOLVED That in the event of either or both the women nominated being unable to serve on the Committee that Mrs: Coldrick and then Mrs: Nock be nominated And in the event of any of the [illegible] other Members being unable to serve on the Committee that Councillor [illegible]. [illegible]illis be nominated.

APPOINTMENT OF FOOD EXECUTIVE OFFICER

Proposed by Alderman Jackson seconded by Alderman Mountford and RESOLVED That the Town Council recommend to the Food Control Committee that the Town Clerk (Mr: L. Gordon Hales) be appointed as Food Executive Officer.

Mayor

4th October, 1939..

BOROUGH OF BEWDLEY

Special Council Meeting 4th day of October, 1939

Report of the General Purposes Committee

Air Raid Precautions

Your Committee have now had under review the existing arrangements for the employment of whole time A. R. P., personnel in the light of the experience gained during the first month of the war.

It has been decided that the number of wholetime workers should be cut down to an absolute minimum in order to effect all possible economy, provided that reasonable security can at the same time be afforded to the inhabitants of the Borough in the event of an air raid.

Certain of the services are well up to strength and can be run entirely on a voluntary basis in view of the size and character of the town. A limited number of whole time workers must be maintained in some of the other services as set out below. A wage of £3., per week is paid to men workers and £2 per week to women.

Air Raid Wardens........................8 mdn
First Aid Parties.......................Nil
First Aid Posts and
Ambulance Attendants....................1
Drivers for Casualty Services...........2 men
Report Centre...........................2 men, 1 woman
(for the present this work will be carried
out by men who will divide the remuneration
available)
Light Rescue Party......................1 driver for lorry
Decontamination Squad...................1 man
Regular Fire Brigade....................2 men
Auxiliary Fire Brigade..................2 men

It may be necessary to reconsider these arrangements if there is any marked change in war conditions in the future. Some reduction in the whole time personnel has to be made and the names of the persons to be employed in future are not at present available. Your Committee recommend that when a final decision has been reached, a list of these names and the remuneration payable should be posted outside the Town Hall.

Arrangements are being made for the whole time personnel to be billeted either at their posts or depots or at 6, Load Street, in order to avoid unnecessary strain on the men working the night shifts. The men will then be free to carry out useful duties in the daytime either assisting and advising householders and the general public or carrying out work under the instructions of the Borough Surveyor.

Your Committee wish to take this opportunity of pointing out that the reductions in the number of whole time personnel employed are being made in order to give effect to the general policy of the Government that work should be found for people who are unemployed as a result of the outbreak of hostilities, provided that efficiency can be maintained. All the whole time personnel have carried out their duties perfectly satisfactorily up to date and your Committee much appreciate what these volunteers have done both on a voluntary basis in the first place and later as paid workers

GRP

Chapter Two

1940
FRANCE FALLS

If the British media and the establishment considered the first few months after September 1939 to be a "phoney war" the thousands of civilian and military already killed by the Nazis belied that description.

By September 1940 seven countries had been invaded and occupied - Poland, Luxembourg, Denmark, Holland, Norway, Belgium and France.

1940 was a dangerous year for Britain and disastrous for France. British political confidence in Prime Minister Chamberlain was undermined by his conduct of the war effort and his previous policy of appeasement. Chamberlain invited Labour to join the Government but Attlee refused, and on 10th May 1940 he resigned. Winston Churchill became Prime Minister.

The British Expeditionary Force retreated to Dunkirk and between 27th May and 3rd June, 300,000 soldiers were saved from capture and evacuated from the beaches back to England by a fleet of civilian and Royal Navy ships.

Hitler's Blitzkrieg of tanks, dive bombers, armoured cars, heavy and light artillery and infantry had devastated all military opposition. On 11th June the French Government left Paris for Bordeaux and on the 14th, Paris fell under Nazi occupation. Prime Minister Reynaud resigned in favour of Marshall Petain. On 16th, Petain asked the Germans for an armistice. Hitler exacted as much humiliation as possible. The Armistice was signed on 22nd in the forest of Compiegne in the same railway carriage as the Germans had surrendered to the Allies in 1918.

Jersey and the Channel Islands were occupied and invasion of Britain was expected. In Bewdley civic life went on. Councillor C.R. Pritchard was elected Mayor for the seventh time and the rate was set at 14 shillings and 8 pence in the pound to produce £12,320, one third to be spent by the Borough Council and two thirds by Worcestershire County Council.

Although tempted, it is not going to be my prerogative to give a comprehensive account of the Second World War. It will be difficult enough to merely relate de Gaulles activities, as condensed as they appear, to Bewdley and his time there with the Free French.

So - we have the situation now that the French Government has capitulated and Marshall Petain, hero of Verdun in World War One, and Laval a previous French Prime Minister, formed a new Government to collaborate with the occupying German forces. De Gaulle and many other French men and women retreat to England. He claims to be the leader of the Free French, broadcasts a message to his people over BBC radio and the fight is taken up.

As the war continued, de Gaulle had major problems gaining and maintaining the 'legitimacy of office'. Others sought to speak for France - Churchill and Roosevelt were not always considered to be de Gaulle adherents. And as for the other major Allied partner Soviet Russia, Stalin obviously would have wanted a communist French leader in exile and in situ after the war had ended. But Britain and England were a safe home for de Gaulle and the Free French in their hour of need - a reason for pride on our own part, particularly in Bewdley which was a refuge and training camp for those brave French who later returned to the fight. Seventy of the two hundred and eleven lost their lives for their cause in Europe and elsewhere.

And so, as Britain organised its retreat from Dunkirk, suffered the horrors of the blitz and prepared for a German invasion, de Gaulle worked tirelessly to organise his Free French Government in exile and the opposition to Marshall Petain's Vichy government of collaboration with the Germans. Ironically De Gaulle was sentenced to death in his absence by Vichy, but finally it was Petain at age 86 who would be himself sentenced to death by the post war French Government (a sentence not carried out) and Laval, who was executed in 1945.

I shall attempt to give coverage to these early "pre-Ribbesford" days and then take the remaining war years in sequence, concentrating of course on the Ribbesford House and Bewdley years of 1942, 1943 and 1944.

CHARLES DE GAULLE

I would like to give the briefest sketch of de Gaulle's life until 1946. Charles Andre Marie de Gaulle was born in Lille on 22nd November 1890. His family were of the minor aristocracy, being strongly monarchist and Catholic, not inclined towards adherence of the Republican revolution, yet holding a deep pride in France with a desire for unity. De Gaulle's grandmother was a prolific historian and novelist, his uncles were academics, his father a teacher at a Jesuit college. De Gaulle wrote that his mother had, "an equal passion" for France and a religious piety.

In 1912 de Gaulle graduated from the Ecole Militaire of Saint - Cyr. He served in World War One and was captured by the Germans in March 1916 during the Battle of Verdun. Whilst in captivity he wrote, "La discorde chez l'ennemi," the first of several military and political books on strategy. In 1921 he married Yvonne Vendroux.

De Gaulle then served on General Weygand's staff, travelling to Poland on a military mission. At Saint Cyr he taught military history, before joining the staff of Marshall Petain. De Gaulle took part in the occupation of the Rhineland and served in Lebanon.

During the 1930's de Gaulle consolidated his position as a career soldier and writer of military books. He advocated mechanised warfare and a military elite. As Churchill and others in Britain argued for military preparedness against Germany, so did De Gaulle in France.

In 1939 de Gaulle was a tank regiment colonel serving in Alsace. In May 1940 he was promoted to brigadier - general. Prime Minister Paul Reynaud appointed de Gaulle Under Secretary of State for War, a Cabinet post. When France fell, de Gaulle's faction in Cabinet opposed collaboration with Hitler and retreated to London. He gave his famous BBC radio broadcast to the free world on 18th June 1940. The new Prime Minister Petain signed an Armistice with the Germans, creating the Vichy regime and in July a court sentenced de Gaulle to death in his absence..

Churchill therefore provided British Governmental support for de Gaulle and the Free French. President Roosevelt was not at first an advocate of de Gaulle, but as the war progressed the cause of the Free French prospered politically.

The French Colonies in Africa were vital components in the fight against Hitler, as were the underground movements in all the occupied nations, including France.

When the British and Americans began their invasion of Africa, they forced the Vichy Admiral Darlan to stop fighting and imposed him as High Commissioner of French North Africa. Darlan was assassinated one month later in December 1942, but the Allies imposed General Giraud. De Gaulle moved to Algiers in May 1943, and organised the French Committee of National Liberation,allowing Giraud to be its co-chairman. Soon, De Gaulle was the absolute leader of the Free French and the Maquis Resistance.

After liberation began with the Allied invasion of France on 6th June 1944, de Gaulle returned to France on 13th June. Montgomery sent a 'Guard of Honour' to meet him at Bayeux. The Politics of the Americans refused to let de Gaulle land in France on 'D' Day. His inheritance was not straightforward. Eisenhower, Roosevelt and Churchill were not entirely convinced he should be given the title deeds of France. Even in the victory, de Gaulle had to fight very hard to ensure France would be delivered to the French nation and not become, even for a short while, administered by the Americans and British.

De Gaulle returned to London and then Washington to meet Roosevelt. Thus began de Gaulle's legitimate ascendancy as Leader of France. In October 1945 he was elected President of the Provincial Government. The Constitution, and reorganising and redrafting the 3rd Republic proved too much for de Gaulle and he resigned in January 1946.

Petain Praises Heroism of Frei

"I THINK OF THE UNHAPPY REFUGEES"

(Continued from PAGE ONE)

Government, the Marshal has constituted the list of his collaborators as follows:

President of the Council (Premier): Marshal Petain.
Minister of State and Vice-President: M. Camille Chautemps.
Minister of National Defence: General Weygand.
Minister of Justice: M. Premacourt.
Minister of War: General Colson.
Minister of Navy and Mercantile Marine: Admiral Darlan.
Minister of Air: General Pujo.
Minister of Foreign Affairs: M. Paul Baudouin.
Minister of Interior: M. Pommaret.
Minister of Finance and Commerce: M. Bouthillier.
Minister of Colonies: M. Albert Riviere.
Minister of National Education: M. Rivaud.
Minister of Public Works: M. Frossard.
Minister of Agriculture and Food: M. Chichery.
Minister of Labour: M. Fevrier.
Minister for Ex-Servicemen and Families: M. Ybarnegaray.

"Immediately after its constitution the Petain Government called a first meeting, presided over by the President of the Republic, to examine the military and diplomatic situation."

Later the French radio stated that Marshal Petain informed the Cabinet of the text of his broadcast to the French nation. "The Government took the decisions necessary in the situation," it was stated.

The broadcast ended with the words, "The resistance of our troops, the coolness of our civilian population, and the greatness of Marshal Petain have maintained the glory of France in the eyes of the world."

"Message from Churchill"

An account of the establishment of the new Government, broadcast by the French radio and quoted by British United Press, stated:

"In the hours preceding the decision, the Government of M. Reynaud had studied the reply of President Roosevelt, and also the military and diplomatic situations existing yesterday afternoon, and had called into consultation General Weygand and Admiral Darlan as well as the Presidents of the Senate and the Chamber of Deputies."

Finally there was read to the Cabinet a message from Mr. Winston Churchill.

British United Press learns in Bordeaux that M. Reynaud's resignation was handed to the French President, M. Lebrun, at 11 o'clock last night after M. Reynaud had been in communication with Mr. Churchill.

The new Cabinet is regarded in Bordeaux as one consisting of experts in their particular departments, says Reuter.

Spain as Mediator?

Speaking on the French radio from Bordeaux immediately after Marshal Petain's broadcast, a commentator of the Columbia Broadcasting System said that the Spanish Ambassador to France would probably act as mediator in the armistice negotiations.

German troops, he said, were understood to be not far away from the place from which the French radio was at present working.

British United Press learns in Bordeaux that a confidential document was handed to the Spanish Ambassador, Senor Lequerica, by the new French Foreign Minister, M. Baudouin, shortly after midnight.

The contents of this document, it is understood, were transmitted to the British Ambassador, Sir Ronald Campbell.

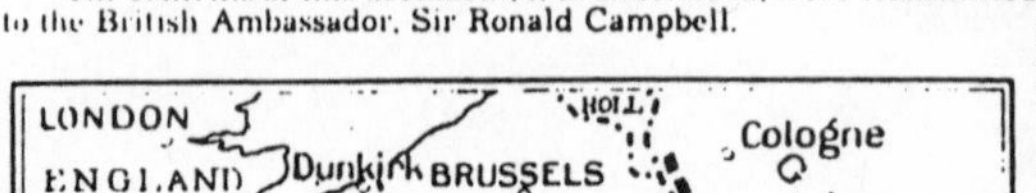

Italian Bombs Kill Egyptians

(Continued from PAGE ONE)

Nairobi reported a successful air attack on Friday by airplanes of the South African Air Force upon Bardera, one of the main towns of Italian Somaliland. This was announced in a communiqué from Air Force headquarters for East Africa.

Much damage is reported to have been done by two direct hits on the town.

Reconnaissance flights over Southern Italian Somaliland revealed no enemy movements whatsoever.

Italian Raids

A communiqué issued to-day by General Headquarters in Cairo states that yesterday Italian aircraft bombed Sollum, Sidi Barrani and Mersa Matruh.

In one raid four Egyptian soldiers were killed and six wounded. Eight Royal Engineer workers were also injured.

All three places are on or near the Egyptian coast not far from the Libyan border.

A Reuter message from Mersa Matruh, a former Egyptian pleasure resort, now an Anglo-Egyptian military and air base, says that the place was raided four times during the day.

Missed Barracks

A British infantry barracks was straddled by bombs in the first raid, but there were no casualties Three airplanes took part. Thirteen minutes later four more bombers flew over attacking the Egyptian barracks

The third and fourth raids, in the afternoon, were made by nine and three airplanes respectively. They dropped bombs across the town from the sea to the desert hinterland

The post office and a number of huts were damaged and eight Egyptian killed.

A number of war correspondents had arrived in Mersa Matruh from Cairo fifteen minutes before the afternoon raids began, and a 200lb. bomb exploded 3ft. from the entrance of the dug-out in which they were sheltering.

American Hurt

An American correspondent and the officer conducting the party were buried by falling debris and were taken to hospital.

A senior British officer who saw the Egyptian troops in action against the raiders said their moral was excellent.

Italian Claims

An Italian war communiqué, quoted by Reuter, to-day said Italian airplanes had bombed Malta, Corsica and the Tunis region.

Italian reconnaissance activity is growing in intensity in the Alps, adds the communiqué. "Successful operations" against the British forces in North Africa were carried out, it is alleged.

Referring to Allied air raids, the communiqué says that at Savona one person was killed and a few were wounded at Cagliari (Sardinia). Some damage was caused to sheds on the aviation fields, six soldiers being killed and 30 wounded.

Says Alien Gave

"Ring Complet Round Enemy Claim Germa

To-day's German Hi mand communiqué by Reuter, stated:

"Fast moving troops r Swiss border near Pontar east of Besancon, thereby ring around the enemy Lorraine and Alsace.

"This completes the en all the French forces def Maginot Line, including heavy fortifications in the Nancy, Epinal and Belfort- which it was unofficially e the beginning of the we paign that upwards of 1,0 were concentrated.

"The French armies, hav down, are pouring back south and south-west in gr gration, closely pursued by

"In those places wher forces succeeded in o ordered resistance, they w back with heavy losses."

"Orleans Captu

It is also claimed that a detachment, led by a divis mander, took Orleans an damaged bridgehead over t

Numerous bridges over were bombed, it is added. columns which had become at these bridges were att bombs and machine-guns

"Motorised troops ope Burgundy and around La gained ground in a south tion," it is added. "Two which there were 39 airpl to take off with bombs were

In the north of Loraine, German troops are appro Mihiel. They are also towards the Rhine-Mar Chateau Salins, Dieuze an are said to have been captu

MAY 10—JU

The German offensive May 10, with the invasion Belgium and Luxemburg. record of its progress:

May 16.—Battle on the M warfare between Namur a

May 21.—Germans rea and Amiens. M. Reynaud Senate "Incredible mista would be punished" had b

May 23.—Germans penetr of Allied army; Abbeville hands; heavy fighting at

May 28.—Belgian army by King Leopold's order.

June 4.—Prime Ministe 335,000 Allied troops res Dunkirk.

June 9.—German rec units reached outskirts of

June 11.—Germans reach

June 12.—Germans clair of Rheims.

June 14.—Germans ent French withdrew to save destruction.

June 17.—Marshal Petain "France must give up the

Belgian's Sui

Because he worried about his country M. G. W. Van aged 47, a wealthy Belg broker, hanged himself wi of his pyjamas in his flat a place, S.W.

At the Westminster Inqu

Evening Standard

Amusements 8
Radio 9

BLACK-OUT 9.47 p.m. 4.1
MOON Rises 6.31 p.m.; Sets 3.

No. 36,125 LONDON, MONDAY, JUNE 17, 1940 ONE PEN

PETAIN SAYS "FR MUST CEASE FIGH

"I addressed myself to the enemy last night"

"A WAY TO END HOSTILITIES"

"It is with broken heart that I tell you to-day that fighti must cease. I addressed myself last night to the enen to ask him if he is prepared to seek with me, as betwee soldiers after an honourable fight, the means of puttir an end to hostilities"

Marshal Petain, the new French Premier, made this announcement to t French nation at 12.30 p.m. to-day.

"Frenchmen! At the appeal of the President, I have assumed from to-d the direction of the French Government," he said.

"Sure of the affection of our admirable Army, which is fighting with a heroism worthy of its noble military traditions against an enemy superior in numbers and in arms, certain that by its magnificent resistance it has fulfilled our duty to our Allies, certain of the support of ex-servicemen, whom I am proud to have commanded, sure of the confidence of the entire nation, I give myself to France in order to mitigate its misfortunes.

"IN THESE SORROWFUL HOURS I THINK OF THE UNHAPPY REFUGEES WHO IN UTTER DISTRESS FLEE ALONG THE ROADS. I EXPRESS TO THEM MY COMPASSION AND MY SOLICITUDE.

"MAY ALL FRENCH PEOPLE RALLY ROUND

R.A.F. RAID ON TOBRUK

Italian Munitic Dump Hit

Most successful raids l beencarried out on Italian naval and air bas Tobruk, Libya, the air of commanding, R.A.F. Mid East, announces.

Displaying great determination airmen persisted in their raid de heavy anti-aircraft fire, until exte damage had been done to an amr tion and a petrol dump.

There were several explosions much black smoke was seen whe

Sunday Dispatch

Radio Page 9.

139th Year. No. 7,234. JUNE 23, 1940. POSTAGE IN U.K., EIRE, CANADA, AND NEWFOUNDLAND .... 1d. OTHER PLACES ABROAD .... 1d. TWOPENCE

FRENCH SIGN ARM

British Government's Grief And A

Hitler's Plan For Britain

By
MADAME TABOUIS

● HITLER, on June 4, informed his staff and his colleagues of his plans for the coming months.

Churchill Appeals To Frenchmen: 'Fight On'

THE FRENCH PLENIPOTENTIARIES SIGNED AN ARMISTICE WITH GERMANY AT 5.30 LAST NIGHT AT COMPIEGNE, FRANCE, WHERE THE 1918 ARMISTICE WAS SIGNED

"The Armistice will not take effect until six hours after a separate French-Italian agreement has been reached," stated a Berlin broadcast, which added that the French plenipotentiaries were expected to arrive at the appointed meeting place in Italy to-day.

No information about the terms of the armistice were known last

NAZIS BOMB US AGAIN

HITLER AND MUSSOLINI GLOAT OVER FRANCE. The dictators celebrated the fall of France with triumphal rejoicing. Hitler ordered flags to be flown throughout the Reich for ten days, and church bells to be rung daily for a week. In Paris, German troops with cameras and guide books wandered about sightseeing. Above, with Goering, followed by German staff officers, Hitler is viewing a captured portion of the Maginot Line; below, Mussolini stands in a camouflaged car, touring the battlefront in South-East France.

Leaders of the French forces

26 June, 1940

FREE FRENCHMEN RALLY TO THE FLAG. Under the inspired leadership of General de Gaulle, who is seen on the left, a rapidly growing army of free Frenchmen was enrolled in England to fight side by side with the British Army against the common enemy. Admiral Muselier (right), who made a thrilling escape from France in a destroyer, was appointed Commander-in-Chief of the Free French Navy. A number of vessels manned entirely by French officers and men took part immediately in successful operations

A TOUS LES FRANÇAIS

La France a perdu une bataille!
Mais la France n'a pas perdu la guerre!

Des gouvernants de rencontre ont pu capituler, cedant à la panique, oubliant l'honneur, livrant le pays à la servitude. Cependant, rien n'est perdu!

Rien n'est perdu, parce que cette guerre est une guerre mondiale. Dans l'univers libre, des forces immenses n'ont pas encore donné. Un jour, ces forces écraseront l'ennemi. Il faut que la France, ce jour-là, soit présente à la victoire. Alors, elle retrouvera sa liberté et sa grandeur. Tel est mon but, mon seul but!

Voilà pourquoi je convie tous les Francais, où qu'ils se trouvent, à s'unir à moi dans l'action, dans le sacrifice et dans l'espérance.

Notre patrie est en péril de mort.
Luttons tous pour la sauver!

VIVE LA FRANCE !

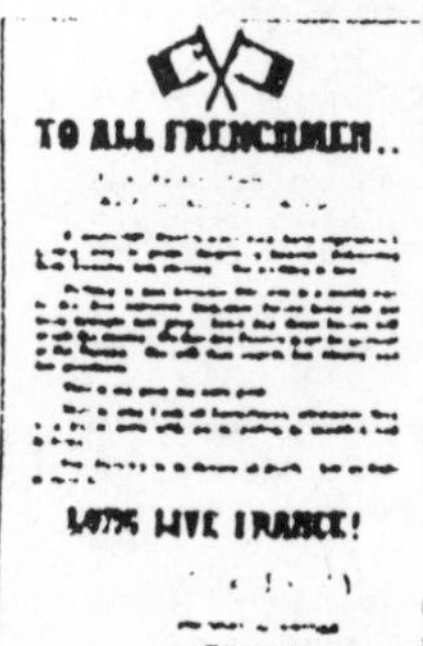

C. de Gaulle.

GÉNÉRAL DE GAULLE

QUARTIER-GÉNÉRAL,
4, CARLTON GARDENS,
LONDON, S.W.1

The Evening Post.

ONE PENNY

Orders of the Commandant of the German Forces in Occupation of the Bailiwick of Jersey.

Dated the 8th day of July, 1940

1. The German Commandant is in close touch with the Civil Authorities and acknowledges their loyal co-operation.

2. The Civil Government and Courts of the Island will continue to function as heretofore, save that all Laws, Ordinances, Regulations and Orders will be submitted to the German Commandant before being enacted.

3. Such legislation as, in the past, required the Sanction of His Britannic Majesty in Council for its validity, shall henceforth be valid on being approved by the German Commandant and thereafter sanctioned by the Bailiff of Jersey.

4. The orders of the German Commandant heretofore, now and hereafter issued shall, in due course, be Registered in the records of the Island of Jersey, in order that no person may plead ignorance thereof. Offences against the same, saving those punishable under German Military Law, shall be punishable by the Civil Courts, who shall enact suitable penalties in respect of such offences, with the approval of the German Commandant.

5. Assemblies in Churches and Chapels for the purpose of Divine Worship are permitted. Prayers for the British Royal Family and for the welfare of the British Empire may be said. Church Bells may ring ten minutes before Service. Such Assemblies shall not be made the medium for any propaganda or utterances against the honour or interests of, or offensive to, the German Government or Forces.

6. Cinemas, Concerts and other Entertainments are permitted, subject to the conditions set out in Order No 5 above.

7. Prices must not be increased or decreased. Any shopkeeper offending against this Order is liable to have his shop closed and also to pay any fine that may be imposed by the Competent Authorities.

8. The sale and consumption of wines, beer and cider is permitted in such premises as are licensed by the Civil Authorities.

9. Holders of Licences for the sale of such intoxicating liquors (wines, beer or cider), shall take the most rigid precautions for the prevention of drunkenness. If drunkenness takes place on such licensed premises, then without prejudice to any other civil penalty, the Island Police shall and are hereby empowered to close the premises.

10. All traffic between Jersey and Guernsey is prohibited, whether direct or indirect, for the time being (other Regulations will follow).

11. The Rate of Exchange between the Reichsmark and the Pound has been fixed at Eight Marks to the Pound.

12. The continuance of the privileges granted to the civilian population is dependent upon their good behaviour. Military necessity, however, may, from time to time, require the Orders now in force to be made more stringent.

For and on behalf of the German Commandant of the Channel Islands

(Signed) **GUSSEK, Hauptmann,**

Commandant, Jersey.

French and Czech troops to fight for Britain — 26 July, 1940

FOREIGN TROOPS RE-FORM IN ENGLAND. Throughout the summer the reconstruction on British soil of foreign units from the occupied countries proceeded apace. On 21 July, Britain recognized the Czechoslovak Government established in London. Above, Dr. Benes, its head, is saluting the colours at a review of Czech troops in Southern England. Below, men of the French Foreign Legion who, after fighting at Narvik escaped to England from Brittany, and joined General de Gaulle's Free French Army, march past at their English camp.

Frenchmen celebrate Fall of Bastille

FRANCE'S DAY OF MOURNING. The 14th July, the anniversary of the Fall of the Bastille in 1789, normally a day of national celebration in France. This year the crowds were sombre and dejected, shown in the picture above of Bordeaux citizens standing in silence before the memorial to those killed the last war. Below, General de Gaulle is reviewing a unit of his force after laying a wreath at the Cenota where his words "Vive l'Angleterre, Vive la France," were taken up and re-echoed by the crov

PETAIN NAMES HIS CABINET AS GERMANY JEERS

MARSHAL PETAIN set up his Fascist Cabinet of France last night while Germany jeered.

"What we expected from France," said a commentator on the German radio was a final denunciation of domination over territories outside her living space, and a recognition of the German task of rebuilding Europe from the ruins of Versailles.

"We are not much interested," he declared, "in the heated discussions of the French Parliamentarians at Vichy.

"The attempt to find a new form of government for France will not distract our attention from the main fact that a German victory has opened the way for a settlement for centuries."

FASCIST STRAIN

Last night, after accepting President Lebrun's resignation and adjourning the Senate and Chamber indefinitely, he published the names of 14 Ministers he had selected for his Cabinet.

Among them were: M. Laval (Vice-Premier), M. Marquet, the Fascist Mayor of Bordeaux (Under-Secretary of State), M. Baudouin, voice of Big Business (Foreign Minister), General Weygand (Defence), and Admiral Darlan (Navy).

Into a new post, Minister of Youth and Family, he put M. Ybarnegaray, close friend of Colonel de la Rocque, head of the old Fascist Croix de Feu movement.

Petain named Laval as his eventual successor.

If Laval is not then available, the next Chief of State will be chosen by the Council of Ministers.

The Cabinet will meet for the first time at six o'clock to-night.

To-morrow is the anniversary of the fall of the Bastille, France's great feast of rejoicing for more than 150 years.

It will be commemorated this year, according to messages from Vichy, as a day of mourning.

TAX-MASTER

Under the new Constitution, Petain gives himself power to:

Appoint and remove Ministers,

Fix new taxes,

Appoint holders of civil and military offices,

Command the armed forces and declare states of siege in any **part of the country.**

Ambassadors and Ministers from other countries will henceforth be accredited to the "Chief" alone, not to France.

A Madrid broadcast last night indicated that the Nazis were well satisfied with the booty they secured in France.

They found enormous quantities of flour, potatoes and vegetables in the occupied territory.

According to the Spanish announcer, arrests are being made all over France.

Politicians, journalists and high officials of the Reynaud Government have been detained.

COASTGUARDS AT WAR

An armed coastguard sets out on patrol at a Southern station. He is one of the many men with sea knowledge who are keeping constant watch for enemy surface and air craft round our coasts.

Police Resent L.D.V. Hold-Ups

COMPLAINTS have been made by police officers that they have been held up, when on duty in uniform, by L.D.V.s.

They say they have had to produce their identity cards.

The matter has been discussed this week by representatives of the War Office, the Commissioner of Police and the Police Federation.

A police-sergeant at Malden, Surrey, is reported to have been stopped while on patrol.

A police car with its illuminated sign was held up on the Kingston by-pass road.

A.R.P. vehicles were also stopped.

The Ministry of Home Security told the "Daily Herald" yesterday:

"If under orders to stop everybody on his stretch of road, an L.D.V. would be within his rights in not excluding persons in police uniform or even in military uniform."

Man And Wife Live As Neighbours For 14 Years

PARTED by a quarrel three months after marriage, a Lincolnshire man and his wife lived as next-door neighbours for 14 years.

Yesterday the husband, Mr. Walter Joyce, of The Limes, Ruskington, was granted a decree nisi in the Divorce Court for desertion.

The wife, Mrs. Mary Joyce, of the Royal Oak Inn, Ruskington, cross-petitioned on the same ground, but her case was dismissed.

After the marriage the couple lived with the wife's parents at the Royal Oak.

The parting came about, said Mr. Justice Hodson, because Mr. Joyce saw his wife, her mother and a man in the cellar at the inn, and took offence for what did not seem to his lordship to be a very good reason.

Went To Parents

Mr. Joyce went out. When he returned later, Mrs. Joyce, who—not unnaturally—was annoyed, and whom he had offended by an observation about the man in the cellar, turned him out.

He went to his parents' home, next door.

Later in 1926 he offered to make a home in a cottage he had bought, but his wife was not willing to live with him.

For a long time the couple did not speak when they met, but in 1932 they were on such friendly terms that, learning that his wife had parted with her wedding ring, Mr Joyce bought her another. There was talk of living together

WAR TOOK ALL

When the aircraft carrier Courageous was sunk Mrs. Jones (right) lost her husband.

In a recent raid on the town in which she lives Nazi bombs wrecked her home. The portrait of her husband remained hanging on the wall (below).

NO MORE BUNS OF

THE Ministry of Food stop making iced

Holiday Visit Barred Here–

IF you own a seaside bu galow or cottage in defence area where entry restricted, you cannot there now for "pleasure holiday purposes."

If you do go you must prod evidence that your visit is merely for those purposes.

But if you are a schoolchild go home there for the holidays, o soldier visiting home there leave, you will be regarded as a son "ordinarily resident" in area.

The prohibition does not apply.

These instances of how the strictions work are given by Ministry of Home Security.

Rumania Building Soviet Frontier

ILET

DIG RY

Home Corps, and mulate ctory" by the Allot-

women any age

uniform, d by the ing the ould be are" on

WAY

100 horti- ban areas. commit- uthorities. orps.

hould be of letters chairmen gardens wing.

llowed up advice in

VEY

would be uses with ultivated, le of use.

adopted by next an 45,000 copies of r.

d by the estimated an Police ardens in wn.

e of food ight well

e 'Sunlight Window'

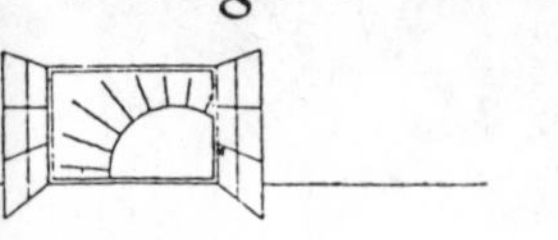

FORTRESS

FREE FRENCHMEN SING —BUT ONLY IN LONDON

"The voice of France is heard —in London."

Bastille Day, 1940

By HILDE MARCHANT

LIBERTE, Egalité, Fraternité—three words that for a century and a half have symbolised the freedom of France—died in France yesterday.

The Pétain Government held a meeting under its puppet dictator, and finished guillotining the Constitution of the Republic.

And for Frenchmen in France Bastille Day 1940 was one of mourning—the death of their liberty.

Yet the voice of France is not stilled. It was heard singing the Marseillaise in the streets of London.

The men of the French Legion came marching down Victoria-street—soldiers, sailors, airmen, who will still fight for France.

They celebrated July 14 in the one corner of Europe where their song could be heard.

Bastille Day has always been celebrated in France with dancing in the streets, flowers, bands, wine.

PICKED TROOPS

Yesterday it began in London with a detachment of picked troops taking the salute at the Cenotaph while General de Gaulle laid a wreath.

No dancing and singing will rescue France. Their arms glistened in the sun, for they must fight their way through Petain's Bastille.

And the English people who watched? They say we are a phlegmatic race.

The pavements and buildings were jammed with people watching. As the troops came into position the edge of French people yelled, "Vive l'Angleterre," "Vive la France."

London. There was a programme of French films for them, with their own stars. There was Mickey Mouse, who seems to be international, and a newsreel.

When the Australian troops were shown there was spontaneous clapping, but it was a picture of the Queen, talking to wounded soldiers, that really roused the house.

The French formed in columns outside in the street while the mounted police kept the crowds back.

FROM "Free Fren[ch] wreath placed General de Gaulle, Legion. You see th[e] the men who will fi[ght] Britons. And below two men of the Legion marching in the Bastille Day parade of French soldiers, sailors, and airmen.

'CONCHIE' TOWN IS ANGRY

Daily Express Staff Reporter

PEOPLE in King's Langley (Herts) are disturbed and angry at a movement in the town encouraging young men to become conscientious objectors.

The parish council have received letters of protest against this pacifist drive. Local firemen were the first to complain. Others have followed suit.

The Rev. Reginald Pym Lemprière Parkin, vicar of King's Langley, said yesterday: "King's Langley is as patriotic as any place in the country. I am certain that I can speak for 90 per cent. of the population, but a certain body is definitely encouraging pacifism.

"I am opposed to any form of pacifism. Not long ago a conscientious objector was dismissed from a printing works. I was asked to sign a form to get him his job back.

"I refused If a man won't fight

25 words of comfort

Fight like a good soldier, and if thou sometimes fall through frailty, take again strength greater than the former, trusting in My more abundant Grace. From "Of the Imitation of Christ," by Thomas à Kempis.

THREE V.C.s

All in one squad

The Daily Telegr

No. 26,555 LONDON, MONDAY, JULY 15, 1940 and Morning Post BROADCASTI

MR. CHURCHILL AND AN INVASION

READY, UNDISMAYED, TO MEET IT

"WE SEEK NO TERMS & ASK NO MERCY"

LONDON IN RUINS BETTER THAN ENSLAVEMENT

Mr. Churchill, in a broadcast to British, Empire and American listeners last night, reaffirmed his confidence in the determination and ability of this country to resist invasion and, when the time comes, to lift the dark curse of Hitler from our age. He declared:

"Be the ordeal sharp or long, or both, we shall seek no terms, we shall tolerate no parley. We may show mercy, but we shall ask none."

U.S. DEMOCRATS MEET TO-DAY

THIRD TERM TAKEN FOR GRANTED

From Our SPECIAL CORRESPONDENT
CHICAGO, Sunday.

Delegates to the Democratic National Convention, which gets off to a slow-motion start to-morrow, have gathered here with three views uppermost in their minds.

The first is that it would be a grave mistake to under-estimate the strength of the Republican candidate, Mr. Wendell Willkie. The second, arising from this, is that Mr. Roosevelt must be nominated for a third term, while the third is that Mr. James Farley, Postmaster-General, must manage the campaign.

Mr. Farley has been national chairman since Mr. Roosevelt's first nomination here eight years ago. He still holds himself remote from the New Dealers, headed by Mr. Harry Hopkins, Secretary for Commerce, who is now here running the Roosevelt candidacy.

Mr. Farley's opposition to a third term has been frequently expressed in the past, and he has also objected to interference by New Dealers in his domain of party organisation and strategy.

The President's acceptance of nomination is now taken for granted by a majority of Democrats.

NAMES ON THURSDAY

FRENCH NATIONAL DAY IN LONDON

Gen. de Gaulle inspecting a French guard o Whitehall before he placed a wreath on the celebration of the French national holiday ye anniversary of the fall of the Bastille. Adml. on the left. (Another picture on Page

EIRE WARNED BY MINISTER

May Soon Be In A Tight Corner

WAR-TIME ADVICE

60-MINUTE AIR BA

LUNDI 26 AOUT 1940
DIRECTION-REDACTION
85, Fleet St., Londres, E.C.4
(adresse provisoire)
Tel.: Central 8843-8477
ADMINISTRATION
Practical Press, Ltd.,
1, Dorset Buildings, Salisbury Sq.,
Fleet St., Londres, E.C.4
Tel.: Central 1555
Journal quotidien paraissant à Londres avec le patronage de l'Association des Français de Grande-Bretagne
Tous les jours - ONE PENNY

FRANCE

LIBERTE • EGALITE • FRATERNITE

LIRE EN PAGE 3:
Nos information de France
EN PAGE 4:
Nos Informations Générales

N° 1

VIVE LA FRANCE!

LA France est aux mains de l'ennemi. Les Allemands occupent la plus grande partie de son territoire. Ils contrôlent directement ou indirectement, tous les moyens d'expression utilisés en France par les Français: la presse, le cinéma, la radio, les livres. Aucune voix venue de France ne peut exprimer librement les souffrances et les espoirs de nos compatriotes.

Un gouvernement français a signé avec Hitler et Mussolini des armistices désastreux, au mépris de l'honneur et de l'intérêt de notre pays, au mépris de nos engagements formels. Des milliers de Français de la métropole, des territoires d'Outre-Mer et de l'Etranger se refusent à reconnaître ces armistices, dont le texte équivaut à une condamnation à mort de la patrie. Ces Français, hommes et femmes, militaires et civils, entendent demeurer, aux côtés de nos alliés, des belligérants

Le Général de Gaulle a eu le courage de faire appel à ces patriotes français, dès les premières heures d'une capitulation honteuse. Il a promis au Monde, en leur nom, que des forces Françaises continueraient la lutte jusqu'à la libération, jusqu'à la victoire. Il tient parole. Quelques semaines après l'armistice de Compiègne, le drapeau tricolore flotte au dessus des camps d'entrainement emplis de troupes. Il flotte au mât de plusieurs bâtiments de guerre. Dans le ciel, nos aviateurs ont repris le combat.

Pour ceux qui se battent.

Ce journal s'adresse, tout d'abord, à ceux qui se battent: aux soldats aux officiers, aux marins, aux aviateurs, à tous les volontaires des Forces Françaises libres. Il s'adresse aux résidents français à l'étranger et, en première ligne, aux plus proches, à ceux de Grande Bretagne, ainsi qu'aux réfugiés qui ont pu échapper à l'occupation allemande. Il s'adresse aussi à tous les Français libres d'Outre Mer, dont il désire l'union. Bien que percevant l'immense disproportion entre sa taille, ses moyens et la tâche à accomplir, il espère atteindre les Français de l'Empire et même ceux de la métropole. En un mot, ce journal est destiné à tous ceux de nos compatriotes qui refusent la servitude et sont résolus à vaincre l'oppression étrangère. Il souhaite d'être lu par tous les amis de la France.

Ce ne sont pas des exhortations ou des conseils que nous désirons offrir aux Français. Nous voulons, plus modestement, leur donner à lire tous les jours, en langue française, des informations exactes. Notre lutte et les sacrifices qu'elle comporte sont justifiés par des faits. Chaque jour, depuis la terrible date de la capitulation, des faits nous affirment avec éclat que nous avons raison d'espérer. La résistance foudroyante de la Grande - Bretagne aux attaques aériennes allemandes, les contre-attaques de la Royal Air Force, le developpement intense et rapide de l'aide américaine, l'organisation, par le Général de Gaulle, des force combattantes françaises, l'esprit magnifique qui anime les soldats britanniques, français, polonais, hollandais, belges, norvégiens, tchèques, canadiens, sud-africains, hindous, australiens, néo-zélandais, réunis en Angleterre, dans le bastion européen de la liberté, les nouvelles, enfin, qui nous parviennent sur la France et sur son Empire, tous ces faits nous prouvent que rien n'est perdu.

Union des Français pour la liberté.

Les Français de la résistance et de la victoire sont dispersés dans toutes les parties du Monde. Ils appartiennent à tous les milieux, à toutes les professions, toutes les religions, toutes les opinions, tous les partis. Il y a parmi eux des paysans et des citadins, des ouvriers et des patrons, des officiers et des soldats. Spontanément, ces hommes et ces femmes se sont mis d'accord sur une tâche très simple et très grande: la libération du territoire français, la restauration de l'indépendance de la patrie, le maintien des libertés qui sont nos plus nobles traditions, la fidélité à notre alliance avec la nation anglaise.

C'est cette noble cause que servira notre journal, avec la volonté de rendre plus étroites chaque jour l'indispensable union et la solidarité de tous les Français libres.

La Redaction

GEORGE VI A PASSE EN REVUE LES FORCES FRANCAISES LIBRES

UN DEVOIR: COMBATTRE

par le Général de Gaulle

Pour ce journal qui nait dans la détresse nationale et qui ne travaillera qu'à la résurrection, aucune titre n'était possible sinon celui qu'il porte: "FRANCE."

Car aucun Français n'a le droit d'avoir aujourd'hui d'autre pensée, d'autre espoir, d'autre amour, que la pensée, l'espoir, l'amour de la France.

Mais quoi? La patrie a succombé sous les armes. Elle ne renaitra que des armes.

Ceux qui voudraient croire ou faire croire que la liberté, la valeur, la grandeur, pourraient se recréer sous la loi de l'ennemi sont des inconscients ou des lâches.

Le devoir est simple et dur: il faut combattre.

Tout ce qui sert à frapper l'ennemi est donc utile et salutaire. Ainsi de "FRANCE" qui veut exhorter au combat.

Ce journal fera son devoir en répandant courage et confiance, en aidant les Français à s'unir dans la guerre, à s'unir avec les Alliés qui combattent auprès d'eux et, en partie, pour eux.

Ainsi, quelque jour, reparaitra la France, lavée de la honte et des larmes, la France tout entière, la France victorieuse.

DEUX VISITES ROYALES

par Eve Curie

Il y a deux ans, lors de la visite des souverains anglais en France, une des plus belles revues militaires que nous ayons jamais vues fut donnée à Versailles, en l'honneur du roi George VI.

L'armée française était intacte. La France était libre, grande. Nous étions les amis, les alliés de l'Empire britannique.

Il y a deux jours, le roi George VI a été reçu "quelque part en Angleterre," dans un camp d'entrainement, par les Forces Françaises libres. Il a passé en revue, aux côtés du Général de Gaulle, des détachements de volontaires.

A la même heure, des canons à longue portée, de fabrication française, établis par les Allemands sur notre littoral, bombardaient, à travers la Manche, les îles britanniques. A la même heure, des avions anglais bombardaient des

Voir la suite en page 4.

FRANCAIS APOTRES de la liberte

par M. Duff Cooper
Ministre de l'Information

J'ai toujours aimé la France, et je ne l'aime pas moins dans ces jours de douleur et d'affliction que je ne l'aimais alors qu'elle était victorieuse et glorieuse.

Je me réjouis de l'arrivé dans ce pays de nombreux patriotes français qui croient toujours le peuple français capable de secouer le joug de la servitude qui lui a été imposé par l'Allemagne. Je suis sur que bonne d'entre eux qui ont eu la bonne fortune de s'enfuir pour quelque temps de leur propre pays et de jouir de l'hospitalité de la Grande-Bretagne représentent des millions de leurs compatriotes dont les espoirs et les désirs reposent maintenant sur la victoire britannique, parce qu'ils savent qu'aucune autre route ne peut conduire à la restauration de l'indépendance et de la liberté de la France.

Je me félicite done de l'apparition d'une nouvelle publication français qui sera la voix de l'opinion non seulement des Français libres qui se sont réfugiés dans notre pays, mais aussi des millions de Français qui sont toujours en France et qui aspirent à redevenir libres.

PORTE-DRAPEAUX

Les Français ont été pendant longtemps les apôtres de la liberté et les porte-drapeaux du progrés. Ils ont été à l'avant-garde de la lutte européenne pour la liberté. Pendant plus d'un demi-siècle, les yeux de tous ceux qui souhaitent la liberté ont été tournés vers Paris. A présent, ils sont dirigés vers Londres, mais ce ne sera que pendant un bref intervalle. La Grande-Bretagne et la France indiqueront de nouveau la voie aux peuples libres de l'Univers et il ne pourrait pas y avoir de meilleur gage de leur union future que la publication à Londres d'un journal français où des Français seront à même d'exprimer les opinions et les idéals qui nous sont communs.

Lire en page 3 le Message de M. Guéritte à l'Association des Français de Grande-Bretagne.

En Page 4, nos informations.

The R.A.F. pound Berlin's heart fo

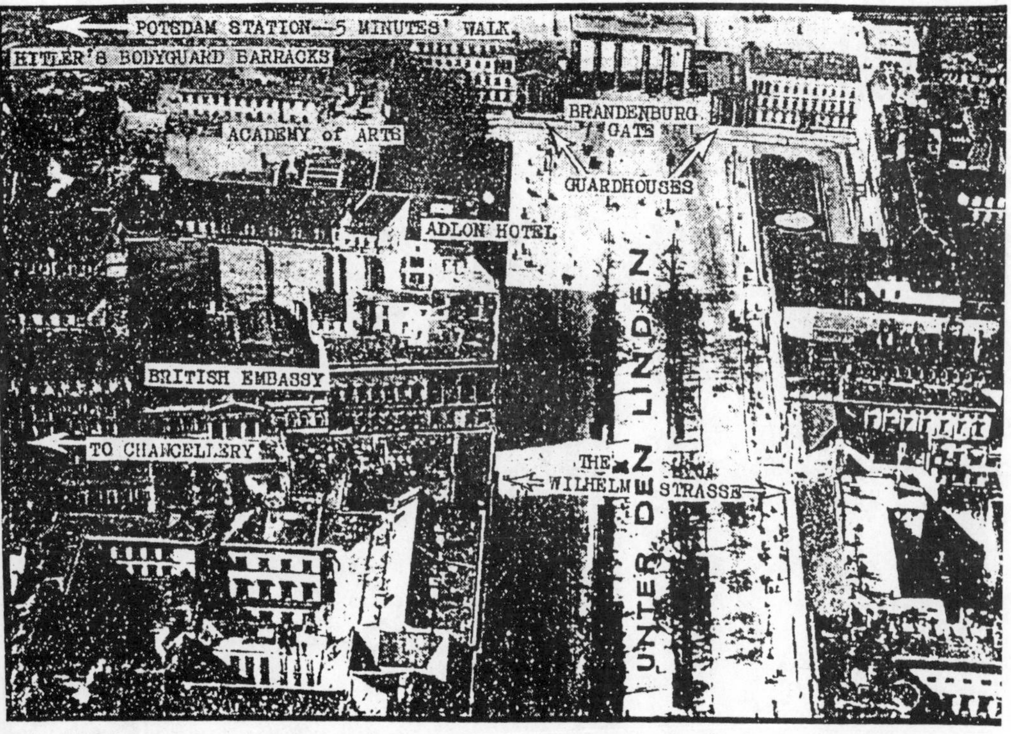

French troops beg for food in Petain's Syria

Daily Express Staff Reporter ALAN MOOREHEAD

CAIRO, Wednesday.

IT is persistently reported here that unrest and revolt against the Vichy Government is spreading along the Mediterranean from Syria to Tunis, Algeria, and Morocco. The movement seems at present small, disorganised, and isolated.

The Vichy Government is doing everything to block it by cutting off all colonies from the outside world to prevent leakage of news. Tunis, Algeria and Morocco are being separated into three completely distinct countries.

Foreign newspapers and correspondence are forbidden: radio sets are banned: travel from one part to another is stopped: private meetings, especially in garrisons have been declared illegal.

Tunis appears to be the storm centre. That is where Weygand and a group of generals were expected to have arrived to clean up disaffected groups in the army.

I understand that Weygand has now who is co-operating with General Aude, the veteran colonial officer formerly at Meknes who is now military governor of Tunis.

In Syria the food shortage is so bad that soldiers are begging in the streets. There is no petrol and no trade overseas or overland.

Italian terror raids, like Monday's attack on Telaviv, in nearby Palestine, which killed 112 people, only stir up resentment. Frenchmen are well aware that the raid was meant as a threat against the m.f they "misbehave," but still they are deserting in some places, and in others have actually begun wearing the de Gaulle emblem hidden beneath their lapels.

Mareth Line against Libya are leading the unrest. They are bitterly protesting against the Italian demand that the Mareth forts must be dismantled and their guns and equipment sent to Tripoli.

Harassed French generals have posted up warnings that disobedience will lead to courts-martial. Many arrests

But the real source of resentment lies in the old, bitter quarrel between the French and the 100,000 Italian residents in Tunis. The Italian colony was crushed two years ago when it started rioting in support cof Mussolini's first wary cry for Tunis, Corsica and Nice.

Now the Italians are taking revenge—publicly jeering at the French, seizing key posts, ejecting Frenchmen from jobs and sitting on military tribunals. Mussolini preferring to let the French straighten out the mess themselves and fearing further disorder, has delayed sending his full military mission.

In Rabat meanwhile, General Nogues is awaiting arrival of a Nazi commission which, I understand, is to be flown out from Germany.

AMERICA

PIERCING defences the two-hour raid t two o'clock yeste pounded the hea man capital. S pilots made glide is a picture that story. The gre station was hit wi several hundr bombs. Reports f

ground. They have the ground now for

"There was desper of these interned ref do between meals bu in their hands and w German commission those they want for of the Gestapo."

BRITISH

Melbourne gi for bomb

MELBOURN

THE City Council day announced to the Lord Mayor tims Relief Fund; has already bee citizens.

DAILY HERALD

No. 7681 THURSDAY, SEPTEMBER 26, 1940

DAKAR EXPEDITION

De Gaulle Would Not Fight His Own Countrymen

By W. N. EWER, "Daily Herald" Diplomatic Correspondent

THE Dakar expedition has been called off, in view of General de Gaulle's unwillingness to engage in serious fighting between Frenchmen and Frenchmen.

It became clear yesterday that the Governor's decision to resist was not a mere gesture.

This decision meant that the port could be taken only after a major operation, not only by the British naval squadron, but by the Free French land forces.

General de Gaulle, as his communique of Monday night suggested, was unwilling to undertake this.

It was, therefore, decided not to continue a useless bombardment of the forts and the French warships, but to call off the whole operation.

Watch will still be kept for any attempt to use Dakar as a German or sea raider base.

The whole affair seems to have been a bad blunder of over-confidence.

MISCALCULATION

It had been rashly assumed that the arrival of General de Gaulle with an appreciable contingent of French troops would induce the authorities to surrender without resistance.

That might have been so if they had not been allowed to receive the reinforcement of the six

HITLER TELLS SPAIN TO JOIN IN WAR

BOMBED OUT OF HOME

Mass Ra[...] Off: 23 S[...]

LARGE German [...] were over En[...] the first time si[...] smashing defeat[...] Once more a ver[...] them was destroy[...]

Twenty-three were [...] were heavy bombers. [...] bombers.

Twenty were shot d[...] English Channel by Spitfir[...] were destroyed by anti-air[...]

Four of our fighters are [...] pilots are safe.

Between one and two hundr[...] enemy bombers and fighters fl[...] north-west just before noon.

Fighter pilots saw two wedg[...] of Junkers 88 bombers flying [...] tight arrowhead formation, abo[...]

...aff Works Knee-Deep ...o Get ...leals

...EBB,
...porter

...ng at Lon-
...hit during
...es the total
...eks.
...ling still goes
...under the ter-
...nigh explosive
...words of one

CLEARING-UP AFTER THE RAID

Nurses use a workman's barrow to wheel away salvaged belongings after their hospital had been hit.

HOMELESS (Moved Away From Jobs) WANT TO WORK

By RITCHIE CALDER, "Daily Herald" Reporter

ON the wall of the rest centre, in a reception district for the homeless, were the "Orders of the Day."

They read something like this:

Kitchen Fatigue: Bill.
Sanitary Squad: In charge, Fred.
Black-out and Repairs: Nobby.

And so on.

The refugees themselves had taken matters in hand and had appointed a committee which made itself r..ponsible for organising the work about the place.

"It's grand, after a fortnight, to have something to do," said Bill, who was manning the ship's galley which had been installed, "but I want to get back to my job."

So did all the men there.

others who were employed in the same locality.

Those who find it difficult to get to work, or who have lost their jobs, as well as their homes, should at once consult their unions.

The unions are in direct touch with the Government and can get immediate arrangements made for transport or for transfe to other work.

Making It Easier

But there are other problems. All the homeless men to whom I have spoken during the past fortnight are keen to go on working.

If they can see their families safely established in new homes they are prepared to go back and face the raids.

The wives are often the difficulty. Many of these stout-hearted women are prepared to face the

ITALY'S 13 DEMANDS TO FRENCH IN SYRIA

From "Daily Herald" Special Correspondent

CAIRO, Wednesday.

THE Italian Commission in Syria has, I am reliably informed, presented a list of 13 demands to the French authorities there.

Negotiations on these demands are proceeding, but only a very few of them have been accepted.

The demands are:—

(1) Demobilisation of the French forces in Syria and Lebanon, especially those suspected of lukewarmness towards the Vichy regime. These include the Foreign Legion.

(2) Repatriation of demobilised officers and men with guarantees that they will not escape.

(3) Repatriation to France of all officers known for their hostility to Germany and Italy.

SURRENDER ALL

(4) Surrender of aerodromes and naval and military bases to the Italians, who will control and use them; also surrender of naval units in Syrian and Lebanon ports.

(5) Maintenance of a military force capable of guarding all Syrian and Lebanon frontiers, and preventing any disaffected officers and men joining British or French forces.

(6) Acceptance of control by the Italian Commission over administration, taxation, censorship and internal order.

(7) Ban on all travelling between Syria and Lebanon on the one hand, and neighbouring countries on the other without special authority.

TO QUELL RISING

(8) Approval of a series of special measures to quell opposition on the part of the local population.

(9) Delivery to the Italian Commission of all stocks of arms, munitions, provisions and explosives in Syria and

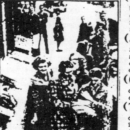

LUNCH—AS USUAL

Cooking over an open fire outside a restaurant in the City. The chef by this method has continued to serve three hundred customers with hot luncheons.

Rest of the News

CLAIRTON, Pennsylvania, was rocked yesterday by an explosion at the factory

A NEW office has been opened by the Fire Brigade Union at 101, Broadhurst-gardens.— Hampstead, N.W.6. Telephone: Maida

›NS
›
TO

›T AIR ARM AT
›NED AS A DEAD

›ass battleship.

›n"
›mist

› for divorce and ob-
›e nisi.
›ough, the co-respon-
›ase was named John

›d's marriage to Lyn-
› consumated, and he
›cree of nullity.
›riage to Dr. Ireland
›st year.

›d, giving evidence on
›d he had twice mar-
›sed woman. After the
› he divorced her.]

› said Lynwood ran
›nd Mrs. Ireland gave
›rable sum of money.

›y Decree

›d Thomas, K.C. (de-
› it true that she
› a single penny by
›at has been proved
›—That is so.

›ow that Mrs. Ireland
›fully kind to Lord
›s poverty and illness,

THEIR BOMBING OF BRITAIN IS FINISHED

Different types of Nazi airmen—prisoners of war—as they passed through London yesterday.

This spectacled studious youth and his—

—companion, both cast

Nurse Heroine Of Raid Awarded G.M.

MISS VIOLET ELEANOR REID is a junior nurse at an asylum. She has been awarded the George Medal for the courage she showed when the place was bombed.

Fourteen others have gained the medal by their bravery during raids.

Among them are ten constables, two firemen, and two railwaymen.

Nurse Reid was seriously injured when one bomb hit a building.

The explosion made her deaf and she was suffering from loss of blood—but she carried an injured nurse to safety and then went back to attend to patients.

Prevented Panic

"By her cool and cheerful conduct," says the official account, "she prevented confusion among the mental patients from developing into what might readily have become a panic."

Others who have been awarded the George Medal include:—

Thomas Bruce, fire brigade superintendent. He rescued three people trapped in a shelter, which was set on fire when a German bomber crashed. While he worked, there were repeated explosions of concentrated petrol vapour. And there was constant danger that bombs in the wreckage might go off.

Constable William G. Hack, J Division Metropolitan Police Force.—A crude oil bomb fell on a factory causing a big fire. Six people were trapped in a shelter. Despite heat, flames, and additional bombs, Constable Hack made a hole in the debris and took out the trapped six.

Then he found a man up to his waist in wreckage which was alight. With the help of two other officers he got the man free.

Saved Trapped Man

TENNIS CHAMPION RECRUITING

Madame Mathieu (left), interviewing the first recruit to General de Gaulle's women's army in London yesterday.

GRACIE TO STAR IN PLAY

By Our Own Correspondent
LOS ANGELES, Friday.

GRACIE FIELDS is to star in a musical play which Monty Banks, her husband, is

Bombed, Must Pay His Rent

A BOMBED tenant who had not served his landlord with a notice disclaiming liability was held liable for the full rent at Edmonton County Court yesterday.

The tenant was sued for posses-

FREE ARMY OF FRENCH WOMEN

By MARY FERGUSON
"Daily Herald" Reporter

FRENCH women in London who were pining to do something for their country went in a constant stream to Westminster House, S.W., yesterday.

Young, middle-aged, rich and poor, they all wanted to join General de Gaulle's new Corps Auxiliaire Feminin—equivalent of our A.T.S.

Madame Mathieu, the French tennis champion, wife of an officer in General de Gaulle's army, has been placed in command of recruiting.

Patriotic free Frenchwomen offered themselves as cooks, nurses, secretaries and chauffeuses.

Want To Work

They did not ask about uniform, the pay of 1s. 4d. a day they brushed aside, conditions of service they ignored—all they asked was, "Please, will you take me?"

"It is wonderful and I am so pleased to see so many of my countrywomen offering themselves for the cause," said Madame Mathieu.

"It is a pity that now we need only a small number of specially qualified women. When we need a great many we shall get them easily."

In the hall, where the women sat waiting to be interviewed, they spoke about brothers and sisters, fathers and mothers, uncles, aunts and cousins still in France and

Stourport Courier

NEWS FOR THE DISTRICTS OF

ARELEY KINGS, ASTLEY, BEWDLEY, DUNLEY, HARTLEBURY, SHRAWLEY, AND WILDEN

EASTER WEDDINGS

PRETTY SCENES AT STOURPORT CHURCHES

Mr. Stanley Baldwin—Miss V. F. Jinks

The Parish Church was the scene of a pretty wedding, on Saturday, when Mr. Stanley Baldwin, son of Mrs. and the late Mr. Enoch Baldwin, of Tan Lane, Stourport, was married to Miss Vera Florence Jinks the third daughter of Mrs. and the late Mr. Jinks, of the School House, Church Avenue, Stourport.

The Rev. W. A. Trippass officiated.

The bride was given away by Mr. James Hodges, and was attended by Miss Iris Jinks (sister) and Miss M. Gwilliam (niece of the bridegroom).

Mr. Harry Baldwin was best man.

Mr. E. R. Kemp—Miss M. Bailey

The wedding took place at St. Michael's Church, on Saturday of Mr. Edward Raymond Kemp, son of Mr. and Mrs. E. R. Kemp, Stroud, and Miss Mary Bailey, daughter of the late Mr. and Mrs. J. W. Bailey, of 35, Vernon Road, Stourport.

The Rev. W. J. Reynolds officiated.

The bride was given away by Mr. J. Bailey, and wore a tweed costume with brown accessories to tone, and an orchid spray.

Mr. Douglas Kemp was best man.

After the ceremony a reception was held at the Tontine Hotel, and later Mr. and Mrs. E. R. Kemp left for their honeymoon, which is being spent in London.

Mr. G. Heybeard—Miss M. Hayward

Another wedding at St. Michael's, on Saturday, was that of Mr. Geoffrey Heybeard, second son of Mr. and Mrs. R. Heybeard, of Areley Kings, who is now serving in the Royal Air Force, who was married to Miss May Hayward, only daughter of Mrs. F. Saunders and the late Mr. J. Hayward, of Vernon Place, Vernon Road, Stourport.

The Rev. W. A. Trippass (vicar) conducted the service.

Given away by her step-father, the bride wore a blue two-piece with navy blue accessories, with a spray of white heather and freesia.

[illegible]

Mr. Don Chell—Miss I. L. Hodges

St. Michael's Church, Stourport, was the scene of the wedding of Mr. Donald Roland Chell, of Stourport, and Miss Iris Lilian Hodges, elder daughter of Mr. and Mrs. R. H. Hodges, of "Denehurst," Bewdley Road, Stourport, on Tuesday.

The bridegroom, who is the eldest son of Mr. and Mrs. D. Chell, Dorsett Road, Stourport, was born in Alberta, Canada, but came to Stourport, the home town of his father, five years ago, and has some fame in the district for hill-billy and yodelling songs at local concerts.

The service was taken by the Rev W. A. Trippass, and Mr. R. C. S. Gregory, Mus.Bac., was at the organ. The hymns, "Love Divine" and "Lead us, Heavenly Father" were sung.

The bride wore a dress of white taffeta with a head-dress of lilies-of-the-valley, and silver shoes. Her bouquet was of white carnations. She was given away by her father, and attended by Miss Gwen Hodges, her sister, and Miss Florence Chell, sister of the bridegroom. The bridesmaids wore lilac coloured dresses with floral head-dresses and shoes to match. They carried posies of anemones.

Mr. George Gibbs, of Kidderminster, was best man.

A reception was held at the Swan Hotel, where about 50 guests were entertained.

Mr. and Mrs. Chell afterwards left for their honeymoon, at Leamington, the bride travelling in a mustard coloured dress and hat with a grey coat.

DUDLEY BRIDEGROOM

For Miss Marjorie Stokes

A pretty wedding took place at St. Michael's Church, Stourport, on Saturday, when Mr. Major Kenneth James Fryer, of 3, Furness Row, Orange Park, Dudley, was married to Miss Marjorie Edith Stokes, second daughter of Mr. and Mrs. A. E. Stokes, of 2, Woodbury Road, Stourport-on-Severn.

The bridegroom, who is the only son of Mr. and Mrs. H. F. Fryer, of Dudley, is on the staff of the Midland Bank, Ltd.

Y.M.C.A. CANTEEN

For Stourport

VISIT OF COUNTESS OF LICHFIELD

The need of a canteen in Stourport was emphasised by Mr. R. P. Vale, chairman of Stourport Urban District Council, when he presided at a public meeting at the Stourport Town Hall, on Friday afternoon. The meeting was in connection with a proposal to establish a Y.M.C.A. canteen in the town, and the Right Hon. Countess of Lichfield, Y.M.C.A. canteen organiser for the county, outlined the work and use of these canteens.

There was a good attendance of ladies of the W.V.S. present, including Mrs. J. A. McLauchlan (Stourport W.V.S. organiser), Mrs. C. Mackie (W.V.S. canteen officer), and Lady Beauchamp (W.V.S. county organiser).

Mr. R. P. Vale, introducing the Countess of Lichfield, said the splendid attendance showed the interest the ladies had in the projected canteen in Stourport. In all parts of Worcestershire and in the neighbouring towns canteens had been started, and he thought it was time one was started in Stourport.

The Countess of Lichfield was showing her interest in their Y.M.C.A. canteen at Stourport, by coming that afternoon to explain the working of the canteens to them.

28 CANTEENS IN MIDLANDS

The Countess of Lichfield explained what the Y.M.C.A. canteens were doing and what they were, as many people did not know about them or why they were formed. Since the beginning of the war 28 canteens had been started and were now running in various parts of the Midlands.

Referring to Stourport, the Countess said they must try to do all they could. The Y.M.C.A. wanted the canteen to be as bright as possible with bright faces to welcome visitors. The Countess described the food served in the canteens.

They did not lay down a hard and fast rule as to the chief items needed, because they found by experience that requirements differed in various districts and they worked to suit the district.

Referring to the canteen staff the Countess said she always found that the ladies liked to be busy and often got bored with nothing to do. They never experienced difficulty in getting volunteers, although some of the canteens were two and a half miles from town, and the ladies had to walk there. Yet in all the heavy snow and terrible weather the ladies continued to man these canteens. The standard must be

FOOD OFFICER

Appointment of Mr. J. W. Moffitt

At a meeting of the Stourport-on-Severn Food Control Committee at the Council House, last Thursday evening, Mr. J. W. Moffitt (deputy food executive officer) was elected Food Executive officer) was elected Food Executive Loft, whose resignation was received at the meeting. The appointment is subject to the approval of the Ministry of Food but the confirmation has since been received.

Mr. E. P. Parker presided at the meeting, and others present were Miss E. M. Capel Loft, Mrs. H. P. Long, Mrs. H. E. Rose, Mr. W. A. Coley, Mr. F. Goode, Mr. A. Griffiths, Mr. A. J. Lewis, Mr. A. Nott, and Mr. I. Nunney.

The Deputy Food Executive Officer submitted the report of the sub-committee.

The Chairman said it was with deep regret that they received the resignation of Mr. A. D. Capel Loft, and proposed Mr. Moffitt be appointed to the position. Mr. Moffitt had been the Deputy F.E.O. since the formation of the committee, and was fully conversant with the duties.

With regard to the enforcement of the rationing order and regulations, a communication was read from the Ministry of Food stating that a divisional inspector for enforcement purposes had been appointed and would be stationed at Worcester. His services would be available for any cases needing investigation in the Stourport area.

Mr. Moffitt also reported on the result of correspondence with the Ministry of Food regarding the request for additional supplies of sugar for employees of Wilden Works. The Ministry were not prepared to accede to the request, but suggested that if a canteen was established at the works they could be registered as a catering establishment, and could obtain special permits for supplies of rationed foods for canteen purposes. Many industrial firms in the Midlands had already established canteens registered as catering establishments.

COUNTY DARTS CHAMPIONSHIP

Stourport League's Team

The following team has been elected to represent the Stourport Darts League in the County Darts Championship, to be held at the Black Horse Hotel, Kidderminster, on Saturday: J. Large and W. Harris (Olde Crown), J. Grennan (Workmen's Club), J. W. Guest (Bay Horse), G. Hardwick and P. Randle (White Lion), E. Kilcour and A. N. Other (Station Hotel) and G. Evans (Manor Arms). Reserves: H. Suellis (Workmen's Club), C. [illegible] (Manor Arms), and [illegible] (Bay Horse).

Only six teams in the league sent in nominations, and the committee decided that the six clubs represented at the meeting should each nominate another player from their club, which was done.

Mr. Dale Thompson, assistant secretary, was elected non-playing captain.

It was decided that the annual meeting of the Stourport League should be held at the Manor Arms, Minster Road, on April 2nd, at 8 p.m., when the presentation of awards in connection with the league will take place.

Mr. J. Nevil Butler, vice-president, has consented to present the prizes.

THE HAVEN CINEMA

"Let Us Live," featuring Maureen O'Sullivan, Henry Fonda and Ralph Bellamy in the principal roles, is the prime attraction for the first three days of the coming week, at the Haven Cinema, Stourport. The story tells how plain average people suddenly find the eyes of the world upon them: innocent people—yet cast in the role of murderers. Universal in its theme "Let Us Live" has already been hailed as "a great love story . . . a powerful drama of everyday people that will be your screen experience of a lifetime."

Hailed by the national Press and the leading critics of the country as one of the greatest films to be made in Britain, "Jamaica Inn," adapted from the book by Daphne du Maurier, is the principal attraction for the last three days of the week.

This dramatic and exciting story of the Cornish wreckers of over a hundred years ago has practically everything that goes to the making of a great popular success. There is action and suspense, with comedy and romance as other essentials of a popular photoplay. Among the highlights are the breathtaking scenes where great sailing ships are lured on to the treacherous rocks by the wreckers.

The cast headed by Charles Laughton is one of the most impressive yet assembled for a British film.

THE GALLANT 8,000

Stourport Saves for Victory

Stourport found itself in the news this week when references were made in the Birmingham papers to the efforts the town is making financially to win the war. One paper begins with a heading: "Sleepy Market Town" Saves £27,810 For Victory. The Gallant 8,000.

Stourport has been described as "a sleepy little market town in which live 8,000 people." But in the week between March 2nd and 9th, the 8,000 inhabitants invested £9,463 in Savings Certificates, Defence Bonds and the Post Office Savings Bank. That is more than £1 1s. a week per head of the population.

"Between November 22nd and March 2nd, £18,347 was invested, so that, since the war finance campaign started, up to March 9th these 8,000 lent £27,810 to help win the war.

Not considering this effort "good enough," the people of Stourport are planning a big campaign to take place before Whitsun—"to encourage the 8,000 to save." Every car in Stourport-on-Severn will carry a savings poster.

"It's the group system that does it: there are more groups of savers here than anywhere else in the West Midland region," said a regional official.

Horticultural Society.—To further the progress of the "Grow More Food" campaign in Stourport, a lecture on "Vegetable Production in War-time" will be given at the Stourport Society meeting at the Swan Hotel on Thursday, April 4th. The lecturer will be Mr. L. F. Clift, N.D.Hort. (instructor in horticulture, Agricultural Education Sub-committee). The meeting will be open to the public.

HEATH'S CHARITY

THE Heath's Charity will be distributed by the churchwardens of Lower Mitton at the Parish Room, Stourport, on Tuesday, April 2nd, at 3 p.m.

Severn Victim.—A body recovered from the River Severn at Worcester on Sunday has been identified as that of Samuel Taylor, aged 75, retired gardener, of 2, Carthouses, Shrawley, near Stourport. The Police had issued a description of the body in which it was stated that a piece of paper bearing a list of cutlery had been found in one of the man's pockets. Taylor, who was a widower, had been missing since March 4th. It is understood that he had left a note with a neighbour, Mrs. Mary Jane Barker, of 3, Carthouses, Shrawley.

p your
CKER
up!

BEWDLEY'S 1940 BUDGET

A 14/8 RATE TO PRODUCE £12,320

AGREEMENT WITH 'BUS COMPANY

BEWDLEY'S budget for the financial year just beginning, and negotiations which had taken place with representatives of the Midland Red 'Bus Company, were the chief topics discussed at a special meeting of the Bewdley Town Council held at the Guildhall on Monday evening.

The Council approved an unchanged rate of 14s. 8d. in the £, which is estimated to produce £12,320, of which roughly one-third will be spent on services administered by the Borough Council, the remaining two-thirds going to the County Council.

The Deputy Mayor (Alderman H. N. Frost) regretted that the Council could not pass on to Bewdley ratepayers the 2d. reduction made by the County Council. He hoped it would be possible to stabilise the borough rates at 14s. 8d. even when the full £44,400 had been raised for the sewerage scheme, which should be in being by June, 1941.

Satisfaction was expressed at the improved 'bus service now operating between Bewdley and Kidderminster, following complaints made at the Council's previous meeting, and a subsequent interview with officials of the Company.

The Mayor (Councillor C. R. Pritchard) presided, and other members present were the Deputy Mayor (Alderman H. N. Frost), Aldermen F. F. Mountford and R. B. Jackson, Councillors J. Bates, T. W. Palmer, F. R. Welch, H. O. Claeck, G. Mortimer Smith and W. Harcourt Webb, with the Town Clerk (Mr. L. Gordon Hales) and the Borough Surveyor (Mr. R. J. Rowe).

An apology was received from Councillor O. H. Wallis.

Alderman Frost was re-elected as the Council's representative on the North-West Worcestershire Assessment Committee and Councillor Mortimer Smith as a representative on the Kidderminster and District Joint Town Planning Committee.

On the Council's behalf, the Mayor extended sympathy to Alderman Frost in the bereavement sustained by the sudden death, under tragic circumstances, of his only sister, who collapsed while on holiday.

The Deputy Mayor briefly acknowledged the condolences.

NEGOTIATIONS WITH MIDLAND "RED"

The Town Clerk recalled that at the previous meeting reference was made to the 'bus service, and said that representatives of the Council had since met the Midland "Red" Company's representatives at his office. Suggestions were made as to how difficulties might be met, and he had since received a letter from the company.

Dealing with the request for additional double-deckers for the evening works traffic from Kidderminster, the company stated that at the present time four double-deckers and four saloons were operated from 5.10 to 5.50 p.m. They had gone into the question of double-deck fleet allocation, but regretted that they could not find another 'bus of that type to substitute for one of the saloons now used. Upon examination of the present service it was found that arrangements were quite adequate for the traffic requirements.

As to the suggestion that a 'bus should be operated from the Hop Pole Inn in the mornings for the Bark Hill estate, the company pointed out that a 'bus leaving the Hop Pole at 7.30 a.m. for Kidderminster was patronised by the Bark Hill people at a fare of 5½d. workmen's return. Their investigations showed that the traffic was being well catered for.

Thirdly, in regard to cheap facilities for visitors to Hayley Green Hospital on visiting days, the letter from Mr. O. C. Power, traffic manager, concluded: "If you will direct the parents of children at the hospital to call at our Kidderminster office before travelling, we shall be pleased to issue them with a half-fare permit. It would be advisable for such applicants to present a note signed either by the Mayor or Town Clerk asking for the concession."

COUNCIL REPRESENTATIVES' VIEWS

Alderman Jackson, who met the company's representatives with the Mayor...

Finance Committee gave very careful consideration to these estimates, and decided to curtail a great deal of the expenditure in order to maintain the rate at the existing figure of 14s. 8d. in the £. These economies included a reduction of £300 in the estimated expenditure on highways. The Borough Surveyor's estimate for £730 for repairs to the 130 Corporation Council houses was also reduced to £463, despite the fact that provision has to be made for the first time for repairs to the 36 houses at Bark Hill, which were erected three and a half years ago. The figure of £463 provided for will utilise in full the statutory allowance of 15 per cent. of the net rents for 1940-41.

"The present estimates show a considerable increase in the sewerage loan charges. Last year the charges were £299; we estimate this year we shall require £783. This is the net figure after allowing for the County Council's grants of 60 per cent.

"Although a considerable saving has been effected as a result of the elimination of street lighting, £114 has still to be paid to the S.W. and S. Electric Power Co. and the Bewdley Gas Co. for maintenance. Provision is made for additional expenditure on the Fire Brigade estimates, as certain provisions of the Fire Brigades Act, 1938, come into operation on July 29th, 1940, which throw an additional burden on the Corporation.

WHEN SEWERAGE SCHEME WILL BE READY

"The cost of night soil removal last year was £614. We estimate the cost will be the same this year, and probably for the next year ending 1942. The engineers have given us a definite promise that, unless anything unforeseen happens, the sewerage scheme will be in being by June, 1941. It will take some months before all the houses are connected to the main sewer and the scheme completed, when we hope to save about two-thirds of the cost of removing night soil. This saving will offset the increase in the sewerage loan charges which will have to be met as the scheme nears completion, and it should be possible to avoid any substantial increase in the rate even when the full £44,400 has been raised for the sewerage scheme.

"There are two items of expenditure included in this year's estimates which are non-recurring: Repairs to Town Hall £235, Bark Hill land and expenses £285. The committee is satisfied that the Town Hall stonework is so dangerous that it must be done. The purchase of the piece of land at Bark Hill will complete our housing estate.

"As none of this expenditure of £520 will have to be provided for in next year's estimates, the consequent saving will offset the further increases in the sewerage loan charges which will have to be met next year.

"We shall probably have additional capital expenditure to meet in connection with the water undertaking, which is likely to be inadequate in the near future. We intend to go into the question of putting down a new engine, with...

"NO DRASTIC CHANGES"

Hartlebury Rector's Policy

Presiding at his first Easter Vestry and annual parochial church meeting as Rector of Hartlebury, the Rev. J. Bewstead Wilson, on Thursday week declared that he did not intend making any drastic changes.

Supported by Commander C. W. Lepper, R.N. (rector's warden) and Mr. J. F. Johnson (people's warden), the Rector, presiding at the Easter Vestry meeting, said he was grateful to them for the extremely cordial and friendly welcome given him and his wife on their arrival in the parish. He hoped their association with Hartlebury would be as pleasant for the parishioners as it was at present for him and his wife. He was glad they were receiving the Rev. H. C. Vial so well and he hoped they would continue to give him their help and support.

The Rector said he was grateful to his predecessor, Canon Noel Paterson, for making it so easy for him to take up his work in the parish, for he knew what a great blow it was for his predecessor to leave Hartlebury after 18 years. He was also grateful to the Bishop and also to the Churchwardens, whose duties had been made more difficult than usual during the change of an incumbent because of the exceptional circumstances. The war, the black-out and the change of times for services had increased their work, and he thought that it was most creditable that, in spite of all their difficulties, they showed a credit balance. This was evidence of the care taken in the management of the parish.

NEW WARDEN

The Rector said he was sorry that Commander Lepper was unable to continue in office, for he and Mr. Johnson had done admirable work together, but he thought he could do no better than nominate Mr. Eliot Howard as Rector's warden, for he was one of the oldest and leading parishioners in Hartlebury.

Mr. Johnson was re-elected people's warden.

At the parochial church meeting the Rector outlined his policy, and declared that he proposed doing nothing in the shape of a drastic change, but both sides would have to give and take. He would have to do things to which he was not accustomed and they might have to do the same.

"I hope I have not given anyone the impression by what I have said or done that I wish to criticise," he added, before thanking Mr. N. Watkins and the choir, to whom he thought he might have appeared irritable, for the way they had taken his suggestions.

NEW VICE-C...

Mr. C. Coombe... Mrs. An...

MEETING OF ... COMMIT...

BARK HILL HOUSES

Bewdley Council and Road Costs

DIRECT LABOUR VIEWS

The cost of road works on Bewdley Council's Bark Hill Estate was discussed at Monday's quarterly meeting, over which the Mayor (Councillor C. R. Pritchard) presided. Other members present were the Deputy Mayor (Ald. H. N. Frost), Aldermen F. E. Mountford and R. R. Jackson, Councillors J. Bates, J. H. Butcher, H. O. Hawley, F. W. Palmer, G. Mortimer Smith, F. R. Welch, G. H. Wallis and Major W. Harcourt Webb, with the Town Clerk (Mr. L. Gordon Hales) and the Borough Surveyor (Mr. R. J. Rowe).

Councillor Palmer said that regarding the road widening at Bark Hill he was not altogether satisfied with the figures—£1,196 for labour, materials and so on, £275 for purchase of land. He thought the amount of time taken to carry out the work was excessive. Sometimes there was one man on the job, next day perhaps four or five. He thought that was one reason why people had so often asked "What will it cost?" The public had taken great interest in it.

The Town Clerk asked why Councillor Palmer was dissatisfied with the figures which he (Mr. Hales) had supplied, adding: "I have given him all he asked for."

"My contention is that had it been put out to contract we might have done it cheaper," said Councillor Palmer.

The Mayor: That is an entirely different matter. The Town Clerk supplied the figures asked for.

Councillor Bates suggested that Councillor Palmer had gone about it in the wrong manner. He should have asked how many square yards of road had been done, and how much it would have cost if put out to contract. The speaker's view was that £1,200 was not excessive. "It generally costs 28s. a square yard, does it not?" he asked the Surveyor.

Mr. Rowe: It depends on the class of road.

Councillor Bates: You have made a first-class road?

Mr. Rowe: Yes, it has all been taken up and re-metalled.

A CONSIDERED OPINION

The Mayor pointed out that when the scheme was first mooted, the whole matter of direct labour or contract was discussed at great length. Various suggestions were made, facts and figures were produced, and the Council—rightly in his opinion—agreed to do it by direct labour, partly to relieve unemployment. They might have been wrong, but they definitely came to that conclusion, and members who joined the Council subsequently must abide by their decision. He could not see any purpose in bringing the matter up now.

The Deputy Mayor said he was quite satisfied the road charges were very reasonable. On the whole scheme they saved money on the original estimates.

Alderman Jackson said the question of direct or contract labour had been before the Council on many occasions. They employed an architect for the Cleobury Road houses, but not for the Bark Hill houses, yet the fees were less for the 100 houses than for the 30 houses. If ratepayers objected, he would like to know who they were. "There is not a penny piece wasted by the finance subcommittee," the speaker added. "We had a lot of unemployed when we started this scheme; we used a lot of them, and I think we saved hundreds of pounds."

Alderman Mountford said that since the Surveyor had been in Bewdley, any work he had undertaken by direct labour had been done economically. He had kept a close eye on expenditure.

WORTH DOING WELL.

"It's all very well to criticise it," said the Deputy Mayor, "but if a job is worth doing at all, it is worth doing well, and a pound or two spent while the job is on may save hundreds later. I don't think there are any better-built houses in the country than those at Bark Hill, and there will be no cost on the roads for some years to come."

Alderman Jackson remarked that the Ministry sent people to see the Bark Hill houses.

Replying to Councillor Palmer, who asked if the work was deliberately spread over a length of time to be more economical, he said it was not finished in one year because the whole of the money allotted had been used up. It was postponed to the next financial year so as not to increase the rates.

Councillor Bates observed that it was not the housing scheme which caused the controversy. All Bewdley people knew it was one of the finest in the country. They grumbled about the road widening scheme because it lasted so long.

"It's all in connection with the one scheme," the Deputy Mayor pointed out.

Councillor Bates: They are not all cognisant of that. People outside have not the knowledge of the inner workings, and I think when they read this explanation in the Press they won't be so quick in criticising what we have ... a good job done well.

T TRADE DIRECTORY

[illegible]

THE CARPET MANUFACTURING CO. LIMITED (Richard Smith and Sons Morton and Sons), New Road, Kidderminster. Manufacturers of Axminster Brussels and Wilton in Piece, Broadlin and Seamless Squares, Chenille Axminster Seamless Squares, Rugs and Mats, Spool Axminster Rugs.
Specialities: The Crompton Axminster in Pieces and Seamless (Pontra) Squares, Takabe Wiltons, Takabe Seamless Wilton Squares, Durbar Axminster, Alcestis Seamless Axminster Squares and reversible Rugs.
Cables and Telegrams: "Carmanco," Kidderminster. Bentley's Code.
Telephone: Kidderminster 2271.
London.—Greenwich House, 10-12, Newgate Street, E.C.1. James Ronald and Sons (Shipping), 3 and 4 Little Love Lane, Wood Street, E.C.
Glasgow.—61-65, Virginia Street, C.1.
Manchester.—Clydesdale House, Turner Street (Retail). Peterkin and Cooke, 9 Chatham Street, Piccadilly (Wholesale).
Newcastle-on-Tyne.—23, Eldon Square.
Leeds.—33, St. Paul's Street, 1.
Bristol.—39, Broadmead, 1.
Melbourne.—Yarra House, Bond Street.
Capetown.—Clarebut Chambers, Progress Lane, Strand Street.
Johannesburg.—613, Stuttaford's Chambers.
Paris.—17, Rue Dereste.
Alexandria and Cairo.—Commercial and Agency Co. of Egypt Ltd., 10 Rue General Earle, Alexandria.
Christchurch, N.Z.—60, Lichfield Street.
Copenhagen.—Nissen and Gronbech, Nyhavn, 14.

THE VICTORIA CARPET CO., LTD.—GREEN STREET, KIDDERMINSTER.
Manufacturers of Seamless Chenille and Axminster Squares, Sofas, Rugs and Mats, Tapestry and Velvet Squares in various grades and sizes. Velvet and Tapestry Hearth Rugs, Mats and Tapestry Stairs.
Telegrams: "Victoria, Kidderminster."
Telephone: 2278 (2 lines).
Codes used: A.B.C. 6th Edition, Western Union 5 letter Edition, Bentley's.
London.—Cathedral House, 8 Paternoster Row. Telegrams: "Pretoneed," London. Telephone: 1818 City.
Manchester.—Clydesdale House, Turner Street. Telegrams: "Thriving," Manchester. Telephone: 8081 Deansgate.
Leeds.—4, York Place. Telegrams: "Invicta," Leeds. Telephone: Leeds 30631.
Glasgow.—John Balton and Son, 21 Wilson Street. Telephone: Bell 3804.
Paris.—A. Witkowski, 18 Rue Des Petites Ecuries.
Copenhagen.—J. Lamberg, Kobmagergade 11.
Capetown.—H. O. Harris, P.O. Box 1095.
Johannesburg.—A. R. Harris, P.O. Box 1199.
Australia.—Melbourne: Thorold Harper and Co., "Qualeta House," 175-7 Flinders Lane; Sydney: Thorold Harper and Co., Brougham House, 181 Clarence Street.
New Zealand.—Auckland: J. R. Sutcliffe Ltd., Corner Lorne and Rutland Streets; Wellington: J. R. Sutcliffe Ltd., 104 Wakefield Street; Christchurch: J. R. Sutcliffe, Ltd., 77, Lichfield Street.

CHILDEMA CARPET COMPANY, LTD.—
Manufacturers of Wilton, Brussels, and Axminster Carpets and Rugs.
Telegrams: Childema Co., Kidderminster.
Telephone 3171.
London.—3 and 4 Little Love Lane, Wood Street, E.C.2, and 11, Rose Street, Newgate Street, E.C.4.

DURHAM

HUGH MACKAY AND CO., LTD.—Manufacturers of the well-known "Takeem" Carpet, also Lisml, "Dursat," "Dursax," "Weardale," other Wiltons and "Welsingham" Axminster. The plain Wilton Carpets "Wiri" (double stitched), "Durmar" and "Neville" are also specialities and are stocked in Durham and London.
Works: Carpet Factory, Durham.
Telegrams: Carpets, Durham.
Telephones: 333-334 Durham.
London.—34, Little Britain, E.C.1.
Telegrams: Pedrawki Cent, London.
Telephones: National 0000-3.
Manchester.—Clydesdale House, 27 Turner Street.
Telegrams: Takram, Manchester.
Telephone: Deansgate 1920.
Birmingham.—County Buildings, Corporation Street.
Telephone: Central 3413.
Telegrams: "Takhom," Birmingham.
Belfast.—Kent House, 2 Kent Street, Royal Avenue. Telephone: Belfast 20000.
Glasgow.—10, Princes Square, Buchanan Street, C1.
Telephone: Centre 3480.
Telegrams: "Dursat," Glasgow.
Leeds.—17, Wellington Street.
Telephone: 22839.
Telegrams: "Durmee," Leeds.
Melbourne.—Flinders Way, 238 Flinders Lane.
Amsterdam.—Vondelstraat, 84, Amsterdam, W.
Telephone: Amsterdam 81770.

HECKMONDWIKE (YORKS.)

HECKMONDWIKE MANUFACTURING CO. LIMITED.—CROFT MILLS, HECKMONDWIKE and WELLINGTON MILLS, LIVERSEDGE. Manufacturers of Chenille Axminster, Jacquard Axminster, Brussels and Wilton Squares and Pieces, Dutch Carpets and Horse Clothing. Makers also of the celebrated Hygienic Untearable Underfelt for Carpets and Stair Pads. Spinners of Worsted and Woollen Yarns.
London Warehouse and Show Room.—94, Newgate Street, E.C.1.
Telephone No. (London Office), City 2700.
Telegrams: Greenside, Central, London. "Croft," Heckmondwike.
Telephone: No. 4, Heckmondwike.

LONDON

GOODACRE, WILLIAM AND SONS, LTD. (Established 1886) — CEYLON MILLS, VICTORIA DOCKS, E.16. Manufacturers of the "Ennerdale and Highgate" Wool Reversible Rugs; also Carlton, County and Regent Axminster Rugs, Kent, Dorchester and Belmont Axminster Squares, Alpine, Bedford and Special Stanley Reversible Hal Carpeting; Mourouk Reversible Cotr Carpets.
London Warehouse.—Boyd's House, 6/7, Friday Street, E.C.
Glasgow.—43, Queen Street.
Leeds.—17, Wellington Street.
Cardiff.—94, Frederick Street.
New York.—295, Fifth Avenue.

ROCHDALE

JOHN BRIGHT AND BROTHERS, LTD.—Tapestry and Hair Squares, Velvet and Tapestry Sofas and Rugs, Velvet Tapestry and Hall Stairs.
London.—St. Alban House, 91, Wood Street, E.C.2.
Manchester.—20, York Street.
Glasgow.—77, Queen Street.
Birmingham.—96, Brairrells Road, Hall Green.
Belfast.—1/2, Clarence Street.
Telegrams: "Brights," Rochdale; "Brit," Central London; "Brights," Manchester; "Grierson," Glasgow.

STOURPORT

WORTH, THOMAS BOND AND SONS, LIMITED — SEVERN VALLEY MILLS

TRADES COUNCIL

Urges Direct Representation on Food Control Committee

The monthly meeting of Kidderminster Trades Council was held on Monday, Mr. W. Davis presiding.

Mr. Maurice Hawind gave a report on the alleged unsatisfactory trading and unloading of meat supplies at the ice works in Dixon Street. He said the position of the store house was bad, being situated close to factories. The loading deck was covered by an awning shed, which could not prevent dirt, dust and other refuse from contaminating meat loaded on the deck before being taken inside. Meat was allowed to lie on the lorries in the open air without any covering. There was cause for complaint about the way in which the meat was taken off the lorries in the streets before being taken to the shops.

While he did not see meat dragged across the floor of the landing stage, he noticed the floor was by no means clean.

He also suggested that greater care might be taken to see that no meat was left without covering, or that it should be left lying on the lorries before being taken inside the ice works, and on no consideration should meat be dragged across the floor of the landing stage.

The Chairman said the report really substantiated the statements made at the previous meeting.

After some remarks by Mr. Rowley and others, Mr. F. G. Poole suggested sending a letter from the Trades Council incorporating the report and asking the management of the ice works for comments. He would rather take that course at the present stage than make an official complaint to the local health authority.

The Chairman said if the matter was taken up it should first go to the Medical Officer of Health.

Mr. A. C. Rowley said he made no complaint against the interior of the ice-works. He thought the Health Department was responsible for seeing that the place outside the works where the meat was placed was suitable.

Mr. Arthur Smith, J.P., said from the report it was clear that everything possible was not done as regards transport cleanliness. He was inclined to think the best course would be to call the attention of the health officer and tell him the Trades Council was not satisfied that meat was handled in the best possible manner.

Mr. A. Whitehouse seconded the motion to approach the Chief Sanitary Inspector and this was agreed to.

FOOD CONTROLLED PRICES

A discussion on prices of controlled food was initiated by Mr. Howard Parker (A.E.U.), who said his members were concerned about the continual rise of prices. He felt that if standard prices were fixed, the lists should be published for all to see.

Mr. F. Rowley explained that maximum prices, subject to control, had to be exhibited, and offenders, whether shopkeepers or assistants, were liable to penalties. The first step for aggrieved persons to take was to send the bill be evidence of excessive charge to the local food controller.

Mr. Hill spoke of a charge of 1½d. for paper carrier bags, to which Mr. F. G. Poole replied that there had been an actual rise of 180 per cent during the last three months on paper carrier bags.

The Chairman advised delegates to make sure of their case before launching complaints which would not "hold water" upon investigation.

Mr. Arthur Smith said the crux of the present food prices control was that no special inspectors were employed so that it was left to the public to find out for themselves, with the assurance that specific complaints would be investigated. He had specimen leaflets for posting near works

Someone here is goin to need your help

Johnny lives in the city. His home may seem safe enough now. But if raids come it will be another matter. Johnny must be moved. It is unthinkable that he should be left to take his chance among the horrors of modern bombing warfare. The Government is going to send Johnny to your district if raids come. This is where your help is needed. To promise now to give Johnny a home, so that the authorities may know he will be cared for. Do not think that because we have not been raided yet, we are not likely to be.

As the year grows older the dang not grow less. These children in t may be needing a safe home next next week, perhaps tomorrow. Whe lo, they will need it suddenly, ur desperately.

All you need do is enrol your nam your local Authority. You may be to take a child now, or your name kept against the time when raids second evacuation necessary. Wh enrol, you will be doing a splendid for the nation.

HALFPENNY A WEEK

Nursing Association Needs Workers' Help

ANNUAL MEETING PLEA

The hope that workers in Kidderminster would each contribute ½d. a week to the Kidderminster Nursing Association, enabling the association still further to expand its useful work, was expressed at the annual meeting in the Council Chamber on Monday afternoon, when Alderman E. O. Eddy presided.

The Hon. Secretary (Miss Hepworth), and the Superintendent (Miss Barrow), read their reports on the work of the past year during which 18,000 visits were paid by the association's nurses.

The Hon. Treasurer (Mr. E. A. K. Perrett) submitted the accounts. After transferring £100 to reserve there was an excess of receipts (£2,270) over payments (£2,263) of £7, compared with an adverse balance of £120 in the previous year. That was mostly attributable to the £120 collected on flag day, and an increase of £110 in fees. The success of their efforts reflected credit on the collectors. There would be no flag day this year, and Mr. Eddy was unable to repeat his donation of £50, so that failing a further increase in subscriptions and collections, there would be a deficit of £100. The Finance Committee was convinced that expenditure could not be curtailed without reducing efficiency. As more and more demands were made on the individual, they might expect a falling away of subscriptions, and the only way to bridge the gap was by an increase in fees.

Moving the adoption of the reports, the Chairman said the association was commenced 50 years ago by the late Mr. Peter Adam and Canon Bladon, for the alleviation of suffering, and helping those who could not help themselves. In Kidderminster they had seven Queen's nurses, who carried sunshine wherever they went.

The association's financial position had improved, but an intensified effort would be necessary this year to raise another £150. Instead of a reduced subscription list, he anticipated an increase, as the association's good work was more widely known. Collectors and ward secretaries had raised £700 despite the worst winter for 100 years, and nurses had paid over 18,000 visits.

"After the war we shall have men returning broken, as well as a large number of unnerved women and delicate children," the speaker continued. "A much greater work will have to be carried on by this association, and for that purpose we shall need more money. Workers contribute 2d. weekly to the hospital. I believe they would pay another half-penny a week to the Nursing Association, to be deducted from their wages weekly or monthly, so that after the war we shall be able to look after the thousands who will require attention and help."

He concluded with a tribute to the officers, thanking the Vice-chairman (Mrs. M. A. Anton) for her generosity in clearing off the debt on the Sister Gregory Memorial Clinic.

Mr. Ernest H. Jones, C.C., seconding the adoption, said he appreciated the association's good work, as did the people of Kidderminster, who had the benefit of the nurses' ministrations. In these times, when destruction seemed the aim of so many, it was pleasing to note the efforts made locally for the amelioration of suffering.

The chairman, vice-chairman, hon. treasurer, hon. secretary, and committee were re-appointed.

VALUE OF DISTRICT NURSING

An interesting address was given by Councillor Miss E. C. Addenbrooke, who traced the origin of district nursing in 1859 and the pioneer efforts of Florence Nightingale, Elizabeth Fry, Octavia Hill, and the Misses Rathbone of Liverpool. The late Dean Boyle, when Vicar of Kidderminster (1867-1880) provided, at his own expense, a district nurse who apparently worked under his wife. When smallpox and typhoid epidemics broke out, the speaker's father (the late Dr. K. H. Addenbrooke, Medical Officer of Health) had the benefit of the nurse's help. He left it on record that had there been district nurses here when he first came to Kidderminster, hundreds of lives would have been saved, as well as untold misery. Many typhoid victims died because their relatives would not carry out the doctor's orders.

In 1870 an enquiry was held into the conditions of district nursing in London. The principle was laid down that for a district nurse, hospital training alone was not enough. Besides theoretical instructions she must gain practical field experience under trained supervision. That principle still held. To-day there was hardly a village but commanded the services of a district nurse.

Miss Addenbrooke described how the three parochial nursing associations in Kidderminster amalgamated to form the present town association, and the improvement during the last 40 years in the inhabitants' attitude towards health and hygiene, with a consequent lessening of the suffering previously caused through ignorance. She had some experience of the amalgamation, as she was at that time secretary of the St. John's Association. With the help of Canon Bladon and the first chairman (the late Mr. Peter Adam), the amalgamation was carried through, and from that day they had never looked back.

LOUD SPEAKER VAN

Two Meetings in Kidderminster

WHAT TO DO IN AN AIR RAID

The first of a fleet of loudspeaker vans touring the Midlands with the object of making known the full extent and purpose of Britain's war efforts halted in Kidderminster on Friday when two open-air meetings were held at the Market Hall steps. The van carried a wide range of posters and photographs appealing for men and women recruits and volunteers for the various national services. Within a few minutes of arriving in the town shortly after noon, the loudspeakers were connected up and music broadcast in order to attract an audience.

The meetings had been arranged by the Midland Regional office of the Ministry of Information. They were addressed by Mr. Gibson Bennett, a native of Tamworth, who in the last war was connected with the Territorial organisation, recruiting the first motor-cyclist signallers for the Royal Engineers in 1914. At the mid-day meeting he was introduced by Alderman E. O. Eddy.

"LEND TO DEFEND"

Emphasising that every man, woman and child in Kidderminster could play his or her part in the effort to beat Hitler, Alderman Eddy said the town was saving £8,000 a week and during the past 24 weeks had lent to defend the sum of £180,000. They could help by becoming "salvage-minded." Kidderminster was taking a leading part in the salvage campaign. Two million tons were wasted every year and if that was utilised it would mean a saving of £1 million. News papers could be saved, and so-called "rubbish" utilised. During April Kidderminster saved 72 tons of paper, 14 tons of crushed tins and 474,000 bottles, in all 84 tons, value £184. The effort had been intensified. During the last 14 days the value of materials salvaged was £107. In proportion to its population Kidderminster was salvaging twice as much as the average for the whole country. Everyone could help—knitting for victory, digging for victory, joining the new Local Defence Volunteers and saving money which would eventually be the means of saving lives.

He appealed to his hearers not to spread rumours. "Gossip as much as you like about the Town Council, but don't gossip about the war," he said. "At all costs we must keep up our production of weapons and materials and we want 100 per cent efficiency. I appeal to you to be cheerful. Keep your spirits up. We want everyone to play their parts."

MAYOR ON PREPAREDNESS

The Mayor (Councillor J. Andrews), presiding at the evening meeting, said Mr. Bennett would speak on what the public should do in the event of air raids. The A.R.P., A.F.S., and other services were ready to do all they could to protect the civilian population, and he was proud that the appeal for local defence volunteers was meeting with such a ready response in Kidderminster, over 200 having joined. He hoped every young man, and older men up to 60, would join one or other of the services. Ladies were doing excellent work, making comforts for the troops and supplies for the hospital. He asked ladies who had not yet done so to offer their services as soon as possible. It was up to each of them to do all they could to help the boys at the front.

Mr. Bennett said as a result of the invasion of Holland and Belgium the German bombers were much nearer to this country. He did not think there was any fear of a German invasion by sea, but by aerial bombardment the Germans might seek so to lower the morale of the civilian population as to make it extremely difficult for the civil defence services to function.

THREE "WAVES" OF ATTACK

He envisaged a wave of planes dropping high explosive bombs, followed by waves of incendiary and poison gas bombs. The A.R.P. services and the A.F.S. would be busy dealing with damage and casualties inflicted by the high explosives, and householders should deal with incendiary bombs. Such a bomb would go through the average roof and remain burning on the top floor, igniting everything within its range, so the first precaution must be to remove inflammable material from attics. In each group of houses neighbours should band together to assist each other in putting out fires started by incendiary bombs. Sand should be used for the purpose, or water sprinkled by a small pump or garden syringe. If a bucket of water was poured on the bomb, it would explode. Buckets of sand and water should be on everyone's premises, and a bath should be filled with water in case the supply was cut off. After the bomb was out, it should be put in the back garden, and the police or wardens would remove it. The third wave of gas bombs would be the enemy's final attempt. The civilian gas mask, however, afforded efficient protection against poison gas. The mask should be tried every day, so as to get accustomed to wearing it. Parents must insist that young children—who generally disliked their gas masks—should wear them for a few minutes at first, and for longer periods each day.

They should observe the black-out strictly, remembering that one householder who failed, endangered the lives of hundreds, and was a traitor to his country. If an air raid took place those

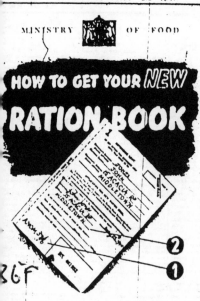

...THS, MARRIAGES, DEATHS

MARRIAGES

...AT--BRISTOW.--On Saturday, ... 29th, 1940, at Mill Street Methodist ...rch, Kidderminster, by the Rev. J. ...nian, Howard Stanley Dean Gartrell ... of Mr. and Mrs. David Gartrell, ...e Hewells," Alveley), to Hilda Janet ...tow (daughter of the late Mr. and ... Albert Bristow, 13, York Street, ...derminster).

...S--LEWIS.--On Saturday, June 29th, ... at Church Street Baptist Church, by ...Rev. L. B. Lewis, Mr. Eric Haines (son ...Mr. and Mrs. H. Haines, "Yesland," ...rport Road, Bewdley), to Miss Dora ...ewis (daughter of Mr. and Mrs. B. ..., Kidderminster).

...--BICKLEY.--On Saturday, June ... 1940, at Aston Villa Methodist ...ch, Birmingham, by the superintendent minister, Mr. Ronald Major Jones ...High Trees, Colwyn Bay), to Miss ... Mary Bickley (daughter of Mr. ... Mrs. J. Bickley, Fawcett's Hill, ...ley).

...NDS--BOND.--On Saturday, June ... 1940, at Ribbesford Church, by the ... C. R. Hollis, Harold John Simmonds ... son of Mr. and Mrs. J. Simmonds, ...ribbesford), to Miss Margaret Bond ...d daughter of Mr. and Mrs. W. ... Red Hill, Bewdley).

...ORD--BINGHAM.--On Saturday, ... 29th, 1940, at St. Mary's Church, ...e Rev. R. J. G. Foster, Mr. Kenneth ...est (son of Mr. and Mrs. J. Stafford, ..., Ashfield Crescent, Wolverley), to ... Doreen Edith Bingham (youngest ...hter of Mr. and Mrs. E. Bingham, of ...adford Avenue, Kidderminster).

...IN--LLEWELLYN.--On June 29th, ... George's Church, by the Rev. P. J. ...n, assisted by the Rev. B. J. Hooper, ...ence Eversfield, son of the late Mr. ... Wakelin, of Handsworth Wood, Birmingham, and Mrs. B. A. Wakelin, of ... Hill, Cleobury Mortimer, to Joan, ...ger daughter of Mr. and Mrs. L. ...ellyn, of Belmont, Chester Road, ...erminster.

...--BRISTOW.--On Saturday, June ... 1940, at Mill Street Methodist ...ch, by the Rev. J. Kinnish, George ...mond Webb (son of Mr. and Mrs. A. ...ebb, Lake House, Alveley), to Annie ...ow (daughter of the late Mr. and ... Albert Bristow, of 13, York Street, ...erminster).

...RS--JAY.--On Saturday, June 29th, ...lden Church, by Canon W. H. Coy, John Richard Withers (only son of ... and Mrs. Richard Withers, of 240 ... Lane, Small Heath, Birmingham), ...ian Christine Frances Jay (youngest ...hter of Mr. and Mrs. Samuel Jay, of ...n, Stourport-on-Severn).

DEATHS

...R.--William Joseph Barker, 88, Peel ..., passed peacefully away Sunday ...30th, aged 73 years.

...--On Friday, June 28th, 1940, at ...n-Hand Inn, Stourport, Benjamin ..., aged 78.

...--On Sunday, June 23rd, 1940, at the ...nce of his cousin (Mr. John Weale, ..., Franche Road, Kidderminster), ...e C. McCoy, for 40 years with Messrs. ...'s Stores, Birmingham, aged 65.

IN MEMORIAM

In loving memory of my dear ..., Alice Onions, who passed away ...ul, 1936. Always in the thoughts ... loving daughter Yvonne, ... and ...

... by day we saw her fade and gently sink away,
... in our hearts we prayed that she might stay.

SATURDAY, JULY 6th, 1940

THAT rumour is a lying jade is a fact which everyone has subconsciously appreciated, but the full extent of that lady's inveracity has been borne in upon us with sledge-hammer blows this week. From all sorts of responsible and irresponsible people we heard stories which purported to be facts but proved instead to be the wildest flights of fancy. Snowball-like, they grew in dimensions as they were passed from mouth to mouth. We can only hope that the rumour-mongers felt crestfallen (and realised the error of their ways) when they read on Tuesday that German planes did not fly over the Midlands on Sunday and that no parachutists were landed. There is absolutely no truth whatever in the story or stories to that effect which were circulated over a wide area. The simple explanation of the report provides a good example of how rumours can grow. It seems that near one Worcestershire village a British aeroplane was flying very low towards rising ground. It was observed by one or two people who thought it had landed, and very properly reported the incident. In the absence of any immediate proof of the plane's identity, and of whether it had landed or not, immediate investigation was made. It was established that there had been no landing in the area indicated, and certainly that there had been no parachutists. Further inquiries established the identity of the plane, and an authoritative denial of the earlier wild reports was issued—but not before much valuable time had been wasted, and many people needlessly alarmed. However, good may emerge if the incident drives home the lesson that it is a patriotic duty in these days to lend no credence to unconfirmed reports of any kind, and to do one's best to check them instead of passing them on. The fact that precautions are taken by the authorities does not mean that the event against which they are preparing has happened. The sooner that is realised by the civilian population the more effective those precautions will be—and the less sleep you will lose.

LOCAL NEWS

Mothers' Union. — At the Mothers' Union meeting at Franche Church on Wednesday, under the presidency of Mrs. Rankle, Miss Peggy Cooke gave an address (by request) on old Kidderminster worthies. It was listened to with great interest.

Gift Days.—Gift days were held at four local churches on Sunday, the approximate result financially being, St. Mary's £160, St. George's £120, Cookley £30, and Birmingham Road Methodist £10. Similar efforts will take place at New Meeting on Sunday, and at the New Church on September 1st.

Engagement. — The engagement is announced, and the marriage will shortly take place, between Squadron Leader Stanley Graham Pritchard (son of the late Mr. Stanley Pritchard and of Mrs. Pritchard, of Torquay) and Diana (only daughter of Mr. and Mrs. Frank Whittone, of Thorney, near Peterborough).

Ramble.—The ramble arranged by the Wolverley Young People's Fellowship on Wednesday was by way of Habberley Valley to Trimpley, and was much enjoyed. Next Wednesday activities will take the form of a dance, proceeds to church funds. An invitation is extended to all. Police regulations insist on gas masks being carried.

St. Ambrose's Social.—To-day (Saturday) possibly the only social of the year

Christadelphian Service.—Mr. A. G. F. Smith will be the speaker on Sunday next, his subject being "The Most High ruleth in the kingdom of men."

Junior Outing.—The Education Committee of the Co-operative Society have decided not to hold the usual junior outing this year; but all activities connected with junior co-operators will be renewed as soon as circumstances permit.

On Committee.—Mr. W. H. Kimberlee, secretary of the Kidderminster Minor Football League, has been elected to the committee of the Worcestershire F.A. Benevolent Fund. The League has received a grant from the F.A., and a meeting will shortly be held to allocate grants to clubs.

Supplementary Fire Party.—St. Mary's Church magazine says:—"Because of the danger to the Parish Church through air raids (now more frequent) the Vicar and churchwardens, after consulting the local authority, have arranged for a supplementary fire party and equipment to be in readiness."

Examination Success.—In the list of passes in the 1st year examination for the Bachelor of Arts degree of Leeds University is the name of Ronald Osmund Jennings. He obtained high marks in Latin, Greek, and Ancient History. Ronald Jennings's home is in Kidderminster, and as a student for Holy Orders he is exempt from military service.

Gift Day.—New Meeting Church gift day will be held on Sunday, when the members of the congregation hope to realise £50. Judged by the results of similar efforts in the neighbourhood who have found the gift day or direct giving—more remunerative than the usual bazaar, it would not be surprising to learn that the New Meeting congregation have realised their object.

Toposcope Removed.—The thousands of Midlanders who ascend Malvern Hills will be surprised to find a well-known landmark has disappeared from Worcestershire Beacon. The indicator on the summit has been removed from the bronze toposcope, in compliance with the order issued by the Home Secretary prohibiting every kind of sign which might help parachute invaders.

Franche Young People's Fellowship.—The meeting on Tuesday evening was presided over by the hon. secretary, Mr. H. Parkes. Mr. W. S. L. Hargrave gave an interesting lecture on "How we got our Bible." The speaker traced the history of the Bible from the manuscripts to the present Revised Version. A vote of thanks to Mr. Hargrave was proposed by Mr. H. Parkes, seconded by Mr. E. Cooke. Games then followed, under the direction of Mr. K. Hudson. A most enjoyable evening closed with dancing to music played by the Fellowship Trio (leader, Mr. A. Moore).

CHECK THOSE RUMOURS!

RUMOURS are the particular weapons of Fifth Columnists and the only way by which any rumour can be checked is by the Authority learning of it immediately. There have been (states the Ministry of Information) reports in various parts of the country that during times when enemy aircraft have been over the British Isles mysterious flares have been seen, indicating guiding signals to any raiders in the area. No such incidents have been reported in such form as would prove the happening, and any such reports idly passed on become dangerous rumours. It is requested that should anyone observe such an incident he should report it immediately to the nearest Police Station, giving the time of the incident, where it was in relation to his position, its nature, its duration, and a confirmatory statement such as name and address of a witness.

Model Railway Club.—Members of "Rosedale" Club (8, Bewdley Hill) hold their first Saturday meeting this week at 2.30 p.m. in the club room. Subject: Model Aircraft. Eric Haughty, Ken Smith, Peter Smith, Alan Jones, Kenneth Hannan, Brian Walker, Ronald Taunton will receive presentation model building sets for enthusiasm. A.R.P.

Important Not... to carefully n... (which appears ... by Mr. J. Haw... and surveyor, al...

Important Not... friends wishing ... of the "Shuttle" ... call or send ... immediately ... address must be ...

St. Ambrose'... called to this ar... place to-day (S... ing grounds of ... Road. Number... been arranged ... gentlemen, ... all.

School Holiday... Education Comm... teachers on Frid... elementary whe... be closed from J... question of holid... ing of the Educ... was decided to ... Advisory Commi... tion.

First-Aid Lec... acquire knowle... would be useful ... vided by four ... Mr. L. R. Baile... by members of ... Brigade) for th... public. Admis... hoped the public ... and time of th... in our advertis...

Sentenced for... Worcestershire ... Monday, John ... of Aston, was ... months' hard la... at Chaddesley C... Eight other of... consideration. ... (20), a metal ... Road, Witton, ... Surman, told t... nald Coventry, ... rather serve a ... the Army. T... him to six mon...

Drumhead Se... Brinton Park ... be held, when ... by Rev. T. B. ... Rev. W. A. Tri... parade will ass... at 2.15 p.m. and ... Oxford Street, ... Road and Sutt... will leave via ... and proceed to ... Bull Ring, Vic... Hall. The Kidd... will be in atten... be taken ... expenses. If w... held in the To...

Senior School... week's discussio... Senior Schools, ... out that Counci... for some year... revision in our ... pointing out the ... children of the ... Empire and its ... Nations. Coun... member of the ... 1933, which ap... ton's "Junior ... Empire," which ... Educational Au... Empire. Now ... children are lik... various parts of ... gain that know... a realisation of ... Empire and wh...

Juvenile Cou... brothers (14), ... cycling offences ... charged with ... out a rear red ... a passenger; ... with being a ... not fitted for ca... Short said the... cycle. Ordering ... 5d. towards co... E. G. Eddy), co... only their own ... people. Another ... indecent on a ... duck with a ... Defendant who ... January, and ... tinued. An eva... to stealing a bi... cycle pump, T... on condition th... his mother.

Use of Schoo... the use of the ... at Kiddermins... children, was m...

UP HOUSEWIVES
AND AT 'EM!

Put out your
PAPER
METAL
BONES
PUT THEM OUT CAREFULLY
Follow the instructions you will receive, save time, space, money.
THEY WILL BE COLLECTED
Councils in districts with a population over 10,000 must arrange for collection. You can help to see that the collection is well and thoroughly done. Send suggestions to your Council.
THEY WILL BE USED
Every scrap that is put out according to instructions and efficiently collected will be used for victory.
This is what your back door should look like on collection day.
METAL
BONES
PAPER
ISSUED BY THE MINISTRY OF SUPPLY

ERCROWDED 'BUS

Borough Court on Friday, Morris, The Cliff, Kinver, was with overcrowding a public service Lill St. on August 8th. He liability but disputed the alleged passengers in excess of its seating

Adams appeared for defendant ... and Midland Omnibus com-

THE NEW CHURCH

Address by Rev. G. W. Wall

In treating upon the subject, "What does your church cost you?," at the New Church on Sunday, Aug. 18th, the Rev. G. W. Wall said he was not speaking merely about money, but rather about what our religion costs in life. The challenge of the knights of the road used to be, "Your money or your life," the Lord's challenge to the members of His church is "Your life, your all." Undoubtedly the church costs us a great deal. It means, says Jesus, the giving up of everything opposed to His work in the world and in the soul; the putting aside of everything unChristlike. That is asking very much of us.

The Church does cost a good deal in money, and it was always intended to do so possibly because we don't like parting with our money, and the Church shows us how to do this gracefully. Really, its demands in this respect are very modest. It only takes a small portion of our means to carry on the Church. How little we spend on it to what we spend on ourselves, not only for the necessities of life, but for our many luxuries. These are right enough in their proper place, but do we spend as much on the church as on them? If not, then our religion is not costing us what it should.

The late Silas Hocking used to tell a lively story about a north countryman who left the Wesleyans and joined the Anglicans. In giving his reason for the change to a friend he said the Wesleyans were always after money; it was give, give, give all the time. Now in the Church of England religion is cheap! Cheap, said his friend? Yes! How much do you think my religion cost me last year? Well, how

CO-OPERATIVE SHOW

Challenge Trophy Won by Mr. S. Callow

Carnations were the only class which failed to attract entries at the annual show of the Co-operative Society Horticultural Section on Saturday. There were over 200 exhibits staged in an admirable show in the Co-operative Hall, potatoes, parsnips, leeks, onions and marrows reaching a high standard. The judges were Mr. A. W. Craddock of The Newlands gardens, and Mr. J. H. Norman, Lincomb Hall gardens. Mr. G. S. Tomkinson was a successful exhibitor in the open classes. Mr. S. Callow won the challenge trophy. The show is practically the only summer show in the town. Mr. F. F. Bryant is secretary. A collection for the Red Cross Society taken by the St. John Ambulance Nursing Sisters realised £2 7s. In an interval, Mr. J. S. Roberts (chairman of the Horticultural section) said though handicapped for space it was a fine show which reflected credit on all concerned.

Mr. E. W. Walters, J.P., president, said the show was one of the best held by the society. Lack of space accounted for the absence of an honorary exhibit by their nursery.

Congratulating competitors Mr. Walters stressed the importance of land cultivation which was going to count for a great deal towards final victory. Credit was due to Mr. S. Callow, winner of the Challenge Trophy, who was frequently on his allotments after a hard day's toil at Wilden Iron Works.

The Challenge Trophy (for most points in Amateur members' classes): S. Callow 32 points.

OPEN CLASSES

Garden flowers: G. S. Tomkinson (gardener F. N. Ray), E. Holder, E. Hemming. Dahlias: E. Holder, W. J. Dunn, G. S. Tomkinson. Gladioli: E. Holder. Roses: G. S. Tomkinson, E. Hemming, W. J. Dunn. Hardy fruit: W. J. Dunn, G. S. Tomkinson, S. Tilsley. Collection of vegetables: 1 G. S. Tomkinson, B. Burford. Potatoes: E. Hemming, G. R. Phillips, E. Bowen. Runner beans: B. Burford, G. S. Tomkinson, E. Bowen. Onions: W. J. Dunn, A. Pardoe, G. S. Tomkinson. Tomatoes: E. Holder, W. J. Dunn, G. S. Tomkinson. Peas: E. Hemming, G. S. Tomkinson, B. Burford.

AMATEUR MEMBERS' CLASSES

Garden flowers mixed: S. Callow, W. H. Willis, G. R. Phillips. Garden flowers: W. H. Willis, G. R. Phillips, W. Southall. Asters: A. Pardoe, W. Southall, W. S. Kindon. Dahlias: W. H. Willis. Gladioli: S. Callow. Sweet peas mixed: W. S. Kindon, W. Southall. Roses: G. R. Phillips, S. Callow, W. H. Willis. Marrows: J. Randle, S. Callow, W. S. Kindon. Cauliflowers: A. Southall, S. Callow, W. H. Willis. Peas: W. Southall, J. Randle, W. H. Willis. Beet long: W. H. Willis, S. Callow, W. S. Kindon. Beet round: S. Callow, W. H. Willis, A. Pardoe. Onions: A. Southall, W. S. Kindon, A. Organ. Potatoes (white and coloured): S. Callow, G. R. Phillips, A. Pardoe. Potatoes white: G. R. Phillips, S. Callow, A. Pardoe. Potatoes coloured: G. R. Phillips, S. Callow, W. Southall. Collection of vegetables: A. Southall, A. Organ, S. Callow. Parsnips: A. Southall, A. Organ, G. R. Phillips. Shallots: W. H. Vaughan, W. S. Kindon, A. Organ. Carrots long: W. Southall, S. Callow, W. S. Kindon. Carrots short: 1 A. R. Powell, S. Callow, G. R. Phillips. Runner beans: S. Callow, J. Randle, A. Southall. Tomatoes: W. S. Kindon, A. Organ, W. H. Willis. Leeks: A. Southall, A. Organ, G. R. Phillips. Mr. J. Allatt's prizes in the potatoe classes were won by G. R. Phillips.

COAL MERCHANTS' OFFENCES

First Cases at Kidderminster

The first cases of their kind were heard at Kidderminster on Friday, when C. F. and F. C. Parsons (trading as Parsons, Green and Company, Church Street, Stourbridge) were fined £1 for supplying coal in Kidderminster, while not licensed for this district, and a further £1 for supplying at a price in excess of that specified for the grade of coal. Defendants were ordered to pay costs amounting to £4 4s.

Mr. Eric Dean, prosecuting for the Board of Trade, explained the orders made by the Board to secure control of coal supplies. Only merchants licensed by the local Fuel Overseer might supply coal retail in any district, and it was an offence for a merchant to supply where he did not hold a licence. The Overseer issued a schedule of prices for his district, and a copy was sent to all licensed merchants. The prices charged in each district were perfectly fair to the retailer, who was prohibited from selling at a price exceeding that specified in the schedule. The orders were designed to protect the public by controlling supplies and prices, and the Board took a serious view of such cases.

Outlining the facts, Mr. Dean said on June 19th the defendants—partners in a Stourbridge firm—supplied and sold to Mr. W. Mountford at a house in Somerleyton Avenue, two tons and one quarter of coal. The firm had never been licensed to supply coal in this district, and a copy

BOROUGH BENCH

FRIDAY, AUGUST 23rd

Before the Mayor, Mr. J. Andrews (chairman), Mrs. M. A. Anton, Messrs. T. Griffin, E. G. Eddy, J. L. Stretton and H. W. Cheshire.

APPLICATIONS

Temporary authority at the "Harp" Inn, Stourbridge Rd., was granted to Arthur Bradley from Arthur Hanswith Hall.

Extension of hours from 10 p.m. till midnight was granted the licensee of the Lion Hotel on Friday, August 30th, for the Spitfire Fund dance.

The licensee of the Queen's Head was The licensee of the Queen's Head, Stourbridge Rd., was granted a music licence.

Mr. Leonard Reynolds, on behalf of St. Oswald's Church Hall, Broadwaters, was granted a music and dancing licence.

LIGHTING OFFENCES

Joan Martin, 65, Shrubbery St., was fined 5s. for not having the front light on her bicycle effectively screened in Vicar St., on Tuesday, August 13th, at 11.55 p.m.

For failing to screen interior lights effectively the following were fined:

Cyril Morris Smith, House Governor and Secretary of Kidderminster and District General Hospital, Mill St., 20s.

James Thomas Penn, Land Oak Inn, Birmingham Rd., 20s.

Georgina Willey, 197 Chester Rd. North, 5s.

John Edward Collins, 1, Bewdley Rd., was fined 20s. for failing to immobilise an unattended motor-car, and for not having lights on the car he was fined 10s. P.C. Gough said the offences took place in New Rd., on August 11th at 10.5 p.m.

Charged with carrying a passenger on a bicycle constructed to carry one person only, Derick William Welding, 4, Goldthorn Rd., was fined 5s. P.C. James said a 10 years old boy was riding on the handle bar when he stopped defendant in Stourport Rd. on August 11th, at 11.20 a.m.

Basil Gill, 31, Claughton St., was ordered to pay 2s. for not having a front light on his bicycle, and for not having a red rear light, in Bewdley Rd., at 10.45 p.m. on August 11th. He was also ordered to pay 2s. costs.

OBSTRUCTION

Winifred Ellen Barrow, of Stanmore, Chester Rd. North, was fined 10s. for causing obstruction with a motor-car which she left in Vicar St., on August 10th from 11.55 a.m. till 12.35 p.m.—P.C. Meredith gave evidence.

WARRANT TO APPEAR

Mr. F. C. Ling, Relieving officer to the County P. A. committee, applied for a further order against Albert Dixon, 32, Goldson Crescent, who was £4 2s. 6d. in arrears under a Maintenance order dated May 5th, 1939, in respect of a mother who had become chargeable.

Applicant stated that although respondent had had spells of unemployment he was now earning £4 6s. 8d. a week and had been in continuous employment since March 29th this year.

The Bench issued a warrant for the attendance of defendant.

DISMISSED

Albert Nuttall, 77, Tomkinson Drive, was summoned for assaulting George William Yarnold, 114, Tomkinson Drive, (a carpet creeler) on the playing field of the Sutton Farm Estate on August 14th.

He pleaded "not guilty," but admitted hitting Yarnold on the head and in the face with his fist because Yarnold pushed Nuttall's son over the back of a playmate and hurt him.

After hearing the evidence, the Mayor said the case would be dismissed.

RUNAWAY HORSE

John Mason, 38, Brinton Crescent, was charged with failing to have control of a horse drawn dray in Church St., on August 9th, when the animal bolted, collided with two vehicles in the Bull Ring and careered up Mill St., before being stopped by the Black Horse Hotel. A police officer was hurt in trying to stop the horse.

P.C. Meredith said the accident happened at mid-day. When interviewed at 1.15 p.m. defendant told him he only left the horse for a minute or two. The brakes were on. Somebody must have frightened the horse whilst Mason was delivering milk up Arch Hill Square.

Witness said two people tried without success to stop the horse after the collision and a Police War Reserve constable sustained certain injuries in his attempt to stop the horse.

Defendant told the Court he was on a milk round down Hall St., and had left the horse-drawn dray by the Baptist Church in Church St. whilst absent up Arch Hill Square. Both traces were broken by the affrighted horse.

Defendant was fined 20s.

SCHOOLBOYS PLAYING WITH AMMUNITION

William Joseph James, 33, Blount Terrace, was charged with possessing ammunition without having a firearm certificate.

He pleaded "Guilty."

P.W.R. Davies said at 1 o'clock on August 8th, a schoolboy gave him a live 22 ammunition cartridge which he said had been given him by another boy. That boy who had five cartridges said he had them off Roy James (son of defendant) who had two left and had lost two.

Three days later, when interviewed, Roy James told witness that he took the cartridges out of a box in his dad's drawer. When seen about the affair defendant

A MONK'S RI... PROPH...

In An Old ...

The following copy ... into our hands ... ness of a local ... that it will be ... to our readers we ... by permission of the ... County Chronicle and ... which it appeared ... received from Mr. Ja... It was originally ... M.S.S. of the ... written in 1600 ... is figured by the ... Leopard, Russia the W... and Austria the Black ... Eagle. The explanati... acceptable in view of ... text, remembering, to... was originally more ... Lion as the badge of ... ment reads as follows

THE AN...

1 Several times he ... recognise him, because ... Lamb resemble each ... wicked are the prec... Wicked One

2 The veritable Anti... the Monarchs of his ti... he will invoke God ... messenger.

3 The Prince of Li... Bible, he will call hi... Most High, chastising ...

4 His innumerable ... as their motto "God ... like the infernal legion...

5 For a long while ... and treason; his spies ... the earth, and he will ... secrets of those in po...

6 He will have Theo... certify and prove his ...

7. A war will furnish ... for lifting the mask, ... which he will make ... Monarch, but another ... recognised by the fa... time it will become ...

8 It will call to ar... Mohammedans, and ev... people. Armies will b... of the world.

9 For men's minds ... angels, and in the ... understand that this ... that they will all bec... not trample down th...

10. The Antichrist w... several marks; he w... priests, monks, women ... people. He will sho... pass along holding a ... barians, but invoking ...

11. His false words ... of Christians, but his ... Nero and the Roman p... be an eagle in his co... will also be in that ... other wicked Monarch.

12. But this one is ... will die cursed by ... who will be elected at ... reign of the Antichris...

13 Priests and mon... seen confessing and ... hatants, because for ... and monks will fight w... and also because the P... cursed the Antichrist, ... that all those who w... will be in a state of g... die, will, like marty... heaven

14. The Pope's be... things will make a gr... cause the death of ... Antichrist's ally.

15. In order to c... more men must be ... ever held; it will requ... lands; for the Cock, ... Eagle would not suf... Black Eagle if they w... prayers of the human ...

16. Never before h... such peril, for the ... christ would be that ... he is incarnated

17. For it has been ... after the Incarnation ... in his turn would be ... threaten the earth wi... the Divine Incarnati... graces.

18. Near the year ... appear; his armies wil... anything before imag... Christians among his ... the defenders of the ... Mahommedans and ...

20. For the first ... entirely red; in the w... world there will not ... not be red, and the ... waters, and even the ... blood will flow in the ...

...ORE EVACUEES

...old of New Influx

...O HOUSEHOLDERS

IS CARPET MAKING ESSENTIAL NOW?

Chamber of Commerce Query

CONFIDENCE IN GOVERNMENT

Kidderminster Chamber of Commerce, at Tuesday's meeting, passed a resolution affirming complete confidence in Mr. Winston Churchill and the Government, and assuring them of its unwavering support in all measures they might think it necessary to take towards the single purpose of winning the war.

The resolution was proposed by the President (Mr. R. K. B. Worth), who said: "We are meeting at the most critical moment in the history of this country, if not in the history of the world. If anyone had told us a month ago that to-day we should find ourselves in our present position, we should have laughed him to scorn. With Holland overrun, the Maginot line turned, if not broken, and a wedge driven between the Allied armies, to-day we learn that Belgium has capitulated to the Germans through her King. Perhaps the strangest thing is that one eventuality which some of us might have expected—Italy's entry into the war—has not come about. I hope it won't, but it seems to me that depends on Mussolini's capacity to see a little farther than some of his countrymen, to realise that spirit counts sometimes more than weight of metal, and that if he throws in his lot with Germany he is in for a bad time whichever way the war goes.

"Our new Government has emergency powers which quite rightly deliver us over, body, soul, and property to the State. There is only one fear that I have about this Government—that they may not drive us hard enough. By us I mean those members of the community who are, at the moment at all events, too old to enter the fighting forces, and who by training are not fitted to take up work in aeroplane or munition factories.

"A SMALL TIME JOB"

"But there must be a lot of work that some of us are capable of doing, and I feel that making carpets is a small time job while the country's fate hangs in the balance as it does to-day. It is my hope, and I am certain you will agree with me, that the Government will be completely ruthless in the demands it makes upon us, and that it will take any man or woman—I had almost said any child—who can be of the slightest assistance. I hope the Government won't hesitate to take over our carpet factories and clear out the machinery if they think it will do good. We need fitters and tuners to keep those factories going, and it may be that those men would be of more value to the country working in armaments factories, even if it means that the carpet factory they come from has to shut down. We must try to keep the export trade in carpets; it's not a very big item in the country's assets, but it's something. If certain factories have to close, arrangements can be made to keep what export trade is left still running."

Mr. O. A. Chadwick, seconding the resolution, said that one of the greatest tragedies of recent years had been the lack of honesty of purpose. He felt that in the present Coalition Cabinet we had at last arrived at honesty of purpose to get something done, and see the thing through. "I hope please God it has not been formed too late," the speaker added.

He recalled that at the time of the Munich agreement he pointed out the need for everyone in this country to be conscripted and told what their job was to be. Some members thought he went too far, and the Chamber sent a more moderate resolution, on the lines that a national

IF AIR RAIDS COME

Is Kidderminster's Shelter Enough?

TOWN COUNCIL DISCUSSION

Whether Kidderminster's air raid shelter accommodation is adequate in the event of aerial attack was the subject of discussion at Wednesday's Town Council meeting, opened by Councillor L. Tolley. He said that in the congested parts of the town, of which there are many, it was impossible for people to construct shelters for themselves owing to lack of gardens. There were no steel air raid shelters here as there were in many towns. In view of the latest developments, were the council satisfied in their own minds that the civil population here had any security or protection at all? It would be a most disastrous thing for Kidderminster if bombs fell. Owing to the lack of protection the civil population would suffer very heavily. He was not trying to scare anyone but felt the urgency of waking up to the fact that, at whatever cost the civil population had a right to expect the local authority to give them proper protection. It did not now exist, and he felt very nervous about it, because in their many congested areas the losses would be terrific if there was an air raid. Protection should be provided at the elementary schools for the children, and for the people who could not provide their own. He asked that a general survey of the whole position should be made immediately, to see what could be done, because it would be no use doing it when it was too late.

Councillor O. A. Chadwick said they did not want to make the civilian population any more unsettled than they were already. The safest place for the public in an air raid was in their own homes. There, against an inside wall, they would be as safe as in many of the shelters that had been constructed.

WHAT HAS BEEN DONE

Alderman A. E. Meredith: The general public should not think that nothing has been done.

Councillor Tolley: I am not suggesting that.

Alderman Meredith: The County Council is the authority, and we are acting under them. We are within 100 of the number we are required to provide air raid shelter for. There are a few more shelters being put up on main roads for travellers, but we are very nearly up to the maximum of shelters we are obliged to provide for the civil population. Schemes have been submitted for shelters to be built, subject to the County Council's sanction. I understand how Councillor Tolley feels, but I don't think he is quite familiar with the immense number of shelters and places made in the town. In some districts we find extreme difficulty in finding suitable places to fix shelters but wherever possible—at public or private cellars, open spaces and vacant land, wherever there is a likelihood—schemes have been submitted. Many have been passed, a lot have been done, and others are ready for construction.

The Mayor (Councillor John Andrews) said provision had been made locally for 3,000 people likely to be caught in the streets. Five large shelters were being erected. No one could say they had been absolutely lacking in the matter—they had been pushing it forward. The County Council had to deal with it, and the Town Council had to look to them, but very good provision was being made. Many cellars and much other accommodation had been converted for children and the general public, and the thing was going forward well.

"There is a good deal in what Councillor Tolley says, but part of our difficulty arises from the fact that we are not our own authority," said Councillor J. E. Talbot.

TRENCHES IN A DANGEROUS STATE

"When the war started quite a number of trenches were dug by wardens and others in different parts of the town. Owing to the weather, they are now in a dangerous state, and in some cases they have actually been filled in. One that has been filled in is not far from the places mentioned by Councillor Tolley, and it would have afforded valuable extra protection to the inhabitants if money could have been spent. As the trenches are not in accordance with Home Office instructions we get no grant, and I cannot help wishing that the Home Office and the County Council would give local authorities more latitude. Small expenditure on some trenches would provide some shelter, better than people would get standing or lying in the open. I hope the urgency of the national peril will impel the Home Office to relax their formalities and give us more latitude."

Councillor Tolley said trenches upon which money was spent at the outbreak of war had caved in, and the sand-bags had been smashed up. Was it not someone's job to preserve those trenches? There was not one in existence now that would be safe for anyone to go in.

Councillor Chadwick said a good deal of voluntary work was done on trenches and shelters to protect the civil population and their children, but what response had there been from parents? They had not stopped their children from spoiling the trenches as fast as they

BOYS ON FARM WORK

Kidderminster and Hartlebury Offers

FARMERS URGED TO ACCEPT

The extent to which schoolboy labour will be available to assist local farmers was indicated at Thursday's meeting of the Kidderminster branch of the National Farmers' Union. The Chairman (Mr. J. R. Pheysey) said boys from Kidderminster Grammar School, Hartlebury Grammar School, and Bromsgrove, could be engaged for farm work during their summer holidays. Some would cycle out to farms within five miles of their homes, others could be billeted with the farmer. There had been requests for boys' services in neighbouring counties, and if Worcestershire farmers did not make up their minds they might find the boys "snapped up." He urged local farmers to get in touch with him if they wanted boys.

Mr. H. Ballard said that despite earlier Government promises that labour would be provided, most farmers were very short of labour, the only supplementary labour available being the Women's Land Army. In Worcestershire local elementary school managers could adjust holidays so as to release scholars for farm work.

Mr. E. W. Gough said it was a move in the right direction, and if farmers did not take what was offered them they might find themselves "in the cart." Dr. Barnardo's Homes had offered 150 boys to the county, as well as those already mentioned, and it would be a thousand pities if they were not made use of. He quoted a case where boys did useful work in singling sugar beet. The sugar beet crop was more than ever valuable to the country this year, and there was every indication that it would be a good one if properly tended.

The Chairman said it was scandalous that men were being taken from the land to work for contractors on unskilled jobs at wages higher than farmers could afford to pay.

IMPORTANCE OF SILAGE

Mr. Pheysey presided, and was supported by Mr. O. P. H. Hingley (vice-chairman).

The Chairman said the Ministry of Agriculture was impressing on them the importance of silage. It could be made quite cheaply, and it conserved the greatest value from the grass or whatever was put in. They had not been meeting recently because it was their job to produce food, not to meet and talk, but that meeting was called to hear from Mr. Wilks, who had been making silage for two or three years, and was one of the leading farmers in the Midlands.

Mr. T. Nelllist Wilks said the farmers' problem was to see what they could do for themselves in the absence of the imported food stuffs they had depended upon for so many years. He did not think they would get from abroad even those supplies they had been led to expect. Shipping could not be spared, even if it was in our possession, to bring annual feeding stuffs to this country, and they must feed their animals from the stuff they grew themselves. European countries lately overrun by Europe, and Germany itself, had for a number of years been feeding livestock on silage and other conserved products. On the other hand we had neglected that for the easier way of buying from abroad at low prices and we had become lazy in not providing our own products.

Good silage could be made by any intelligent person quite cheaply, and from a great variety of products, excluding cabbage and kale, which did not ensile easily. It meant conserving the stuff they grew themselves at the right time in such a way that it would be used at any time they wanted it. Good silage, made in the proper way, was next in value to dry products, and probably the cheapest of all conserved products to make. Certainly it was the easiest to store, it would keep, and pests had no effect upon it.

Mr. Wilks caused some amusement by a reference to the "pleasantly sour" smell of silage, and the reception one was likely to get in the house if one went in with silage on one's boots. He countered with "rather a bad smell in a house than a big bill in the office."

An interesting discussion followed in which many questions were answered by Mr. Wilks.

Members were advised that if they wanted to make silage treacle could be had.

Mr. Wilks said silage could not be set on fire under any circumstances—which was important in view of the possibility of enemy attempts to set fire to crops.

Mr. Gough said that last year he was in New Zealand, where they had the best climate in the world for making hay. Notwithstanding, the New Zealand dairy farmer made nearly all ensilage, which was conclusive proof of the value of hay versus ensilage.

A NEW APPOINTMENT

The Chairman, expressing thanks to Mr. Wilks, spoke of the remarkable work he had done in reclaiming farm from forest. He had recently been appointed to a very important official position in which he would have charge of 600 acres to improve grass land. What he did not know about grass land was hardly worth knowing.

Mr. Wilks said farmers would be told about the job in due course, and he hoped

TO THE GENERAL ...

AIR RAID PRECAU...

THE PUBLIC are requested ... ticular ATTENTION to the ... given by the BBC and pamp... from time to time, and to ... the recent publication "Your Air Raid Shelter." Instruction ... the Regional Office, Civic Hou... ham should be read with ca...

If in doubt on any point ... with the Air Raid Warden in ... who will give you all infor... help possible.

WHEN A WARNING IS ... your duty to take shelter.

BELOW is a LIST OF PUBLIC ... provided to give protection ... caught in the street during ...

GEO. RAINER ...

PUBLIC SHELTERS provide... protection to persons caught ... during an Air Raid.

Retail Mkt. Basement, High St...
Town Hall Basement, Vicar ...
Wise Radio Base't (Turk's Hea...
Wrenson's Base't (Turk's Head...
Free Library Basement, Mark...
Mr. Jensen's Basement, 18, Ch...
25 & 26, Worcester St. Base...
Mr. Shingler's Horsefair ...
Conservative Club, Park Butt...
Tunnels, Mr. J. H. Smith's ya... Stat...
Tunnels, Radcliffe's Brewery, ...
Tunnel, Rock, Mill Street ...
Parkers Arms Basement, Castl...
Swan Street, rear of 10, High ...
Swan Street, rear of 12 & 13, ...
Swan Street, rear of 3, High ...
Co-op. Dairy Basements, Fran...

SHELTERS UNDER CON... ready in a few days.

French Shelter, Green, Blake...
Surface Type Shelt...
Green, Blakebrook.
Broadwaters (bottom Bernsley ...
Near Pumping Station, Gree...
Land Oak House grounds, B...
Top of Barnsley Hill, near Hur...

SHELTERS to be commenced ... Surface Type Shelte...
Mill Street Car Park.
Jerusalem Walk playground. ...
Adjoining Brinton Park, Stour...
At Proud Cross.

(Signed) J. H. ... Borough Engineer & ...

LORD DUDLEY'S M...

WAGES AND ALLOW...

Council and Its Servi...

MANUAL WORKERS' R...

Kidderminster Town Council ... day agreed that a detailed re... be given at the next meeting ...

SPITFIRE UNDER THREE WEEKS

NOW TO MAKE IT £6,000!

YOU HAVE DONE IT! Exactly three weeks ago to-day (Saturday), at your request, the "Kidderminster Shuttle," in conjunction with the "Kidderminster Times," acceded to your request to sponsor a fund through the medium of which you could express your admiration of the R.A.F. It was decided to aim at raising £5,000 in 28 days, but the response has been so generous that by Thursday afternoon, when the third list closed, the total stood at £5,199 3s. 5d.

There is still a week to go before the fund closes, and it is hoped that efforts will not be relaxed, so that a cheque for perhaps £6,000 might be sent to Lord Beaverbrook. It is a magnificent result, and congratulations are due to the people of Kidderminster and Bewdley boroughs, Stourport urban and Kidderminster rural districts, on the readiness with which they have demonstrated, through this fund, the enthusiasm which prompted us to sponsor the scheme.

The final efforts towards the £5,000 mark were greatly assisted by Sir Herbert Smith, Bart., of Park House, who gave 100 guineas, and Messrs. T. Bond Worth and Sons, Ltd., of Severn Valley Mills, Stourport, who contributed £100 although the directors of the firm had already given generous support.

Launched a fortnight ago last Saturday, the Kidderminster, Bewdley and Stourport Fighter 'Plane Fund reached the £4,000 mark on Tuesday, and its object of raising £5,000 in 28 days was accomplished with a week to spare.

For this happy result all classes of the community share in the joy of a common effort for a worthy cause. In the ordinary sense, there has been no appeal for funds, but the townsfolk of Kidderminster, Bewdley and Stourport, as well as those living in the outlying district, have taken the scheme to their heart so completely that the newspaper offices have been besieged daily since it was launched. Last week, thanks to a handsome donation from Mrs. Lilian Hooper and her aircraftman son, Ronald, the £4,000 was in sight. Since then workpeople's collections (Carpet Trades, Ltd. £50) among others, have sent up the figure sharply, so that by Tuesday night £4,250 was realised.

Messrs. Steel Stampings, Ltd., Cookley, showed their interest with a gift of £50, in addition to a donation of £25 from Mr. and Mrs. Forty. Messrs. T. and A. Naylor, Ltd., sent £50, in addition to donations from the two directors; Messrs. Greatwich, Ltd., sent £20, in addition to donations of two directors.

Mr. Joseph Howard, of Holbeache, made a generous contribution of £20. Smaller sums came in from collecting boxes, as well as donations from the rank and file.

"With the deepest admiration of the boys of the R.A.F." was one eulogy; while a retired tradesman sent a generous gift "wishing the scheme all the success it deserves." A lady summed up the general view when she forwarded a small donation "to the fund for helping the brave boys who are proving themselves such heroes."

FROM AIRMEN'S PARENTS

Among the early subscribers this week was Major Laughton Goodwin, head of the firm of Messrs. Laughton Goodwin and Co., the Kidderminster garage proprietors, whose two sons, Pilot Officer Barry Goodwin and Flight-Lieutenant Henry Macdonald Goodwin, were killed within two months of each other while on active service.

The Wolverley mother of twins in the Services said she hoped her small contribution would assist in some way in bringing her sons back home unharmed, and a small boy handed in 3s. 6d. as a token of admiration for his airman father.

Touching tributes came from the office cleaners of Messrs. Brintons, Ltd., and nine old age pensioners from Rack Hill.

A lady, whose father was a borough official, sends two guineas from Birmingham; an industrious collector filled three boxes; and Mr. C. D. Chadwick's savings stall totalled £20; while a son of a former Kidderminster carpet manufacturer identified himself with the effort. Two children sent their books of savings certificates.

Mr. Frank Stone honoured his promise by sending £50; and among valued help came boxes full of contributions from wardens' sites at Hartlebury. A former well-beloved Catholic priest, though

"By far the best collection in clubs and public houses goes to the credit of Stourport Workmen's Club, who have this week sent along £65 8s. 9d., and intimated that their efforts are continuing and that a further donation might be forthcoming next week. This is indeed a splendid effort, and one that is much appreciated.

Accompanying a 1914 gold half-sovereign from a Wilden lady was the following note: "A treasured possession of the last war, which I hope will help a little in winning this one."

With a five guineas donation was a note: "With our best wishes for the continuance of your success in this splendid and worthy effort."

Another example of what can be done socially for the fund is provided by Mrs. Charge and Mrs. Williams, of Drayton, Belbroughton, who have promoted whist drives and held them alternately at their homes. As a result of this effort £3 has been raised.

Kidderminster Rotary Club (at one of whose meetings the idea of a local "Spitfire" Fund was first broached publicly) decided on Tuesday to give a donation of ten guineas. The suggestion came from Mr. Geo. Rainsford, and was seconded by Mr. A. K. Nicholls. The proposer remarked that while Rotarians had supported the fund as individuals, he felt they should be identified with it as a club.

Gifts continued to come in on Wednesday, as varied as the positions of the senders. For instance, two ladies brought in sums which did them credit, "from two 85-year-olds"; and school children from a small private school brought in contributions which included 44 farthings—one child (2s. 6d.) "to help to bring daddy home quickly."

At the other end of the scale, Sir Herbert Smith, Bart., of Park House, handed in a cheque of 100 guineas; and the young firm of Messrs. W. and R. R. Adam, Ltd., sent £50—both welcome contributions at the interesting stage of the scheme.

Another welcome gift was from a carpet employee, representing his family and a volunteer billeting with him. The useful suggestion accompanying this gift was that billeting hostesses, able to afford it, should give one week's billeting charges to the fund, in the name of their guests. Brintons' workers, and employees from other factories, brought in further boxes—result of the collections. In some cases the letters and messages received were so stimulating in character as to deserve full mention, but space forbids.

£105 Sir Herbert Smith, Bt., Park House.

£100 Messrs. T. Bond Worth and Sons, Ltd., Stourport.

£50 Messrs. Steel Stampings Ltd., Cookley; Messrs. T. and A. Naylor, Ltd., Green St.; employees of Messrs. Carpet Trades, Ltd., per Mr. C. H. Andrews (Mill St. branch £33 5s. 2½d., Long Meadow Mills £9 10s. 8d., Lea's £8 1s. 1½d.).

£50 Messrs. W. and R. R. Adam, Ltd., Birmingham Road.

£35 13s. 6d. Bewdley Spitfire Fund (per the Mayor (Councillor Chas. R. Pritchard). Donations from Mr. E. Teague, 2s. 6d., Window Cleaner, £1; J. Smith, 2s.; Master J. Smith, 1s.; Miss Drew, 2s. 6d.; Miss Robinson, £1 1s.; Anon, £1; Miss Hallett, £2; Mrs. Wilcox, 10s.; Mrs. Jeffs, 2s.; ex-P.S.

£5 Messrs. Laughton Goodwin and Co., motor engineers; Mr. H. G. Kimberley, Worcester Chambers, Worcester Street; Mr. W. Hawker, Offmore Road; Major F. E. Durcher, Pitton Street; Councillor Fred Wilson, Stourbridge Road; Mr. J. E. Tate; Ladies of the afternoon whist drives, Stourport Public Assistance Institution staff (per Mr. A. J. Burton); Mr. and Mrs. Harry Richards, Parker's Arms, Park Lane.

£4 17s. 6d. Scholars of Lea Street School.

£4 13s. 0½d. Mr. C. Lincoln Potter's collection box.

£4 12s. 3d. Wardens No. 6 site, Hartlebury.

£4 10s. 8d. "Shuttle" and W. H. Smith and Son's collecting box.

£3 10s. Mrs. Cowper, Circassian House, Muxtow Green.

£3 3s. Mrs. M. Van Moppes, New Tree House, Chillerminster; Messrs. A. Bennett and Sons, Garage, Coventry St., Kidderminster; Mr. C. J. Goodwood, Wolverley Lodge, Kidderminster; Mr. and Mrs. J. Miller Perrin and Joan, 8, Comberton Terrace; Mr. and Mrs. F. K. Bullus senior and the Misses D. F. and M. G. Bullus, 4, Bexley Av.; Mrs. Florence Weston, Ridge End, Lea Bank; Mr. H. M. Westcott, 462, Chester Rd.; Mr. and Mrs. George Rainsford, 7, Russell Rd.; Mr. and Mrs. L. W. Southall, Riversdale, Severn Rd., Stourport.

£3 3s. Mr. and Mrs. L. G. O. Stingsby.

£3 Proceeds of Drayton whist drives promoted by Mrs. Charge and Mrs. Williams; Messrs. J. Page and Sons, Home-stone, Bewdley.

£3 Mrs. S. M. Lawson, Kudell, Burnetts Lane; Castle Inn (darts and customers), Park Lane (per H. Corbett); Mr. H. Leloup, 8, Silver St.; Messrs. Oakes and Sons, Churchfields; Mr. and Mrs. H. G. Hill, Three Crowns and Sugar Loaf, Franche, J.P.

£2 17s. 10½d. Mrs. Gwilliam's collecting box.

£2 16s. 8d. Mrs. Edwards, Belle Vue, collecting box (including donation from Mr. and Mrs. T. Cox and daughters).

£2 13s. 1d. Collection by Mrs. Codding and Mrs. Morris on Broadwaters Estate.

£2 10s. Mr. and Mrs. G. Brimfield, 41, Crescent Road.

£2 8s. Employees of Mr. H. Blunt, Kidderminster and Stourport shops.

£2 4s. Customers of New Inn, Stourbridge Street.

£2 2s. Mrs. Mytton, Minster House, Stourport; St. Mary's Boys' School (per Mr. Hodgkins); Mr. T. Potts, 70, Coventry St.; Miss C. Pouget, Holy Trinity Convent; Mr. Percy Dougall, Blakebrook; Kidderminster Co-operative Society (2nd donation); Mr. and Mrs. H. H. Johnson, 24, Blakebrook; Mr. and Mrs. H. W. Lavis, 10, Birmingham Rd.; Mr. and Mrs. F. G. Tanner, 25, Connaught Av.; Mr. and Mrs. F. K. Bullus, junior, c/o E. Weaver and Son, 58, Oxford St.; Mr. and Mrs. Albert E. Horton, High St.; Mr. and Mrs. W. H. Perks, Estell, Chaddesley Rd.; Mr. T. H. Child, 29, Birmingham Rd.; Messrs. Hardiman and Co., Comberton Hill Stores; Mrs. Tibbetts, 24, Pentham Rd., Birmingham; Mr. and Mrs. A. Grainger, 190, Bewdley Rd.; Mr. George H. Southall, Haselwood, Roden Av.; Mr. and Mrs. Edward Pugh, Woodfield Crescent; Miss Hughes, Aspen House, 14, Park Lane; Mrs. Amy Jackson, 1, Vernon Rd., Stourport; Mr. H. K. Harper, Corner Garage, Stourport; Mr. and Mrs. W. J. Bowdler, Norwood, Chester Rd.; Mr. and Mrs. A. J. Mason, 274, Greenhill; Miss A. Burbery, 116, Bewdley Rd., Stourport.

£2 2s. The Chief Constable and Mrs. R. Hodgkinson, Franche Road; Mrs. C. R. Mitchell, St. John's Avenue; Mrs. and Miss Mountford, Bewdley; Mrs. M. E. Porter, Lickhill Farm, Stourport; Mr. and Mrs. W. F. Roberts, 94, Coventry Street; Staff of the Pearl Assurance Co. (Kidderminster District Office); Messrs. Hepworth Press, Ltd., Mill St.; Mr. and Mrs. Handle, 28, Milton Gardens, Stourport; Mrs. C. H. Wright, 237, Chester Rd.; Mr. A. Jordan, Malt Shovel, Chapel Street.

£2 1s. 1½d. Messrs. W. and R. R. Adam collection.

£2 Mr. and Mrs. R. Corbet Perrin, The Firs, Stourport; Mr. A. K. Hunt, 57, Franchise Street; Mrs. F. Reynolds, 41, Bank Street; H. and F. M., Stourport; Mr. and Mrs. A. W. Smith, 110, Bewdley Street.

£2 Mr. W. D. Lloyd, Wood House, Areley Kings; Councillor Charles Tepper, R.N., Charlton House, Hartlebury; Mr. and Mrs. J. Edwards, 26, Mill St.; Mr. and Mrs. H. Cartwright, 434, Stourport Rd.; Mrs. and the Misses Cooper, 345, Hurcott Rd.; Mr. and Mrs. E. E. Walker, 33, Reservoir Rd.; Lea St. Infants' School (per Miss Duffield); Mr. and Mrs. A. E. Weston, 6, Blackwell St.

£1 15s. Residents of Park Crescent, Stourport.

£1 12s. Collection of 12 members of Conservative Club (per Mr. Ralph Rogers, 66, Tomkinson Drive).

£1 11s. 6d. Mr. and Mrs. H. R. Morris, 313, Hurcott Rd.

£1 10s. "Two 85-year-olds."

£1 6s. 3d. Stourport Horticultural Society

£1 Mrs. A. E. Hunt, 57, Franchise Street; Mrs. Clara Charles, 130, Greatfield Rd.; Miss E. Perkins, Tall Trees, Comberton; Miss R. Perkins, Tall Trees, Comberton; Mr. J. Aylesbury, 130, Bromsgrove Street; Mr. and Mrs. Jack Beral, 18, Habberley Street; Mr. and Mrs. G. W. Beral, 7, Mason Road; Mr. W. H. Crane, Westcroft, Stourport; Mr. David McBride, "Gladsheim," Dunley Road, Stourport; Mr. and Mrs. V. Fisher, Moorhall Estate, Stourport; the Rev. E. J. G. Foster, 252, Chester Road; Mr. and Mrs. G. Evans, 257, Chester Road.

19s. 6d. Miss Blundell, Bewdley Hill.

18s. 6d. Mrs. Pitman-Pells, 49, Sutton Park Rd.

17s. 6d. Mr. and Mrs. B. Brazier, 66, Wood St.

15s. Kenneth French, 29, Brinton Crescent, collecting box; Mrs. and Miss Dovey, 26, Mill Street; Redstone House, Astley Cross; No. 4 Section, A Company Home Guard, Kidderminster; Mr. and Mrs. W. A. Bennett, 116, Chester Rd.

14s. 8½d. John Evans, 132, Tomkinson Drive collection.

13s. 11½d. Clarence Harris, 28, Poplar Rd. collection.

12s. 6d. Mrs. A. Morgan, 150, Offmore Road.

12s. 5d. Ralph Rogers, 66, Tomkinson Drive, collection.

11s. 6d. Rushmore School children (per Mrs. Heath).

10s. 6d. Mrs. and the Misses J. and M. Wyer, Franche Road; Mr. C. B. Griffiths, Deputy Town Clerk.

10s. 6d. Mrs. B., Stourport; Mr. and Mrs. J. B. Lawley, Sudford, Chaddesley Road; Mr. H. E. Parratt, Races Lodge, Chaddesley Rd.; employees of Bradley and Turton's (second donation); Master John Bignell, Mare and Colt Garage; Miss Joan Bignell, Mare and Colt Garage; Mr. and Mrs. H. Whitehurst, 27, Peel Street; Baldwin's Reelbearing Department (per J. Connolly) second donation; Mr. and Mrs. A. C. Bletsoe, 822, Chester Rd.; the "Chetwynd" Inn; Miss M. Hughes, Aspen House, 14, Park Lane; Mrs. and Miss Southerton, 13, Summerfield Rd., Stourport; Mr. and Mrs. Neal, 71, Bewdley Rd., Stourport; "Wychbold," Hurcott Rd.; Mr. and Mrs. M. K. Fryer, Stourport.

10s. "From the Dugouts," Arley Kinglish; Mrs. T. W. Bayliss, Berris, Sutton Park Rd.; Mrs. Evans, The Grove, Arley; Holy Innocents' Mothers Union; Mr. and Mrs. W. Mallard, 72, Aggborough Cres.; John and Graham Beral, 7, Mason Rd.; Mr. and Mrs. M. Greatley, 68, Aggborough Crescent; Mr. and Mrs. David C. Wilson and Mrs. W. H. Large, 28, Warwick St., Stourport; Y.O.M., Kidderminster; Mr. and Mrs. B. Bishop, School House, Astley; Mr. and Mrs. J. Griffiths, 28, Lorne St., Stourport; Mrs. L. Burdett, Wilden; Mr. and Mrs. M. K. Viggers, 184, Stourbridge Rd.; Workmen of T. Vale and Sons at Smethwick Dept.; Postings Anon; Mr. and Mrs. W. Reyes, 30, St. John's Ave.; Leslie Ronald Reyes, 30, St. John's Ave.

10s. Miss F. E. Field, 80, Lickhill Rd., Stourport; A.B.C.; Mrs. B. Brooks, 102, Hurcott Rd., mother of an airman "My week's pension"; F.C.J., Greenhill; K.M.J., Greenhill; Mr. and Mrs. C. Postans, Larchfield Hill, Chaddesley Corbett; Mr. Harry Postans, Larchfield Hill, Chaddesley Corbett; Mr. J. Dunn, 98, Baldwin Rd.; The Beacon, James Rd.; Mr. and Mrs. H. Morris, 10, Swan St.; Mr. W. L. Powell and family, Tanwood Cross, Chaddesley Corbett; Mr. Price, Springbank House, Coventry St.; Mrs. Price, Springbank House, Coventry St.; Miss Margaret Morris, The Bungalow, Worcester Rd., Titton; anon; Mr. and Mrs. F. J. Carpenter, 9, Findon St.; Miss H. Timmis, 23, Mill St.; Miss L. Hooper, 98, Baxter Avenue; Mr. A. Leloup, 8a, Silver St.; Mr. and Mrs. H. B. Edmonds, Cobden St.; Mr. John Ellis, 296, Hurcott Rd.; Mrs. W. T. Wilkes, 9, Turton St.; Mr. and Mrs. G. Payne, 334, Hurcott Rd.; Miss V. Cartwright, 434, Stourport Rd.; Mrs. Godfrey, Bettyne, Northwood Lane, Withybenhall; Mr. and Mrs. T. J. Beeston, Cookley; Brintons office cleaners; Mr. and Mrs. J. Wilkes, Dalham St.; Mr. and Mrs. Clarence Handle, Sutton Rd.; Mr. John Pratt, The Pound, Astley; Mr. F. Freeman, Far Forest; Mr. and Mrs. H. Parker, 35, Turton St.; Mr. F. Burford, 847, Chester Rd.; 82-years-old old age pensioners, Mr. and Mrs. S. Barratt, 170, Marlpool Lane; Miss M. Wright, 202, Birmingham Rd.; Mrs. E. A. Thomas, Somerleyton Av.; Mrs. A. Phevey, Reynolds, Leap Gate, Wilden, H.B.; Miss E. M. Bolton, Bath House, Comberton Hill; Mr. and Mrs. Oakcott, Treganon, Wilden; Mr. and Mrs. T. Knowles, Astley; Mr. and Mrs. Adams, 23, King Rd.; Mr. and Mrs. E. Stuart, Prince Albert Inn; Miss Florence Ayres, 41, Crescent Rd.

9s. Nine Old Age Pensioners, Hackfields.

8s. 7d. Mrs. Williams and Mrs. Griffiths, Mill Lane.

8s. 6d. Mr., Mrs. and Miss Cupper, 33, Lorne St., Stourport.

8s. Mr. F. Ralley, 47, Mill St.; Mrs. E. Ralley, 47, Mill St.

7s. 6d. Mr. and Mrs. L. O. and Mr. Hayton, 17, Highfield Rd.; Mr. O. J. Stokes, 62, Worcester Rd.; Mrs. H. A. Morris, Bewdley Rd.; Mrs. L. Deakin, Grosvenor Ave. Nurseries; Frank Roberts, Grosvenor Ave. Nurseries; Mrs. and the Misses Nuttings, 138, Hurcott Rd.; Mr. Sam Powell, Dunley; all at Rosedale, 27, Castle Rd.

7s. 6d. Mr. and Mrs. H. Tai...

OUR "MODERN" SCHOOLS

To Open on Tuesday

The new schools at Habberley Road and Hurcott Road for senior children will be called the Kidderminster Modern School and the Sladen Modern School, it was decided at Tuesday's meeting of the Borough Education Committee and they will open on Tuesday.

The Selection Sub-committee recommended that the rooms used by the County High School of Clacton-on-Sea at Habberley Road be reduced this week to eight class rooms (four each in the boys' and girls' departments), and that the head master and the Worcestershire County Council be informed that the school must leave Habberley Road not later than Christmas next. The committee agreed.

It was further agreed that the schools be not open for purposes of instruction on Monday, and that the Borough Surveyor be requested to move furniture now used by senior children to the new schools between the time of closing school this Friday and the time of opening school on Tuesday. Teachers will be in attendance on Monday.

It was decided that the following assistant teachers be transferred to the new schools as from Tuesday: To Hurcott Road, Mr. Walter, Mr Miller, Mrs. Jeffrey, Misses Hanland, Carless, Smallman, Hill, Hodgkiss; Habberley Road Girls, Mrs. Edwards, Misses MacDonald, Barnes, H. Barth, W. Barth, Monaghan, Williams, Simmonds, Quick and Duignan; Habberley Road Boys, Messrs. Hardy, Thrustle, Lawley, A. Handley, Foxall, Longmore, Edwards, Wridgway, Misses Seager and Tipper.

"We met the head teachers yesterday," remarked the Chairman (Alderman H. W. Cheshire) "and these are some of the assistant teachers who will go to the various schools. The opening will have to be done as best we can, because we have not got the new furniture. Furniture will be taken from the other schools, and we are arranging now for the children to be transferred to the various schools. I hope a start will be made on Tuesday, so we are now getting a move on with it.

TRIBUTE TO CANON SLADEN

"Yesterday, at the meeting the question arose as to the names of the schools. It had been mentioned to me before that the head teachers rather object to the word 'Road' being included. They think it would be better if each school had a name of its own. Well, some of us had a brainwave with regard to the Hurcott Road School, and thought it would be a very nice gesture indeed to call it the Sladen Modern School—(hear, hear). It was unanimously accepted by us, and we have even gone a little further and seen some members of the management of the Hurcott Road School. It is unanimous with all the managers, and I hope it will be unanimous with this committee. It is a very well sounding name. 'We know all the work Canon Sladen has done in connection with the Hurcott Road School, and I think we might be able to overcome his objection to calling it by his name. It would be very acceptable in the whole of the town."

Canon L. B. Sladen made another suggestion. He recalled that the site of the school was given by Canon William Lea, of Overbury, who formerly worked in Kidderminster (as a curate). Would it not be better to call the school the Lea Sladen School which would bring in the name of the man who started the thing by giving the site some years ago? Sladen sounded rather bald by itself, he thought.

The Chairman said the majority of Kidderminster people had forgotten Mr. Lea. It was a Church of England School, which had come into being through the efforts of Canon Sladen, who was Vicar of Kidderminster. He really did not think they could do better.

Alderman O. W. Davies said they had a precedent at Worcester, where the senior schools were named after his uncle, Mr Christopher Whitehead, who was chairman of the Education Committee there for 30 years.

The suggestion that the school at Hurcott Road be called the Sladen Modern School was unanimously agreed to.

The Chairman did not think they could have a better name than Habberley for the other school; Habberley was well-known all over the world.

"So is Kidderminster," remarked Alderman Davies.

Councillor J. E. Talbot pointed out that Habberley was not in the borough, and Alderman A. E. Meredith said the school was not at Habberley, but at Kidderminster. Previously they had agreed that it should be called the Kidderminster Senior School.

The Chairman said "Modern" had rather superseded "Senior" and the vice-chairman's proposal that it be called the Kidderminster Modern Boys' and Girls' School was agreed to.

The Chairman said the decision would please the head teachers

The Committee agreed that Miss Douglas, head mistress at Habberley Road, be allowed, temporarily, the use of a flat

THROUGH THE CENTURIES

Rotary Address on Mayor and Corporation

A fascinating glimpse of Kidderminster in the olden days was given by Mr. A. J. Perrett at Kidderminster Rotary Club on Tuesday, when he told an interested audience how civic rule has grown up through the centuries in a talk which he called "The Mayor and Corporation."

The President (Rotarian F. H. Stone), presiding, welcomed as visitors Lieut Kennedy, Messrs H. Hill, G. Forrest, G. Watkins and A. Carr.

Mr Perrett said that just before the war began he was collating hundreds of old documents which were to be preserved in a muniments room at Caldwall Hall. He abandoned his researches into local history because the present was no time for delving into the past. However, at Mr North's request, he agreed to address the club that day on the Mayor and Corporation of Kidderminster—proposing not to enter deeply into the history of the town, but to bring to the notice of his hearers one or two salient facts. He had a few documents from the Borough Librarian, which he exhibited. The first was the toll book of Kidderminster Horse Fair, containing entries between the years 1691 and 1710. He contrasted its bulk with the modest little volumes containing the minutes of the Corporation for a much longer period—from 1764 to 1827—complete with the signatures of the various High Bailiffs, Aldermen and "Assistants" (corresponding to the Town Councillors of to-day) who held office during that period.

Mr. Perrett went on to examine the circumstances under which Kidderminster became a borough, suggesting a Celtic origin. Probably a town arose on the site principally because the route from London into Wales lay through Oxford, Worcester and Bridgnorth (the first place at which the Severn could be bridged), and Kidderminster provided a bridge head over the Stour. The second factor was its possession of a rich bed of clay suitable for "fulling," a process which removed grease from cloth, gave it "body" and made it amenable to dyeing. The speaker suggested that even to-day that extensive bed of clay, stretching from the Retail Market to Wilden, might be utilised for the extraction of aluminium or the making of cement, both commodities sorely needed in war time.

Tracing Kidderminster's chequered ownership, Mr. Perrett said in the eighth century it came into the possession of the church, and so remained for the better part of 200 years, when it reverted to the Crown, as was shown by a reference in Doomsday Book, "the King holds Kidderminster." In 1159 it passed into the hands of a Lord of the Manor. A document, "The Composition of the Manor and Borough of Kidderminster," now to be found in the Mayor's Parlour, gave details of the government of the borough in the Middle Ages. About 1300 appeared the first known Bailiff (predecessor of the Mayor). He was Philip the Clerk, at a time when surnames were just coming into vogue. The borough had evidently acquired a degree of independence, for the bailiff was chosen, not by the Lord, but by the inhabitants. To assist in the government of the town the Bailiff had 12 burgesses, "catch-poles" serving as policemen, and "victual-tasters" whose task it was to see that the bread was of proper weight and quality and the beer up to strength. The Bailiff had the right to hunt and kill two couple of rabbits three days a week, whereas the ordinary townsman was restricted to one rabbit.

In Elizabethan times the Bailiff acquired the title of "gentleman" when his year of office terminated. That was why William Shakespeare's father was John Shakespeare, gentleman, in the old records, and not because of any noble blood that ran in the poet's veins.

PELTING THE BAILIFF

From time immemorial the choice of the Bailiff was made on the first Monday after Michaelmas, and the town developed the curious custom of the "lawless hour," the interim between the old Bailiff vacating the office and his successor taking over. The hour's rioting reached its climax when the populace pelted the new Bailiff with apples and cabbage stalks.

"I am all in favour of reviving these old customs," remarked Mr. Perrett, amid laughter, with a glance at the Mayor-elect, Mr. O. W. Davies. "There may be a shortage of apples to-day, but there are plenty of cabbage stalks!"

The 17th century saw a major change in the history of the Corporation. The Lord of the Manor was getting hard-up (like the landed gentry of the 20th century), and thought to relieve his embarrassment at the expense of the Corporation. As Kidderminster had no written right to any of its claims, the Corporation sought to legalise its position by asking for a charter. King Charles I duly granted the charter in 1636, and for the next 200 years, the Bailiff (now the High Bailiff), 12 Capital Burgesses or Aldermen, and 25 Assistants, ruled the town. The 12 picked the 25, and between them they formed the Common Council. When a member died a member of the 12 too often filled the

HOSPITAL IN WAR TIME

Heavy Drain on Finances

War-time problems of finance facing the Kidderminster General Hospital were mentioned at Tuesday's meeting of the Contributory Scheme Committee, when it was stated that new income of £1,800 plus the 25 per cent of workers' contributions which nearly all manufacturers had promised would help to offset the mounting costs.

The Chairman (Mr. J. Wright) said the hospital's accommodation had been increased by 71 beds, or 50 per cent, and despite war-time difficulties its work proceeded. Three members of the medical staff had been called up for service but in the clinics the hospital still had good consultants. There was no service it could not offer patients. As in every walk of life expenditure was mounting, and a lot more money must be spent to keep the hospital going. However, the sub-committee, which had been working hard for some months had succeeded in raising £1,800, one way and another, towards the hospital's income. It was a splendid effort, and the money would go a long way towards offsetting the increased expenditure they had to meet. In addition to that sum, they hoped for subscriptions from employers of labour at the end of the year. Almost all the large firms had promised to give subscriptions equivalent to 25 per cent of their employees' contributions. Only one or two of the big firms had not yet accepted that principle, and it was hoped they would do so before long. He could not see anyone standing out when the hospital's wonderful work was realised.

Mr. Wright said income from the contributory scheme had come in well, but owing to the war it was difficult to forecast what would be the total for the year. The House Governor (Mr. C. M. Smith) anticipated that unless anything unforeseen happened, it would not fall short of last year's record, £10,850. One did not know if Mr. Smith was too optimistic, but if that figure was maintained in present circumstances it would be a fine achievement. Certainly people had come into the town, small firms had sprung up and private subscribers had come along in fairly good numbers.

The fact that they were unable to have a carnival this year was a serious blow, as last year it brought in over £380. The Licensed Houses Competition, which last year realised £86, was being held again.

Mr. Wright referred to letters received from patients in the hospital, who praised the way in which the nurses and the staff generally manned their posts.

CONTRIBUTORS AND THE NURSING HOME

He announced that if a contributor or the dependant of the contributor wished to go into the nursing home attached to the hospital, the Contributory Scheme would make an allowance of 35s. a week towards the cost, which was £5 5s. a week. They would have their own doctor, and there was no extra charge except for him. They had tried to get an inclusive fee, but up to the moment had not succeeded.

Mr. T. Brighton said he was extremely concerned about the nursing home. It was true that 5s. a day had been granted, but unless additional benefit was obtained he was afraid it would lead nowhere. He urged that they should push for an inclusive fee—not as a demand, but as a hope. He believed it was being done in other districts, and did not see why Kidderminster should lag behind. It might be a matter of medical etiquette, but with a little human feeling they could get over that difficulty."

"We are trying to get an inclusive fee for the home and the doctor," the Chairman assured him, "and I cannot see any real difficulty, but unfortunately some doctors do."

After commenting that he would have liked to answer criticisms, but that the absence of any seemed to show that members were satisfied with the running of the hospital, the President (Mr. William Johnson) went on: "Even at the present time we don't see eye to eye with affairs in the institution. Mr. Brighton has raised a strong point regarding the nursing home and the scheme for taking in members of the Contributory Scheme for treatment there. But there is one thing you must remember. A member has the option of going into the home and getting the privacy of treatment which some people like, and the same allowance is made to those entering the nursing home as we would have to pay if they went to hospital in Birmingham. That is a step in the right direction. It gives the contributor an opportunity to choose for himself, and a little help to meet the bill. But some members of the medical staff, not only in Kidderminster but in other towns, still think that you are treading on their rights and prerogatives if you suggest to them that they should do an operation or give treatment for which they should only charge a limited sum. Some of them who look at it from a broader point of view are prepared to charge an inclusive fee for a certain number of weeks, and

READ"

t Festival

giving for the
nday last and
y. There was
vegetables, and
ook very bright
nd the singing
's service was
nd was well
given by the
ising he spoke
bread, and why
, showing that
ded as one to-
plying that we
for the day—
can only live
ount of anxiety
ny good. 'Some
orry about the
suffering from
's teaching not
rrow is quite

KIDDERMINSTER FOOTBALL LEAGUE

RESULTS

Tomkinsons 4, Wilden 4.
Carpet Trades 1, Steatite 1.
Stourport Swifts 5, Kidderminster Athletic 0.
Pike Mills "A" 9, Bewdley 3.
A.A. Workshop 1, Pike Mills "B" 7.

FIXTURES

Wilden v. Pike Mills "A"—E. Millward. Kick-off 3.
Steatite v. Tomkinsons—W. A. Bennett. Kick-off 3.30.
Stourport Swifts v. Carpet Trades—D. Bowman. Kick-off 3.
Pike Mills "B" v. Franche—F. B. Cope. Kick-off 3.30.
R.A.F. (Hartlebury) v. "A.A." Workshop—W. D. Tranter. Kick-off 3.

LEAGUE TABLE

P W L D F A Pts

BEWDLEY

The returns for the week
ember 9th, are as follows.
ficates, £1,111; Defence Bonds
s Bank £378. Total £1,658
Parcels for Troops.—Now that
over, the Mayoress and hel-
oncentrating on making up
arcels for the troops. Rela-
wdley and Wribbenhall men
in addresses immediately,
men serving in the near East
Sales.—In spite of wet
other unfavourable conditions
les are likely to reach nearly
al of £72, which was a record.
10s. 9d. has been paid into
nd included amounts from
h collecting boxes. One girl
and another over £5 5s., when
ere emptied. Other contribu-
ning along.
ay Service.—The two minutes
bserved in St. Anne's Church
cial Armistice Day service on
ducted by the Rector (Rev.
The Mayor and Mayoress,
sellers, attended the service
week wreaths have been laid
morial by the Mayor and
Bewdley, Bewdley and Wrib-
itish Legion, Bewdley. Old
ciation, R.A.O.B., Bewdley
number of private wreaths
it.
e.—On Wednesday an enjoy-
drive was held at Hoarstone
zes were given by Mrs. Neale,
Miss Hindmarch (Stockport),
Mrs. Hignell, Mrs. Kent, and
Winners were: Mr. Jesson, Mrs.
Baldwin, Mrs. Aston, Mrs.
Mrs. Kent. Competitions
Mrs. S. Smith, Mrs. Lawson,
liams. After distributing the
ing knitted garments for the
in the forces, Mrs. Gray
company for their support
ded to hold the next whist
ember 27th.
for Seventh Time.—Mrs.
ayoress of Bewdley again, is
ested in Poppy Days which
anised in Bewdley for many
ost successfully—for her hus-
rman of the County Executive
sh Legion. A Worcestershire
Mrs. Pritchard has since this
great personal interest in the
s Fund, which she has orga-
brought to a pitch of great
he is chairman of the Nursing
and takes part in the affairs
women's section of the Conser-
ation. Of her it has been said
nurse, secretary, and driver
nd," who has a legacy of war
1914-18. Her relaxations are
ading and music.
unday.—The usual procession
ildhall to St. Anne's Church,
Sunday, was not held, but a
rvice was conducted by the
lain (Rev. C. Raymond Hol-
yor and Mayoress (Councillor
rd and Mrs. Pritchard) were
by aldermen and councillors,
als, and many representatives
ganisations. The Rector gave
ddress on "Citizenship." The
0 9s.) was for the Bewdley,
iation and Wribbenhall Dis-
Association. The Mayor
et that it was impracticable

STOURPORT

Funeral to-day (Saturday).—Mr. William Ernest France of Severnside, died on Tuesday at the early age of 52. Funeral takes place at St. Michael's Church, Stourport, to-day (Saturday).

Death.—Mr. Edgar Henry Quarterman, formerly of Astley Cross where he carried on business as a butcher for years, died on Wednesday at the home of a daughter in Prospect Road, Stourport, aged 67. The funeral took place at St. Bartholemew's Church, Areley Kings, on Friday afternoon.

War Savings.—Efforts are being made by the Stourport Savings Association to raise £2,000 before Thursday next, and thus complete the £100,000 aimed at when the campaign was launched a year ago. Savings last week reached £2,029 (certificates £717, Defence bonds £430, Post Office Savings Bank £882), bringing the aggregate to £97,378.

Haven Cinema.—Patrons have a treat in store during the coming week for on Monday, Judy Garland, Frank Morgan in "The Wizard of Oz" is screened. This is a remarkable piece of screencraft, filmed in technicolour. On Thursday for three days, "Ten Days in Paris," featuring Rex Harrison and Karen Verne—a story of the British Secret Service.

Armistice Day.—At the War Memorial on Monday representative wreaths were laid by several town organisations including the British Legion, the V.A.D. Nurses, members of the Stanley Baldwin Lodge, M.U. Oddfellows, members of the Stourport Co-operative Women's Guild, first Stourport St. Michael's Boy Scouts. A number of private poppy wreaths and flowers were laid by relatives of men who died in the Great War.

Football Match.—No. 3 Platoon, "A" Company, Stourport Home Guard versus Canaries XI to-day (Saturday), at Astley School. Kick-off 2.45 p.m. Home Guard team: W. Hunt; W. Greaves, W. Haynes; W. Andrews, S. Millward, J. Price; G. Lucas, W. Badham, W. Dorrell, S. Coombs, T. Cox. Reserves: P. Ward, G. Griffiths, E. Merrick, O. Thomas.

Armistice Day Observance.—There was no united service on Monday, but at St. Michael's Parish Church the Vicar was the celebrant at Holy Communion, when intercessions were offered for those who died in the Great War and the present war. In the afternoon, at the Congregational Church, Mrs. H. J. O. Potter made reference to Remembrance Day and the meaning of Armistice observances.

Co-operative Women's Guild.—A whist drive was held in the Town Hall on Saturday, in aid of troops funds. Donors of prizes were Mr. Gilbert Foster and Mrs. Whiteman. Prizewinners were Miss Bandall, Mrs. Such, Mrs. Gregory, Mrs. Piper, Mrs. Dunn, Mrs. Bevan; consolation prize, Mrs. Lashford. A competition was won by Mrs. D. Darby. Mr. Blower was M.C., and Mrs. C. L. Southall (secretary) presented the prizes. A cooking demonstration by the Electric Power Company will be given on Wednesday, November 20th, at 3 p.m.

Town Comforts Fund. — Arrangements are now being made for the despatch of parcels for Christmas to all local serving men. The hon. secretary (Mr. F. G. Rowley) emphasises the necessity of sending in any new address without delay, as it is hoped to start sending almost immediately. Addresses can be left at Miss Lennard's shoe shop, Mitton Street, or sent to the secretary at the Legion Club. It should be stated whether the man smokes or not; and care should be taken to see that full address is given, to avoid loss of parcels. Collecting boxes will be re-issued this week-end.

Armistice Remembrance Day. — The Chairman (Mr. R. P. Vale) and members of the Urban District Council, with officials, attended the special service in St. Michael's Parish Church, on Sunday afternoon, for observance of the annual Armistice Remembrance Day. The congregation included Home Guard, British Legion, and ex-Servicemen, Scouts, Guides, and other organisations. On the instructions of the Police, a parade through the town was cancelled. Service was conducted by the Vicar (Rev. W. A. Trippass) who read the names of over 120 men, whose names are inscribed on the War Memorial, and included two who died during the present war. Mr. W. P. Matthews, lay reader, read the lessons and the choir sang an anthem "Save us, O Lord." The preacher

BLOOD DONORS WANTED

Lady Beauchamp at Stourport

How women can help the nation in wartime was explained at a largely attended meeting in Stourport Town Hall on Friday, when attention was called to a scheme of enrolling blood donors.

Mr. R. P. Vale (chairman of the U.D.C.) presided, supported by Countess Beauchamp, the W.V.S. County Organiser, Mrs. Rom, County Secretary, Mrs. J. A. MacLauchlan, Area Organiser, and Dr. R. S. MacArthur.

The Chairman, in welcoming the large gathering, said he had received a letter from Lord Woolton, Minister of Food, who stressed the importance of providing communal feeding centres in all towns where there was or might be definite needs as the result of enemy aerial attack. At present, the Minister stated, we were very well off for food; in fact, as regards supplies we had hardly felt the effects of war, except that we had been rationed in certain directions. Although we were some distance through the war, we still had a considerable distance to travel before we reached the end of that journey, and we might have to put up with even more severe trials as the result of enemy destruction of ships, or through food stores being damaged by incendiary bombs.

In view of those contingencies, the Minister suggested that local authorities should make arrangements for suitable centres from which at least one hot decent meal could be served to people bombed out of their homes.

TRIBUTE TO W.V.S.

Mr. Vale said he mentioned the matter because they had met under the auspices of the W.V.S. The work of running any scheme of community feeding locally would rest on the broad shoulders of Mrs. MacLauchlan and W.V.S. helpers.

Countess Beauchamp began her address with a tribute to Mrs. MacLauchlan and helpers and the W.V.S., who had done far more voluntary work than was realised. In the present war the civilian population played an important part because the women had to carry on important services whilst their men were with the armed forces or on other National work.

The W.V.S. was finding suitable opportunities for women to help the National effort. They had already offered to do about thirty different jobs related to branches of Civil Defence, A.R.P. services, as nurses, and at first aid work, auxiliary hospitals, evacuation, transport services, etc. They were doing many reponsible tasks in conjunction with local authorities, under the direction of the Government authority concerned.

If emergency help was required the authorities could 'phone the nearest W.V.S. office, where a register was kept of the different help available, and what trained helpers could be sent. A great many women's organisations who had done good work in peace time, were also anxious to help in wartime.

In Worcestershire the W.V.S. had 8,000 members without reckoning over 1,000 in Worcester City.

Already they had a stock of second hand clothing and stores for meeting any great emergency. They were now collecting new clothing, mostly from the American Red Cross Society, who had been generous with food, clothes, shoes, etc. America had sent 9,000 lbs. sugar, 8,000 lbs. flour, 2,000 lbs. rice, over 9,000 pieces soap, 5,000 tins of milk—gifts for distribution through W.V.S., of which this county got its share. The speaker described arrangements for giving emergency help to evacuees and refugees.

Lady Beauchamp, after detailing the many agencies within the W.V.S., spoke of the clerical work, most of it done at report centres, and of the transport service, which would mean a great deal in connection with blood transfusion. She assured would-be donors that blood transfusion was not dangerous. A cousin of her husband had offered his blood on 23 occasions, and been the means of saving 18 lives, and still looked as healthy as ever.

After referring to the sad plight of evacuees, who had been rendered homeless by enemy bombs, she mentioned what had been achieved by the Salvage Campaign, during which 1,000 tons of scrap aluminium were collected throughout the country, including 141 tons from Worce-

MAYOR-MAKING AT BEWDLEY

Councillor Pritchard Elected for Seventh Year

Though Bewdley Mayor-making ceremony on Saturday, in the Town Hall, was shorn of some of its pageantry, there was no doubt about the heartiness of the welcome given to Councillor C. R. Pritchard, who was elected for the seventh consecutive year.

Reference was made to the ever increasing duties devolving upon civic authorities, in all of which Mr. Pritchard had taken his full share, and warm tribute was paid to Mrs. Pritchard, not only for special war work undertaken at the sacrifice of much valuable time and trouble, but also for the unstinted support she gave to her husband in the discharge of his Mayoral duties.

Members present were Aldermen H. N. Frost, J.P. C.C., Alderman F. A. Mountford, Alderman R. B. Jackson, Councillors C. R. Pritchard, J. Bates, H. G. Gazely, P. W. Palmer, G. Mortimer Smith, Major W. Harcourt Webb, with the Town Clerk, Mr. L. Gordon Hales, M.O.H., Dr. U. W. N. Miles, Surveyor-Sanitary Inspector, Mr. S. J. Rowe, Borough Treasurer, Mr. B. T. Webster, Mayor's Chaplain, Rev. C. R. Hollis, the Mayoress, Mrs. C. R. Pritchard.

The Deputy Mayor, was first voted to the chair.

Rising to propose the re-election of Councillor C. R. Pritchard as Mayor, Councillor Palmer said there was no doubt that Bewdley Town Council was critical of their Mayor, for it had been given to few people to hold that office during the past twenty or thirty years. Referring to the length of service of Mr. John Green, Alderman Frost, and Lieutenant Pritchard, the speaker said it would seem that at Bewdley once a Mayor, always a Mayor. Mr. Pritchard had served an apprenticeship in the office, which contrasted with the practice in towns of "mushroom" growth, where a Mayor held office for two or three years only. Councillor Palmer said if the Mayor had kept a diary detailing the time given to his civic duties, it would amaze both the Council and the townspeople to find so many-sided services Mr. Pritchard rendered. In all his work the Mayor had received valued help from Mrs. Pritchard, quite apart from her duties as Mayoress.

Mr. G. Mortimer Smith seconding, said they all appreciated the time and efforts of the Mayor, for they realised that his duties became more onerous each year.

The vote was unanimous, and the Mayor, after robing, made the statutory declarations. He was installed by the Deputy Mayor, who paid warm tribute to the Mayoress for all the help she gave her husband in various ways. Wishing the Mayor a happy year of office, Alderman Frost said they hoped Mr. Pritchard would have health to carry on as well physically as in other respects, for he was most capable in public service.

The Mayor first thanked members for the great honour the borough and Council of Bewdley had conferred upon him by his election to that office for the seventh consecutive year. He little thought, on taking office the first time, that it would have lasted so long, but one never knew what fate had in store. The Mayor said he particularly wished to thank Alderman Frost for all the encouragement given him through increasingly difficult years, and also the Council for their support. He would continue to give of his time and the best of his abilities in discharging the duties of the office.

The warnings given so frequently reminded them of the terrible and difficult times through which they were passing.

FACING NEW PROBLEMS

A problem never before faced was that of dealing with people from bombed areas and evacuees from danger zones. In facing that problem he could assure them, on behalf of people of all classes in Bewdley, of their sympathy with the homeless people in distress. While expressing his readiness to carry on to the best of his ability, the Mayor said he hoped they would forgive his shortcomings and accept his assurance that he and the Mayoress would be given credit in their efforts to uphold the honour and dignity of the borough of Bewdley.

The Mayoress was presented with a bouquet inscribed, "To the Mayoress, with many thanks from her helpers and admirers." She afterwards placed the bouquet on the war memorial.

The Mayor re-nominated Alderman Frost as Deputy Mayor.

Acknowledging the appointment, Alderman Frost said he had not actually been called upon on many occasions to deputise for the Mayor, although they knew Mr. Pritchard had suffered greatly. He had managed to attend to civic duties during the past six years, with whole-hearted enthusiasm. Work in connection with Bewdley Council was ever increasing. Given health and strength, he was quite prepared to do his part in dealing with the extra duties put upon their shoulders, especially on the aldermen and chairmen of committees. Whatever might be said of extra work in the last war it was nothing

LEA BANK FA

Czech Struck by N

How a Czech refugee
tuary in this country aft
employment at the Suga
met his death through an
Bank in the early hours
inc. was described at Th
minster inquest on A
(39), of "Shirley," Stourp
ley.
Schneider was a laboure
the sugar factory, and w
11 shift on Saturday, lea
midnight. He was walkin
was knocked down from
driven by an Army officer
to Bewdley without stoppi
was pushing his machin
heard the bump, and by
moon saw Schneider lyin
of the road. He pulled
man to the side of the r
up Dr. J. W. Stretton, wh
borough ambulance. Sch
to hospital, and died t
night without regaining
The inquest at the Tow
day was conducted by t
tershire Coroner, Mr. F. P
the driver of the car wa
Mr. N. H. Capel Loft.
Evidence of identificati
the widow, Mrs. Alice Sch
in broken English and
tressed. She said her h
fect health, eyesight and
home at two o'clock on S
to go to work, and would
night. When she saw in
never able to tell her wh

HEARD A "B

Charles William Paton,
Avenue, said he was push
Lea Bank about 12.45 a.m.
he heard footsteps appro
hill, and saw the lights
car. Next he heard a bu
car swerve violently acros
which gave him the im
had been on its wrong
stop, but carried on
going rather fast, and pa
time." When the car swe
40 yards in front of him.
Witness said it sudde
that the footsteps had ce

BOROUGH OF BEWDLEY

Quarterly Council Meeting 29th day of January, 1940

QUARTERLY REPORT OF THE MEDICAL OFFICER OF HEALTH

Bewdley
27th January, 1940

To the Town Council of Bewdley.

Gentlemen,

During the quarter ending 31st December, 1939 there were only six deaths registered giving a rate of 1·3 per 1000 of the population for the quarter or 5·2 per annum. They were all over 65 years of age, except one infant, which only lived a few minutes.

There were 28 births registered during the quarter, giving a rate of 6·2 per 1000 of the population for the quarter, or 24·8 per annum.

There were notified during the quarter two cases of Scarlet Fever, both of which were isolated at their own homes; two cases of Erysipilas; one of Whooping Cough, which has recently been made a notifiable infectious disease, and three of Pulmonary Tuberculosis.

The Ministry of Health has decided that the work on the new Sewerage Scheme is to go forward, as it is considered to be urgently necessary in the interests of the public health.

I remain, Gentlemen,

Your obedient Servant,

(Signed) U. W. N. MILES

Medical Officer of Health

Committees (Continued)

EVACUATION - To consist of the following members of the Council, that is to say - the respective Chairman of the various Committees appointed by the Council to whom be delegated the consideration of all matters relating to Evacuation within the Borough whether by Government Schemes or individual arrangements.

That each of the Committees now appointed by this Council and hereinafter mentioned, viz:-

General Purposes
Emergency
Finance
Water and Health
Highways
Housing
Lighting and Fire Brigade
Rating and Valuation
Air Raid Precautions
Evacuation

shall continue in office until the 31st day of October, 1940 unless this Council shall at any time otherwise order, and shall have power to engage the services of such officers, clerks, collectors, servants, workmen and others, as may be necessary to help them to carry out the various matters entrusted to their care by this Council and shall also have power to transact any business which has been heretofore committed by this Council to any Committee in the like behalf and is not yet completed, and that the said Committees respectively may, for and on behalf of this Council, do and direct all such acts, matters and things as may be necessary or incident to the execution of the powers, authorities, and directions given or committed to them respectively and this Council doth hereby delegate to the said Committees its powers and duties in relation to the matters aforesaid.

TOWN PLANNING - To consist of the following members of the Council that is to say - Aldermen Frost, Mountford and Jackson; Councillors Wallis, Wallis, Gazely, Bates and Palmer, to whom be delegated all matters pertaining to the Town and Country Planning Act, 1932.,

LIBRARY - To consist of the following members of the Council that is to say - Aldermen Frost and Jackson; Councillors Bates and Palmer: the Secretary for the time being of the Bewdley Institute and Mr: H. R. Mountford.

And That the Meetings of the General Purposes Committee be held on such days and at such times as the Mayor may decide and that the other Committees do meet on such days and at such hour as they respectively may appoint.

GUARDIANS COMMITTEE

7. Proposed by Councillor Gazely seconded by Councillor Mortimer Smith and RESOLVED That the Mayor (Councillor Charles Rodman Pritchard) be and he is hereby nominated for membership of the Guardians Committee in accordance with Clause 6 (4) of the Administrative Scheme for the County under the Local Government Act, 1929 for the ensuing year.

NORTH WORCESTERSHIRE JOINT HOSPITAL BOARD

Chapter Three

1941
Britain fights on; Russia Invaded; U.S.A. at War

The consequences of Hitler continued to be felt on an ever-wider scale. The German Axis invaded Russia, and Japan entered the War against the United States by bombing Pearl Harbour in Hawaii on December 7th 1941. World War was then a reality.

The Kidderminster Shuttle carried an advert urging readers to, "Kill that rat - its doing Hitlers work." In March, the Rotary Club received Franz Fischer, a Czechoslovac refugee, to talk about their predicament and give thanks to the people of Kidderminster for their kindness to Czechs and "other refugees". In the issue of 27th December, reference was made to a meeting at the Youth Club on December 6th being "Free French Night". Speakers were Mrs Nairac and Mrs Knowles (no relation) of the Kidderminster branch of Friends of the French Volunteers. The Borough of Bewdley reported news of its Evacuation Committee. The W.R.V.S. were thanked for their help.

Books of the Day

NEW FICTION

By GEORGE W. BISHOP

***The Captain from Connecticut.* By C. S. Forester.**
(Michael Joseph. 8s 6d.)

JUST before the end of the war between the United States and Great Britain the American frigate Delaware broke through the blockade and was a menace to British shipping in the Atlantic.

Out of this incident Mr. Forester has made a rousing and colourful tale. The interest is centred in the captain of the Delaware, Josiah Peabody, who has emerged from a cruel, embittered childhood into a fine, courageous figure of a man. Behind his stern sense of discipline there are many endearing qualities, and when romance leaps into his life he grasps it with the impetuosity of a poet. So well is the character drawn that one accepts his lightning marriage.

There is a slight feeling of anti-climax at the end. For this history must be blamed: the encounter with the British man-of-war, Calypso, does not take place because the news arrives that peace has been declared. But there are a number of stirring fights in the first half, and throughout the book one is again impressed by Mr Forester's uncanny knowledge of a sailor's life in the early part of the 19th century.

***They Went on Together.* By Robert Nathan. (Heinemann. 6s.)**

In Mr. Nathan's short sensitive novels understatement is extremely effective. Here all the horrors of an evacuated people before an invading army are presented in the microcosm of a small group: a mother and her two children and one stray girl who has lost her parents. There are bombs from the sky and guns in the distance, roads cut off by destroyed bridges; but the real tragedy lies in the mother's awful weariness and concern and the nightmare that there is no end in sight to the grim journey.

***Ramping Cat.* By Christian Mawson. (Cape. 9s 6d.)**

Before one has got far with this very interesting first novel one realises that it is a historical romance in a new dress. The subject, in fact, is the last days and fall of Thomas Cromwell, the organiser of the ruthless tyranny of Henry VIII, and destroyer of the monasteries. The "ramping cat" is the family nickname of Katharine Howard, who married the King so as to bring about Cromwell's destruction.

The whole story, however, is transferred to the surroundings of to-day; the names are the same, and the characters talk of 'phones, taxis, cheques, cigars, cinemas, saloon-bars and even No. 10, Downing-street. Mr. Mawson draws an unobtrusive but evident parallel between Cromwell's machinery of despotism and Hitler's, with the whole country under a stifling terror of espionage

***Call the New World.* By John Jennings. (Hamish Hamilton. 9s 6d.)**

This narrative of the career of an American soldier of fortune is an admirable piece of history without tears. Having been cashiered from the American army after the war against Britain in 1814, Mr. John Jennings's misjudged and blameless hero assists in the liberation of Venezuela, Chile and Ecuador from the Spanish yoke.

In spite of its length, the tale moves quickly. Between battles Peter Brooke wins the hearts of no fewer than three ladies. Mr. Jennings's rather pedantic style does not always match his romantic material, but he can tell a story

***Little Ladyship.* By Ian Hay. (Hodder and Stoughton. 8s 3d.)**

In Ian Hay's play dealing with the girl who married a busy surgeon and

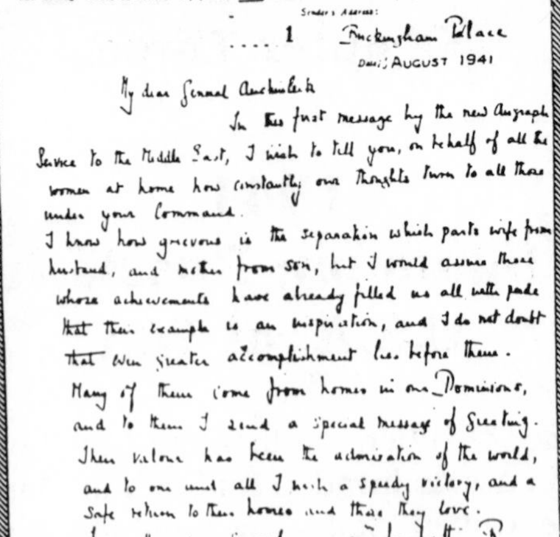

The message should be written very plainly above the double line.

Sender's Address:

. . . . 1 Buckingham Palace

Date: AUGUST 1941

My dear General Auchinleck

In this first message by the new Airgraph Service to the Middle East, I wish to tell you, on behalf of all the women at home how constantly our thoughts turn to all those under your Command.

I know how grievous is the separation which parts wife from husband, and mother from son, but I would assure those whose achievements have already filled us all with pride that their example is an inspiration, and I do not doubt that even greater accomplishment lies before them.

Many of them come from homes in our Dominions, and to them I send a special message of greeting.

Their valour has been the admiration of the world, and to one and all I wish a speedy victory, and a safe return to their homes and those they love.

I am, Yours very sincerely Elizabeth R.

Write address in large BLOCK letters in the panel below. Nothing else should be written below this line

GENERAL SIR CLAUD AUCHINLECK, GCIE. ETC
COMMANDER-IN-CHIEF.
MIDDLE EAST FORCE.

The message which the Queen sent to-day to Gen. Sir Claud Auchinleck C.-in-C., Middle East, to inaugurate the airgraph service from London to the Middle East.

VICHY FLOUTS ARMISTICE IN SYRIA

From CHRISTOPHER BUCKLEY
Daily Telegraph Special Correspondent
CAIRO, Thursday.

A deliberate breach of the armistice terms by Vichy leaders in Syria and their adoption of a policy of planned obstruction has been established up to the hilt by a series of episodes now disclosed.

Gen. Dentz was arrested because on the eve of and during the actual armistice negotiations he had British officers removed from Syria and in some instances handed over to the Axis Powers.

A more flagrant act of bad faith within the letter of the law can hardly be imagined on the part of a commander seeking the cessation of hostilities.

Gen. Sir Maitland Wilson the British C.-in-C. in Syria, has also had evidence of three definite breaches of the armistice:

Gen. Dentz denounced as deserters all Vichy troops who opted for the Free French.

Families and baggage of many troops were removed against their consent to embarkation ports thereby virtually giving them no opportunity for opting.

After signing the armistice the Vichy officers sold a considerable quantity of military material to the civil population rather than allow it to pass to the Allies.

ALLIES TAKE ACTION

IMPROVING THE FARMLANDS

LARGE INCREASE IN FOOD PRODUCTION

From Our Agricultural Correspondent
NOTTINGHAM, Thursday.

Five thousand miles of farm ditches are being cleaned out in Nottinghamshire as part of the agricultural war effort.

About 2,000 miles have already been dealt with.

Mechanical excavators are used, doing the work of many men.

Men of the Pioneer Corps here and elsewhere are giving valuable help in improving Britain's farmlands. Within a week or so Italian prisoners of war under armed guard, will be available in gangs of 25 for land reclamation and drainage.

Three Nottinghamshire parishes covering 6,000 acres, that had barely 50 acres of ploughland between them before the war, now have 1,500 acres.

It is in such cases that the county war agricultural executive committee's mobile forces of men and machines have proved invaluable to

U.S. HAS "JUMP ON HITLER"

COL. KNOX ON VALUE OF NAVAL AIR ARM

FROM OUR OWN CORRESPONDENT
NEW YORK, Thursday.

"We have the jump on Hitler," declares the Secretary of the United States Navy, Col. Knox, in an article appearing in this week's issue of Collier's Magazine, in which he sets forth his reasons for believing that the United States should maintain an independent naval air arm.

"The Naval and Military Intelligence," writes Col. Knox, "estimates that, if Hitler wins in Europe and Britain, his shipbuilding capacity will be at least four times our own.

"In addition, all Europe will become Hitler's aircraft factory. It would then be in his power to build a sea and air navy bigger than our own.

"But we have had the jump on Hitler in ships and ship-based 'planes in the 'know how' of training, and most particularly in the high morale and intelligence of our personnel. The American people should demand that we must keep the jump on Hitler—and jump on him first where there is any doubt about it."

Col. Knox reveals that an American naval observer was aboard the American-built Catalina flying boat which spotted the German battleship Bismarck.

TWO QUESTIONS ASKED

Two questions, he says, are often asked:

Should the navy give up its aviation arm in favour of a unified air force?

Has the European war proved the 'plane to be mightier than the battleship?

"The first of these questions," he states, "is generally answered by citing the brilliant feats of the R.A.F. and the crushing devastation wrought by the Luftwaffe in mass attacks over Britain.

"Further, there is evidence that Great Britain, in the midst of a life and death struggle, is finding it necessary to adopt our methods of using its sea and air arms as a single co-ordinated striking force.

The unanimous report of our naval observers has been that, to be effective, the naval air arm must have 'planes developed by the navy for naval uses, 'planes flown under naval command to attain naval objectives, 'planes flown by naval-trained pilots.

"Our observers have expressed the belief that England's early failure to develop an independent, powerful sea air arm has been primarily responsible for nearly every reverse suffered by Britain so far in the war at sea."

FINE FILM OF RUSSIA

97 CAMERA-MEN

By Our Film Correspondent

London and the provinces will shortly see a film projection of the life of Russia as she likes to see herself. Ninety-seven camera-men contributed to the super-documentary "A Day in the Life of Soviet Russia" which was flown here in a bomber carrying the Russian Military Mission.

The film, which lasts more than an hour, is a conscientious presentation of as many phases of Russian life as can be welded into an artistic whole.

The vast resources and extent of the Soviet Union, "on which the sun never sets," are revealed in a series of flashes ranging from the Behring Straits to the Ukraine at harvest time.

Roosevelt welcomes Lord Halifax

NEW BRITISH AMBASSADOR IN AMERICA. The death of Lord Lothian, Britain's representative, in Washington, on 12 December, 1940, left a diplomatic gap which was filled a fortnight later by the appointment of Lord Halifax. The selection of so prominent a statesman as Ambassador was unprecedented, and was received with deep satisfaction in the United States. Lord Halifax, who crossed to America in the battleship "King George V," was met in Chesapeake Bay by President Roosevelt, who journeyed from Washington specially to welcome him. Above, the President and the new Ambassador are seen together shortly after the latter's arrival.

Daily Telegraph and Morning Post

4 A.M.

AUGUST 15, 1941 — Printed in LONDON and MANCHESTER — PRICE 1½d.

.S. UNITED ND PEACE

AND PREMIER RIC MEETING

DECLARED IN NT CHARTER

evelt have met at sea. After a series of y have drawn up a momentous eight-point s of Great Britain and the United States. eeting was broadcast yesterday to a world tancy by Mr. Attlee, Lord Privy Seal and

sclosed that President and Premier were officers who were not named.

ne the news that among those who left Mr. Harry Hopkins, administrator of the nder Cadogan, the Foreign

of Supply, who

GERMANS SHOW THEIR DISMAY

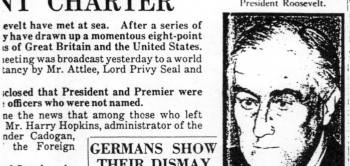

The latest portrait of Mr. Churchill and (below) President Roosevelt.

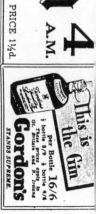

FRANK REVIEW OF WAR STRATEGY

STAFF OFFICERS' PART IN TALKS

ATLANTIC AND FAR EAST PROBLEMS

By Our Diplomatic Correspondent

Perhaps the most important feature of the meeting between Mr. Churchill and President Roosevelt is the simple fact that it should have taken place at the present juncture in the war.

Although the heads of the two principal Governments associated in the war against Hitler's Germany have had countless conversations on the Transatlantic telephone, they had never met in their official capacities as President and Premier.

Reports reaching London show beyond doubt that this first contact was altogether happy.

The two men took kindly to one another from the outset and, as the talks developed from day to day, an always greater community of interest and understanding was established.

Where democratic nations are concerned this fact is of great importance.

SUPPLIES FOR BRITAIN

Since Britain first started large-scale purchases of war supplies from the United States, and to receive them under the "Lease-Lend" Act, British demands have been most diverse. On this side there may have been some lack of co-ordination between the great purchasing departments, creating in the United States the impression that British orders were not being placed in accordance with a settled plan.

The announcement that Lord Beaverbrook, Minister of Supply, took part in the conferences at sea and has arrived in Washington "to discuss further details with appropriate authorities" emphasises the import-

FIGHTING ALL ALONG RUSSIAN FRONT

UKRAINE TOWNS EVACUATED: HITLER'S VISIT

From OSSIAN GOULDING, Daily Telegraph Correspondent

STOCKHOLM, Friday Morning.

Fighting has flared up fiercely along the whole of the vast Russian front from the White Sea, in the Arctic, right down to the Black Sea.

This was announced in the midnight communiqué from Moscow. It added that in the Ukraine the Red Army had evacuated the towns of Kirovograd, about 120 miles north of the Black Sea port of Nikolayeff, and Pervomaisk, on the River Bug, north-west of Nikolayeff.

The evacuation of Kirovograd suggests that the German army has made a 95 miles thrust to the East from Uman. Stating that the Russian air force continued to deal heavy blows at enemy troops and aerodromes, the communiqué claimed that on Wednesday 74 German aircraft were destroyed in combat or on the ground.

The Red Air Force's loss was 27 'planes.

"In the Baltic Sea," the communiqué concluded, "one of our warships sank a German submarine."

HITLER IN UKRAINE

Hitler has established his headquarters with Field-Marshal von Rundstedt "somewhere in the Ukraine."

The Berlin newspapers yesterday printed this announcement prominently on their front pages.

This is the first time since the Russian war began that Hitler's whereabouts have been even hinted at by semi-official German circles

DOCKS BOMBED AT BOULOGNE

NAZIS LOSE 14 'PLANES TO 5

In two daylight sweeps by the R.A.F. over Northern France yesterday 14 enemy fighters were destroyed and five of our fighters are missing.

In the first raid big groups of R.A.F. 'planes crossed the south-east coast early in the afternoon at a great height. They were over France for nearly an hour.

Blenheims, escorted by fighters, bombed docks at Boulogne. One

KNOCKED DOWN BY AMBULANCE

Soldier Killed on Christmas Night

"I cannot see that the driver of the ambulance has any reason for self-reproach," remarked the Coroner (Mr. F. P. Evers), at Friday's Kidderminster inquest on Lance-Corporal Arthur Brindle (43), The Essex Regiment, who died in hospital from multiple injuries caused when he was knocked down by the borough ambulance in Mill Street on Christmas night. "The verdict is one of 'Accidental death'—it is particularly sad that this tragedy should fall upon the man's relatives at this season of the year," added Mr. Evers.

Mr. J. M. Thursfield associated himself with the condolences, on behalf of the Chief Constable (on whose instructions he represented the officer driving the ambulance).

Evidence of identification was given by a brother, Private John Brindle, 7, Bulgaria Street, Armley, Leeds (the same home address as deceased). He said deceased had good health, sight, and hearing.

Another soldier, Private Richard Hopkins, of "The Newlands," Franche Road, said he saw Brindle at 8.30 p.m. on Christmas evening in the Bridge Inn and they each had 3½ pints of beer. Witness did not know what deceased might have had earlier. He left at 10 o'clock, but did not see Brindle after that—he only saw him go out through the door. Witness walked along Mill Street, and near the car park saw an ambulance turning round. Next he saw a man lying on the pavement on the right hand side facing Franche.

P.C. Worrall said at 10.20 p.m. he was driving a police car along Mill Street towards the Bull Ring and the borough ambulance was in front of him. Both vehicles were travelling at about 15 miles per hour. The ambulance was being driven on the near side of the road. When near French's electrical shop he saw a shower of sparks coming from the side of the ambulance, as if from a cigarette. The ambulance went on a few yards and then stopped against the near side kerb. Witness also stopped and then saw P.C. Jones jump out of the ambulance and come towards him shining an electric torch. P.C. Jones bent over the figure of a man lying on the footpath. Witness saw it was a soldier, who appeared to be seriously injured. The ambulance turned round and conveyed the soldier to hospital. The width of the road was 26 feet 6 inches.

In reply to the Coroner witness said the body lay about two yards to the rear of the ambulance. A mark 12 yards long had been made by the man's clothing as it dragged along the footpath, diagonally from the gutter to the wall. Apparently the man had been knocked across the footpath by the force of the impact. The ambulance had not been on the footpath. The near side head lamp bracket was broken, the radiator was slightly dented, and the spot light was pushed back.

P.C. Charles Powell, who was driving the borough ambulance from the hospital towards the Bull Ring, said two side lights were on, the offside masked head lamp and the ambulance sign was lighted. Driving at 15 miles per hour he suddenly saw a figure a yard or a yard and a half in front of the ambulance, slightly to the near side, but could not say which way the man was walking. "Before I had time to apply the brakes or do anything to avoid a collision, I collided with him," added witness. "I stopped immediately."

"Had you mounted the footpath at all?" asked the Coroner.

"No, sir," replied P.C. Powell. He added that it was a very dark night and there was a slight mist. The ambulance sign—a white light behind red lettering—could be seen for a distance by people in the opposite direction.

Dr. Hugh Mackie, senior house surgeon at the Kidderminster Hospital, said deceased was unconscious on admission at 10.30 p.m. and died a few minutes later. The man was suffering from a compound fracture of the right leg, fracture of the left knee, fractured right arm, and fractured upper jaw. Several teeth were knocked out. There was a scalp wound at the back of the head, and a number of abrasions about the face.

Asked by the Coroner if there were any indications of how the man had spent the evening, witness said just before death he vomited and there was a smell of alcohol. Death was due to shock following the multiple injuries described.

SPRING GROVE FATALITY

Inquest on Kidderminster Man

A verdict of "Accidental death" was returned at Friday's Kidderminster inquest on George Rankin McKay (56), of 7, Lea Bank Avenue, a sugar boiler, who died in Kidderminster Hospital on Christmas Eve, from injuries sustained an hour or so earlier, when he was knocked down at Spring Grove by a car which Ronald George Newman, of Park View, Gravel Hill, Ludlow, was driving towards Bewdley (in the opposite direction to that in which McKay was walking).

The inquest was conducted by Mr. F. Percival Evers (District Coroner for North Worcestershire). Mr. N. M. Capel Loft appeared for the widow, and Mr. I. R. Whittingham, a Birmingham barrister (instructed by Messrs. T. Haynes Duffell and Co.) was for the driver of the car.

Evidence of identification was given by the widow, Mrs. Mary McKay, who said her husband enjoyed good health. He was short-sighted, and wore spectacles. On Christmas Eve he went shopping, after which he was going to a farm to fetch a chicken for Christmas).

Mr. Loft: Your husband was very fond of walking?

Mrs. McKay: Yes.

Was he always very particular about walking on the footpath?—It was a passion of his. He was always practising it and preaching it, and warning others to walk on the footpath. He said people did not realise they could not be seen if they walked in the road.

Dr. Alice McElvott, junior house surgeon at the hospital, said McKay was admitted at 9.50 p.m. He had a fracture of the base of the skull, an open fracture of the left leg, and lesser injuries. He died 30 minutes after admission, from shock following the severe injuries.

Answering Mr. Loft, Dr. McElvott said the injuries were consistent with the man having been run into by a car, but she could not say whether he was run into from the front or behind.

CAR DRIVER'S STORY

The driver of the car said he and his fiancée left Barnt Green at 7.50 on Christmas Eve to drive to Ludlow, and had reached a point midway between Kidderminster and Bewdley an hour later. He was driving on his correct side, between the white line and the verge, at a speed which he put at 20 to 25 miles per hour.

"The road appeared to be clear," Newman continued. "I saw nothing in front of me until I heard a bump, and saw a figure on the offside of the bonnet. I applied my brakes immediately, and stopped. I found the man stretched right across the middle of the road, with head towards the verge, left behind the car.

Mr. Loft: I must put it to you that your recollection of what happened on this night is quite wrong, and that in fact the deceased man was on the footpath on your offside of the road when you struck him, and that you came back off the footpath, carrying the man on the bonnet to the centre of the road?

The Coroner: Is there any evidence of this coming forward?

Mr. Loft: I have evidence of certain marks on the offside footpath.

Mr. Evers: I think they are quite immaterial.

Mr. Loft: I think they are very material. Glass from the man's spectacles was found on the offside.

Mr. Evers: All this is before me, and the police statement. All these things can be very easily accounted for, apart from what you suggest.

Mr. Loft (to witness): You agree that driving under these conditions, it is easy to lose the road?

Newman: Not for me. I do a great deal of black-out driving.

TYRE MARKS ON VERGE

Are there Goodyear tyres on your car?—Yes, in perfect condition.

Have you been shown the marks of Goodyear tyres mounting the grass verge 26 yards from where the man was found lying, and leaving it 14 yards from where he lay?—No. On police instructions, several cars were driven off the road on to the verge, including my own, next morning.

Did you know that at the point where Goodyear tyres left the verge, 14 yards from the body, pieces of deceased's spectacles were found embedded in the offside grass verge?—Yes, the police showed me where they were found.

In further cross-examination, witness said that immediately after the collision he found a parcel containing a chicken, with parsley trimmings, lying in the centre of the road near the man, and also his hat.

Mr. Loft said that some parsley, apparently off the parcel, was found embedded in the verge.

"How far could you see in front of the car?" he asked witness, who replied: "About 25 yards."

Mr. Loft: How do you account for not seeing this man before he was on your bonnet?

Newman: He must either have been in the centre of the road, or walking across the road into me. My masked head lamp gives an excellent light from the white line to the grass verge.

Asked how many cars besides his there were driven on the grass verge, coming from both directions, Newman said: "There seemed to be dozens." He could not tell what sort of tyres they had.

Mr. Evers: The Goodyear is a fairly common sort of tyre?

Witness: Yes. I have Goodyear tyres only on the back, and [illegible] tyres on [illegible].

PASSENGER [illegible]

Miss Queenie [illegible], "Lindsworth," Barnt Green, a passenger in the car, corroborated the driver's evidence, and said she had nothing to add to it.

Mr. Loft: Did you feel the bump?

JUVENILE DELINQUENCY

1940 Was Town's Worst Year

The year just ended was the worst on record for juvenile crime in Kidderminster. It was stated by the Chairman of the local Juvenile Court (Mr. E. O. Baldy) at their sitting on Friday. He said the number of juvenile offences had risen from 90 in 1939 to 137 last year, and cases of larceny (83) were 30 more, [illegible] 44 courts [illegible] against 25. Although the town had spent £40,000 on education this year (£22,000 more than in 1939), it had possibly the worst record of juvenile crime of any town in the Midlands.

To check the spread of juvenile delinquency, Mr. Baldy (who is local President of the Boys' Brigade and other youth organisations), suggested an extension of boys' clubs, and the showing of educational films on Sundays to keep children off the streets, as there seemed to be a lack of religious education. He thought there ought soon to be a technical school where boys could be trained for the staple industry of the town.

[illegible] the [illegible] grave concern at the number of boys appearing before them, the Chairman said he felt the offender's name should be published if he made a second appearance, so that the townspeople should know what boys were spoiling the town's record.

Two boys aged 13 and nine, who [illegible]

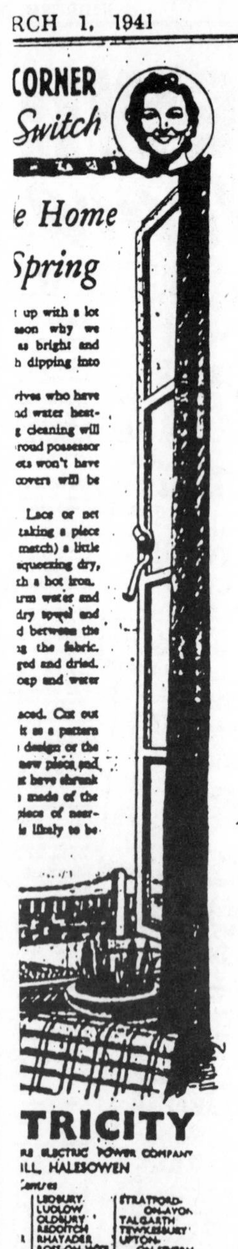

"CZECHOSLOVAKIA" HERE

Refugee's Address at Rotary

The kindly reception accorded to Czech and other refugees in Kidderminster was gratefully acknowledged by one of their number, Mr. Franz Fischer, at Kidderminster Rotary Club, on Tuesday, when he called his talk "Czechoslovakia in Kidderminster." He said that he and his friends who worked in the town, did not need assistance in the material sense, but would welcome a committee to explain to them aspects of English life which appeared strange to foreigners. A promise was given that the setting up of such a committee would be considered.

The President (Rotarian F. R. Stone) presided, welcoming as visitors Rotarian Powell (Brierley Hill), Mr. Franz Fischer and Mr Rudolph Hantush (Czechoslovakia), Messrs. L. G. French, Leslie Fletcher, George Watkins, and S. F. Nash. He called on Mr. French (manager of the local Ministry of Labour office) to introduce the Czechoslovakian visitors.

Mr. French said it was part of his official duty to control the employment of aliens in his area, and thus he was brought in contact with refugees and all other aliens in the district. Because of that, Mr. T. L. Watkins and their hon. secretary mentioned to him the suggestion that a refugee committee should be set up locally for the welfare of alien refugees. Arising out of that, he suggested that the club might invite two Czechs—Mr. Fischer who had been editor of a paper in Czechoslovakia and was a representative black-coated worker, and Mr. Hantush, an industrial worker who was a trade union leader in his own country. They were fairly representative of the Czechs with whom the speaker had come in contact. "I am pleased to say that 98 per cent of them have justified not only the friendly official attitude, but also the more personal interest that I have been able to show in them—giving motive power to the official machinery," added the speaker.

CZECHS FLED FOR THEIR LIVES

Mr. Fischer began by thanking members for their invitation, and saying what a pleasure it was to be among Rotarians again. He recalled that when he and his friends came to Scotland in 1938, the Dunfermline Rotarians were among the first friends to look after the Czech refugees and extend hospitality to them.

The question most often put to them was: "Why was it necessary for you to leave your country in 1938?" The simple answer was "Because of our anti-Nazi activities," but those few words did not explain the deeper sense of the question. The speaker read extracts from British newspapers published at the time, showing that after the German triumph, Social Democrats in Sudetenland had to leave the country in order to save their lives. Speaking of the Czech "group" in Britain, Mr. Fischer said every one was registered with the Czech Refugee Trust Fund, a semi-official institution, the manager of which was an English gentleman. The Czech representative on that body recently visited Kidderminster to see them, and to discuss certain questions with Mr. French. The group comprised industrial workers, shopkeepers, journalists, and professional men of all kinds, and locally they all knew each other from Czechoslovak days. They were all very glad to be in this country, to which they were not "alien" in the common sense of the word. Not only were they very friendly aliens, but at last they were allies with Britain in the fight against the common enemy.

"We are helping your country in several ways," the speaker continued. "Our friends are in the R.A.F., the Czech Air Force, the British Pioneer Corps, the Czech Army, and the British Merchant Navy. Others are busy in different industries vital to the war effort. Before we came to Kidderminster we were living near Cleobury Mortimer. One day in November 1939, Mr French came to see us, and gave a helping hand to get us jobs in Kidderminster. Most of us are now at the local sugar factory, working under the same conditions as do other workers. It was a new job for most of us, but we soon got used to it, partly because in our Czech training schools we were made familiar with the whole course of production, and not merely our own branch of it.

KIDDERMINSTER'S KINDNESS

"In this kind town ...

MR. E. C. HODGKINS' RETIREMENT

Glowing Tributes at Presentation

Glowing tributes to the work done by Mr. E. C. Hodgkins as headmaster for over 30 years of St. Mary's Boys' School, a position from which he has just retired, were paid at a gathering in St. Mary's Chantry on Saturday, when he received gifts from friends and well-wishers.

Speaking from his half-century of teaching experience (39 years of which have been spent at Kidderminster), Mr Hodgkins suggested that the paramount need of the age was that religion and education should go hand in hand.

From the clergy, congregation, school managers, and friends he received the Victoria edition of the history of Worcestershire, by Mr. J. Willis Bund, F.S.A., and an engraved silver salver; old boys of St. Mary's School presented him with a handsome barometer.

Mr. O. H. Walter was hon. secretary and treasurer of the general presentation fund, and Mr. V. A. Cale was hon. treasurer of the Old Boys' fund.

The Vicar (Canon L. B. Sladen), presiding, said they had met to express respect, affection and gratitude to Mr. Hodgkins for the splendid, self-denying, and successful work he had done for a great many years in the parish and town, as schoolmaster at Franche and at St. Mary's Boys' School. He was most grateful for the help and loyal services of Mr. Hodgkins during the 32 years he had been vicar of the parish. All kinds of people, the congregation at St. Mary's, the school managers, and many others were associated with the presentations that afternoon. He wished to thank Mrs. Hodgkins for her co-operation with her husband in the work he had done for many years. The History of Worcestershire was Mr. Hodgkins' own choice. The second gift, a silver salver, should be regarded as a memento of what was due to Mrs. Hodgkins.

Mrs. A. F. Dauglish, in making the presentations, said but for her husband, the Rev. A. F. Dauglish, Mr. Hodgkins might not have come to Kidderminster and they might never have had the benefit of the good work he had done there. As her husband was not well enough to attend she had taken his place. At the beginning of 1903 the managers of Franche School were in a predicament in finding a successor to Miss Grant, who had served the school faithfully for many years. The new curate was the Rev. A. F. Dauglish, and he had two or three candidates "up his sleeve" for the vacancy, Mr. Hodgkins being the favourite.

She had been a friend of Mr. and Mrs. Hodgkins for nearly 40 years. Her eldest brother, Alderman Herbert Tomkinson, who was a manager of Franche School at the time of Mr. Hodgkins' appointment, was at an important meeting of the County Council that afternoon, which explained his absence. Mrs. Dauglish said that since returning to the town she had resumed membership of the Education Committee. She was also a manager of St. Mary's Schools, and thus once again was in touch with Mr. Hodgkins. She admired him for his faithfulness, for he had set a good example to the young under his charge, and to his staff.

Although he had retired he was not leaving the district, but was remaining to give them advice on gardening and lots of things he was going to unearth about the history of Kidderminster. Mr. Hodgkins had kept touch with his old boys and received wonderful letters from them, and in retirement he would have time and leisure to pursue his hobbies. Retirement came at an opportune time, because under the new educational system the character of the Boys' School had changed since the opening of the Sladen Modern School in Hurcott Road.

The speaker added a tribute to Mrs. Hodgkins for help in all sorts of capacities which had enabled her husband to concentrate on activities of interest to others.

Alderman H. W. Cheshire, J.P. (chairman of the Education Committee) said he was glad to express his appreciation of Mr. Hodgkins in the cause of education. A schoolmaster could be judged by the quality of his boys, and in that respect the percentage was high at St. Mary's School. There must be hundreds throughout the world who had reason to be thankful to Mr. Hodgkins for what he had done for them when they were at

. Speaking for his wife an
Hodgkins said the predomi
in their minds that aftern

SATURDAY, MAY 17, 1941 KIDDERMINSTER SHUTTLE AND STOURPORT COURIER

Come on Bewdley!

Pull Your Weight!

LEND ALL YOU CAN DURING

WAR WEAPONS WEEK

MAY 17TH TO 24TH 1941

£25,000 AND MORE

FOR FIVE FIGHTERS

THE WHOLE OF THIS SPACE HAS BEEN SPONSORED BY BEWDLEY TRADESPEOPLE, the following having contributed:

fined £1

of Astley Cross, 10s for riding a light

Wilden Top Wilden, an unauthorised A police officer said cycle gave a light

9, Crown Street, motor-lorry on the engine running,

said defendant had been spoken to about said: "It's a pity better to do," he only left the

Products, Ltd., to screen a pole line pleaded "Not Taylor, chief engineer after the fuses had had replaced not discover who circuit for the firm said caused by the firm £5

Johnson, 373, Bristol Birmingham, pleaded to give his name address of the owner certificate of insurance do so by the police defendant said he was Case dismissed on

Avenue, Fernhill for driving a car licence.

Yarhampton, Stourwith being drunk in Constable Smart defendant dead drunk had to be carried and he snored on

not drunk on beer wine given me for I would drink it me clean out It got home—laughter happy—(renewed

This man has three times since disgustingly drunk Fined £2

Marjorie Alice Burton, Dunley, was charged money from Irene Burf Stourport Dorothy Tandy of gave evidence that wage packet, conput in into her hung up where was near defendant's On leaving work, and set off for She felt something She got off her her pocket, found separate shillings.

Saturday: Children's Matinee 2.30 p.m.

BEWDLEY

Savings.—A total of £477 was invested up to Saturday last.

The Health of the Mayoress. — The Mayoress (Mrs R. B. Jackson) wishes to thank her many friends for kind inquiries about her health. We are happy to learn that she is now somewhat better.

Aid to Mrs. Churchill's Russia Fund.—This Fund now exceeds £200 which includes the result of the flag day. Grateful thanks are due to all who so readily assisted this most worthy fund.

Methodists' Social Hour.—Rev. J. S. Bushby was the speaker and Mrs. Legge the tea hostess at the social hour on Wednesday in High Street Methodist Church. Fortnightly attendances at this pleasant function are well maintained.

Mayoress's Gift Fund.—The Mayoress's Gift Fund for soldiers serving now amounts to £107 10s 7d., which sum has been received within three weeks as a result of an appeal by the Mayoress and social events. Over 270 souvenirs have been sent to the troops—soldiers, sailors and airmen—from the ancient borough. Already many grateful acknowledgments have been received from the men on service.

Evacuees' Social Centre.—On Thursday, December 11th, the Women's Club held their Christmas supper at the W.V.S. rooms in Load Street. A meat pie and a rabbit pie had been cooked by Mrs. Wright, an evacuee from Coventry, jam tarts by Mrs J. T. Smith, of the W.V.S. The tables looked bright and cheerful, and everybody present enjoyed themselves. After supper games were played and community singing took place. At the close "Auld Lang Syne" was sung.

Gift Shop.—A shop to aid Mrs. Churchill's Appeal for Russia has been opened at the W.V.S. centre in Load Street. The shop was organised under the supervision of Mrs J. T. Smith and Mrs Malam. Voluntary contributions were made of goods of all descriptions including trinkets, silver cigarette cases, pewter and bric-a-brac. The people of Bewdley also gave a fine range of Christmas toys for the children. Up to Thursday over £100 had been raised for the fund.

Local Will.—Mr. William Nigel Gresley, of Cutey, Kingston St. Mary, Taunton, Somerset, and of Winterdyne, Queen's Avenue, Dorchester, Dorset, who died on the 24th August, aged 81 years, son of the late Major Francis Gresley, of Winterdyne, Bewdley, left gross estate value £5,152 11s. 4d., with net personalty £4,992 15s 11d. Capt William McGowan, late Royal Guernsey Artillery and Engineer's executor. Testator left £50 to his nephew, William McGowan. His furniture and personal chattels to his sister, Susan Isabel Garstin Payne-Gallwey. The residue of the property upon trust for his sisters Susan and Mary during their lives

preached farewell sermons in the Parish Church on Sunday before leaving to take up new duties at St. Peter with St. Nicholas Church, Droitwich. His subject was Fellowship centred in the Eucharist and he spoke of the many friends he was leaving at Stourport.

Children's Toy Service.—Members of the Children's Church at St. Michael's parish Church and their friends are bringing gifts to the annual to service to-morrow. The Vicar, Rev. W. A. Trippass states that the whole of the offerings, which he hopes will include plenty of books and games, are to be sent to the children, who use the St. Martin's Church play centres in Birmingham.

War Savings.—The grand total of war savings to date is £361,563 and includes £1,413 for the past week, consisting of certificates £638, defence bonds £510, Post Office Savings Bank deposits £265. Christmas savings cards of pretty designs proved popular and these may be obtained at the Post Office by purchasing savings stamps or on application from the various street savings group secretaries.

W.V.S. Activities.—The appeal of Mrs. J. A. McLauchlan for knitters to report at the Town Hall centre met with a gratifying response, and she will now be glad to enrol volunteers for the camouflage netting class which will meet early in the New Year. Although the needlework must be accurate, the materials are easy to handle. Ladies who can look in for an hour or two should give in their names as the work can be allocated to meet their convenience.

Town Comforts Fund.—The Hon. Secretary (Mr F. G. Rowley) gratefully acknowledges the following donations to the fund: Members of the Burton family and friends £5 5s (their third donation), Mrs Whitefoot £2 5s (for prisoners of war), Mrs P. Danby 5s, Mrs W. Chadwick 2s 6d and Mr A. R. Rowley 2s. The Hon. Secretary also thanks Mr F. Pinnegar for the gift of a beautiful model of a Wellington bomber, which will be disposed of as soon as possible in aid of the fund.

Penny-a-Week Fund.—The honorary secretary, Mr W. Rowbotham, states that since the list of November collections was received, £2 4s. 10d. has been collected by Mrs. J. L. Hatchett, making the total for November £68 16s 4d (£22 3s 7d more than October) which reflects credit upon the voluntary helpers. There are still a few streets in the town not covered by collectors. Mr. Rowbotham, Council House, would be glad to hear of ladies willing to undertake this work, especially in Brindley Street, Warwick Street, and Areley Kings.

Church Gift Tree.—The massive Christmas tree in the Congregational Church is to serve a dual purpose on Sunday. At the afternoon service the scholars will bring gifts for the Worcester Orphanage and in the evening adult church members will place gift envelopes for the Church Fund on the tree, which will be stripped during the service by Mrs A. E. Stokes. The choir, under Mr. L. W. Lashford, will render excerpts from Handel's "Messiah."

CHALLENGE FOR THE DAY

On Sunday morning at Baxter Church, the Rev. S. J. Hooper preached a vigorous sermon on the subject "When wrong triumphs." It was so topical that members of his congregation asked that it might appear in the "Shuttle," thus reaching a larger congregation.

Mr. Hooper said: The Pharisees wanted a reputation for generosity so they stood in public places, flourished trumpets and let everyone see how much they gave away. They got what they wanted. They wanted a reputation for piety, so they stood at street corners to pray, and adopted a "lean and hungry look" so that everyone could tell they were fasting.

Jesus was very severe in His criticism of them, but He quite frankly admitted that they were successful.—He said they had their reward—they did get what they set out to get.

If we start with the idea that God is good and reigns over all with sovereign power we are apt to assume that therefore evil will habitually fail and righteousness always succeed. But the facts of life do not bear out that view

... law and custom is one thing; lack of preparation for probable, if not certain, risks is another. The first is regrettable though generally inevitable; the second is unpardonable since it is the seed of defeat.

It is to the second that Dr. Goebbels has had to plead guilty. He explicitly admitted (1) the failure to strike a balance between the provision of clothes and munitions; (2) failure to overcome the difficulties of transport in Russia, and (3) failure to make an provision for a winter campaign.

"Old rags may be used for linings, even single gloves are valuable!" Such admissions would lead to the downfall of any government whic was not a dictatorship.

OLD NEWSPAPERS Bought, 3lbs a 1d. Old Magazines, Periodicals, etc. 4lbs a 1d. Bundle them up and bring them to the "Shuttle" Office. We will pay cash.

... Radcliffe & Co., Cross Brewery, ... Messrs. A. H. Smith (Radford Avenue), C. Coombes, Misses Adam, Hitterhill, Bewdley, Miss Chapman, 25, Castle Street, Bridgnorth, and anonymous.

Members present were: Chairman and vice-chairman, Mrs. H. N. Frost, Mrs. C. Pagett, Messrs. Harry Bridges, E. H. Jones, G. S. Chadwick, R. A. Knight, H. E. Rolley, W. H. Jennings, G. N. P. Humphries and W. A. Coley (Stourport) with the clerk Mr. A. A. Mumford. Apologies were received from Messrs. John Page, J. Dalley, F. Wilson, and C. R. Pritchard.

Between now and the end of May Canada expects to send us about 230,000,000 eggs.

A monster sperm whale has been washed ashore at Ballyhealy, on the South Wexford coast, Ireland. Nearly 60 feet long, the whale is believed to have been killed through striking a mine.

... small spanner all of which were found in his coat pocket. After admonishing the man the Mayor said the Bench was taking a merciful view of the case and the offender would be fined five pounds! The defendant thanked the Bench for their leniency!

There is an objection to the term "standard" in connection with the new Government "utility" cloth which will, it is expected, be available in early spring. The Board of Trade points out that there are many qualities of "utility" cloth all procurable in various colours and patterns. Every piece of cloth is identifiable by a special Government mark to be found every few yards along the selvedge. On the made-up garments there will be a tag bearing the mark. All prices are controlled and will vary according to the quality. Women are assured by the Board of Trade that they will have plenty of choice in colour.

KIDDERMINSTER BOROUGH EDUCATION COMMITTEE

ABSTRACT OF THE ACCOUNTS of the above Committee for the year ended March 31st, 1941 (which Accounts have been audited by J. STANDEN, ESQ., Assistant District Auditor, and have been certified by him to be correct.

ELEMENTARY EDUCATION

INCOME.

	1941 £ s. d.
Balance at commencement of year	8400 17 7½
Rates	20224 10 0
Grant from Board of Education	25387 10 0
Caldwall Hall	10 0 0
From School Managers	86 16 10
Sale of Needlework	62 4 10
Parents' Contributions	57 3 3
Domestic Centre Sales	54 2 8½
Miscellaneous	191 10 0
Total	£54983 15 3

EXPENDITURE.

	1941 £ s. d.	£ s. d.
Public Elementary Schools:		
Salaries of Teachers	26300 17 6	
Contributions, Sec. 9 (1) (b), Teachers Superannuation Act, 1925	1285 16 1	
Books and Stationery	1084 11 0	
Fuel, Light and Cleaning	2820 6 0½	
Upkeep and Repairs to Buildings	406 4 7	
Rent, Rates and Taxes	806 12 2	
Furniture and Apparatus	70 0 3	
Other Expenses of Maintenance	144 1 7	
Organisation of Physical Training	84 7 4	
		33006 16 6½
Playing Fields		285 10 4
Education (Institution Children) Act		37 14 11
Medical Inspection and Treatment:		
Salaries	1053 18 0	
Other Expenses	319 19 11½	
		1373 17 11½
Schools for Blind and Defective Children—Contributions to:		
Other L.E.A.s	157 0 0	
Other Bodies	329 6 7	
		487 6 7
In Respect of Loans:		
Interest	3335 16 5	
Principal Repaid	3510 3 2	
		6845 19 7
Administration:		
Salaries	894 1 6	
Other Expenses	683 0 0½	
		1577 1 6½
Other Expenses:		
Domestic Centre Purchases	52 13 2½	
Approved Schools	314 11 11	
A.R.P.	2449 14 1	
Evacuation Refund	25 14 8	
Miscellaneous	1 0 0	
		2843 13 10½
Transfer to Loan and Capital Account		1125 12 4
Total Expenditure		47583 13 8
Balance at end of year		7400 1 7
Total		£54983 15 3

HIGHER EDUCATION

Income	£ s. d.	Expenditure	£ s. d.
Balance at commencement of year	29 0 0	Aid to Student	6 0 0
		Balance at end of year	23 0 0
Total	£29 0 0	Total	£29 0 0

LOAN AND CAPITAL ACCOUNT

Income	£ s. d.	Expenditure	£ s. d.
Balance at commencement of year	1810 19 1	Public Elementary Schools	20186 11 9
Loans	17924 0 0	Balance at end of year	673 19 8
Transfer from Revenue Account	1125 12 4		
Total	£20860 11 5	Total	£20860 11 5

LOAN DEBT ACCOUNT

Income	£ s. d.	Expenditure	£ s. d.
Loans	110597 6 0	Instalments paid	29395 3 1
Loan raised during year	17924 0 0	Instalments unpaid	99126 2 11
Total	£128521 6 0	Total	£128521 6 0

December, 1941. W. H. RODEN, Clerk.

...campaign ... further
Hitler wants to renew his attempt
his régime by making peace with
ritain. He is using now Goering's
wn relations with the circles of
ional finance to launch a fresh
n for an immediate peace. This
tler dangles before us the bait of
llowed to concentrate our whole
against Japan. This new man-
as absolutely no chance of being
ul. The war is going on until the
nd.

ELGIAN ARTISTS' WORK

Mayor Opens Exhibition

arming exhibition of work by a
f Belgian artists may be seen up to
3rd next at Kidderminster Art
and those members of the public
ve an artistic eye would do well
it. The paintings are the work
J B Van Genechten Mrs Jean A.
and Mr John Gerard, and they
scenes in the countryside in
including many in Worcester-

xhibition was opened on Friday by
yor (Alderman O W Davies).
Herbert Clist, F.R.I.B.A., presided,
r welcoming the Mayor for coming
t notice, said: "I do feel that the
ts here may give him more pleasure
ome manifestations of art seen
es in this gallery and sometimes
re in the past. It is absorbing to
way in which the artists, of
have captured the spirit of the
countryside. Some of our wonder-
ntryside is very difficult to portray
these pictures will remind you
the coming reconstruction of this
—which is bound to come—we
preserve these beauties of our
and not let them be destroyed
oiled. We may have all sorts of
ble industries planted in the
of the countryside and far from
if we are not careful. There are
tches in the towns of England and
be a temptation to re-build them
countryside. If it is necessary to
nt industry from the towns in
o clear up the slums let us not
n such a way as to over-weight
al communities with the evils of
fe. In the reconstruction of our
et us make open spaces and have
awns and flowers. I was sadly
nted to see the last shrub visible
y office in Exchange Street uprooted
extension of a 'bus stop outside
n Exchange."
atulating the artists Mr Clist said
d admirably portrayed the scenes
was up to Britishers to use their
e with the object of preserving the
of rural England.
Mayor, responding to a hearty
, said the pictures on view certainly
him much more than a great
of those he had seen on some
. They showed life, beauty, and
At some previous exhibitions he
n a lot of straight lines mixed
some arrangement one could not
it. However, those he saw on this
reminded him of others he saw
the last war in an art gallery
sels—some wonderful paintings and
rrible to look at as regards their
fascinating though the subjects
The exhibition contained works of
isitors from abroad who came into
trict. It was up to all to do
e in preserving the beauties of
rict. He felt the greatest pleasure
ring the exhibition open.
B. Van Genecten, a noted Belgian
hanked the Mayor and the officials
ble for organising and staging the
n.

RITISH ISRAEL WORLD FEDERATION

Address at Kidderminster

King's Daughters" was the title
ddress given by Mr G. E. Weaver
Oddfellows Hall, Callows Lane,
mber 10th. The speaker said that
ing's Daughters" he referred to
t the beloved children of our
King, but Biblical princesses, one
n was the instrument by which
ord was fulfilled. Contrary to

... the death of the Monarch, the
Antichrist's ally.

15 In order to conquer the Antichrist more men must be killed than Rome has ever held; it will require an effort from all lands; for the Cock, the Leopard, and White Eagle would not suffice to overcome the Black Eagle if they were not helped by the prayers of the human race.

16. Never before has humanity been in such peril for the triumph of the Antichrist, would be that of a demon in whom he is incarnated.

17. For it has been said that 20 centuries after the Incarnation of the Lord, the Beast in his turn would be incarnated and would threaten the earth with as many evils as the Divine Incarnation had brought it graces.

18. Near the year 2,000 the Antichrist will appear; his armies will surpass in numbers anything before imagined; there will be Christians among his hordes, and among the defenders of the Lamb there will be Mohammedans and savage tribes.

20 For the first time the Lamb will be entirely red; in the whole of the Christian world there will not be a space that will not be red, and the heavens, the earth, the waters, and even the air will be red, for blood will flow in the sphere of the four elements at the same time.

19 The Black Eagle will throw himself on the Cock which will strike heroically with its spurs, but lose many of its feathers; it would soon be annihilated were it not for the help of the Leopard and its claws.

21 The Black Eagle, which will come from the land of Luther, will surprise the Cock from another side, and will invade the land of the Cock, taking one-half.

22 The White Eagle, which will come from the North, will surprise the Black Eagle and the other Eagle, and will completely invade the land of the Antichrist from one end to the other.

23 The Back Eagle will be forced to leave the Cock to fight the White Eagle, and the Cock will pursue the Black Eagle into the land of the Antichrist to help the White Eagle.

24. The battles waged until then will be small in comparison to those that will take place in the land of Luther, because the Seven Angels will at the same time pour fire from their burners on the land (image taken from the Apocalypse), which means that the Lamb will order the extermination of the Antichrist race.

25 When the Beast sees he is lost he will become furious during the months, the beak of the White Eagle, the claws of the Leopard, and the spurs of the Cock must harass him.

26. Rivers will be crossed on stepping stones of corpses, which in some places will change the course of the water. Only great noblemen, superior officers, and princes will receive burial, for to the carnage caused by firearms will be added the piling up of those who perished by famine and plague.

27 The Antichrist will several times sue for peace, but the Seven Angels, who precede the three animal defenders of the Lamb, have said "Victory shall only be recorded on the condition that the Antichrist be crushed like straw on the threshing floor."

28 Executors of the Lamb's justice, these three animals cannot stop fighting as long as any soldier remains to the Antichrist.

29 The reason the senttence of the Lamb is so implacable is that the Antichrist has pretended to be a Christian and to be acting in His Name, so that if he did not perish the fruit of the Redemption would be lost and the gates of Hell prevail against the Saviour.

30. It will be seen it is not a human war which will be waged when the Antichrist forces his arms. The three animal defenders of the Lamb will exterminate the Antichrist's last army, but the battlefield will become as an altar of sacrifice larger than the greatest of the Cities, and the corpses will have changed its shape by raising in it chains of mounds.

31 The Antichrist will lose his crown and will die demented and alone. His empire will be divided into twenty-two states, but none will have either a Royal house, an army or vassals.

32 The White Eagle will, by Michael's order, chase the Crescent from Europe, where only Christians will remain; it will occupy Constantinople.

33. Then an era of peace and prosperity

goes for all the anti-aircraft troops.

FOR THE FREE FRENCH

Meeting at the Youth Club

Saturday Dec. 6th was Free French Night at the Kidderminster Youth Club, when the speakers were Mrs. Nairac and Mrs. Knowles of the Kidderminster branch of the Association of friends of the French Volunteers.

Mrs. Nairac explained that France was now split into three separate parts—the Occupied and Unoccupied zones and Free France. It was of the latter that she was going to talk. It was only just over a year ago that General de Gaulle arrived in this country as a general without an army and without friends; now, however, he commanded an army of 60,000 men, a powerful navy, and one third of the French colonial empire. General de Gaulle served with distinction under both Pétain and Weygand in the first world war, before being taken prisoner by the Germans, from whom he made no less than five separate attempts at escape. In his absence, the Vichy authorities had condemned him to death for treason and, to add insult to injury, fined him 100 francs (about 11 shillings). Mrs. Nairac spoke of the many young Frenchmen who were escaping to this country from France, of whom a large number were even younger than many of the boys among her audience.

Mrs Knowles who is a native of Dieppe, then told in detail of some thrilling escapes from occupied territory. A typical story was that of 17-year-old Pierre, who live in La Rochelle. When the Armistice was signed, Pierre worked his way southwards along the coast, vainly trying to find a ship. Eventually he was lucky enough to fall in with soldiers of the Polish Army, who were pracically the last Allied unit to leave France. The Poles befriended him and smuggled him aboard ship in a borrowed uniform, and so Pierre came to join the forces of Free France. Mrs Knowles emphasised that Pierre, in common with most of his comrades, was no dardevil, but a peaceful sort.

In conclusion Mrs Nairac asked her audience to imagine the difficulties confronting these patriots, who had left behind friends, home and all that they held dear, in order to aid our cause. Their great need was friendship, and the speaker appealed to those present to support the Association of Friends of the French Volunteers, which existed to help these men in every possible way.

The speakers were thanked for an especially interesting talk by John Moore.

TRUSTEE SAVINGS BANK

Help in War Savings Campaign

At the annual meeting of the Trustees of the Kidderminster Trustee Savings Bank, held at 8, Tower Buildings, Kidderminster, on December 16th, an increase in deposits of over £40,000 was reported. Alderman ... presided, supported by Messrs. G. W. Goucher, F. W. Yates, A. E. Nicholls, and E. W. Gough, with J. E. Tyzack, chief actuary, and F. D. Grant, manager.

The fourth Annual Report stated that the business transacted during the year resulted in an increase in the amount due to depositors of £40,645, compared with an increase of the previous year of £21,312, making a final total of £94,956 and bringing the number of accounts open to 1,019. The Government Stock and Bonds had increased substantially, the figure amounted to £13,055 bringing the total amount held by depositors to £26,897. Although pleasing to report such great increases in deposits it was still more pleasing to show outstanding progress in the number of accounts and transactions for these demonstrated that the bank was ever widening its circle of influence, and being of increasing use to the people it endeavoured to serve. This progress by Kidderminster Branch was considered most satisfactory.

Every bank in the amalgamation had

BOROUGH OF BEWDLEY

Quarterly Council Meeting — 27th day of January, 1941

Report of the Evacuation Committee

Your Committee beg to report on their proceedings during the past quarter, as follows:-

Alderman R. B. Jackson has been appointed Chairman for the ensuing year.

The Chairman attended a conference at Worcester on the 16th December, 1940 with the Evacuation Officer (Mr: W. Evans).

On the instructions of the Ministry of Health the following premises have been requisitioned for housing evacuated families:-

Sandbourne
Salentum
Weatherheads
40, Load Street
Rookery Cottage.

When a large number of evacuees is sent into this town from either the Birmingham or London areas it will be impossible to billet large families on individual householders if the evacuated mothers wish their families to be kept together. The requisitioned premises are expressly set aside for accommodating such families.

Equipment has also been purchased for these premises to provide for the normal household needs of the evacuees.

Your Committee have received great assistance from the Women's Voluntary Services in carrying the proposals of the Ministry of Health into effect.

Thirty eight homeless refugees from the Birmingham area have now been billeted at Sandbourne, Salentum and Rookery Cottage. These refugees were brought to Bewdley on the 6th December, 1940 and food and hot drinks were immediately supplied at the Baptist School Room, High Street. The use of this room was kindly given by the Deacons and voluntary workers made excellent arrangements for the reception of the refugees and prepared the meal that was served.

Miss D. I. Lovesey has been appointed as Social Worker for evacuation purposes in the Borough of Bewdley and has been instructed to supervise the domestic arrangements at Sandbourne. A scheme has been put into operation whereby coal is stored and issued to the various families and paid for weekly and Miss Lovesy is taking steps to see that the various regulations laid down for the proper running of the establishment are observed.

Miss Lovesy will also endeavour to make arrangements for communal meals where required and organise general recreational facilities for the evacuees in conjunction with the W.V.S.,

Your Committee recommend that this Report be received and entered on the Minutes and adopted by the Council.

relating to Evacuation within the Borough whether by Government Schemes or individual arrangements.

That each of the Committees now appointed by this Council and hereinafter mentioned, viz:-

General Purposes
Emergency
Finance
Water and Health
Highways
Housing
Lighting and Fire Brigade
Rating and Valuation
Air Raid Precautions
Evacuation

shall continue in office until the 31st day of October, 1940 unless this Council shall at any time otherwise order, and shall have power to engage the services of such officers, clerks, collectors, servants, workmen and others, as may be necessary to help them to carry out the various matters entrusted to their care by this Council and shall also have power to transact any business which has been heretofore committed by this Council to any Committee in the like behalf and is not yet completed, and that the said Committees respectively may, for and on behalf of this Council, do and direct all such acts, matters and things as may be necessary or incident to the execution of the powers, authorities, and directions given or committed to them respectively and this Council doth hereby delegate to the said Committees its powers and duties in relation to the matters aforesaid.

TOWN PLANNING - To consist of the following members of the Council that is to say - Aldermen Frost, Mountford and Jackson; Councillors Wallis, Wallis, Gazely, Bates and Palmer, to whom be delegated all matters pertaining to the Town and Country Planning Act, 1932.,

LIBRARY - To consist of the following members of the Council that is to say - Aldermen Frost and Jackson; Councillors Bates and Palmer; the Secretary for the time being of the Bewdley Institute and Mr: H. R. Mountford.

And That the Meetings of the General Purposes Committee be held on such days and at such times as the Mayor may decide and that the other Committees do meet on such days and at such hour as they respectively may appoint.

GUARDIANS COMMITTEE

7. Proposed by Councillor Gazely seconded by Councillor Mortimer Smith and RESOLVED That the Mayor (Councillor Charles Rodman Pritchard) be and he is hereby nominated for membership of the Guardians Committee in accordance with Clause 6 (4) of the Administrative Scheme for the County under the Local Government Act, 1929 for the ensuing year.

NORTH WORCESTERSHIRE JOINT HOSPITAL BOARD

8. Proposed by Councillor Webb seconded by Councillor Bates and RESOLVED That the Mayor (Councillor Charles Rodman Pritchard) be and he is hereby nominated for membership of the North Worcestershire Joint Hospital Board in accordance with Clause 4 (2) of the North Worcestershire Joint Hospital Order, 1938 for the ensuing year.

C R Pritchard
Mayor

27th January. 1941.

BOROUGH OF BEWDLEY.

Quarterly Council Meeting. 28th July, 1941.

Report of the Lighting and Fire Brigade Committee.

Your Committee beg to report on their proceedings during the past quarter as follows:

A call was received from the Home Guard on the 4th May reporting a fire at Deasland Rock. The Brigade turned out and although a thorough inspection was made of surrounding woods andbuildings no trace of fire was found. Later a further message was received from the Home Guard reporting that the fire had been located close to Smethwick School Camp and had been extinguished by the Home Guard.

Both the Regular Brigade and the Auxiliary Fire Service took part in a general A.R.P. practice held on the 8th May.

A Guard of honour was formed by men of both Brigades for Lord Dudley at the Garden Cinema on the 14th May on the occasion of the opening of Bewdleys War Weapons Week.

The Superintendant has reported that the pressure on the hydrants in Wribbenhall is not satisfactory as a result of inspection carried out by the Brigade on the 15th May. Your Committee have accordingly resolved to make application to the Home Office for the provision of a large tank or dam to provide supplementary water supplies.

The strength of both Brigades has been seriously depleted during the past quarter as a number of men have been called up for military service. New volunteers are urgently required for the Auxiliary Fire Service in Bewdley.

The Superintendant reported to your Committee that several hydrants in the Borough were defective after inspection had been carried out by the Brigade and your Committee have accordingly given instructions for the necessary repairs to be carried out.

Leaflets and handbooks giving advice on fire precautions have been issued to shop keepers and leaders of fire parties respectively within the Borough, and your Committee have also had cards printed and issued to householders for the information of Wardens and other members of the various A.R.P. Services, and for assistance after premises have been damaged by enemy action.

Approval has been received from the Home Office for the construction of air raid shelters and accommodation for telephonists at the Fire Station and Auxiliary Fire Post. Arrangements have been made for this work to be completed as soon as possible.

Chairman.

J Bates.

BOROUGH OF BEWDLEY.

Quarterly Council Meeting **28th July, 1941**

Report of the Air Raid Precautions Committee.

Your Committee beg to report on their proceedings during the past quarter as follows:

Wardens Service - W. Ince one of the whole-time wardens in the Borough applied to your Committee for permission to resign his position in order to take up employment in a factory in Kidderminster on work of National importance. Your Committee decided to release Warden Ince and have appointed Mr. F. Gardner in his place. Mr. Gardner has had experience during actual raiding conditions in Birmingham where he was a voluntary A.R.P. worker. Warden Ince will continue to act as a voluntary part-time warden.

Your Committee have made an application to the County A.R.P. Department for a telephone to be installed in the house occupied by the Head Warden (Mr. [illegible] Bradley) as no A.R.P. post manned at all times of the day and night is situated anywhere near Mr. Bradley's house and it is felt that it should be possible to get in touch with the Head Warden by telephone at a moments notice if required.

Air Raid Siren. - Arrangements have now been made by the County Council for the air raid siren at Bewdley to be put on remote control. A flick test will be made every Wednesday morning at 12.30 hours.

Messenger Service - Your Committee have had under consideration a circular from the Ministry of Home Security referring to the Civil Defence (outdoor) Messenger Service together with a report from the Head of the Bewdley A.R.P. Messenger Service (Dr. H.N. Miles).

There is an urgent need for more recruits for the Outdoor Messenger Service in this Borough and your Committee have requested the W.V.S. and the Leader of the Bewdley Girl Guides to endeavour to obtain female recruits over 16 years of age.

Salvage of Property. - Your Committee have had under consideration a circular from the Ministry of Home Security referring to the removal and storage of household effects from houses damaged by enemy action and have instructed the Chairman and the Borough Surveyor to ascertain what premises are available within the Borough to provide emergency storage accommodation so that they can be earmarked for this purpose.

Public Shelter Rules - Your Committee have given instructions for copies of the public shelter rules issued by the Regional Commissioner to be framed and hung in all the public shelters within the Borough and copies have also been issued to all A.R.P. Wardens for their information.

Chairman.

28th July, 1941.

BOROUGH OF BEWDLEY

Quarterly Council Meeting 28th day of July, 1941

Report of Water and Health Committee

Your Committee beg to report on their proceedings during the past quarter, as follows:-

Corporation Waterworks - Your Committee have had under consideration the increasing demands that are bound to be made on the existing pumping plant and machinery at the Blackstone Pumping Station when the joint sewerage scheme is completed and a considerable number of new connections to the drainage system made in both Bewdley and Stourport-on-Severn. It is clear that some additional provision will have to be made at the pumping station to meet this increasing demand. After consulting the technical advisors to the Ministry of Health, your Committee advertised for tenders for the sinking of another borehole and the provision of new electric pumping plant at the waterworks. Seven tenders were received and your Committee have resolved to accept the tender sent in by C. Isler & Co: Limited of London. Your Committee recommend that application be made to the Ministry of Health for sention for the raising of the necessary loan to cover the purchase of additional ground adjoining the waterworks and the erection of a new pumping plant.

Hern's Nest Hostel - At a Meeting of the Joint Committee appointed to adminster the Hern's Nest Hostel held on Tuesday, the 17th June, 1940 the following recommendations were made:-

1. That the existing Joint Committee be dissolved and a new Management Committee appointed by the Town Council to include two representatives from each outside Authority in addition to the representatives appointed for the Borough of Bewdley.

2. That the Town Council be responsible for the appointment or dismissal of the Matron provided that full representation be given to the Management Committee when this matter is under discussion.

3. That the appointment or dismissal of the cook and subsidiary employees be in the hands of the Management Committee who would also be responsible for the general administration of the Hostel provided that any action taken in regard to the appointment or dismissal of staff and admission or removal of children should be reported immediately to the Town Council.

4. That the Management Committee meet each month at the Hostel, and submit a report every month to the Town Council. The Matron and the Doctor for duty to attend these Meetings.

The Management Committee also wished to report the fact that the present paid staff of one matron, one cook, one odd job man and one woman for washing is sufficient for present requirements, but that it may be necessary for an additional nurse to be employed if children under five were admitted to the Hostel.

Your Committee resolved to approve the above proposals and appointed the existing representatives for the Borough of Bewdley on the old Management Committee to continue to act on the new Management Committee until November, 1941 when all Committees will be appointed for the following twelve months.

British Restaurant - At the request of the Ministry of Food your Committee have prepared proposals for setting up a British Restaurant at premises at the rear of Messrs. [illegible] Load Street, Bewdley. These proposals have now been approved by the Ministry of Food and instructions have been given for the scheme to be carried into effect.

Borough of Bewdley

Quarterly Council Meeting — 28th day of July, 1941

Report of Water and Health Committee (Contd:)

British Restaurant (Contd:) - A great deal of the heavy equipment will be supplied from the Ministry of Food's pool and authority have been given for the Town Council to purchase the other goods such as crockery, cutlery and kitchen utensils. Orders for these goods have been placed after consultation with representatives of the W.V.S., Arrangements have also be made for certain structural alterations to the premises which have been approved by the Ministry of Food to be carried out as soon as possible.

Joint Sewerage Scheme - Your Committee are pleased to report that they have received a communication from the Ministry of Health that the work comprised in the Kidderminster Bewdley & Stourport-on-Severn Joint Sewerage Scheme have been placed by theWorks and Buildings Priority Sub Committee of the Ministry of Health in list W.B.A., for the highest degree of acceleration. This means that the Local Representative of the Ministry of Labour will give every assistance in the finding of the necessary labour andthat difficulties in obtaining materials will the more readily be overcome.

Your Committee recommend that this Report be received and entered on the Minutes and adopted by the Council.

R. P. Jackson

Chairman

28th July, 1941.

MINUTES OF THE PROCEEDINGS AT A SPECIAL MEETING OF THE COUNCIL FOR THIS BOROUGH DULY CONVENED AND HELD AT THE GUILD HALL ON WEDNESDAY THE TENTH DAY OF DECEMBER, 1941 AT FIVE O'CLOCK IN THE AFTERNOON.

PRESENT

Alderman	Robert Bertie Jackson (Mayor)
"	Henry Neal Frost (Deputy Mayor)
"	Fergus Edward Mountford
Councillor	Gerald Mortimer Smith
"	William Harcourt Webb
"	Charles Rodman Pritchard
"	Harry George Gazely
"	Henry William Windsor
"	Joseph Bates
"	Frederick Reginald Welch
"	Percival William Palmer

RESIGNATION OF COUNCILLOR BUTCHER

10. The Mayor referred to the resignation of Councillor Butcher and several members also spoke with regard to the services rendered by Councillor Butcher during his term of office on the Council.

Proposed by Alderman Frost seconded by Councillor Pritchard and RESOLVED that the record of the appreciation of the work done by Mr. Butcher during the fourteen years in which he had served as a Councillor for the Borough of Bewdley be entered on the Minutes.

MINUTES

11. Proposed by Councillor Palmer seconded by Councillor Webb and RESOLVED that the Minutes be taken as read and signed by the Chairman.

ELECTION OF A COUNCILLOR FOR THE SOUTH WARD

12. After some discussion with regard to the legality of the proceedings it was proposed by Councillor Pritchard seconded by Councillor Palmer and RESOLVED that the Council proceed with the business of the election of a Councillor for the South Ward.

Proposed by Councillor Palmer seconded by Councillor Bates and RESOLVED that the voting be by ballot and that the Town Clerk be appointed to act as scrutineer.

Councillor Gazely then proposed and Councillor Pritchard seconded the proposal of the name of Mr. William John Godwin, Baker and Grocer, of Catchems End, Wribbenhall, Bewdley, and Alderman Frost proposed and Councillor Webb seconded the proposal of the name of Mr. Harry Roden Mountford, of Grendon, Kidderminster Road, Bewdley, Schoolmaster, for election as Councillor for the South Ward for the Borough of Bewdley to fill the vacancy arising on the resignation of Mr. J.H. Butcher.

The voting was then conducted by ballot and Mr. Harry Roden Mountford was duly elected Councillor for the South Ward by a majority of 6 votes to 5.

R.B. Jackson

Mayor

Chapter Four

1942
THE FREE FRENCH AT BEWDLEY

The War dominated every part of life. The fighting was ferocious in Africa, Europe, the Far East and Soviet Russia. Hitler reformed the Vichy Government in France, Laval was made Chief of Government with Petain Chief of State. De Gaulle gained credibility and his Free French became established at Ribbesford House near Bewdley, though he was not in situ, rather in London and Abroad. After being based briefly in Malvern, the Free French would stay at Ribbesford for the next two years, and Ribbesford became the Ecole Militaire des Cadets de la France Libre.

A Shuttle advert gave information, 22nd August 1942 "For the Public in the event of Invasion".

Another advert declared carpet production had almost ceased, and the factories of Kidderminster were armament producers on a large scale.

The Rotary Club was host to a meeting addressed by a Commandant serving in the Free French Army.

From then on references to the Free French became more noticeable and frequent. I would also like to note the political debate in local newspapers, and have included references to the Labour Party, Tory Party, Communist Party, Liberal Party, Aid to Russia etc. The debates persisted throughout the War. Finally on 20 July 1942, De Gaulle paid an official visit to Bewdley.

I decided to keep as much of the photographic coverage of the Free French and De Gaulle at Bewdley in one section. The year 1942 is as apt as any. Please forgive the fact that some of the photographs and newspaper coverage might not appear in exact chronological order. However, such a definitive categorisation would sit nicely in a museum showcase, but for the benefit of my desire to finish the book, I have taken perhaps one or two liberties.

1942
continued

The following photographic pages represent aspects of life at Ribbesford House between 1942 and 1944. Some are obvious others not so. We have for instance, a Passing - Out Dance Card; Leave Pass; part of an essay written by a Cadet about Napoleon; a map of Ribbesford House Grounds; artifacts including Cherry Blossom Boot Polish; Turf Cigarettes; France Libre match box etc; Ration Book; Free French Badges; Buttons; Ribbons; a programme for "Les Jour Heureux," Souvenir of the H.Q. Club London; air mail cover; F.F. drawing of uniform; map of the World showing route taken by F.F. officer from Afganistan to Bewdley; A photograph of Free French Cadets at Malvern with the hills as a backdrop, F.F. marching in (probably) London; De Gaulle taking the salute outside Bewdley Town Hall 20 July 1942; De Gaulle sitting; De Gaulle + F.F. - London; De Gaulle at Ribbesford House with Staff Car; De Gaulle with officers at Ribbesford House; De Gaulle inspecting Cadets at Ribbesford House; 2 cadets with machine gun; cadets running; inspection for cadets; same-showing more cadets; the whole F.F. company outside Ribbesford House; motor cycles on the drive at Ribbesford House; photo of Patrick Beaufrere a one time Bewdley F.F. cadet killed in August 1944; a French soldier inspects a grave cross of Mielkarfe, of the F.F.

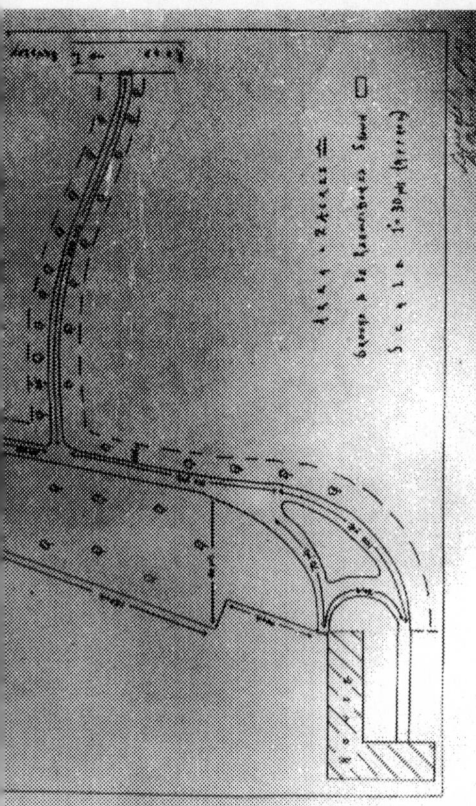

Forces Françaises Libres.
Free French Forces.

PERMISSION
LEAVE - PASS

No.

Corps et Unité / Corps and Unit: ECOLE MILITAIRE DES CADETS, [illegible]

Grade, Nom, Prénoms du Bénéficiaire / *Issued to*

Nom et adresse complète de la personne chez qui se rend le permissionnaire / *To go to*

Durée / *Valid for a period of* ………… Jours / Days

Le bénéficiaire devra rejoindre son unité avant le / *The bearer is to be back at his unit before* ………… 19 … à / at ………… heure / o'clock

Transport par / *Travel by* ………… à titre gratuit (permissions trimestrielles) / *with a free warrant (quarterly)*

EN CAS D'HOSTILITE TERRESTRE EN GRANDE BRETAGNE, le bénéficiaire devra rejoindre immédiatement son unité.

IN THE EVENT OF LAND WARFARE DEVELOPING IN THE UNITED KINGDOM, the bearer of this leave permit must at once report to his Unit.

Fait à / *Issued at* [illegible] 194

Signature

Grade et Nom de l'officier signataire / *Rank and Name of Issuing Officer* [illegible]

OBSERVATIONS.

Gare de départ : ………… Heure

DECOMPTE.

£	s.	d.

Ecole Militaire des Cadets — No 29.

Composition d'Histoire.

Date: Vendredi .. Mai 1943

Le Général Bonaparte et la Campagne d'Italie

La Promotion Sortante
de
L'Ecole Militaire des Cadets
have the pleasure to request your presence at their Passing Out Dance to be held on Tuesday, 6th June, at 8 p.m.

Ribbesford House, Bewdley

Transport will be provided
from
Kidderminster, Lion's Hotel, 7-30 & 8 p.m.
Bewdley, George Hotel, 7-30, 7-45 & 8 p.m.
Stourport, Swan Hotel, 7-30.

This card has to be shown at Control.

CHERRY BLOSSOM BOOT POLISH
WILD WOODBINE CIGARETTES
PLAYER'S NAVY CUT
CIGARETTES MEDIUM
"TURF"
CIGARETTES
CHERRY BLOSSOM BOOT POLISH

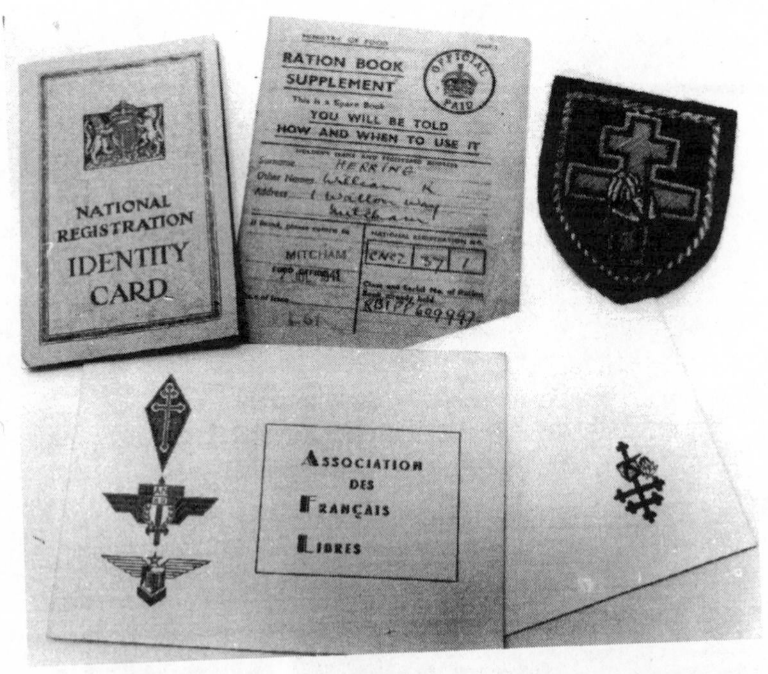
NATIONAL REGISTRATION
IDENTITY CARD
RATION BOOK SUPPLEMENT
OFFICIAL PAID
This is a Spare Book
YOU WILL BE TOLD HOW AND WHEN TO USE IT
HERRING
MITCHAM
Association des Français Libres

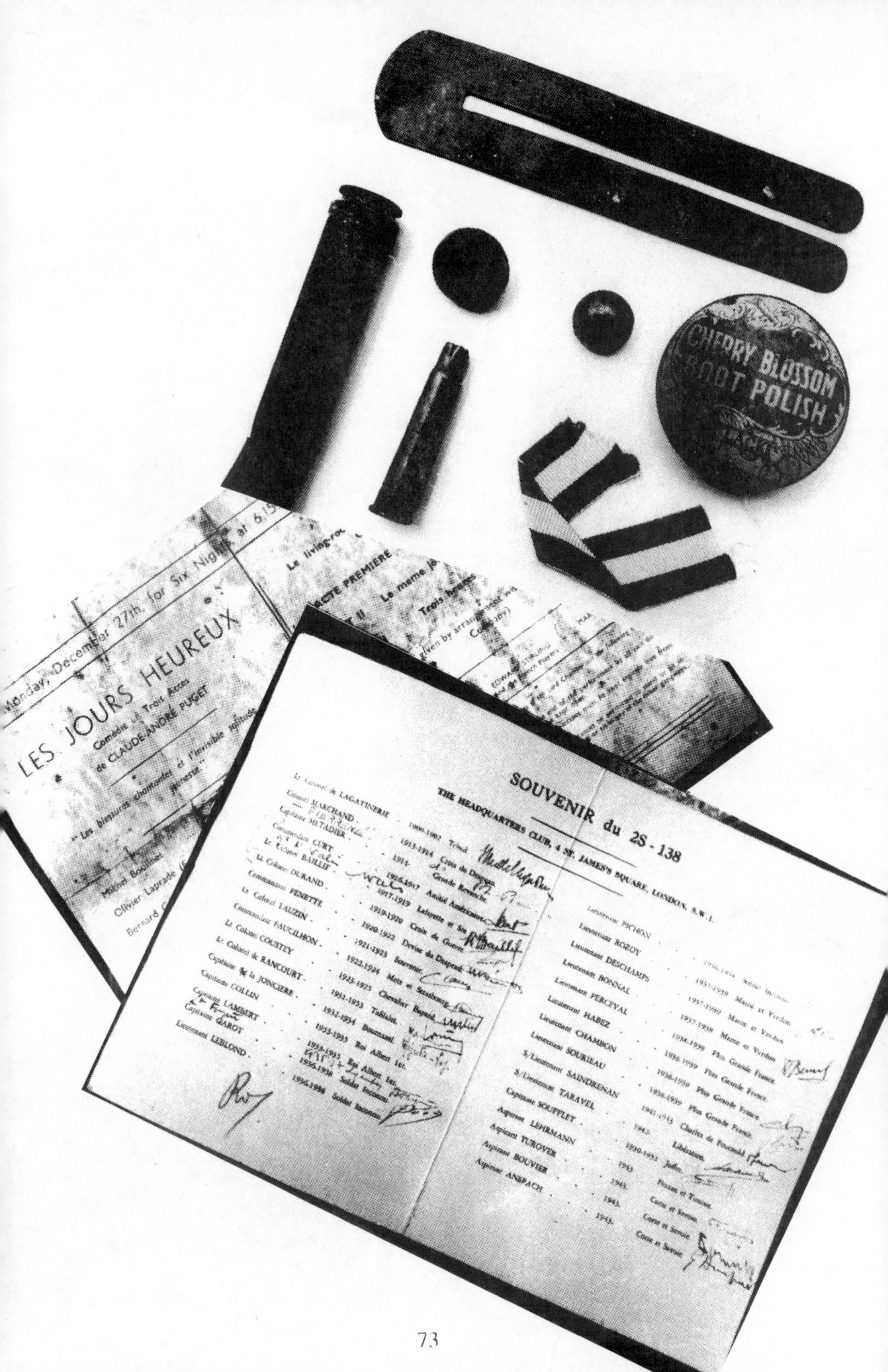
CHERRY BLOSSOM
BOOT POLISH
Monday, December 27th, for Six Nights at 6.15
LES JOURS HEUREUX
Comédie en Trois Actes
de CLAUDE-ANDRÉ PUGET
"Les blessures chantantes et l'invisible solitude ... jeunesse"
ACTE PREMIERE
Trois heures
SOUVENIR du 2S - 138
THE HEADQUARTERS CLUB, 4 ST. JAMES'S SQUARE, LONDON, S.W.1.

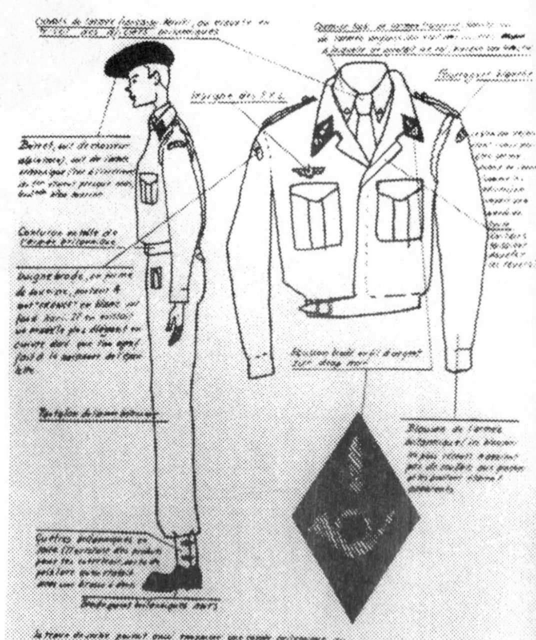

…rme de sortie des Cadets de la France Libre

…e la tenue des Cadets de la France libre (juin 1942, juin 1944) d'après un …an d'ex. Albert Blin (promotion « 18 juin »).

PATRICK

BEAUFRÈRE

dit STAEHLE

dit CHARLES DUROC

Né le 9 août 1922
à Trégastel (Côtes-du-Nord)

MORT POUR LA FRANCE
LE 23 AOÛT 1944
PRÈS DE [illegible] (VAR)

Le grand-père de Patrick Beaufrère est le poète Léon Durocher qui sut, jadis, unir dans un même amour la Bretagne et la France.

Son beau-père, M. Hans Staehle, dont il voulut porter le nom, est à l'époque attaché au Bureau International du Travail, à Genève. Mais, en 1938, il s'en va professer l'économie politique à l'université américaine de Harvard, et le jeune Patrick se trouve ainsi transplanté aux États-Unis, où il achève ses études secondaires avant de s'inscrire au cours de géologie de Harvard.

Les malheurs de la France affectent profondément ce jeune Breton exilé. Avec quelques amis, il prend l'initiative d'un groupement d'étudiants qui s'affilie à l'Association *France for ever*.

Mais sa décision est déjà prise. Dès qu'il a vingt ans, il informe ses parents qu'il va rejoindre en Angleterre le général de Gaulle. Arrivé à Londres, il s'engage dans les Forces Françaises Libres sous le pseudonyme de Duroc, hommage rendu au souvenir de son grand-père, dont les amis abrégeaient familièrement ainsi le nom de Durocher.

« Charles Duroc » est envoyé à l'École Militaire des Cadets d'où il sort aspirant, en décembre 1943, avec la promotion « Corse-et-Savoie ».

À sa sortie de l'École, l'aspirant Duroc opte pour les Zouaves et est dirigé sur l'Afrique du Nord. Pourtant, c'est dans les rangs du 1er Bataillon de

81

14 April, 1942 **Pro-German government formed in Vichy**

LAVAL COMES BACK TO POWER. On 14 April Berlin and Vichy announced that Laval would return to office and that Petain had decided to reconstitute the Vichy cabinet on a new basis. This reorganization was forced upon Petain by Hitler who, it was said, used the French prisoners of war in Germany and threats to starve the French people as bargaining weapons. With a pro-German head in Vichy, Hitler doubtless hoped to obtain the services of French workers for essential war work in German factories, and even to obtain the use of the French fleet, which had been disarmed under the armistice terms. The new cabinet, in which Laval held the post of Chief of Government, and the Ministries of Foreign Affairs, the Interior, and Information, was formed on the 17th, and on the same day President Roosevelt recalled Admiral Leahy, U.S. Ambassador to the Vichy Government, "for consultation." Petain retained the nominal title of Chief of State. Laval's appointment led to disturbances in Paris and Northern France, and on the 16th thirty-five German soldiers were killed in a troop train that was derailed near Caen. The picture above, doubtless a piece of German propaganda to prove the success of the new arrangement, shows French "volunteers" in German uniforms leaving Versailles for service on the Russian front. On the left, Marshal Petain and Laval are seen together shortly after the new government was formed.

AXIS GARRISONS SURRENDER. The town of Bardia, which had been occupied by the New Zealanders on 22 November and reoccupied by the enemy on 1 December, surrendered unconditionally to British and Imperial forces on 2 January after a brilliant attack in which Polish and Free French forces took part. Over 7,000 Axis prisoners were taken, including Major-General Schmidt, administrative head of the Afrika Korps. British casualties were only sixty killed and 300 wounded. Having reduced Bardia, the British forces turned

Keystone Press

Keystone Press

LUNDI 26 AOUT 1940
DIRECTION-REDACTION
85, Fleet St., Londres, E.C.4
(adresse provisoire)
Tel.: Central 8043-8477
ADMINISTRATION
Prestford Press, Ltd.,
1, Dorset Buildings, Salisbury Sq.,
Fleet St., Londres, E.C.4
Tel.: Central 1355
Tous les jours - ONE PENNY

FRANCE

LIBERTE ▪ EGALITE ▪ FRATERNITE

LIRE EN PAGE 3:
Nos information de France
EN PAGE 4:
Nos Informations Générales

N° 1

VIVE LA FRANCE!

LA France est aux mains de l'ennemi. Les Allemands occupent la plus grande partie de son territoire. Ils contrôlent directement ou indirectement, tous les moyens d'expression utilisés en France par les Français: la presse, le cinéma, la radio, les livres. Aucune voix venue de France ne peut exprimer librement les souffrances et les espoirs de nos compatriotes.

Un gouvernement français a signé avec Hitler et Mussolini des armistices désastreux, au mépris de l'honneur et de l'intérêt de notre pays, au mépris de nos engagements formels. Des milliers de Français de la métropole, des territoires d'Outre-Mer et de l'Etranger se refusent à reconnaître ces armistices, dont le texte équivaut à une condamnation à mort de la patrie. Ces Français, hommes et femmes, militaires et civils, entendent demeurer, aux côtés de nos alliés, des belligérants.

Le Général de Gaulle a eu le courage de faire appel à ces patriotes français, dès les premières heures d'une capitulation honteuse. Il a promis au Monde, en leur nom, que des forces Françaises continueraient la lutte jusqu'à la libération, jusqu'à la victoire. Il tient parole. Quelques semaines après l'armistice de Compiègne, le drapeau tricolore flotte au dessus des camps d'entrainement emplis de troupes. Il flotte au mât de plusieurs bâtiments de guerre. Dans le ciel, nos aviateurs ont repris le combat.

Pour ceux qui se battent.

Ce journal s'adresse, tout d'abord, à ceux qui se battent: aux soldats, aux officiers, aux marins, aux aviateurs, à tous les volontaires des Forces Françaises libres. Il s'adresse aux résidents français à l'étranger et, en première ligne, aux plus proches, à ceux de Grande Bretagne, ainsi qu'aux réfugiés qui ont pu échapper à l'occupation allemande. Il s'adresse aussi à tous les Français libres d'Outre Mer, dont il désire l'union. Bien que percevant l'immense disproportion entre sa taille, ses moyens et la tâche à accomplir, il espère atteindre les Français de l'Empire et même ceux de la métropole. En un mot, ce journal est destiné à tous ceux de nos compatriotes qui refusent la servitude et sont résolus à vaincre l'oppression étrangère. Il souhaite d'être lu par tous les amis de la France.

Ce ne sont pas des exhortations ou des conseils que nous désirons offrir aux Français. Nous voulons, plus modestement, leur donner à lire tous les jours, en langue française, ces informations exactes. Notre lutte et les sacrifices qu'elle comporte sont justifiés par des faits. Chaque jour, depuis la terrible date de la capitulation, des faits nous affirment avec éclat que nous avons raison d'espérer. La résistance foudroyante de la Grande-Bretagne aux attaques aériennes allemendes, les contre-attaques de la Royal Air Force, le developpement intense et rapide de l'aide américaine, l'organisation, par le Général de Gaulle, des force combattantes françaises, l'esprit magnifique qui anime les soldats britanniques, français, polonais, hollandais, belges, norvégiens, tchèques, canadiens, sud-africains, hindous, australiens, néo-zélandais, réunis en Angleterre, dans le bastion européen de la liberté, les nouvelles, enfin, qui nous parviennent sur la France et sur son Empire, tous ces faits nous prouvent que rien n'est perdu.

Union des Français pour la liberté.

Les Français de la résistance et de la victoire sont dispersés dans toutes les parties du Monde. Ils appartiennent à tous les milieux, à toutes les professions, toutes les religions, toutes les opinions, tous les partis. Il y a parmi eux des paysans et des citadins, des ouvriers et des patrons, des officiers et des soldats. Spontanément, ces hommes et ces femmes se sont mis d'accord sur une tâche très simple et très grande: la libération du territoire français, la restauration de l'indépendance de la patrie, le maintien des libertés qui sont nos plus nobles traditions, la fidélité à notre alliance avec la nation anglaise.

C'est cette noble cause que servira notre journal, avec la volonté de rendre plus étroites chaque jour l'indispensable union et la solidarité de tous les Français libres.

La Redaction

GEORGE VI A PASSE EN REVUE LES FORCES FRANCAISES LIBRES

UN DEVOIR: COMBATTRE

par le Géneral de Gaulle

Pour ce journal qui naît dans la détresse nationale et qui ne travaillera qu'à la résurrection, aucune titre n'était possible sinon celui qu'il porte: "FRANCE."

Car aucun Français n'a le droit d'avoir aujourd'hui d'autre pensée, d'autre espoir, d'autre amour, que la pensée, l'espoir, l'amour de la France.

Mais quoi? La patrie a succombé sous les armes. Elle ne renaîtra que des armes.

Ceux qui voudraient croire ou faire croire que la liberté, la valeur, la grandeur, pourraient se recréer sous la loi de l'ennemi sont des inconscients ou des lâches.

Le devoir est simple et dur: il faut combattre.

Tout ce qui sert à frapper l'ennemi est donc utile et salutaire. Ainsi de "FRANCE" qui veut exhorter au combat.

Ce journal fera son devoir en répandant courage et confiance, en aidant les Français à s'unir dans la guerre, à s'unir avec les Alliés qui combattent auprès d'eux et, en partie, pour eux.

Ainsi, quelque jour, reparaîtra la France, lavée de la honte et des larmes, la France tout entière, la France victorieuse.

DEUX VISITES ROYALES

par Eve Curie

Il y a deux ans, lors de la visite des souverains anglais en France, une des plus belles revues militaires que nous ayons jamais vues fut donnée à Versailles, en l'honneur du roi George VI.

L'armée française était intacte. La France était libre, grande. Nous étions les amis, les alliés de l'Empire britannique.

Il y a deux jours, le roi George VI a été reçu "quelque part en Angleterre," dans un camp d'entrainement, par les Forces Françaises libres. Il a passé en revue, aux côtés du Général de Gaulle, des détachements de volontaires.

A la même heure, des canons à longue portée, de fabrication française, établis par les Allemands sur notre littoral, bombardaient, à travers la Manche, les îles britanniques. A la même heure, des avions anglais bombardaient des

Voir la suite en page 4.

FRANCAIS APOTRES de la liberte

par M. Duff Cooper

Ministre de l'Information

J'ai toujours aimé la France, et je ne l'aime pas moins dans ces jours de douleur et d'affliction que je ne l'aimais alors qu'elle était victorieuse et glorieuse.

Je me réjouis de l'arrivé dans ce pays de nombreux patriotes français qui croient toujours le peuple français capable de secouer le joug de la servitude qui lui a été imposé par l'Allemagne. Je suis sur que bonne d'entre eux qui ont eu la bonne fortune de s'enfuir pour quelque temps de leur propre pays et de jouir de l'hospitalité de la Grande-Bretagne représentent des millions de leurs compatriotes dont les espoirs et les désirs reposent maintenant sur la victoire britannique, parce qu'ils savent qu'aucune autre route ne peut conduire à la restauration de l'indépendance et de la liberté de la France.

Je me félicite donc de l'apparition d'une nouvelle publication français qui sera la voix de l'opinion non seulement des Français libres qui se sont réfugiés dans notre pays, mais aussi des millions de Français qui sont toujours en France et qui aspirent à redevenir libres.

PORTE-DRAPEAUX

Les Français ont été pendant longtemps les apôtres de la liberté et les porte-drapeaux du progrès. Ils ont été à l'avant-garde de la lutte européenne pour la liberté. Pendant plus d'un demi-siècle, les yeux de tous ceux qui souhaitent la liberté ont été tournés vers Paris. A présent, ils sont dirigés vers Londres, mais ce ne sera que pendant un bref intervalle. La Grande-Bretagne et la France indiqueront de nouveau la voie aux peuples libres de l'Univers et il ne pourrait pas y avoir de meilleur gage de leur union future que la publication à Londres d'un journal français où des Français seront à même d'exprimer les opinions et les idéals qui nous sont communs.

Lire en page 3 le Message de M. Guéritte à l'Association des Français de Grande-Bretagne.

En Page 4, nos Informations.

Ruins of Sevastopol

A CITY IN RUINS. The fall of Sevastopol was a severe blow to the Russian cause. The great naval base, home of the Black Sea Fleet, was of the utmost strategic importance to the enemy, for not only did its capture remove the last remaining threat to his right flank, but it gave him a base from which he could in the future carry out landing operations south of the Caucasus Mountains. This would threaten the port of Batum and the vital oil centre of Baku. In addition its loss would seriously restrict the free movements of the Black Sea Fleet, which was now well within the

bend fought fierce rearguard actions whilst retiring to their main defensive positions along the lower reaches of the river, but by the 16th fighting was taking place before Voroshilovgrad, and two days later the enemy was only seventy miles north-west of Rostov, and still advancing rapidly. On the following day Voroshilovgrad was evacuated by the Red Army in order to avoid encirclement. The pictures show: left, Russian sappers on the Voronezh sector crawling forward to clear a gap in a minefield for the passage of their tanks and infantry, and right, Soviet infantry equipped with automatic weapons, awaiting the enemy in a village in the southern sector.

U.S. MARINES LAND IN THE SOLOMONS

7 AUGUST, 1942

In the early hours of 7 August warships and aircraft of the U.S. Pacific Fleet opened up a heavy bombardment on the Japanese positions in the Tulagi area of the Solomons, and U.S. marines went ashore in landing barges. By nightfall they had gained strong positions on Guadalcanar, Tulagi, and Florida, after having overcome fierce enemy resistance, and on the following day they extended the occupied area of Guadalcanar and captured a vital aerodrome. On Tulagi almost all resistance had been overcome and huge quantities of munitions and supplies had been captured. By noon on the 10th the marines were in firm control of Guadalcanar, Tulagi, Gavatu, Tanambogo, Makambo and Florida, and were engaged in mopping up enemy forces who had retired into the interior. During these operations long-range U.S. bombers carried out extensive reconnaissance besides bombing enemy ships and air bases in New Britain, New Ireland, and in the Solomons area. The pictures show: left, U.S. marines landing on Guadalcanar, and below, left unloading transport vehicles and supplies. Amphibious tanks that were used by the attackers are seen coming ashore, below right

Congress members arrested in India

9 August, 1942

RIOTING IN INDIA. After the failure of Sir Stafford Cripps's mission to India, the Congress Party, on 10 July, issued a resolution demanding immediate British withdrawal. Shortly afterwards the Government of India raided Congress headquarters and seized the records of its proceedings. Amongst the documents confiscated was Gandhi's origina draft resolution, submitted to the Working Committee on 27 April, which contained a statement to the effect that if India were free one of her first steps would probably be to negotiate with Japan. The Government published the text of this draft on 4 August, and on the following day Congress passed an amended resolution restating its demand for British withdrawal and threatening a mass civil disobedience campaign if its demands were not met. As a result the Government, on the 7th, issued an order forbidding the closure of shops dealing with vital necessities, and on the 9th arrested 148 Congress leaders, including Gandhi, Pandit Nehru, and Dr. Azad. Rioting broke out in Bombay and other cities and the police and military were called out to deal with the disturbances. Altogether 658 people were killed and 1,003 wounded by police and military action. Government forces casualties amounted to thirty-one police and eleven military killed, and a large number injured. The pictures show: above, the Yervada Palace, Poona, where Gandhi was imprisoned, and below, a picture of Gandhi taken in London in 1931.

24 August, 1942

Premier visits Moscow and the Middle East

CHURCHILL MEETS STALIN AND SMUTS. On 17 August it was announced that important conversations had taken place in Moscow between Mr. Winston Churchill, Mr. Averell Harriman and M. Stalin, and that a number of decisions had been reached concerning the conduct of war against Germany. On his return journey the British Premier visited the Middle East where he conferred with Allied leaders and visited Allied troops on the desert battle-front. During his stay he met General Smuts, who presented him with the hat he is seen wearing. In the top picture Mr. Churchill (third from left) is seen in Moscow with Mr. Harriman (centre), M. Stalin and M. Molotov.

EIGHTH ARMY DRIVES THE AXIS WESTWARDS. Many daring and highly successful actions were fought by British and Dominion troops as they continued their advance through the Libyan Desert from El Alamein in pursuit of the much-harassed German and Italian armies. This dramatic action picture was taken during General Montgomery's great outflanking movement on the road towards Matratin between El Agheila and Sirte. It shows British advanced infantry with bayonets and rifles charging through a smoke screen to storm an enemy position.

reinforcements from Sicily and Italy. This was the prime reason for the delay in the whole campaign; the initial advantage was unavoidably lost by the Allies.

From the German point of view the Tunisian campaign could have been nothing more than an attempt to stage a large-scale delaying action. The German High Command were trying to hold the Tunisian bridgehead for as long as possible so as to prepare the defence of Sicily and Southern Italy, which, once the Allies had gained Tunis and Bizerta, would become the objective of attack from the other side of the Mediterranean. But a decisive stage was reached directly the Eighth Army broke through the Mareth Line, where General Montgomery repeated the same successful outflanking movement as at El Alamein. The subsequent advance by the Eighth Army northwards through Sfax and the link-up with the British First Army and the Americans from the west, sealed the fate of the Axis in Tunisia. With the occupation of Tunis and Bizerta the retreating enemy was trapped in the narrow Cape Bon peninsula with his back to the sea and little chance of escape. All resistance ended on 13 May; Africa was at last set free from Nazi and Fascist tyranny. Malta, whose people had so long and valiantly borne the Nazi air terror, was now relieved.

Meanwhile, in the far north of Russia the Red Army had scored another notable victory. On 18 January, following a fortnight's heavy fighting, the siege of Leningrad was raised after sixteen months. The Russians launched their two-pronged offensive on 12 January from the west bank of the Neva and from the area south of Lake Ladoga. Aided by the Red Fleet and coastal batteries, the land forces penetrated powerful German defences to a depth of nine miles, and on 18 January the siege was raised when the two Russian armies linked up. At least five German divisions were routed, and over 13,000 of the enemy killed. While the siege lasted the people of Leningrad suffered great privations. The only link between the beleaguered city and the rest of Russia had been by air and across the frozen ice of Lake Ladoga, over which food, fuel and munitions reached the four million inhabitants. Nevertheless, the normal life of Leningrad went on, and many of its

FRANK RICHARDS AND HIS BLUE RICARDO BAND.
No reduction in price
No admission after 10.5 p.m.

DON'T FORGET THE
[B]ABBERLEY GOLF CLUB
[V]ALENTINE DANCE
TO-NIGHT (FRIDAY)
at the Black Horse Hotel
[FRA]NK RICHARD'S No. 1 BLUE RICARDO BAND.

[K]idderminster Cricket Club
DANCE
[Blac]k Horse Hotel, Kidderminster
[Sa]turday, 21st February, 1942
7.30 p.m.—11.45 p.m.
JOHN HAY AND HIS BAND.
[Tic]kets 2/6 (payable at the door) 229

[St.] John Ambulance Brigade
DANCE
Town Hall, Kidderminster
SATURDAY, MARCH 7th
RAPCATS BAND
[By] kind permission of Lt.-Col. E. T. C. [S]mith, O/C Detachment R.A.P.C.)
Tickets 2/6. Forces 2/-. 240

[HO]LY INNOCENTS' CHURCH
[Mo]nday, February 16th, 7.30 p.m.
SOCIAL EVENING IN THE
[H]ALL FOR CONGREGATION
[MI]LITARY WHIST. MUSIC. GAMES. 276

[T]HE SALVATION ARMY
DUDLEY STREET.
February 14th and 15th
[YO]UNG PEOPLE'S WEEK-END
[MEE]TINGS on SATURDAY, 8 p.m. and [SUN]DAY at 11.0, 3.0 and 6.15, led by LIEUT.-COL. W. KITCHING. [Nat]ional Young People's Sec., London. 2[..]

youth club. Y.P.F. Boys' Brigades, and Girls' Life Brigades are fitting into the Government scheme, and are arranging to train the young people in various forms of national service. The Girls' Life Brigade. 1st Kidderminster Company, Milton Hall, Lorne Street, hope to recruit new members under the scheme, any girls, or parents, interested, may obtain information from: Capt. Mrs. L. Dudley, 98, Chester Road South, Lieut. Mrs. E. Grealey, 64, Aggborough Crescent; or Rev. T. J. Rowlands, The Manse, 14, Lorne Street. The company has been running for over 10 years, and has three sections—cadets 6-10 years, junior 10-14 years, senior 14 years and over (no set age limit).

From Premier's Wife.—A happy child must be Beryl Darkes, who has received a letter from Mrs. Churchill, thanking her for the contribution sent for the "Aid to Russia" fund. Beryl, who is the daughter of Mr. and Mrs. W. Darkes, of 7, Serpentine, is a scholar of Harry Cheshire Modern School. She made wax flowers and sold them to friends, and sent the money to Mrs. Churchill, who sent the following letter: "Dear Beryl,—Thank you very much for your gift which I have just received. I am most grateful to you for the trouble you have taken to help the brave Russians in their terrible struggle, and in the glorious defence of their country.—Your sincere friend, Clementine S. Churchill." Beryl, we understand, during the last twelve months has raised about £3 for various charities.

Good Work.—Nine boys and girls of Kidderminster have raised ten pounds for the Merchant Navy Comforts Service by giving several entertainments during the Christmas vacation. The cheque was sent to National Appeal Headquarters, 62, Heath Street, London, N.W.3, by Mr. Anthony Balmforth, of St. John's Vicarage, 11, Blakebrook, Kidderminster. His associates are the Misses Eileen Evans, Gwenyth Meredith, Dione eMredith, and Doris Roberts, and Messrs. Paul Balmforth, Martin Steward, Joseph Steward, and John Grove. Lord Leathers, Minister of War Transport is opening at the Baltic Exchange, London, E.C.3, on February 23rd, a fortnight's exhibition of the work of the Comfort's exhibition of the War Libraries, and the Ship Adoption Society

circuit, where he has been most successful in his work, and is a "brother beloved," while his relations with Nonconformist ministers and Anglicans have been particularly happy. Mr. Kinnish came to Kidderminster from the Halesowen and Hasbury Circuit, and had many years of ministerial duties in the Midlands to his credit. Born in the Isle of Man, he received his theological training at Hartley College, Manchester, and entered the Primitive Methodist ministry at Hyde. The Manchester fifth circuit, Ashton-under-Lyne, Clay Cross, Londale Street, Stoke-on-Trent, Dudley Road circuit at Wolverhampton, Ford Street circuit at Coventry, and Halesowen and Hasbury district are the circuits he has served. He has done a considerable amount of district work and has filled the office of secretary of the Birmingham and District Temperance and Social Welfare Committee. His charm of manner, combined with a keen business brain, has made him an efficient and sympathetic superintendent.

Free French Tea Reception.—The committee of the Association of Friends of the Free French Volunteers (Kidderminster Branch) attended a tea reception held in honour of General de Gaulle at the Queen's Hotel, Birmingham, on Saturday. The function, which was most enjoyable, was largely attended, and the guest of honour was accorded an enthusiastic welcome. The tea reception was tendered the General that he might have an opportunity of meeting some of the French colony and sympathisers in Birmingham and its precincts. General de Gaulle was accompanied by Monsieur Heritier, Civil Representative for General de Gaulle in Birmingham, Free French Officers and Personnel. In a sincere and spirited address the General appealed for continued support of the Franco-British Entente. Lord Dudley, Regional Commissioner, also addressed the gathering. The Kidderminster visitors to the tea reception included Mrs. Bessbane (chairman), Mrs. Lamb, Mrs. R. Brinton, Mrs. M. L. Nairac (hon. sec.), Mrs. G. Knowles, and Mr. H. H. Whitehouse (honorary treasurer). Periodically the Association of Friends of the Free French Volunteers (Kidderminster Branch) despatches comforts to the Free French Forces. Contributions of knitted goods will be gratefully received.

by Mr. R. R. Adam C.C. (president of the hospital), Alderman E. G. Eddy, J.P., Alderman L. Tolley, Mr. William Johnson (past president), when references were made to the excellent work now being carried on at the institution. Sutton Arms were first in the competition, Worcester Cross Hotel second, and Highley Men's Club third. The amount collected by the first named was £26 6s. 5d. The cups and the framed diplomas were presented and duly acknowledged by Mr. Harry Knight. Arthur Howley's Party was a decided attraction, and the evening was most enjoyable.

Mayor's War Charity Fund.—The Mayor (Alderman O. W. Davies) recently admitted that he is a great beggar, and we have pleasure in giving some results of "The Mayor's War Charity Fund." This embraces many excellent causes, and the total raised is over £735. The statement, audited by Mr. S. R. Edwards, chartered accountant, was submitted to a meeting in the Mayor's Parlour on February 4th. It was stated that 1,532 lbs. of wool had been given to the ladies, from which they had made 5,135 garments, woollen comforts, pyjamas, etc. A flag day will be held on Saturday, March 14th, for the fund. With regard to the receipts to the Mayor's fund to 31st December, the following are the main items of income: Dances, entertainments, etc., £91 17s. 10d.; Sale of Flowers (per Mrs. J. Ballantyne), £64 19s.; collecting box, minesweeper, £1 0s. 9d.; donations, £11 12s. 9d.; from Sunday cinema entertainments, £180; donations for Red Cross fund, £9 5s. 6d.; flag day, collections and donations, £160 3s. 3d.; sale of wool (per Mrs. S. Goodwin), £94 3s. 2d.; British Sailors Society, flag day, £112 4s. 8d.; total, £735 12s. 11d. The expenditure showed that £288 12s. 1d. had been spent on wool. The balance in hand was £206 5s. 8d. In the Lord Mayor of London's Air Raid Distress fund, donations of £3 5s. 6d. were received, and £275 resulted from the flag day, collections and donations.

KIDDERMINSTER FOOTBALL LEAGUE
Fixtures for Saturday.
Kidderminster Athletic v. Hoobrook A.
Hoobrook "B" v. Wanderers.
Pike Mills v. Stourport Swifts.
Castle Rangers "A" v. Chestonians "B".
RESULTS.
Wilden 4, Chestonians "A" [..]
Stourport Swifts 8, R.A.S.C. [..]

NURSING ASSOCIATION

Owing to war conditions and the difficulty of collecting, the Committee appeal to Subscribers who have not had their boxes opened recently to take their box and card to their Ward Secretary, or, if unable to do so to send a post card. See list Ward Secretaries, Page [illegible]

FREE FRENCH FORCES

Officer's Address at Rotary Club

An unusually large gathering at Rotary club on Tuesday heard an address by a Commandant serving in the Free French Army under General De Gaulle on the part played by French loyalists in co-operation with the Armed forces of Great Britain and her Allies. At the close of his talk the Commandant asked the Mayor (Rotarian Osman W. Davies) to accept a badge of the Free French Association as a token of thanks for the welcome the Free French Volunteers had received in this country.

The speaker said he came for a round table chat on the activities of the Free French Force and the Anglo French Association whose motto and aim is service as that of the Rotary movement itself. His service started many years ago and he had the privilege of being the oldest volunteer in his Corps which went through the last war and this. Although people did not see or hear much of the Free French, that armed force consisted of Army Air Force and Navy. French infantrymen had foreseen a great deal about mechanical warfare and difficulties in the use of tank. At present the Free French Forces in Syria were helping the Allied British Army in Libya, and others saw service in Norway. The Free French Air Force was much larger than the Infantry. Some members were in Scotland operating under the Command of the British R.A.F. and making a good show in achievements. More were being trained in various schools for the Air Force.

The Free French Navy of about fifty ships was not large numerically, but of good calibre and the submarines were most active.

The Free French Association regarded the moral side of welfare as most important. Their work in co-operation with the British Allies was intensely worth while. They were mindful of the value of helping men physically and morally. A great deal of help in comforts for their soldiers, sailors and airmen came from the man in the street, from bus conductors and the like who readily contributed to the organised welfare work for the Free French. General De Gaulle's forces also included women volunteers working exactly like the A.T.S., but not of exactly the same status. They were concerned with the welfare of relatives and families of Free French in this country, some having children.

The Mayor expressing thanks, said the Commandant had given them a lot of information about the Free French Movement and the Anglo French Association. A very good organisation existed in Kidderminster and was helping those bodies. The speaker could take back with him assurance to General De Gaulle that the people of Kidderminster and district were pleased to co-operate, for all appreciated the difficulties under which the Free French must be working. He was astonished at the daring with which French people had flown over to this country. It showed that France was still living. He hoped the Commandant's visit to Kidderminster would prove a happy one as it ought from what he had known of the generosity of local people during the last two years in helping good causes. Rotarians sent best wishes for the success of the Free French movement. The President (Rotarian W. J. Hammond) said the real heart of France still [illegible]

the hospitality of [illegible] letter. The Boy Scouts are assisting [illegible] the collection of old books [illegible] magazines. They have organised themselves into a "Press Gang" and hope to squeeze some of the householders of Kidderminster on January [illegible] and 31st. Many old books [illegible] come off the shelf to be dusted, they may cause a momentary wrench on parting, but our country is in need. Will readers kindly spread this appeal?

JOHN W. STRETTON

(District Commissioner of the Kidderminster Boy Scouts)

OUR WATER SUPPLY

Address by Mr. Alan Moody to Franche Y.P.F.

On Tuesday an address on "Water Supply" was given to the members of Franche Young People's Fellowship by Mr Alan Moody (deputy borough surveyor).

The speaker said water [illegible] had always been the "Cinderella" of [illegible] services and had never commanded so much attention as gas or electricity [illegible] but actually it was the most important of all. It was used in the home, [illegible] fire fighting and in the [illegible] plentiful supply [illegible] craft of water engineering [illegible] one. The Romans [illegible] remains of their [illegible] today. The consumption [illegible] of water per person [illegible] with the present [illegible] per person per [illegible] olden days were [illegible] washing as the Romans [illegible] century most British [illegible] washing as a [illegible] in [illegible] successive outbreaks of [illegible] the cause was traced to bad [illegible] water and [illegible] the [illegible] taken up.

The main Public Health Act [illegible] in 1875. Mr Moody then [illegible] the ways in which water [illegible] collected [illegible] stored. The rainfall in [illegible] the world varies. In [illegible] 600 inches while in other [illegible] scarcely anything at all. [illegible] chief methods of collecting [illegible] reservoir. The water ran [illegible] reservoir from the high land [illegible] it. This was called the catchment [illegible] and was often planted with trees which helped to prevent too much [illegible] down with the water. [illegible] of rainfall was collected [illegible] soaking into the ground.

The speaker described [illegible] dams and mentioned several failures in recent times which had caused great loss to life and property. There was now adequate legislation which provided a safeguard against poorly built dams. Other sources of supply were rivers and lakes. In one part of a river sewage might be discharged, but a town farther up the bank might take its water supply from the same river. Waste material always kept to one side and left the water in the middle perfectly pure.

Springs as a source of water supply were very erratic. Many towns such as Kidderminster pumped their supplies from wells sunk underground. In Kidderminster the borehole was 500 feet in depth and the water from such depth was always perfectly pure and cold. Boreholes in soft sandstone had a casing of steel gauze, but those in hard rock did not need such a casing. In tropical regions, where rainfall was slight, many ingenious ways of collecting water were devised. For instance in Gibraltar 40 acres of land were covered with sheets of corrugated iron which collected dew, which was condensed and drained away. The sources of water arranged in order of purity were spring water, borehole, upland surface water and, least of all, river water. There were many ways of purifying water, but quantity was of paramount importance and also in any scheme the economic side must be considered.

Mr Moody concluded by saying that if his talk had aroused in his listeners a feeling of appreciation of the work behind the turning on of a water tap he would be well repaid.

Questions then followed, and the Rev. [illegible], who presided, heartily thanked Mr Moody for a most instructive lecture. He also congratulated Mr Moody [illegible]

DIG

VICT

KIDDERMINSTER SHUTTLE AND STOURPORT COURIER

DINGS

EDDING

Miss Welch
Mr. and Mrs.
Welch, of
Miss Sheila
d Major the
R.A.C.D.," at
sh Church,
nesday.
taken in the
resque cere-
was prettily
s, and other
wore khaki
n the Argyle
hlanders kilt
of the ushers
it and the
egiment also
is chairman
ural District
Controller, a
Town Council,
llor, for the
on. Educated
Sussex, Miss
outbreak of
her in W.V.S.
ities.
ajor the Rev.
e son of the
d Mrs Lloyd,
yn, Anglesea.
ler, an old
end of the
ld, and the
r A. N. W
Argyle and
lers.
s given away
a gown of
with crystal
ne veil. Her
orchids. Her
ssed in blue
necklet, and
She carried
were the Rev.
puty Assistant
nd the Rev.
ector of Rib-
y and Dowles.
oral. Mr. F.
organ played
ing Handel's
march from
processional
f Jacob," and
as the introit.
e Rector read
The closing
ds, heavenly
the proces-
h the church
ister the orga-
ohn's Wedding
attended by
d friends was
of the bride's
ve the toasts
bridegroom,
and hostess,
nthusiastically
R. Lloyd are
ymoon at an
. The bride
ide and white

COOKLEY

lliss L. B.
Cookley, was
y wedding on
Lily Beatrice
er of Mr. and

GIRLS HIGH SCHOOL

As a result of the sports and demonstration held on the grounds of the school on Wednesday afternoon, pupils of the Girls' High School will send a cheque for £20 to the Children's Country Holiday Fund. This is the highest amount the school has collected for this cause and reflects the highest credit on all who have spent time thought and preparation in arranging and carrying out the programme. In making this kindly gesture the girls help other children, less fortunately situated, to enjoy out-door recreation under happy conditions. The centre of the playing grounds, conveniently marked, roped off, and and spaced with flags in the school colours (green, yellow and purple) was flanked with chairs for spectators. By 5.15 p.m. about 750 interested parents and friends had assembled and the young competitors in their black gym shorts and blue shirts were waiting eagerly for the signal to commence the programme of events. Organisation, supervision and judging were under the control of the Sports Committee, and Mrs J. Gethin, with the aid of a megaphone, announced the results of each race.

The programme was a lengthy one and contained 28 events. The girls, who put plenty of zeal and effort into their sports, showed a healthy spirit of goodwill and comradeship, and there were some commendable achievements. The usual friendly rivalry for the school shield was evident and the three houses, Chad, Clare and Cyniberht worked hard for the coveted honour, Chad being successful with 144 points.

Among those present were the Mayor (Ald O. W. Davies), Miss M. C. Oldfield M.A., (headmistress), Ald. E. G. Eddy, O.B.E., Miss H. M. Roden, B.Sc. (Alice Ottley School, Worcester), Miss E. C. Addenbrooke, J.P., Mrs. Daughish, Miss L. Douglas (Harry Cheshire Girls School), Mrs. T. N. Ballantyne, Rev. Small (Droitwich), Mr. G. A. North, Mr. J. Moffitt (Clerk to U.D.C. Stourport) and many others.

Diversion was provided by the many novelty races. In the salvage race, in which the junior pupils classified salvage and placed it in respective sacks was highly amusing. The washing race caused much laughter among the onlookers and a great deal of concentration on the part of the little folk who pegged clothes on a line. "Late for the train" a race in which entrants had to change shoes, put on a coat, beret and gloves, open an umbrella and run to the "station" was another popular event. The sack races were great fun for competitors and spectators alike, and the relay races proved exciting.

The mothers' race—egg and spoon—was an amusing interlude while the fathers' sack race was responsible for some exhausting jumping on the part of the fathers and much hilarity on the part of those who watched.

A display of Greek and National dancing by pupils of the school pleasingly demonstrated the attention being paid to this branch of physical training. The girls, dressed in summer frocks, danced on the grass with bare feet. The dancing was graceful, hand and wrist movement being particularly good. The dancing was under the direction of Mrs. J. Gethin with Miss J. Newbold as pianist.

At the conclusion of the sports, Miss M. C. Oldfield, M.A. (head mistress) introduced Miss H. M. Roden, B.Sc. (Alice Ottley Girls' School, Worcester), who distributed the trophies and awards.

Miss Roden who has done a great deal for children in Worcester and is chairman of several youth committees, smilingly shook hands with the successful competitors as they collected their prizes. She was presented with a bouquet of roses by one of the junior girls, Ann Davies, and in acknowlegment said she had spent a very happy afternoon

"SHUTTLE" PORTRAIT GALLERY No. 25

Alderman Louis Tolley

No more resolute fighter for Socialism in the public administration of Kidderminster can be found than Ald Louis Tolley, the "Father of the Town Council," and his life story which is told this week will arrest the interest of every member of the working class and indeed of his political opponents. Here we have a Socialist, who is as much a party man as the most blue-blooded ultra-Tory and all his life he has striven for the amelioration of conditions of the working classes of Kidderminster. Although at first blush Louis Tolley may appear to be in some measure almost blinded by prejudice in favour of his Socialistic ideals, yet there is always a ring of genuine sincerity about his public utterances and about his strivings to carry out social reforms with their flavour of the Socialistic doctrine about them. Now in his 53rd year, Ald. Tolley is an alert spare figure, full of activity with a ready brain and an equally ready tongue, who can always be relied upon to give a good account of himself in the debates at the Town Council meetings, where his speeches are listened to with interest.

Mill House, Hurcott, where his father, the late Mr. Joseph Tolley, was the engineer-in-charge of the paper mill, was the scene on November 4th, 1889, of the birth of the subject of our sketch. His parents were both natives of Kidderminster, and he is the youngest of a family of eight children—four sons and four daughters. Mr. Tolley was one of the first scholars to attend Broadwaters Infant School when it opened under a woman teacher. From there he went to St. George's School. He left school at fourteen, and was apprenticed to the engineering trade, indentures for seven years being signed with the firm of Messrs. Bradley and Turton, engineers. He commenced at the Clensmore works, and later moved, when the firm took over their Park Lane works. He continued as a journeyman for 14 years, leaving them in 1920 to take up a position as an engineering hand with another Kidderminster firm.

On November 1st, 1919, he was elected a member of Kidderminster Town Council for Rowland Hill Ward, in the Labour interest, and thereby hangs a tale. His election as one of the first Labour councillors—Mr. Tom Field had been elected a few months before—led to Mr. Tolley being dismissed by his firm, which caused quite a furore in the town. What was described as a "Town's Indignation Meeting" was held in the Town Hall "to protest against the treatment of Councillor Tolley by his late employers in not being allowed time to attend the Council and committee meetings of the Corporation."

The meeting passed a resolution reading, "That this meeting, having heard the statement of Councillor L. Tolley, expresses its strong indignation at the action of his employer; it further expresses the opinion that the State or the municipality is entitled to the services of its citizens in prior right to that of private employers, and that the action of capitalists who seek to deprive their workers of the right to take part in the administration of civil affairs is

Allied Workers, and has held the position of president of the Kidderminster branch for fourteen years.

In 1923 Mr Tolley was a candidate for Parliamentary honours for the Kidderminster Division, and fought in the Labour interest against Sir John Wardlaw-Milne and Mr. H. G. Purchase (Liberal). The figures at the poll were: Sir John Wardlaw-Milne, 15,469; H. G. Purchase, 9,663; and Louis Tolley, 3,990.

Mr. Tolley was one of the founders in 1921 of the Kidderminster Trades and Labour Club in P[illegible] Street, the opening ceremony of which was performed by the late Mr Arthur Henderson. Mr. Tolley became president and served on the committee for some years.

To emphasise the public work of Ald. Tolley it is only necessary to say that he is chairman of the following important committees: Baths; Food Control; Borough Restaurant, vice-chairman, Waterworks and Drainage; Joint Burial, and Farms Committee and in addition is a member of the following committees: Watch; Higher Education, Finance; Estates and Development; Parks and Assessment.

"I have had a keen desire to see housing conditions in Kidderminster improved," said Ald. Tolley to the "Shuttle" representative, "and was privileged to be vice-chairman of the Building Committee when municipal houses were first erected in the town. I have been associated with the erection of over 1,000 houses, and hope that after the war a very extensive programme will be put forward and carried out for houses for our lads returning from the war."

It was primarily through Mr. Tolley that the new baths in Castle Road were constructed, which have undoubtedly proved a great boon and of immense value to the town, a matter about which Mr. Tolley is very proud.

Mr. Tolley took a prominent part in the initiation of the Kidderminster sewerage scheme, which was only brought about after a great fight. On his first election programme Mr. Tolley expressed the view that the antiquated method of sewage disposal in the town should be abolished in favour of a more up-to-date method. He has been vice-chairman of the Kidderminster Hospital Saturday Fund Contributory Scheme, and a member of the Management Committee of the hospital, and is also a member of the Employment Exchange Management Committee. Prior to taking up his work with the Co-operative Society, Mr. Tolley was a member of the Management Committee for about ten years, and also served on its Education Committee, for five years, at one time being chairman.

With such a busy life Mr Tolley finds time for some hobbies. He is keenly interested in horticulture, and as an amateur gardener, is cultivating 1,400 square yards of allotment ground. He has won no less than 1,200 prizes at various shows in the district for his produce, which includes food, flowers, and vegetables. He has also been a member of Stourport-on-Severn Horticultural Society for eighteen years and on one occasion secured the Baldwin Challenge Vase for the best cultivated allotment. For many years he has been a member of the Kidderminster Bagatelle League, playing for the Labour Club. He is also interested in the game of bowls, and sport generally. In his younger days he gained two championship medals in the Kidderminster and District Cricket League when playing for Baxter Church Cricket Club. For fourteen years he has been actively associated with the Kidderminster Amateur Swimming Club and four years ago was honoured by being made a life member of the club for the valuable services rendered to that organisation.

Mr. Tolley lives with his wife and daughter at 26, Larches Rd., Kidderminster. In 1912 he married Miss Beatrice Blanche Gower, who comes from the Netherton district, near Dudley. There were two children, but the elder of two daughters died about five years ago. The surviving

86, Stourport Rd., Foley Park.

TOTT — HEATHCOCK. — At St. Michael and All Angels' Parish Church, Stourport, on Saturday, June 20th, 1942, by the Rev. W. A. Trippass, Vicar, Sergt. H. Stott, R.A., son of Mr. J. Stott and the late Mrs. Stott, 8, Tweedmouth Rd., Plaistow, London, to Beatrice Alice, second daughter of Mr. and Mrs. E. Heathcock, 102, Lickhill Road, Stourport.

DEATHS

COOKE.—On Monday, June 15th, Marjorie, beloved daughter of Mr. and Mrs. Cooke, of 44, Anchorfields, aged 19. Rest in peace.

LANE.—Janet, formerly of Prospect Road, Stourport, passed peacefully away June 21st, 1942. Interred Kidderminster Cemetery June 24th, 1942.

SMART.—On Monday, June 22nd, 1942, at 20, Woodfield Crescent, Bertha (beloved wife of Mr. W. A. Smart), aged 65 years.

IN MEMORIAM

CATER.—In loving memory of our dear dad, who passed away June 22nd, 1941. Always remembered by his daughters Floss, Beat, and Doris. At rest.

DANCE; BETTRIDGE.—In memory of Mrs. E. Dance, beloved mother of Mrs. and Mr. Bettridge, 44, Vine St., Kidderminster, passed away June 27th, 1930. Peace after much suffering. Also Bramwell, dearly-loved son of Mr. and Mrs. Bettridge, who passed away June 7th, 1930. Greatly missed.

HOBRO.—In loving memory of a dear father Frederick H. Hobro, 9, Albert Rd., who passed away June 23rd, 1940. Ever remembered by Nina and Eddie. In the garden of memory we meet every day.

HOBRO.—In loving memory of my dear husband, Frederick H. Hobro, 9, Albert Rd., who passed away June 23rd 1940. Always remembered by his wife and children.
Hearts that loved you never forget,
In memory you are with us yet.

HOBRO.—In memory of our dear father, Frederick H. Hobro, 9, Albert Rd., who passed away June 23rd, 1940. Ever remembered by John and Beryl.
We think of him in silence,
We often speak his name.
What would we give to hear his voice
And see his smile again.

HOOPER.—In loving memory of my dear father, William Hooper, of 39, Woodfield St., Kidderminster, who fell asleep on June 16th, 1941. Also of my dear mother, who entered into rest on June 29th, 1939. Ever remembered by their daughter, Alice. God's greatest gift—remembrance.

MILLS.—In loving memory of James Mills, late of Back Queen Street, who passed away June 27th, 1931. Not forgotten by his wife and children. Also Harry, son of the above, who died July 8th, 1928. Always remembered by mother, sisters, and brothers. In silence we remember.

PARDOE; ROSE.—Happy memories of Walter Allen Pardoe, who passed away June 23rd, 1941. Also of dear mother, Fanny Rose, died June 15th, 1940. Sadly missed by Alice, 18, Avill Grove.

PIERCE.—In loving memory of my dear husband, John, who passed away on June 25th, 1933. Always in the thoughts of his loving wife and family, 136, Sutton Park Rd. Memories cling.

SMITH.—In loving memory of my dear husband William Henry Smith (late fruiterer Bewdley St., Kidderminster), who fell asleep June 24 1937; also of William Arthur Smith our only son, who passed to his rest June 29, 1906. Ever in my thoughts.—Until we meet again.

TAYLOR.—In ever loving memory of a dear husband and father, Herbert Taylor who passed peacefully away June 25, 1935. Always in the thoughts of his wife, sons and daughters, 52, Hemming St., Kidderminster "Too good in life, to be forgotten in death."

TEALE.—Treasured birthday memories, June 30th, of our dear son and brother, Charles, who passed away June 25th, 1936.
The presence of our loved one
Is with us when we tread
The pathways of remembrance
In the Garden of the Dead.

...STAFF.—In loving memory of

...and transport facilities. A heavy volume of salvage has been collected and disposed of for war purposes, the total to date being nearly 4,000 tons.

The scheme for a supplementary water supply—in case of an emergency—by linking up with the Birmingham main water supply is progressing well. The work of the Town Council regarding allotments has been good and many plots have been taken up, though there are more available.

The Home Guard is well up to full strength and the police service is satisfactory, although, on account of its numbers being depleted through men being needed for the Army, it is under strength. All this work—much of it unseen by the public eye—has been creditably carried out.

• • • •

When a country is engaged in a desperate war there is always a danger of people losing their sense of perspective and proportion. For instance, there are people who take the view that our war workers in the West Midlands and elsewhere ought not to have a holiday at all in view of the military situation, but the Government is quite clearly not of the same opinion. The English are not easily stampeded. The war has now been going on for two years and ten months, and our factory workers have been Trojans in sticking to their jobs, working long hours, often including Sunday. The time has arrived when these men and women are fully entitled to a rest and a holiday so that they do not break down in their efforts, but get fresh zest and vigour for the rest of the year. An old saying is "All work and no play makes Jack a dull boy," and it applies very much at the present juncture. The Kidderminster Town Council was fully justified this week in deciding to spend up to the proceeds of a half-penny rate in providing entertainments for the workers to have a "holiday at home." The arrangements were relegated to a special committee, upon which will be co-opted workers' representatives, and, with the use of some commercial acumen, attractions can no doubt be thought out by which entertainments can be provided for the holiday-makers who will gladly pay for them. If this is done it is possible that the cost of the full proceeds of a half-penny rate, which amounts to about £357 10s., will not have to fall upon the town, but that profit from, at any rate, some of the entertainments will reduce the suggested expenditure. The chief point of the "holiday at home" is to save petrol on the roads and coal on the railways, also in the latter case the use of rolling stock required for more important, and indeed, vital purposes.

The protest by Ald. E. G. Eddy, at the Town Council meeting on Wednesday against permitting gambling games for boys and girls at the Fair held in the Cattle Market last week is not trivial, but one of substance. Parents, when they allow their children to visit the fair, held under the auspices of the Corporation, expect them to enjoy a little fun. It is a serious matter however, when through attending the fair the children are introduced to the besetting sin of gambling. At the fair there were several stalls at which children were invited to roll pennies in the hope of winning a money prize. The game can scarcely be contended as being one in which there is any element of skill. In fact it is a pure gamble, and scores of children soon lost their precious pennies. Ald. Eddy urged the game was calculated to create the spirit of gambling among the young people and said he thought the town authorities, without being adverse to the fair as such, should deplore that it should be

...Broad, Evelyn Clark, Ruth ... Muriel Davies, Doris D... Harold Eales, Stanley Foster, ... Horton, Winifred Hughes, ... jorie Hughes, Kathleen ... phries, Mary Jefferies, Mo... Jones, Gwendoline Morris, R... Moule, Harold Price, M... Pritchard, Muriel Pri... Florence Shewry, Gertrude ...ton, Olive Turley, Helen ... Joan M. Weavers, Isabella W... Pendants: Walter Cross, D... Dudley, Edith Jones, Ena ... Olive Morgan, Elsie Price, ...gery Shellis, Ernest G. ... Edith Taylor.

Be Careful.—With the adv... summer and the cons... drying of grass and underg... it is necessary to be doubly ... ful with cigarette ends ... matches. On Monday eveni... prompt action of Mr. Buck... Franche Road, prevented ... might have proved a dan... fire in the hedge and fence ... Rugby field at Whitville. ... in his garden Mr. Buckler ... smoke issuing from the ... under the hedge opposite ... almost immediately flames ... to spread along the fence. ... the help of a passing cycl... fire was quickly under c... and no damage was done. ... safe to say that a cri... dropped cigarette end or a ... match was responsible f... fire which, but for Mr. Bu... quick action, could hav... serious consequences.

Appeal to Students.—An ... to students to help on wa... during their summer vacati... been made by the Minis... Labour and National S... There is a special need ... Midlands for men to do ... labour in factories, or as ... bers of mobile gangs, a... women to do factory work, ...tic work in hospitals and ... and clerical work in factori... Government offices. For s... living in districts where lit... work is available, free tra... warrants can be issued to th... of work if it is beyond ... travelling distance, and acc... dation will be found. Wa... be the ordinary rates for t... Any student willing to ta... work should apply at the ... Employment Exchange. ... registration arrangements ... been made at a number of ...sities and similar establish...

Preferment.—The Rev. ... Gerald Holbeche, M.A., Pr... charge of St. James' Churc... December, 1940, and a mer... St. Mary's Parish Church ... who acts as Chaplain to the ... and the P.A. Institution, h... mated his acceptance of th... of St. Luke, in the Prittlew... trict of Southend-on-Sea. ... thus returning to the Dio... Chelmsford, where he ... ministerial duties four yea... Educated at St. John's ... Durham, he took his B.A. ... in 1937, and the Diplo... Theology in the following ... when he was ordained ... Bishop of Chelmsford and ... to a curacy at St. Paul'... Ham, East London. Subse... he was at Shoebury. H... move was to Coventry, on ... ment as assistant priest ... Margaret's. He had only ... in shortly before the dev... blitzes which wrecked parts ... city. Mr. Holbeche is at ... off holiday. Crockford's ... Directory states that the ... value of the living of St. L... £400 gross with house, and ... pre-war population of 8,00...

Scouting.—Mr. F. C. ... seretary of the Boy Scout ...ciation in Kidderminster, ...bably one of the oldest s... the district. His zeal and ... for the many years he h... associated with the movem... earned him a place of high

Y

death occu-
ospital during
derick Oakes
dland "Red"
on pension
Mr Oakes
ed a stroke
uncillor H R
reports that
igh for week
as follows
defence
onds £2,700

report the
ged 56, wife
30 Severn
ich occurred
took place
on Thursday
ear in our

n S. Harris,
wles Road,
pil of King
hool, Kidder-
ed up for
ore complet-
Birmingham

URBAN DISTRICT OF STOURPORT-ON-SEVERN

SALVAGE COLLECTION

NOTICE TO HOUSEHOLDERS

The collection of salvage has recently revealed that many householders are still placing dirty tins, rags, and bones in the Salvage Bags. This creates considerable difficulties at the Sorting Depot.

WILL ALL HOUSEHOLDERS PLEASE NOTE:—

(a) That tins should not on any account be placed in the Bags, but should be placed in the refuse bins.

(b) That rags for salvage should be free from dirt and vermin.

(c) That bones should be dried and placed in a separate receptacle.

Dated this 15th day of July, 1942.

(Signed) JOHN W. MOFFITT,
Clerk of the Council.

The Council House,
Stourport-on-Severn.

QUEEN ELIZABETH'S SCHOOL (HARTLEBURY)

SPORTS DAY

Will Parents of Present Boys, Old Boys, and Friends of the School please note that in order to save paper no formal invitations are being sent out this year. Sports Day will be held on Wednesday, July 22nd, commencing at 2 p.m. Presentation of cups at 4.45 approximately will be made by Lady Baldwin. Speech Day will this year be held in the Autumn Term, and the date will be announced later.

STOURPORT

To Help Sailors.—Retiring collec-

Old Elizabethans' Association.— Hartlebury Grammar School Old Boys' Annual Re-Union takes place at the school on Saturday, July 25th. Tea will be provided, annual meeting of the association, 6 p.m.

The late Mr. A. F. Hutton.—A one minute silence was observed on the Old Anchor Bowling Green at eight o'clock on Saturday, during a match in tribute to the late Mr Arthur F Hutton, of 51, Lorne St., whose sudden death whilst on Home Guard duty at Wilden Iron Works was reported last week. Deceased was vice-captain of the home club. Similar tribute was paid at all matches played under the auspices of Kidderminster District Bowling League.

Gardeners and Garden Pests.—The loan exhibition of photographs of garden pests on view in the show window of J. Nevil Butler, Ltd., Bridge St., has attracted interest this week, arranged by Mrs. Trippass, in conjunction with Stourport Horticul-

Stourport Congregational Church

MISSIONARY GARDEN MEETING

at The Heath, Lickhill Road

(by kind permission of Mr. and Mrs. A. D. Capel Loft)

Friday, July 24th, 7.30 p.m.

(If wet in Congregational Church).

Speaker:

REV. HILARY WILSON, B.A.

Chairman: DR. LLOYD JOHNSTONE (late of China)

MUSICAL INTERLUDE by MALE VOICE CHOIR.

Collection for L.M.S. 135

HORTICULTURAL SOCIETY

Earl Baldwin to Open Stourport Show

Members of the Stourport Horticultural Society, as well as the general public, are asked to note that the annual show will be held on Saturday, September 5th, and will be opened by the president, the Rt. Hon. Earl Baldwin of Bewdley, K.G.

Lieut.-Col. J. A. Dyson Perrins has kindly given permission to use the Drill Hall, which will allow for better spacing and more room to walk round the exhibits. It is expected that larger entries will be received, owing to the amount of vegetables now being grown by members.

At the monthly meeting held on Thursday, July 2nd, Cllr H. G. Southall, who presided, offered his congratulations to exhibitors.

An interesting lecture was given by Mr. G. Van Frachem on "Fruit trees and pest control," and dealt with the subject from the point of view of the small gardener. He urged members to allow plenty of space when planting bush fruit, so that vegetables could be planted between, thereby making the best possible use of the ground. Advice was given on buying, planting, staking, manuring, pruning, and the lecturer also dealt with the pests which attack the various fruits, in each case giving a detailed description of the pests and their habits.

The judges for the monthly competitions were Mr A. W. Craddock and Mr. W. Bullock, who in their remarks on the exhibits, said the quality was good.

The secretary stated that allotment sites had been tested for lime, and were all found to be very acid. In view of this, the allotments committee were assisting the society to purchase a quantity of lime for distribution in the autumn, and orders should be sent in at once to

NATIONAL SAVINGS

Special Efforts by Bewdley and District

The summer drive by the savings groups in their "Tanks for Attack" efforts starts next week, Monday, July 20th, and the hon. sec., Cllr. H. R. Mountford, reports that the stage is now set for an intensive campaign during the ensuing ten weeks period until September 26th.

The Borough of Bewdley and the external Rock area are now 100 per cent covered by savings groups after a wide search for public-spirited group officers who have undertaken this important work. Here is the opportunity for every member of the local community to play the part in the national struggle, and incidentally to benefit themselves by their investments in small savings, including Defence Bonds, National Savings Certificates, and National Savings Stamps, and P.O.S.B. Deposits. Information will be readily forthcoming from the hon. sec., group officers, post offices, or banks. Remember the aim of the drive is 30 per cent increase on the corresponding sales last year, which will provide two of the largest "Churchill" tanks to be named after Bewdley and Rock. There will be no entertainments organised, but all interests should be directed towards the maximum investment of small savings of idle money which may otherwise serve no effective purpose. Just pay it in from next Monday onwards.

Street Group Officers (all volunteers) herewith.

Habberley Road (A): Misses Tomes, Chester Terrace.

Habberley Road (B): Mrs. Smithson, "Greenacres."

Catchems End: Mrs. H. R. Mountford, "Grendon."

High Bank: Mrs. Bloomer, "High Bank."

Spencer Avenue: Mrs. Murray and Mrs. Colley, 3, Spencer Avenue.

Kidderminster Road (A): Mrs. Pountney, "Oban Cottage."

Kidderminster Road (B): Mrs. Hartwell, Beales Corner.

Westbourne Street: Mrs. Heath, Police Station.

Stourport Road: Mrs. E. F. Roden, "Brookfield."

Acacia Avenue: Miss O. Pritchard, "Gemmill."

Northwood Lane: Mrs. Sollum, Northwood Cottage.

Springfield: Miss Watkins, Spring-

GENERAL DE GAULLE

Official Visit to Bewdley on Monday

General de Gaulle is paying an official visit to Bewdley on Monday, July 20th.

Arrangements are being made for an official welcome to be afforded to General de Gaulle by the Mayor (Alderman R. B. Jackson), and Corporation outside the Town Hall at 11.30 a.m., when the General passes through Bewdley. The Mayor hopes that the aldermen, councillors, magistrates, and officials will make every possible effort to support him on this important occasion. The Mayor will receive General de Gaulle outside the Town Hall.

It is hoped to provide a guard of honour outside the Town Hall from local Military Units, the Home Guard, N.F.S., Civil Defence Services, A.T.C., Scouts, and Guides.

"A SPLIT SECOND"

Child's Tragic Death at Bewdley

The story of how a little girl, Lilian Rose Genner, in company with her mother, ran across the road into the side of a Midland "Red" 'bus at Welch Gate, Bewdley, and was killed instantly, was told at the inquest at Bewdley on Friday. The fatality occurred on Wednesday evening, July 8th. The child was the daughter of Mr. and Mrs. George Edward Genner, 44, Sandy Bank, Bewdley.

The inquest was conducted by Mr. N. H. Capel Loft. Mr. O. Neville Weston (Kidderminster) represented the 'bus driver and the Birmingham Omnibus Company.

Mrs. Nellie Genner, 44, Sandy Bank, Bewdley, said she was walking down Welch Gate with her little daughter and gave the child a threepenny piece to buy some chips from Mrs White's shop on the other side of the road. Near the Anchor Inn the child loosed her hand and started to run across the road. No vehicle was in sight when she looked round and she did not hear any horn sounded. The child was well across the road when the 'bus came and struck the child, who was then 1½ yards from the path on the opposite side.

Dr. H. Newton Miles, Load St., Bewdley, who arrived at 6.15 p.m., said the child was dead, death being due to laceration of the brain following a fracture of the

TOWN COUNCIL TOPICS

LABOUR MAYOR CHOSEN

THE principal public matter decided at a meeting of Kidderminster Town Council on Wednesday was the choice of Alderman Louis Tolley as mayor for the ensuing municipal year. Alderman Tolley was elected by ballot, and he will succeed the present Mayor, Alderman Osman W. Davies, who has held the position as a Conservative for two years. The selection of Alderman Tolley was made when the Council had gone into committee after the ordinary business.

The Mayor (Ald. O. W. Davies) presided and those present were: Cllr. J. Andrews (deputy mayor), Aldermen O. Anton, H. W. Cheshire, E. O. Eddy, A. E. Meredith, and L. Tolley; Cllrs. Miss E. C. Addenbrooke, J. Bristow, J. Brown, F. D. H. Burcher, G. S. Chadwick, J. Dalley, J. Ferguson, S. Goodwin, W. H. Jennings, F. Martin, A. Smith, F. R. Stone, J. E. Talbot, G. N. Weston, F. Wilson; officials: The Town Clerk (Mr J. H. Thursfield), Borough Treasurer (Mr. A. Shiner), Borough Surveyor (Mr. J. Hawcroft), Chief Sanitary Inspector (Mr. G. A. North), Chief Constable (Mr. H. Hodgkinson), Director of Education (Dr. Chapman), and the Deputy Town Clerk (Mr. C. B. Griffiths).

The Mayor said it would be the wish of the Council that sympathy should be expressed with Councillor G. N. Weston, in the death of his mother, whose husband had served on the Parks Committee and who was much respected in the town.

It was agreed that the Town Clerk should write to Cllr. Weston and his sister a letter expressing the sympathy [illegible] members of the Council felt with them in the bereavement they had suffered.

HOME HOLIDAY PLAN

The Mayor: I should like to refer to the three weeks entertainment plan which is starting next Saturday for the workers to have a holiday at home in order to save transport on the railways and other means of transport. The arrangements are in hand and I think they will provide a lot of pleasure to the people of the town. One or two very good bands are coming to the town. The school children are being well looked after. I should like to express my appreciation to the members of the teaching staffs who are giving up part of their holidays and who are going to act as stewards and look after the children, four of them every afternoon and four of them every evening. We want the help of every member of this Council to take part in the carrying out of the programme and to show an interest. We also want the people themselves to enter into the spirit of the thing. For the purpose of getting helpers together, Alderman Tolley has undertaken to look after Brinton Park, and Cllr. Burcher to look after St George's Park.

Ald O. Anton: Are you having a hand book or a printed programme?

The Mayor: No, we are advertising in the Press and putting posters up in conspicuous places to tell the people what events there are and when they may see them.

A letter was read from the Borough Surveyor concerning the criticism raised at the last meeting of the Council respecting the removal of iron railings from property in Kidderminster by the Ministry of Works and Buildings. The Surveyor wrote that he had now received a letter from the Emergency Works Officer in which that official confirmed the promises made at a recent interview and which he had reported to the General Purposes Committee to improve the quality of the re-instatement and in bad cases to make adjustments to work already carried out.

In moving the quarterly report of the Education Committee, Ald. H. W. Cheshire (chairman) said that they hoped now that they had a Director of Education to improve the education of the town.

TRADES COUNCIL AND GAMBLING

A letter was read from Mr. J. S. Moseley, secretary of Kidderminster Trades and Labour Council, on the question of gambling stalls at the recent annual fun fair. The letter

Chamber. That wire has been there for weeks—at least two months—and it is now in a state of rust and does not look to be worth anything. There is enough tin there to keep a factory going. Possibly there are transport difficulties but surely when we have made such a drive, we can get the stuff away.

Invited by the Mayor as to whether he had anything to say about the matter, Mr. G. A. North (chief sanitary inspector) said that the position was that at Hoobrook, they had their main centre, and personally he would like to see that heap six times the size. They were getting away from there 40 tons a month and at the present time there would not be 80 tons on the site. There were three men working 15 hours a day and on Sunday mornings. Another point they had to bear in mind was that during the last two months, the furnaces and yards had been stocked out with railings which had been the cause of the trouble. This was nothing compared with what some authorities had to deal with. At Worcester there was over 150 tons. The wire mentioned by Ald. Meredith came from Stourport, and the furnaces could not take it at present owing to the congestion of railings.

Alderman Meredith: It is deteriorating.

Mr. North: There will be no deterioration in the value of it if it stops there for five years.

UNWANTED DAY NURSERIES

Cllr. Andrews moving the report of the Maternity and Child Welfare Committee said the Committee had given further consideration to the subject of day nurseries. The Committee, who had been helped very much by Cllr. Arthur Smith had investigated particulars supplied to them by several firms in the district of persons, who, it was stated, desired to make use of the facilities of a Day Nursery. Out of 37 cases investigated it was found that only 4 persons would use a Day Nursery if provided. Many had made satisfactory arrangements for the care of their children and had no desire to send them to a nursery. Other mothers were unable to go to work by reason of ill health and others lived outside the Borough, at Bewdley, Stourport-on-Severn and other places.

The Committee placed these facts before the Council in support of their previous recommendation that the time is not yet ripe for the provision of Day Nurseries in the borough.

Ald. Meredith moved the minutes of the Drainage and Waterworks Committee, which stated that the agreement with the Birmingham Corporation for an additional water supply came into operation on June 9th last, when the first supply was taken into the mains of the Town Council. The Sewage Disposal Committee reported that the whole of the work in connection with the above scheme had now been completed, with the exception of the finishing of the tarmacadam surface to the approach road to the Disposal Works and a certain amount of painting of plant at the latter. The former would be completed this week, and the latter would be finished within the next two or three weeks.

The Committe regret that it had not yet been possible to put the works into operation owing to the difficulty of obtaining the necessary labour, but are making application to the District Man-Power Board and the Ministry of Labour for the necessary staff to be provided.

MORE SERIOUS READING

The report of the Library and Museum Committee stated that during June 15,575 books on fiction and 33,393 non-fiction books had

OBITUARY

LIEUT. F. W. NORTH, R.N.

The utmost sympathy will be felt with Mr and Mrs Harold North, and Mrs Fred North, of 6, Comberton Terrace, Kidderminster in the tragic bereavement they have sustained by

the death of Lieut. F. W. North, R.N., elder son of Mr and Mrs. Harold North, who, it is officially reported, has lost his life at sea. He had a brilliant scholastic career and seemed set for a highly successful career of usefulness, and was personally popular in every sphere. The details [illegible] are not yet known, but Mr. Harold North and [illegible] are pursuing every avenue to ascertain the facts.

Just 25 years of age, Lieut. North married on [illegible] 1940, while on leave, Miss Millicent Dowling, [illegible], with whom the utmost sympathy will be felt.

Lieut. North was educated at [illegible] Grammar School and at Birmingham University; he took his B.Sc. degree for engineering in 193[illegible] and commenced an engineering training with the [illegible] Co., Rugby. During his educational course he played cricket occasionally for Kidderminster and was captain of the Birmingham University hockey team 193[illegible], and of the cricket team in the same year.

When the war broke out he volunteered immediately and joined up on September [illegible], 1939, and after a months training at Portsmouth was posted to the Ark Royal and served on that historic vessel until November, 1941. In January of this year he was appointed chief engineer (at 25) on an American cutter engaged on convoy duty.

Mr and Mrs North's younger son, J. H. P. North, is serving as staff Sergeant in the R.A.O.C.

NEWS OF SERVING MEN

Pictured reading the "Shuttle" while on leave in Cairo is Private Albert Hartland, who is serving in the M.E.F. His wife, Mrs. A. Hartland, of 24, Mill St., has received the welcome news that he is safe

and well. Pte Hartland, who, in civil life was an employee of the Kidderminster Corporation, has been abroad three years, and has served in the Crete and Abyssinian campaigns, and in the Anglo-Egyptian Sudan.

Mrs. S. Knott, of 36, Bromsgrove St., has received news that her husband, Corporal Samuel Thomas Knott, Worcestershire Regiment, is

reported missing in the Middle East since June 20th. An airgraph received by Mrs. Knott two or three days previous

Mrs. B. Gane, of 1, Coun[illegible] Mill Lane, Wolverley, has [illegible] news that her husband, [illegible]

Gane [illegible] ing [illegible] Middl[illegible] since [illegible] 20th. [illegible] Gane [illegible] eldest [illegible] Mrs. [illegible] and [illegible] Mr. A[illegible] 37, [illegible] Kidde[illegible] He jo[illegible] Forces [illegible] two [illegible] and h[illegible] about [illegible] month[illegible] M[illegible] East. news is anxiously awaited.

Our soldiers, sailors and [illegible] all speak eloquently of the ho[illegible] received when on service [illegible] week new evidence of this [illegible] comes from a letter writt[illegible] lady in Durban. Some of ou[illegible] had occasion to spend a sho[illegible] in this country and the lad[illegible] R[illegible] gave pleasure to [illegible] when she sent this letter [illegible] Vaux of 166, Marlpool Lane[illegible] husband is in the R.A.F. Sh[illegible] "I promised your hubby [illegible] would meet him and two [illegible] in the canteen and since th[illegible] had some nice outings in [illegible] I [illegible] enjoyed it as much [illegible] have. Your husband is loo[illegible] and well, and the people of [illegible] go all out to make our b[illegible] as happy as possible. They [illegible] on buses and trains and all [illegible] with reduced fees at cinemas[illegible] canteen is connected wi[illegible] Wesleyan Church and we giv[illegible] [illegible] sandwiches, mince [illegible] cakes and cigarettes [illegible] have a free concert every [illegible] hope to see England some [illegible] am a Londoner, but have li[illegible] for 2[illegible] years. My son is in th[illegible] African Air Force as a[illegible] instructor."

Among the many who a[illegible] awaiting further information co[illegible] [illegible] news has been [illegible] this week by his wife, Mr[illegible] [illegible] Bryn Stour, Cookley, [illegible] husband Pte. Arthur Charle[illegible] [illegible]ershire Regiment, [illegible] [illegible] believed a prisoner of [illegible] the Middle East, since Ju[illegible] Pte. Perry, who is the secon[illegible] Mr. and Mrs. R. C. Perry, 7[illegible] side, Stourport, served thro[illegible] evacuation of Dunkirk and [illegible] Faroe Islands. Before join[illegible] Forces he was employed at [illegible] Bradley and Turton, Ltd.[illegible] minster.

Mrs. Wilfred Prosser, of 20 [illegible] Avenue, has received t[illegible] that her husband, A.C.1[illegible] Prosser, R.A.F., has arrived [illegible] Middle East, after a long [illegible] in Durban, when the party [illegible] there the townspeople trea[illegible] boys with great hospitality. [illegible] letter to his wife, the young [illegible] said he had received the fir[illegible] after four months. He met [illegible] A.C.1 J. Vaux, at Durban, a c[illegible] with whom he had spent ne[illegible] years of training. Although [illegible] in the journey overseas, the[illegible] each other on landing. A[illegible] Prosser married Miss Doris [illegible] Cook[illegible] and was employed [illegible] Kalt[illegible] department of Carpe[illegible] before joining the Forces.

Ronald G. Chadwick, [illegible] elder son of Mr. and Mrs[illegible] Chadwick, "Westfield," Co[illegible] Avenue, is now a pilot office[illegible] R.A.F. A cable received th[illegible] states that he is posted in [illegible] Sydney, Nova Scotia.

Mrs. E. A. Harris, of 7, [illegible] St. writes on behalf of [illegible] band, Stoker J. Harris, now [illegible] on one of His Majesty's [illegible] "somewhere at sea." In [illegible] received last week he refers [illegible] "Shuttle," which he is now [illegible] ing. He says how very int[illegible] it is to read the local ne[illegible] nearly 12 months at sea.

W.V.S. CONGRATULA[illegible]

Visit of the Dowager Mar[illegible] of Reading

Warm praise was given to [illegible] W.V.S. by the Dowager Mar[illegible] of Reading when she paid [illegible] anticipated visit to Kiddermi[illegible] Thursday morning. For so[illegible] it had been hoped that La[illegible]

DDING IN INDIA

[illegible] Martin Barker—Miss M. Borebank

and Mrs. W. W. Barker, of Spring Grove Crescent, minster, have received news le that their youngest son, H. Martin Barker, of the ershire Regiment, was mar- Counoor, India, on Saturday ith, to Miss Margaret Bore- daughter of Mrs. and the late ebank, Inspector of Excise) bridegroom, who is an Old n, passed on to Goldsmith's preparatory to taking up the ic profession and was in his ear at college. When his up was called up, he joined eived his papers on his 21st r. he served in the ranks me and afterwards proceeded hurst where he obtained his sion. He served in Ireland, ne back to the Midlands, and India last August. In June year he was at Karachi.

nd Mrs. W. W. Barker have s and one daughter. One n the R.A.S.C., in Ireland, and ns have been in Australia ears. Mrs. Barker made a Australia six yeads ago to em.

[illegible]UAL PRIZE-GIVING

Street Junior Mixed School

ednesday afternoon the annual ing at Lea Street Junior School was attended by the (Alderman O. W. Davies). The ings were enlivened by an t programme by the scholars. Mayor, who distributed the made a few helpful remarks scholars. Evidently good work g done at this school under admastership of Mr. Harold nd his loyal staff. Regret was ed that Miss Badland, who has taken the utmost interest in ool, was unable to be present to indisposition. An apology so received from Miss M. E.

Headmaster, after heartily wel- the Mayor and other friends, review of the year's work. erred in appreciative terms to vices of Mrs. Evans, a Smeth- acher who joined the staff last Five boys had gained hips at the Grammar School— Butler, John Goodyear, Gordon ay, Brian Moore and Raymond y. R. Frankish had been a scholarship by the Birm- L.E.A., and four girls had ntrance scholarships to the chool—Valerie Scott, Margaret Lorna Grove and Mary Taylor. other scholars had been d as fee-paying pupils at local ry schools. Among news of holars, it was stated that Woodgate was taken prisoner ya, but after two days he d to escape and return to the lines.

efforts for charity included collections for the following Overseas Tobacco Fund, and Strays Society, Hospital's Day, Red Cross, R.S.P.C.A., C., Y.M.C.A., and others. Of scholars, 167 were members Savings Association, and last er £501 was invested. Scholars ing 153 availed themselves of ilities for milk. Mr. Jones d to parents to provide either s or rubber-bottomed shoes for d games, and announced that orts heats would be run in Park on August 6th with the week later. There were 133 from the girls and 96 from rs. He also referred to the cy feeding arrangements and for more volunteers.

Mayor (Alderman Osman W. thanked the audience for their , and congratulated the staff excellent scholarship record. t boys were going to his old and he would watch their s with interest. He referred arrangements for dental treat- nd appealed to parents to see hildren's teeth were cared for. npliment the school on its t record, and referred to his H.M.S. "Vansittart," whose

OBITUARY

MR. THOMAS BAKER

After an illness of some 12 months' duration Mr. Thomas Baker (beloved husband of Mrs. Eliza Baker), passed away at his home, 12, Lark Hill on Thursday, July 16th. Mr Baker, who was 74 years of age was on the staff of Messrs J. P. Harvey and Co corn merchants for 16 years, and later became an employee of Messrs Clement Dalley and Co. At the time of his retirement five years ago he was working for the Kidderminster Corporation. Gardening was his hobby.

The funeral took place on Saturday, July 18th, at the new cemetery the Rev. E. J. G. Foster conducting the service.

Floral tributes were received from: His wife; Beatrice, Harry, and Bryan, Violet, Alf, and Graham; Lena, Joe, Doreen, and Mrs. Munn; Sid, Winnie, and children; Mr. Marchant, Doll, Charlie, and kiddies; little Nigel; Mr and Mrs. Young and Kath; Mr. and Mrs Edwards; neighbours of Lark Hill and Eddy Road; Mr and Mrs. Read; Margaret, Harold, and David; Mrs. Stanton and children; Mr. and Mrs. Houghton, also Maggie, Beat and old friends; Arthur, Annie, and Phyllis; Mrs. Hopkins; Mr. and Mrs. B. Bingham.

MRS. CAROLINE RANKLE

The funeral of Mrs. Caroline Rankle, wife of Mr. George Rankle, 101, Franche Rd., took place on Saturday, a choral service in St. Barnabas' Church, Franche, being followed by interment in St. John's Churchyard. The deceased lady, who died at home on Wednesday last week, after a long illness had been a tireless worker for many good causes. Since coming to the carpet borough 40 years ago she and her husband have done a great deal in the religious and social life at Franche where for several years Mr. Rankle has been people's churchwarden at St. Barnabas' Church. She often deputised for the enrolling member of Franche Mothers' Union besides giving an effective lead in other organisations. The greatest sympathy is felt with her husband and daughters in their loss.

The cortege was met at the church gate by the Rev. Gwynfor John (priest-in-charge), Mr. G. S. Tomkinson (vicar's warden), and the robed choir preceded by cross bearer. The choir was augmented by girl choristers, under Mrs. Greaves. At the organ Mr. W. H. Parker, M.Sc., played "O rest in the Lord" (Mendelssohn). The opening hymn was "How bright those glorious spirits shine." Psalm 23 and the Nunc Dimittis were chanted, and the closing hymn was "For ever with the Lord." The organist played Handel's Largo as the procession left the church, and the congregation lined the church walk in farewell tribute.

The family mourners were: Mr. George Rankle (husband), Mabel, Mary and Kathleen (three daughters), Mr. W. H. Parker and Lieut. H. B. Hunt (sons-in-law), Mrs. Fellowes (sister of deceased), Mrs. Baskerfield, Mr. and Mrs. Arthur Holloway (brother and sister-in-law), Mrs. W. Billson, Mrs. W. Corbett and Mr. Walter Rankle (all three of Halesowen), Flight Officers Lamb and H. Morgan (A.T.C.).

In the congregation and at the graveside were the Rev. A. P. Dauglish (Franche school managers), Mrs. G. John (Franche Mothers' Union E.M.), Mr. W. Greaves (St. Barnabas' Church Council), Mrs. Greaves (school staff), Mr J. Woodbury (president Franche Village Club), Cllr. G. S. Chadwick, C.C., Mrs. C. Pagett (representing British Red Cross Society collectors), Mrs. H. Hardwicke, Mrs. Fred Smith, Mrs. G. S. Tomkinson, and several contingents from Franche Church and village organisations. Mr. A. Turner represented the churchwardens of St. Mary's Parish Church.

Letters of apology were received from Mr. E. C. Hodgkins (formerly of Franche) and from the local committee of the A.T.C.

Floral tributes were from: Dad; Mabel, Billy and Sandy; Mary, Stanley, and Patsy; Kathleen, Bert, Valerie, and June; granny Holloway and Harry; Jennie, David, and Reg; Dolly; Jim, and family; Arthur, Polly, and Audrey; Annie, Dick, and family; Florrie, Bob, and family; sister Lizzie and family; Walter, Annie and family; Polly and Percy Rankle and family; Sarah and family; Mr. and Mrs. Billson and Peter; Polly, Ivy, and Jack; Dot and Jim Mr. and Mrs. Bert MacFarlane; Mr. and Mrs. S. Macfarlane, Leslie, and Peggy; Mr. and Mrs. E. Foster, and Mary; Percy

EXIT COMMUNIST DELEGATE

AT TRADES AND LABOUR COUNCIL MEETING

AN incident of major importance to the trade union movement not only locally but nationally, took place at a meeting of Kidderminster Trades and Labour Council on Monday evening, when a delegate representing that powerful trade union, the Amalgamated Engineering Union, was expelled because he is a self-avowed Communist.

The delegate in question is Mr. Maurice Everall, branch secretary of the Kidderminster Communist Party, and after the decision was asked to leave the meeting and walked out. The expulsion occurred at the instigation of Cllr. Arthur Smith, J.P., who, when Mr Everall entered the room produced a copy of the rules of the Trades Council, and said he wished to raise a point of order.

Cllr. Smith: My point of order is concerning Mr. Everall who has now arrived. Mr. Everall is the branch secretary of the local Communist Party and I raise the point as to whether he should be here to-night. The rules say "In no circumstances shall a Trades Council co-operate with or subscribe to the funds of the Communist or Fascist parties or any subsidiary organisation of these parties or any industrial organisation which has been proscribed by the Industrial Council."

The Chairman: I do not think that we can take it that the Trades Council is co-operating with the Communist Party just because a member is a member of any other organisation.

Cllr. Arthur Smith: Going back to the year 1934 the trades unions were receiving circulars from the Trades Union Congress on this very question. In that circular it says "Trades Councils have been informed that the recognition of Congress will be withdrawn from any Council which accepts delegates connected in any way with either Communists or Fascists or any ancillary bodies." That is official from the T.U.C. in 1934. It adds "The General Council hope that you will assist them to the utmost of your ability."

The Chairman (Mr. W. Davis): Yes but Mr. Everall is a delegate here of the A.E.U. and rather than take any action against Mr. Everall even if I thought fit, I would sooner their local branch should consider the point first because, after all, the Trade Union Congress has not got a clean sheet in this matter because we know that many of the organisations affiliated with and paying fees to it are what we call proscribed organisations. I think that rather than that we should have any conflict in our Council at the present moment we would let the matter go on the grounds that Mr. Everall is a delegate of the A.E.U. I think it is for the T.U.C. to show us a policy or a pattern on what they term a clean slate before they can expect us to do something on those lines ourselves. The point that Mr. Smith raises is a correct one—there is no doubt about that—but I am not going to ask Mr. Everall to leave this room.

Cllr. Smith (heatedly rising from his chair and collecting his papers): Then in that case Mr. Chairman I shall leave myself and I shall request my delegate to withdraw, also the secretary who is in my union.

The Chairman: Just one minute Mr. Smith.

Mr. H. B. Preston: I respect Mr. Everall, but I think he must withdraw.

The Chairman: Quote me any one question is a member of the Communist or Fascist Party or any subsidiary organisation of those parties. I shall have to ask you to leave the meeting Mr. Everall. I do not want to ask you to leave if you wish to make a statement first.

Mr. Everall: I would like to make a statement. I would like to say that I am the secretary of the local Communist organisation. I have not attempted to hide it. I expected this to happen this evening. In view of what is happening on the Eastern front in the world to-day if the rule which has been quoted links up Communists with Fascists—and because of that rule in a time like this I have to be expelled—I shall have done good in coming here to-night. I will say good night.

The Chairman: Good night, Mr. Everall.

Mr. Everall then left the meeting.

The Chairman: Personally, I am very sorry this has happened because if this matter is pursued it is going to strengthen the Tory Party.

Mr. M. R. Jones: There would be no Trades Councils in this country to-day if it had not been for the Communist Party in Russia, which is fighting our battles to-day. I think we ought to get down on our knees and thank God that there is a Communist Party.

Cllr. Arthur Smith: I have no objection to the Communist Party or anybody who wishes to belong to it. My objection is to members of the Communist Party coming into the Trades Council, where they are not entitled to sit under the rules. I have no objection as to where the Communists hold their meetings but I have seen so much of the Communist Party that gets into other organisations and splits them up, that I think that if there are others present who belong to the Communist Party or any other of the proscribed organisations they should not wait here, but their own consciences should tell them to resign. I hope if there are any present, that they will take that step. I can say that I have given my support to the Russians as far as I could. I do not interfere with anybody's form of government, but I do say this, when I belong to any organisation I believe in sticking to the rules and when I cannot stand to the rules I resign.

Mr. M. R. Jones: I think that the T.U.C. should alter that rule.

Cllr. Arthur Smith: If the T.U.C. alters the rule then I will welcome Mr Everall back.

Mr. H. G. Parker: I think we are looking at this matter from a very narrow point of view. Mr. Everall has done a lot for this Trades Council. I am going to move that we send a resolution to the T.U.C. asking that this rule shall be amended as quickly as possible. In doing this thing to-night, although it is by rule, we are certainly playing into the hands of the Tory Party, which has been one of our biggest enemies throughout the trade union movement.

The Chairman: We cannot ask the

BOROUGH OF KIDDERMINSTER

Information For The Public In The Event Of Invasion

The following is supplemental to the information given in the pamphlets distributed by the Government informing the public what to do if invasion comes:—

1. A LOCAL COMMITTEE has been set up under the Chairmanship of the Mayor, and this Committee will make all arrangements possible under invasion conditions for the welfare of the inhabitants.

2. IF the necessity for action arises, the Committee will require the assistance of many persons in carrying out special work required to be done, and all able-bodied persons who are not engaged on essential work will be asked to REGISTER THEIR NAMES AND ADDRESSES at the TOWN HALL, when they will be directed to the job for which they are most suited.

3. FOODSTUFFS are stored in the district sufficient to maintain the population for some weeks, but as there will undoubtedly be some dislocation of the transport and distribution services, you are advised to KEEP ENOUGH FOOD AND WATER in your house to enable you to maintain the family for 48 hours.

4. YOU are asked to continue in your usual occupations as long as you possibly can, and it is essential that you KEEP OFF THE ROADS so as not to hamper preparations being made for defence. You should KEEP UNDER COVER AT NIGHT.

5. SHOULD the DISTRIBUTION OF NEWS through the usual channels become dislocated, arrangements have been made to issue official bulletins, which will be posted on the official notice boards throughout the town, and also conveyed to you by other means. DO NOT SPREAD NEWS WHICH IS NOT OFFICIAL, as this is a fifth column trick designed to help the enemy.

6. IF YOU ARE IN DOUBT as to what you should do, get in touch with your Warden or the Police whom you know, and either will give you advice on your problem and help you as far as lies in their power.

7. YOUR DUTY is to:—KEEP CALM, BE PATIENT, AVOID PANIC, and carry out the instructions given from time to time by the Invasion Committee, the Members of which are:—

The Mayor and Deputy Mayor of the Borough
Alderman A. E. Meredith, J.P.
Lt.-Col. F. D. H. Burcher
Councillor F. R. Stone
Chief Constable (Mr. H. Hodgkinson)
Controller (Capt. Geo. Rainsford, O.B.E.)
Food Executive Officer (Col. J. H. Thursfield, M.C., T.D.)
The Commander of 6th Worcs. Batt. Home Guard (Lt.-Col. R. W. A. Painter, M.C.)

J. H. THURSFIELD,
Town Clerk.

21st August, 1942.

"TO BE CALLED FOR"

A Visit to a Day Nursery

At one end of the large garden I found the Day Nursery. The little folk were playing happily in the sand-pit under the apple trees that golden morning, and Nurse Harrison was teaching 14-months-old June to fill a tiny bucket with leaves. She came forward to greet me.

"O, yes, we are expecting you," she said, as I introduced myself. "Will you come this way?" I followed her through the building to meet Mrs. H. Spencer-Sales who is the nurse-in-charge. She welcomed me brightly, and, for a little while, we sat in her office and talked about the Nursery, its service, and its possibilities. Mrs. Spencer-Sales is an enthusiast. Her engaging personality radiates kindness and friendliness, and it is quite evident that she thoroughly enjoys her work. Over a cup of tea (which I found very welcome after my long walk) I learned some interesting facts concerning the creche.

Conducted under the supervision of Dr. Wyndham Parker of Worcester, it is a unit in the Worcester County Council Nursery Scheme, and is the pioneer nursery of the Kidderminster district. Opened on July 12th, it is devoted exclusively to the service of war-workers, and has accommodation for 30 children between the ages of one and five. Seventeen are already in attendance. The creche is open daily, except Saturdays.

THE STAFF

The staff includes Mrs. H. Spencer-Sales (nurse-in-charge), Nurse Jean Harrison (Norland-trained) and a rota of helpers, principally from the W.V.S., who give their time voluntarily. Dr. McEvett (who also gives her services voluntarily) visits the nursery at least once a week for inspection, etc.

Because mothers must be at work on 8 a.m. the staff is on duty early, and the little folk are fed and cared for throughout the day until mothers call for them just after 5 p.m. The food, prepared and cooked at a near-by canteen, is sent to the nursery in special hygenic containers. Meals are varied as much as possible, vegetables and milk naturally playing an important part in the diet.

All the children attending the creche have been inoculated against diphtheria — a wise precaution to which mothers have readily agreed.

The little people are divided into two groups—the "tinies" (between one and two years) and the two-to-four-year-olds.

"Now," said Mrs. Spencer-Sales, "Would you like to see the building and the children?"

I had already made a mental note of the cream and blue colour scheme of her office and, to my delight, found that it was used throughout the entire nursery. Surely no scheme could be more suitable or charming! I later learned that an architect with a flair for modern ideas had converted and decorated the building.

Next to Nurse's office was the isolation room. Though, as yet, there has been no occasion to use it, a room of this description is obviously a necessity. There was a small cot with blankets (blue of course!) and other equipment; and a convenient window connecting the isolation room with the office was useful for observation purposes. The staff retiring room adjoined.

One of the most important rooms at the nursery was the wash-room, where little folk are taught to be as useful and self-reliant as possible. The "tinies" have their own bath-room and rest-room and are washed and cared for by Nurse Harrison but the two-to-four-year-olds are taught greater independence and, under tactful supervision they wash themselves.

Along the wall on one side were rows of little pegs, each having an animal token pasted above it. On the pegs hung individual towels, and facecloths, and on a shelf above, were [illegible]

"HOLIDAY[S AT HOME]"

Conclu[ded]

Saturday ni[ght] "Holidays at [Home]" its success ... satisfaction to the launching the project. the scheme ... The entertain[ments] high order ... tions drew ... Admission, ... all, but bowls competitions while at the ground the ... Mitchells and one of the be[st] season.

Over three ... the children's interest of ... amusements ... the unusual ... the various ... much a comp... the average ... as it was ... played for the ...

Those who ... their holiday ... well as patr... satisfaction ... feature was a ... unity of pur... way to happ...

[BRI...]

A second ... petition was ... noon, and on ... large number ... interesting ... Kenneth Nic... Street, and ... a play-off wa... of the previo... Booton, 108 ... and fourth ... Cyril Priest. The winner's was 15.

Miss Elsie ... staged the fin... certs they ha... "Holidays at ... the Town Ha... noon. There ... ance and th... enthusiastical...

An open co... held on ... attracted a la... including se... including the ... by Lady Ward ... in the breez... Mr. Frank A... Proctor were ... keen competi... emerged the ... 28 and he wa... of 15s. (a Sav... he generousl... president of ... to the four ... the Shelter ... sporting gest... cocks and Mr ... for second pl... decided again ... sented Mr. B... second prize ... has a gold c... Mr. Sam Tyl... years ago w... brook Olymp... they created ... seven cups in ... people will ... an umpire ... Public Scho... League cricke... chairman of ... will present ... afternoon wh... Old Pals to ...

[ST. G...]

The conclu... pairs compe... before, were ... Play started ... presence of ... number of s... the Mayor ... which took ... certificates. his indebted... (Mr. J. Gilch...

ST. GEORGE'S OLD PALS

Welcome Home to Mr. W. H. Mountford

Gratitude for recovery from a serious operation was the explanation given by Mr. Will Mountford, hon. treasurer of St. George's Old Pals' Society, in entertaining members and friends on Saturday to a war time tea. The company included Mrs. G. R. Woodward, president and patron, and the Rev. B. J. Isaac, M.B.E., chaplain, who was home on leave, and others. An apology was received from the Rev. P. J. Martin, who was on holiday.

Mr. W. Cox who took the chair in the unavoidable absence of the octogenarian Chairman, Mr. E. Gwynne, said they were delighted to see Mr. Mountford back again. Another pleasant surprise was to see their president, Mrs. Woodward.

Mrs. Woodward responding to a

MINISTER RETIRING

Farewell Gifts to Rev. John Kinnish

The Rev. John Kinnish completed his ministry as superintendent in the Kidderminster and Stourport Circuit on Sunday, preaching at both services in the George Street Methodist Church, of which he has pastoral charge. Both services were well attended, notably that in the evening, when the church was nearly full and a real Methodist atmosphere of fellowship prevailed. Mr. Kinnish preached in the morning on "The abiding Christ," stressing particularly the influence of Christ on civilisation and in Christian experience.

In the evening a special feature was the heartiness of the congregational singing and the fine solo work of Mrs. Morris of Bewdley, in "How lovely are Thy dwellings" and "Abide with me," and Mr. Tom

Cllr. Arthur Smith: The only exception I can see is that it did not go through the proper committee rather than go through open Council. That would have been the correct procedure.

The Mayor: It is more a matter of courtesy than anything else.

The report was adopted.

Ald. Eddy moved the adoption of the Medical Officer of Health's report (for nine weeks) which showed that there were five cases in Hayley Green Isolation Hospital from Kidderminster.

DAY NURSERIES

The report of the Maternity and Child Welfare Committee was moved by its chairman Cllr. J. Andrews who referred to the question of day nurseries for children. He read a list of names of persons who were supposed to want day nurseries for their children and which had been submitted to the Council for investigation. The names were submitted as being those of workers at a certain factory. Inquiries had proved that none of the persons worked at the place and that they had actually been approached in their own homes by a person from the factory to put their names down to swell the figures. Eleven names were given, but one name was included in the previous list considered by the Council, so actually there were ten. Of these five would use the nursery, one could not be traced two were expectant mothers, and three others had merely been asked to put down their names to swell the total. Inquiries had proved that those three had not the slightest idea of going to work, and were not likely to do so. "I think," said Cllr. Andrews "that there is something wrong with this nursery business. People are trying to press it when to my mind, there is no need for a day nursery. If that need should come, we should be only too happy to go on with it, but in such circumstances as these, I think you will agree that it is quite impossible. Even the names submitted did not materialise. This matter has given us no end of trouble in making the necessary investigations."

Cllr. Wilson said he thought there was a need for kindergarten schools for children between three and four abeyance.

DEFINITELY NO DEMAND

Ald. Eddy: I raised this matter in the Council 18 months ago and very extensive inquiries were made. It was definitely proved that there was no demand and in view of the report which has been submitted by Cllr. Andrews this morning that has also been confirmed. At Redditch, where they have 40 children, there is a wage bill alone of £850 a year, and until there is a demand in Kidderminster, I think the best thing to do is to let the matter lie in obeyance.

Ald. Tolley: We gave our reasons at a recent meeting why we have not established day nurseries. The unfortunate thing is that certain people seem to have nothing better to do than to try and pour ridicule on the town of Kidderminster to establish a day nursery. You know where it has all originated from. How long are we going to tolerate these people coming down here trying to establish day nurseries for which there is no demand. We have spent no end of time to find out if there is any need for them. Cllr. Andrews has given us plain facts. We are no longer going to continue to allow people to attack this town publicly in an effort to make us start a day nursery in defiance of the fact that there is no need for one. I should ignore any other appeals to establish such a thing until the right appeal comes from the mothers themselves.

Cllr. Chadwick: Regarding Cllr. Wilson's remark about kindergarten schools that is irrelevant to this matter and is in the hands of the Education Committee.

The Mayor: I may say that a deputation called upon me on this matter, and I told them if they submitted names, I would be able to see if there was any demand. I quite agree with all that has been said and especially with what Ald. Tolley has said.

Cllr. Andrews: People do not realise

"A JOURNALIST'S REBUKE"

TRIBUTE FROM EARL BALDWIN— "I RESPECT YOU"

A letter which appeared in the "Kidderminster Shuttle" last week from the pen of one of our reporters, Mr. Walter Watson, protesting against an article which appeared in the "Sunday Pictorial," making a personal attack upon Lord Baldwin when, in his years of retirement, he very kindly came out of his house to open the flower and vegetable show at Stourport, has caused much favourable comment from over a wide area. Mr. Watson was not writing from a political angle, but confined his observations to the importance of maintaining a decent standard of journalism.

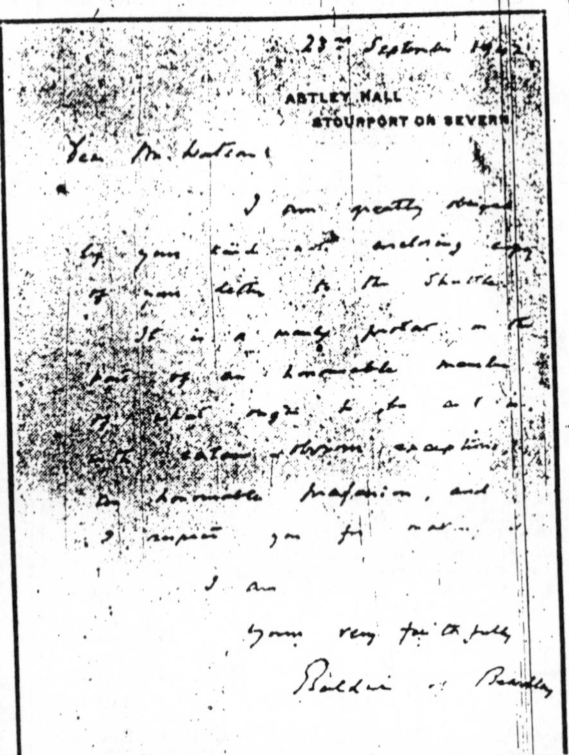

23rd September 1942

ASTLEY HALL
STOURPORT ON SEVERN

Dear Mr. Watson

I am greatly obliged by your kind note enclosing copy of your letter to the Shuttle.

It is a manly protest on the part of an honourable member of what ought to be and is, with certain obvious exceptions, an honourable profession, and I respect you for making it.

I am

Yours very faithfully

Baldwin of Bewdley

The letter is as follows — "23rd September 1942. Astley Hall, Stourport-on-Severn. Dear Mr. Watson I am greatly obliged by your kind note enclosing copy of your letter to the 'Shuttle.' It is a manly protest on the part of an honourable member of what ought to be and is, with certain obvious exceptions, an honourable profession, and I respect you for making it. I am yours very faithfully, Baldwin of Bewdley."

On Thursday Mr. Watson received the letter shown in facsimile above from Earl Baldwin, and below we give some of the number of expressions of opinion on the matter.

A JOURNALIST REBUKED

To the Editor

Sir,—The "Shuttle" has been my weekly companion every year since

MOTOR TYRES

To the Editor

Sir,—Referring to the letter by Mr. J. Southern in last week's "Shuttle," I would like to add a few words about motor tyres in local road blocks. I believe there have been more than 900 used in this way locally. What is the weight, I wonder?—10, 15 or 20 tons? I frequently pass several of these road blocks and think how small was my

Security For Everybody In Britain

PLAN TO ABOLISH POVERTY

Below we give a brief summary of the Governing Principles submitted by the Trades Union Congress to the Beveridge Committee on Social Services.

There should be an inclusive scheme to cover unemployment, sickness, maternity, non-compensatable accidents, invalidity, old age, blindness, death and widowhood and orphanhood.

There should be a flat rate of benefit which for a commencement should be £2 per week plus dependants' allowances, this to be the amount payable to adults in respect of unemployment, sickness, maternity, invalidity, non-compensatable accidents, widowhood, blindness and old age.

UNEMPLOYMENT BENEFIT should be implemented with a scheme for transfer allowances (lodging, removal, etc.) to make it possible for people to move when their industry has closed down.

WIDOWHOOD.—A young widow of working age with no children should not continue to receive benefit if she finds employment, but should inherit her husband's insurance rights under the scheme and have equal employment opportunities with men.

OLD AGE PENSIONS should begin at 65 for men and 60 for women as at present, and the pension should only be paid on retirement from work at the determined age. If a pensioner returns to work he should forfeit the pension whilst working.

MATERNITY.—The cash benefit of £2 per week should be paid for the maternity period, subject to any scheme which may be worked out.

DEATH.—The amount in view is £20 on the death of the insured person.

[illegible]HOOD.—The figure in mind is 15s. per week up to the age of 16 or as long as the child remains at school.

Benefit should continue during the whole period of the contingency provided against.

The scheme should come under the direction of one Ministry with special arrangements for health services.

A comprehensive national medical service covering everything that medical science can command for prevention and cure of sickness should be provided by the nation and be made available to everybody in the State.

To implement these recommendations, Parliamentary Legislation is necessary. Your active interest and support is the bulwark upon which this Legislation will be built.

ISSUED BY THE KIDDERMINSTER AND DISTRICT TRADES COUNCIL

OBITUARY

MR. T. R. BADLAND

As briefly stated last week, Mr. Thomas Renshaw Badland, of "Fern Villa," Somerleyton Avenue, passed peacefully away unexpectedly on Thursday, October 1st, in the Kidderminster Hospital, following an operation. The greatest sympathy is felt with his wife and two daughters in their loss.

Mr. Badland was 58 and a Manchester man who came to Worcestershire in his early days. Of a quiet disposition, he had a useful record of service. Formerly leading chorister at Stone Parish Church, he served with the Worcestershire Regiment in the Western Front in the last war and was awarded the Military Medal with Bar. On demobilisation he returned to Kidderminster and began business as a market gardener. Since last year he has been engaged at a maintenance station and was a member of "F" Company, Home Guard. For many years he has been an active church worker in St. George's parish as Sunday school teacher, chorister, and churchwarden both at St. Andrew's Mission Church and later at the restored Parish Church. He showed interest in the Young Men's Club and other parochial organisations, and was people's churchwarden and joint hon. treasurer for several years. A member of Kidderminster Club and Institute and a keen chess player, he often played in the club's teams.

MISS ENID PARSONS

The death took place, on Saturday, September 26th, of Miss Enid Parsons (only daughter of Mr. Harold Parsons, of New Rd., Caunsall). The funeral was conducted at Cookley Church on Thursday, October 1st, by the Rev. W. L. Gutch. The chief mourners were: Mr. H. Parsons (father), Mr. George Parsons (brother), Mrs. Walker (grandmother), Mrs. Toone (aunt), Mrs. Evans (aunt) H. Evans (nephew), Mrs. Page (friend), Mrs. Taylor (friend), Mrs. Cyril Davis (cousin).

Wreaths were sent by father; brother George; Mr. and Mrs. Cyril Davis, Mrs. and Mr. A. Smith and Brian, Mr. and Mrs. Beaves; Mr. and Mrs. A. J. Houseman; Mr. W. Page; Mr. and Mrs. H. Page; Mr. and Mrs. Woodward, Norman and Maud; Mrs. Powell, Mrs. Shenton, and Miss Derby; Jack; Mrs. Pagett and all at Blackwell St.; friends from 26, 27, and 29, Blackwell St.; uncle, aunt, Gert, Bert, Harold and Edna; Gran and auntie Agnes; fellow workmates at the Fellowship and workmates; Steel Stampings; babies, Edith and Albert Taylor; patients at Hill Top Sanatorium, Bromsgrove; Mr. and Mrs. Barker and customers; Anchor Inn, Caunsall; Mrs. Gwillian and Mary.

MISS LOUISA OAKES

The funeral of Miss Louisa Oakes (daughter of the late Mr. and Mrs. William Oakes, of 13, St. George's

LETTERS TC

TRANSPORT OF TROOPS

To the Editor

Sir,—Under the above heading [illegible] I. C. Barker [illegible] motorist [illegible] V.T.S. [illegible] have been conveying members of His Majesty's Forces, coming home on leave, and stranded en route after Public Transport has shut down at night.

Had I. C. Barker paid his tribute and left it at that,—no comment would have been forthcoming from elsewhere—but he went on to add that his "good natured" transporters belonging to Birmingham and Stourbridge organisations had told him that Kidderminster motorists had failed to co-operate in the scheme.

Doubtless he repeated that slander in ignorance,—but I am afraid that those who originated it—belied their good nature and marred their good works.

The facts are as follows.—Early in 1940 I was asked to create a Kidderminster V.T.S. group and by April of that year we had an active organisation maintaining a regular service.

From that date until Petrol and Rubber restrictions in August 1942 caused cessation of activities for all groups,—the Kidderminster organisation made over 900 journeys, carried [illegible] members of the forces to their homes and covered just over 27,000 miles—all between the hours of 10.0 p.m. and 4.0 a.m., fog, rain, snow, or moonlight.

Our ultimate collecting commitments covered the following—all service passengers arriving in the town by the last train into Kidderminster from the South, all ditto arriving on the last train into Stourbridge Junction Station from the North, and all ditto leap frogged into Kidderminster Police Station from New Street, Birmingham by the joint activities of the Birmingham and Stourbridge groups.

Our delivery destinations went as far afield as Tenbury, Cleobury Mortimer, Ludlow, Bridgnorth, Wolverhampton, Droitwich, Worcester, and a host of lesser known places in the vicinities. All these activities of the Kidderminster group were well known to the Stourbridge organisers.

It would seem, sir, that Kidderminster V.T.S. members have not only hidden their identities but also their good works, and while I do not take this opportunity to mention individual names, I do take the occasion to express thanks and gratitude both to them and the Borough Police Staff whose co-operation has been invaluable to the successful operation of the Kidderminster V.T.S.

FRANK R. STONE

A NEW ZEALANDER'S IMPRESSIONS

To the Editor

Sir,—In last week's issue of the "Shuttle" appeared a letter from a gentleman resident here, but giving a Northern Ireland address.

This gentleman objected to my impressions of Ulster, given, he says, "in a series of articles headed 'A New Zealander's Impressions.'" May I remind the writer of this letter that the only article on Ireland from my pen appearing to that date was one on Londonderry?

As for my supposed attack on the climate, in a previous account I happened to mention of the Northern Irish that "I learned to love the people and hate the climate." Am I to take it then that the gentleman in question considers my opinion of the weather of more consequence than my regard for the people?

A TILT AT

To

Sir,—I am
writer who s
Kidderminster
evacuees and
somewhere to
and it seems
opportunity fo
for those with
mutual advan

TO THOSE

To

Sir,—It take
a world, but
few who tilt
This town, n
of their inc
butter, and
under a nom
afraid to dec
should try t
their surroun
others to m
come from t
have experien
does not know
I have found
a friendly am
glory of one
counties

Tilters ma
and shame
grateful.

Aggboro Cr

A TILT AT

Sir,—May I
ate Mr. Taih'
I have been
of "Dear Ol
over a perio
entitled to
the people o
first went to
stranger and
shall never
received then
upon Kidde
town

I will close
ing lines:

"Twas t
days
For that
The peop
The kind
How ofte
griev
While in

Starbotton.

AID

To

Sir,—Stalin
Cassidy ano
thought
offensive be
Not long ago
ference in
present were
Laval, Degre
leagues of c
instructed to
against Brit
and to sprea
German prep
seaboard.

Those in
the death o
the parties
ment, the
tionists, w
England's h
would appe
applied thes
own conduct

How can
front when
tives hob-no
Bank for In
Wendel Will
of the aver
these peopl
needed "p
dilly-dally
Europe rush

premiers who were
in a former war,
on the same side
Nazi aggression.
really a review of
the war and the
ugh which Great
ssed, especially on
lamentable fall of
as the text of the
cerned there were
in it, and Smuts,
considered as an
ther a man who
mple soldier, gave
plans away. But
of the speech was
ed like a tonic on
e British Common-
a masterly survey
effort which Great
ade in this war,
e air and on the
course of the war
upon in the shape
announcement, but
Smuts did indicate
defensive war of the
about over, and
approaching the
n on the war fronts
e fronts in enemy
ituation is ripening
developments."

Committee. — A
alled on Sunday of
o support the form-
lo-Soviet committee
ter. Most of the
affiliated to the
were invited. Mr.
ll, Secretary of the
rty in Kiddermin-
brief outline of the
Anglo-Soviet com-
that its chief func-
ep before the people
the full meaning
oviet Alliance. The
chairman (Miss M.
F. Bayliss, respec-
lected pro tem, and
enerally that there
y of support in the
ng will be held on
mber 6th, at the
Hall, and a sub-com-
elected to arrange
as decided that a
be called of repre-
m every organisa-
n to be held in the
ittee Room, Town
n 27th October, at
ayor has kindly co-
ida.

scholars who are members is little more than half the number at school. Locally the schools are doing exceedingly well. Addresses are being delivered by the honorary secretary, and excellent support is being given to the movement by the teachers. Associations continue to be formed: Kings Estate (secretary, Mrs. K. M. Simpson); Woodward Road (secretary, Mrs. E. Brown, 45, Woodward Road); Blakeshall No. 2 (secretary, Miss L. M. Cheshire, The Barn House, Wolverley). At the High School the credit amount of stamps has had to be increased from £25 to £50. Locally £5,464 was invested in Certificates last week, and £4,465 in deposits. The grand total now invested is £2,412,793. Sir Theodore Chambers, vice-president of the National Savings Committee will speak in the Council Chamber on Friday, October 30th, at 6.30 p.m. All savings workers are invited.

The New Christian Council.—A lively debate took place on Monday in the New Meeting Vestry on the motion "that this meeting considers that our Church should not be represened on the United Christian Council." The motion was proposed by Mr. J. Bill, and seconded by Mr. W. J. Church, the leaders of the opposition being Mr. H. S. Beresford and Mr. H. Winbury. Points made in support of the motion were that the New Meeting's traditional independency would be limited by such an association; that in any event the Council could serve no useful purpose; and that the word "Christian" in its title was ambiguous, the Church of England having some years ago officially limited its meaning to include only those who believed in the deity of Jesus. The opposers retorted that doctrinal questions were not involved; that the Council was being formed for the practical purpose of applying Christian moral principles to the town's life by "prodding" the proper authorities into making necessary reforms and improvements; and that if others did not exclude the New Meeting there was no reason why it should stand aloof. The motion was defeated by a majority of nine votes. The presence of Mr. A. G. Mumford and Mr. Carter, of St. Mary's, was appreciated—the former taking part in the debate.

... Speke, of Maripool Lane, Kidderminster, informs us that the sum of £113 15s. 3d. was realised as a result of the effort promoted a few weeks ago at the Franche Church Hall, in aid of the Merchant Navy. Mr. Weavers, of Stourbridge Road, was kind enough to give a duck (won by A. Warner), and a bag of potatoes (won by J. Bentley). These gifts realised £15, and added to the fine total already assured. Mrs. Powell's gift of a duck was secured by K. Hudson, and the spoons by Violet Prosser. Sergeant Speke and P.C. Radcliffe are to be specially thanked for their able assistance. It will be recalled that earlier in the summer Mrs. Powell and friends raised the sum of £125 for the P.O.W.R.A.

The Fighting French.—Members of the Association of friends of the Fighting French met in the Library Hall on Thursday. The Colonel de Lagatinerie addressed the gathering on the occasion of the society's second annual meeting. Mrs. Beakbane presided. With her were the Colonel de Lagatinerie, the Mayor (Alderman O. W. Davies), Mrs. Nairac (secretary), Mrs. Whitehouse (treasurer), Mrs. Lamb, Miss. Knowles, Mrs. R. S. Brinton, Miss. J. Anton, and M. Heritier. The chairman welcomed the speaker and the Mayor. The Secretary and Treasurer presented their reports. The Colonel de Lagatinerie congratulated members on the splendid lead they had given to other branches, and asked for increased membership because France was in great need of friends. Their spirit and courage were not sleeping. They were live flames, and resistance within the country was steadily growing. France would arise again. The association, under the leadership of General de Gaulle, was giving great help. Last year there were 17 branches and 8,000 members; this year the numbers had increased to 34 branches and 15,000 members. Great demands were being made on the finances which looked after the welfare of French people in this country, and assisted mothers with young children, aged people, prisoners of war, the French Merchant Navy, and French fishermen. Thanks to the speaker were expressed by the Mayor and Mr. G. S. Tomkinson. We hope to give a fuller report in our next issue.

POPULAR FIREMAN RETIRES

Mr. Harry Arthur Owen, Fire Brigade Station Officer, will retire this week-end after 20 years' service. A son of the late Mr. George Owen, of Franche, he attended the village school when Miss Grant was the headmistress. He was also a chorister in St. Barnabas Church choir, when the late Rev. T. P. Monahan was priest-in-charge and the late Mr. R. E. Grove organist-choirmaster. On leaving school he was with Dr. E. H. Addenbrooke and then became chauffeur to the late Dr. Bertram Addenbrooke. In the last war he served in the Motor Transport Service for four years and 10 months, and while in France and Belgium was staff car driver to Brigadier-General Tredcroft, and later acted as despatch rider to the 37th Division. Upon demobilisation he returned to Kidderminster and was a taxi driver before joining the Borough Fire Brigade as a "retained" man in February, 1922. After the carpet manufacturers and spinners of the town presented the Town Council with a Dennis fire engine in 1923, Mr. Owen was appointed driver-mechanic and for several years had charge of the equipment at the rear of the Police Station yard, which was formerly the home of the Fire Brigade for generations. There he also had charge of the first (green) borough ambulance, presented to the town through Mr. W. Todd, a former councillor. When the new Fire Station was opened he became whole-time resident station officer, remaining there until the new N.F.S. came into operation. He holds the National Fire Brigade Medal with bar and expects to receive the silver medal for 20 years' service.

Mr. Owen, who now lives at 28, Worcester Road, married Miss Ada Lewis, of Wolverhampton, who has been a splendid helpmeet at the station recreation room and at numerous functions in the Town Hall and elsewhere promoted to raise funds for the Fire Brigade Benevolent Institution and other causes.

Mr Owen has attended over 400 outbreaks of fire, including the following notable ones: St George's Parish Church (November, 1922), Richard Hughes, Ltd, Park Lane timber yard, Hagley Hall, Hurcott Paper Mill, Broome's spinning mill, Brintons, Ltd canteen, jam factory, starch house, etc. Witley Court, Mawley Hall, near Cleobury Mortimer, Holbrook's Vinegar Works, Stourport, Brockencote Hall Chaddesley Corbett, Bewdley timber yard, Pensax Saw Mills Winterdyne, Bewdley, The Elms, Abberley, Jelleyman's Carpet Factory, Franche Village Club, Candle Factory, Radcliffes Cross Brewery.

Fireman Owen and his colleagues have assisted at Hospital carnival parades in Kidderminster, Stourport, Bewdley, Stourbridge, and Bromsgrove.

good wishes, and blankets, sea-boot stockings, socks, helmets, etc., knitted by the children and staff, are sent regularly to the crew. A photograph of the former skipper, Captain H. Harrison, a treasured possession, has been framed and hangs in a prominent place in the hall, and interesting letters are received from time to time from Chief Petty Officer J. Beecroft.

There was tremendous excitement at the school when, at morning assembly, the headmaster (Mr. C. V. Rose) announced the success achieved by the "Lovania," and the building rang with cheers and prolonged clapping. The incident was explained and the children thrilled to the knowledge that their "very own ship" had been in action and given such an excellent account of herself. A telegram of congratulation was immediately sent to the "Lovania" expressing the school's pride in her success.

When a "Shuttle" reporter called crowds of eager little people and a delighted staff extended a cheery welcome and readily told all there was to tell. It was learned that, prior to the adoption of the trawler, the Foley Park School had helped the High School's ship, the "Glen Kidston," by sending contributions of blankets, but when Captain H. Harrison was transferred from that ship to the "Lovania" it was decided to adopt the trawler as the school's "own ship."

Collections of knitted garments, etc., for Christmas are now well in hand and will be despatched to the crew shortly. Kidderminster will join in the felicitations of the children and staff of the school, and send H.M.T. "Lovania" heartfelt congratulations and good wishes for jolly sailing, good hunting, and every success.

PETROL LORRY OVERTURNS

Hundreds of gallons of petrol ran into the road when a lorry, descending the incline of the railway bridge at Foley Park, between Kidderminster and Stourport, on Wednesday crashed over the footpath towards a garage, knocked down a pump, overturned, and finally stopped with its nose in the garage doorway. Police and N.F.S. officials were soon on the scene, and all passing vehicles were stopped within 50 yards, and the drivers and occupants instructed to put out pipes and cigarettes. The garage is that of the Foley Park Service, the proprietor of which is Mr. H. Pocknell. Firemen also poured large quantities of water and sand on to the petrol. The driver and his mate had a miraculous escape by managing to crawl out of the cab.

MAYOR MAKING DAY

ALD. L. TOLLEY'S CALL FOR A NEW VISION

THE election of Alderman Louis Tolley as Mayor of Kidderminster, in succession to Alderman O. W. Davies, took place on Monday in the Council Chamber. The entrance stairs to the Council Chamber were decorated with a magnificent display of chrysanthemums, and there were also floral decorations on the central table in the Council Chamber itself.

The public gallery was crowded and many prominent Kidderminster people had to stand owing to all the seating accommodation being filled. There was a number of boys and girls from the local schools, including the Grammar School and High School.

Promptly as the Town Hall clock struck the hour of 12 the Mayor entered in his crimson robe, wearing his chain of office, accompanied by the Town Clerk (Mr. J. H. Thursfield) in wig and gown. Each wore their war medals.

The Mayor: The first business of the meeting is the election of the Mayor of Kidderminster for the ensuing year.

PROPOSAL FOR NEW MAYOR

Cllr G. S. Chadwick, who was dressed in Home Guard khaki, then rose and said: "At a time such as this when we are about to write another page in our municipal history, I should like to make myself perfectly clear in proposing the name of Ald. Tolley as mayor and leading citizen of this borough and to say that we meet to-day to honour the man and not his politics. At this time of the year we sometimes find the fogs limiting our visibility, but we do not anticipate that those fogs should enter into our municipal affairs. Should I for one moment become politico-economically minded, I am sure that my colleagues on this Council will fully understand when I say, as past records show, that my association with that of the Conservative and Unionist cause in this borough is of longer standing than that of any sitting member of this Council, yet at the same time I can propose Ald. Tolley as Mayor and Chief Magistrate of this town, because I appreciate his efforts on behalf of this borough—(applause). I am not unmindful of many influences. For instance, I think there is something after all to be said for the spirit of the old school tie; that spirit that teaches people that the game of cricket does not consist of being bat in hand all the time, but it teaches us that we have to field as well as bat for the team, for the side that we represent. We in this borough have watched for many years Ald. Tolley taking his part on the municipal cricket field. We have seen him in the long field, we have seen him in the slips, we have seen him at mid-on, we have seen him at cover-point. I am not going to say, Mr. Mayor, that on occasions in the past we ... Ald. Tolley

The Mayor, Ald. L. Tolley

Kidderminster has been very fortunate in the men who have served the town as chief citizen. They have been men of international repute, like Rowland Hill, and if you look down the long list of mayors in this Chamber you will see the names of men whose life work has made Kidderminster industry, and Kidderminster itself, famous all over the world. I do submit that in electing Ald. Tolley this morning to the highest post that you can give him in the borough that the present election will be no exception to the rule. His undoubted zeal, his absolute sincerity, and his unwavering support for the causes in which he believes with his heart and soul, as well as his business ability, will stand him in good stead during the coming 12 months. I am confident that when he leaves office he will leave the name Tolley amongst the long list of men who have served Kidderminster so well. I have great pleasure in seconding the name of Ald. Tolley as Mayor for the coming year—(applause).

The Mayor: Any other nominations?

There was no other nomination.

The Mayor: I will put it to the meeting that Ald. L. Tolley be Mayor of Kidderminster for the ensuing year.

The resolution was carried unanimously amidst applause from all parts of the Council Chamber.

The newly-elected Mayor, with his sponsors, Cllr. Chadwick and Cllr. Ferguson, together with the retiring Mayor and the Town Clerk, then left the Council Chamber and entered the Mayor's Parlour. Here the Chief Constable divested Ald. Davies of his chain of office and placed it on Ald. Tolley, who also assumed the crimson mayoral robe. The party then returned to the Council Chamber where the new Mayor was loudly applauded on his entry.

NEW MAYOR'S VISION

The new Mayor, Ald. Tolley, then re-entered the Council Chamber, wearing the Mayoral crimson robe and chain of office, together with his mover and seconder, Cllrs Chadwick and Ferguson. He then took the oath and signed it witnessed by the Town Clerk and followed by taking the oath as a Justice of the Peace for the Borough.

The Mayor: Cllr. Chadwick and Cllr. Ferguson, aldermen and councillors, and ladies and gentlemen, to-day, you have honoured me by electing me as Mayor of this my native town for the ensuing year. I convey to you my sincere thanks for the honour thus conferred. I wish to thank most sincerely the proposer and the seconder of the resolution to make me Mayor, as well as to thank all present for the manner in which that nomination was received. Time was when the newly elected Mayor gave a resume of the work of the Council during

I can see, when the war is over, a vision of the future world. I see our country filled with happy homes, with firesides of content, the foremost in all the world. I see a world without a slave, man again is free, and where all these powers of earth and air are the tireless toilers for the human race. I see a world of peace, adorned with every form of art, while lips are rich with words of love and truth and where labour reaps its true reward. I see a race of people without disease of flesh or brain, and, as I look, life lengthens, and over all the grey dawn shines the eternal star of human hope. The cynic will say—a dream—a Utopian dream. But no. Some months ago, two great statesmen met in mid-Atlantic. They did not need to discuss war aims or war strategy. They met to discuss a new world, when the war was over, and out of their deliberations came the Atlantic Charter—the world that is to be. To the members of this Kidderminster Town Council, to the chairman and members of the Housing and Town Planning Committee, and of the Health Committee, and of the Estates Committee, I would say "Let your vision be my vision," because I regard that Atlantic Charter as the foundation stone out of which my vision came into being. You can plan now, and I hope you will plan now for the world that is to be.

I look forward to my year of office with every confidence, born of the knowledge that I shall receive the whole-hearted support of every member of this Council, and of its officials and workmen. But more than that, out of the many kind expressions given to me during the past few weeks since it was known that I was to occupy this position, I am satisfied to feel that the people of this town are eager and anxious to aid and assist in every possible way, not only myself, the members of this Council, and the town in particular, that we might make Kidderminster the greatest city in the world. And why not? I can only hope in my endeavours during the coming year that I shall maintain the dignity of the office, so that when my time comes to hand over, you will be able to say and say sincerely, that you are in every way satisfied and that the choice which you made to-day has not been misplaced—(loud applause).

TRIBUTE TO EX-MAYOR

Ald. A. E. Meredith: Some two years ago to-day, it was my privilege, and a very great pleasure, to submit a name to this Council for the choice of Mayor. I venture to suggest that subsequent events during the whole of that period—which has been a very trying and hard one indeed—have shewn that our choice was a wise one. In submitting the name of Osman W. Davies two years ago, it was from the fact that he had earned during his association with the council, by his ability and his devotion to public duties, together with the most courteous manner and keen business acumen, the right of nomination. The services he has rendered in his official capacity, as leader and chief magistrate of this borough, has amply repaid us for that nomination and choice—(hear hear). Having passed through the chair myself during peace time, I am in a position to know the enormous amount of duties entailed even in peace-time in that office. The layman has no conception whatever of the duties and the responsibilities of the Mayor. During the last two years with the war conditions which have prevailed, I suggest that no previous Mayor has had such a worrying and such a severe strain put upon him as Ald. Davies. I will not attempt to enumerate many of the things which he has done. The members of this Council know the amount he has done, but some of the most vital work he has put in has been in connection with the war, the Invasion and the Civil Defence committees. I happen to be an executive member of these two, and I can truthfully talk about the enormous time and energy Ald.

Quarterly Council Meeting

27th day of April, 1942

Your Committee beg to report on their proceedings during the past quarter as follows:

Water Supply, Stourport-on-Severn - The amount of water consumed by Stourport-on-Severn U.D.C. for the quarter ending 31st March, 1942 was 35,026,000 gallons, an increase over the last quarter of 2,102,000 gallons, and an increase of 6,368,000 gallons over the corresponding quarter last year.

Waterworks Extensions - The Minister of Health confirmed the Borough of Bewdley (Waterworks Pumping Station) Compulsory Purchase Order, 1941, on the 26th day of March, 1942. The order was confirmed as made by the Town Council in the first place, subject only to an undertaking being given to grant access between the fields lying on either side of the strip of land to be purchased for the access road to the Waterworks Pumping Station.

After the order had been confirmed negotiations for the purchase of the ground required in connection with the scheme were re-opened with the Owners and your Committee are glad to report that agreement has been reached for the purchase of all the ground required for the sum of Six hundred pounds (£600).

Your Committee recommend that authority be given for the Corporate Common Seal to be affixed in the presence of the Mayor and the Town Clerk to the conveyance and any other document that may be necessary in connection with the purchase of the ground coloured pink on the map marked Borough of Bewdley (Waterworks Pumping Station) Compulsory Purchase Order, 1941.

Permission was obtained for the Corporation to enter into possession before completion in view of the urgent need for the scheme to be completed as soon as possible and work was commenced on the new bore hole on Tuesday April the 14th, 1942. It will now also be possible to proceed with the erection of the chlorinator at the Waterworks Pumping Station.

British Restaurant - The British Restaurant has now been open for approximately two months and very satisfactory progress is being made. There has been a small but steady increase in the number of meals served, and very favourable reports have been received both from officials of the Ministry of Food and members of the general public who have taken advantage of the facilities offered.

Arrangements are being made with the Education Department of the Worcestershire County Council for the school children to be fed at the schools. It will be some time before these arrangements can be carried into effect but it is hoped that the result will be of advantage both to the school children and to the members of the public using the Restaurant.

A wireless has been provided in the dining room at the British Restaurant and a licence obtained from the Performing Rights Society permitting its use.

Your Committee are of the opinion that the excellent facilities and the reasonable prices charged at the British Restaurant are not generally

REPORT OF THE A.R.P. COMMITTEE

Quarterly Council Meeting 27thday of July, 1942

Your Committee beg to report on their proceedings during the past quarter as follows:

Civil Defence Exercise - A Civil Defence Exercise was held within the Borough on Wednesday, June 17th, when four incidents were staged. Several members of the Kidderminster Civil Defence Services were good enough to come over and act as umpires and submit comprehensive reports on the work of the Bewdley Civil Defence Services at the various incidents. One incident in particular was on a big scale and several services were in action simultaneously. The umpire stated in his report that the work at this incident was first class, and it certainly appears as a result of this A.R.P. Exercise that considerabl progress has been made by the Bewdley Civil Defence Services which have now reached a very satisfactory standard of efficiency.

Your Committee have resolved to hold another exercise towards the end of August as it is felt that these exercises serve a very useful purpose and should be held at regular intervals in order to provide reasonably frequent opportunities for the various services to practise operating together.

Messenger Service - Despite all attempts to recruit new volunteers for the Messenger Service the present number enrolled is very much below the authorised establishment. Since the last Quarterly Meeting of the Council a number of air training cadets have offered to turn out in the event of a raid in Bewdley and act as A.R.P. Messengers, but at least twelve more messengers are required for general duties, including A.R.P. Practices.

General Organization - After a conference at which the County A.R.P. Officer was present, your Committee resolved to effect a re-organization in the headquarters staff for Civil Defence in the Borough, and the following appointments have been made:

Senior Deputy Sub-Controller - Alderman H.N. Frost,
Additional Deputy Sub-Controllers - Alderman F.E. Mountford,
Councillor W. Harcourt Webb,
Councillor H.W. Windsor,
The Town Clerk,
The Borough Surveyor.

The office of Joint Executive Officers has been abolished and the Town Clerk has been appointed to act as Administrative Officer and the Borough Surveyor as Co-ordinating Officer. Mr. W.C. Bradley has been appointed as Training Officer and Mr. J.F. Hanglin as Deputy to Councillor H.W. Windsor, Officer in charge of the Report Centre.

Defence Regulation 29BA - The Chairman of your Committee, together with the Town Clerk and the Adjutant of the Bewdley Company of the Home Guard, attended a conference at the office of the Ministry of Labour and National Service at Kidderminster, when the direction of persons registering into the Home Guard and Civil Defence, in accordance with the provisions of Defence Regulation 29 BA, was considered, and it was agreed that men in the younger

Special Council Meeting   26th day of October, 1942.

Report of the General Purposes Committee

Your Committee beg to report on their proceedings during the past quarter as follows:

Invasion Committee - On the instructions of the Regional Commissioner an Invasion Committee has been set up by the Town Council for the Borough of Bewdley to ensure that the plans of the Military and Civilian Services within the area covered by the Committee have been formulated and are properly dove-tailed into a local defence scheme.

Several meetings of the Invasion Committee have already been held, and it is hoped that it will soon be possible to arrange for a public meeting at the Town Hall in order that the inhabitants of the Borough may be informed of the various tasks which they will be called upon to perform under invasion conditions.

Bus Shelter, Load Street - Your Committee have for some time past had under consideration the question of the provision of a bus shelter in Load Street. Arrangements have now been made with the Midland Red Bus Co., and Mitchell & Butlers Ltd., for the erection of a shelter at the side of the forecourt to the Angel Hotel, Load Street, by the present bus stop. It is hoped that the work will soon be put in hand and the shelter provided for the benefit of the inhabitants using the bus service before the advent of winter conditions.

Midland Red Bus Co. - Representations have been made to your Committee as a result of the restrictions on retail deliveries that the lack of a bus service running to the Bark Hill district occasions general hardship to inhabitants living in that district. Your Committee have made an application to the Midland Red Bus Co., asking for a bus service to be run up to the Bark Hill Council houses two or three times each day.

Your Committee have also drawn the attention of the Midland Red Bus Co., to the fact that several complaints have been received with regard to the time spent by buses waiting at the top of St. Anne's Church, Load Stree with a result that the buses eventually leave Bewdley in a great hurry and endeavour to make up time at the intervening stops between Bewdley and Kidderminster, and buses often move on before passengers wishing to alight have time to step right off the bus.

Bewdley Food Control Committee - Your Committee have had under consideration the provisions of the Food Control Committees (Constitution) Order, 1942, which provides that the existing members of Food Control Committees shall continue in office until the first day of January, 1943. In the meantime the Town Council have to prepare a list of names of persons for appointment as members of the Committee for the new year commencing on the 1st January, 1943, and the Order provides that the Town Clerk shall deliver this list of names to the Divisional Food Officer on or before the 31st October. Final appointment of the members of the Committee for the new year will be made at the next Quarterly Meeting of the Council, after any observations received from the Divisional Food Officer with regard to the list submitted to him have been considered.

Under the provisions of the new Order a person who is carrying on or engaged in the business of a catering establishment may be appointed as one

R.B.J

Report of the Finance Committee

Your Committee beg to report on their proceedings during the past quarter as follows:

Rate Arrears - Your Committee again gave consideration to the question of arrears outstanding before the end of the current half year in accordance with the recommendations made by the District Auditor, but it was only found necessary to institute proceedings against one rate payer as there has been a considerable improvement in the general position during the half year ending 30th September, 1942.

The following is a statement of the arrears of rate, water rents and housing rents during the three half years ending 30th September, 1941, 31st March, 1942, and 30th September, 1942, respectively:

	September, 1941	March, 1942	September, 1942
Rate	£251. 9. 1.	£50.18. -.	£14. 5. 7.
Waterworks	£ 65. 3. 9.	£23. 8. 7.	£ 6.12. 9.
Housing	£ 5. 9. 2.	£ 1. 7. 6.	£ -. -. -.

National Society for the Prevention of Cruelty to Children - Your Committee have resolved to make a contribution of £2. 2. -. to the funds of the N.S.P.C.C. in recognition of the excellent work done by that body within the District.

Painting of Beales Corner - Mr. S.H. Smith, the Vice-Chairman of the Berkhamsted Urban District Council has presented to the Corporation a painting which was in his possession of old houses at Beales Corner. Your Committee have given instructions for this picture to be framed and hung in the Town Clerk's Office and a letter of appreciation has been sent to Mr. Smith.

Municipal Offices, Hours of Employment - Your Committee have had under consideration the question of the hours of employment for the staff at the Municipal Offices in war time, including a report submitted by the National Joint Council for Local Authorities, Administrative, Technical, and Clerical Services. Arrangements have been made for the clerical staff at the Municipal Offices to work 46 hours a week and additional remuneration will be paid for the extra time put in at plain time rates of salary, based on the difference between normal peacetime hours and 46 hours a week.

Flags of the Allies - The flags of Great Britain, America, U.S.S.R., China and the Fighting French have been purchased and instructions have been given for these flags to be flown around the bandstand and on the bridge.

Waterworks Extensions Loan - Application has been made to the Ministry of Health for the issue of the final sanctionsfor the raising of the necessar loan now that the sinking of the borehole has been completed and the test has proved satisfactory. Application will be made to theP ublic Work Loan Board in accordance with the previous resolution of the Town Council as soon as the sanctions have been received.

26th October, 1942. Chairman

BOROUGH OF BEWDLEY

REPORT OF THE HOUSING COMMITTEE

Quarterly Council Meeting 27th July, 1942.

Your Committee beg to report on their proceedings during the past quarter as follows:

Camping Sites - Your Committee have had under consideration the provisions of Section 269 of the Public Health Act, 1936 relating to the licensing of camping grounds within the Borough, and also Section 53 of the Public Health Act, 1936 relating to buildings constructed of short-lived materials as defined by the Borough Building Bye Laws.

Applications have been received for certain camping grounds within the Borough to be licensed by the Local Authority and your Committee have resolved to grant the following licences:

Mr. Gardner, Dog Lane Camping Ground,
Mr. Hurst, Butt Town Meadows Camping Ground,
Mr. Carr, Council Hill Camping Ground, and
Mr. Birch, Wyre Hill Camping Ground.

These licences have been made expressly subject to the strict observance of the Bye Laws with respect to tents, vans, sheds and other structures used for human habitation, and the Sanitary Inspector has been instructed to report to the Committee any breach of these Bye Laws.

Your Committee do not wish to prevent visitors from enjoying the amenities of the Borough and have no desire to keep people away from Bewdley who are likely to make purchases in the town, but the Local Authority have double responsibility in this matter in that they must see that reasonable precautions are taken on grounds of Public Health on all camping sites, and also that the amenities referred to are not destroyed by uncontrolled camping within the Borough.

A small Sub-Committee has been appointed to consider the exercise of powers vested in the Local Authority to control the erection of buildings constructed of short-lived materials within the Borough. There is some indication that a number of people are erecting such buildings without application to the Council for approval of plans and your Committee are determined to see that both the provisions of the Public Health Act, 1936 and the Borough Bye Laws are observed in all cases, and it is not right that property owners who have spent a considerable amount of money on a good sound building built according to plans approved by the Council should find the rateable value of the district reduced through the erection of miscellaneous dwellings without any planning or control.

Allotments, Council Houses - Applications have been received from time to time for extra land for wartime allotments. Your Committee have agreed to the provision of extra ground at Cleobury Road for seven tenants and also five extra allotments on the Bark Hill Estate.

Chapter Five

1943
THE ALLIES PLAN FOR VICTORY

Politics, as well as War, was pursued with mortal vigour during 1943. The British and Americans cooperated as never before. Mussolini was freed from prison by German paratroopers and he was presented to Hitler in September. At Tehran from 28 November until 1 December, Churchill, Roosevelt and Stalin met and committed themselves to total victory against the Axis nations. Before then in North Africa on 21 November, Churchill and Roosevelt met with Chiang-Kai Shek of China to pursue the war against Japan.

De Gaulle had met General Giraud on 14 January 1943 at Casablanca, as Churchill and Roosevelt met. De Gaulle and the Free French therefore were included in the summit fight back against the Axis. The Kidderminster Shuttle 25 December 1943, records with photograph the 1st wedding I believe of an American Serviceman, Pte Anderson of North Carolina, to Miss P.J. Taylor of 38 Tomkinson Drive, Kidderminster.

Bewdley Town Council's Air Raid Precaution Committee continued its work, noting the need for more young people to go forward into the Borough's Messenger Service.

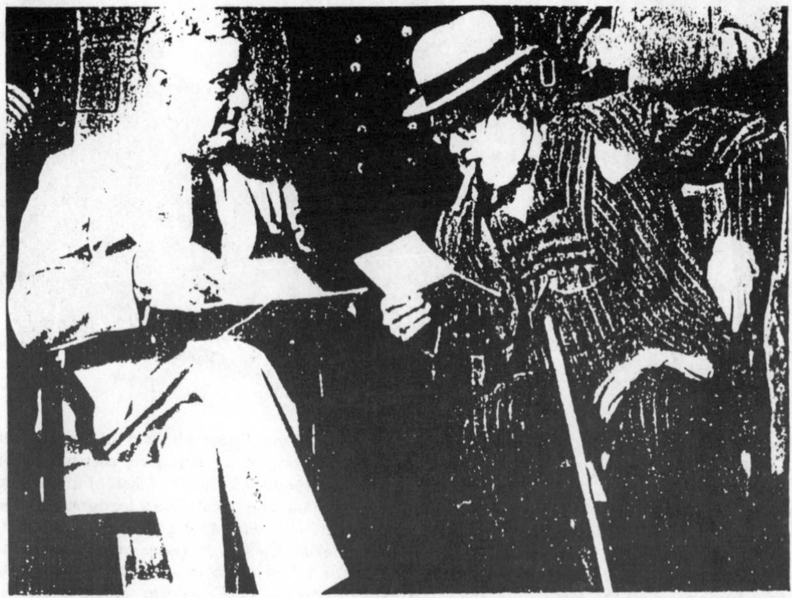

ALLIED CONFERENCE AT CASABLANCA. On 14 January the Prime Minister of Great Britain and the President of the United States met at Casablanca, in French Morocco, for important discussions on the future Allied operations in the war. They were accompanied by the combined Chiefs of Staff of the two countries and their expert advisers. This was the fourth wartime meeting of the two great Allied leaders. Although Marshal Stalin was invited to join in the talks he was unable to leave Russia owing to the offensive operations of the Red Army which he was directing. Nevertheless, he was fully informed of the decisions made, one of the objectives of which was to relieve pressure on the Russian forces. The far-reaching importance of this meeting in North Africa may be judged by the fact that it was the greatest gathering of Allied war chiefs called since the outbreak of the Second World War. Mr. Churchill left Britain on 12 January in the same "Liberator" which took him on his 14,000-mile trip to the Middle East and Moscow in August, 1942. President Roosevelt arrived in North Africa on 14 January after making the 5,000-mile flight across the Atlantic by "Clipper" plane. During the conference, which lasted ten days, the whole field of the Second World War was surveyed in detail, and all Allied resources were marshalled for the more intense prosecution of the war by land, sea and air. Mr. Churchill and President Roosevelt and their respective staffs arrived at complete agreement regarding plans for offensive operations which were to be undertaken by the Allies against the Axis in the 1943 campaign. The conference also provided an opportunity for a meeting between the Fighting French leaders, Generals de Gaulle and Giraud. These pictures, taken at Casablanca, show: top, left, General Nogues (France) and General Patton (U.S.A.); bottom, left, President Roosevelt with Mr. Churchill; above, Generals de Gaulle and Giraud.

Generals Giraud and

DE GAULLE ARRIVES IN NORTH AFRICA. General de Gaulle, leader of the Fighting French since the fall of France in 1940, arrived in North Africa on 30 May for talks with General Giraud, Commander-in-Chief of the French forces in North Africa. This visit of General de Gaulle was the result of several months of negotiations between the French National Committee in London and General Giraud. The long-range exchange of views, effected through General Catroux, who had travelled to and from Britain with proposal and counter-

de Gaulle at Algiers

30 May, 1943

proposal, led eventually to General Giraud's agreement to a meeting at Algiers to discuss the co-ordination of Fighting French effort. Above, the two leaders of Free France are seen together. Their discussions culminated later in the establishment of the French Committee of National Liberation, presided over by the two Generals jointly. Meantime the French forces in North Africa, under General Giraud, were playing their part in the final Tunisian fighting. The picture on the left shows French troops unloading mules on the way to the Tunisian front.

...he Daily Telegrap...

MONDAY, MAY 31, 1943 — and Morning Post — Printed in LONDON and MANCHEST...

...TACTICS ...-BOATS

ALLIES HAMMER ITALY'S ISLAND BASES AGAIN

NO AXIS FIGHTERS ENCOUNTERED

ALLIED FORCE H.Q., N. AFRICA, Sunday.

Unchallenged by Axis fighters, bombers of Gen. Doolittle's Strategic Air Force yesterday struck new hammer blows on Italy's anti-invasion bases of Sardinia and Pantellaria, without loss to themselves.

Enemy fighter opposition appears to have been completely beaten down since last week, when our pilots met packs of Axis planes, sometimes as many as 50 of them together.

Docks and railway installations were heavily bombed during several attacks yesterday by Mitchells, Marauders, Lightnings and Warhawks.

More fires and explosions were observed in the dock area of Pantellaria, which has been pounded by the Allies for 18 days. Shipping and the airfield there were also hit.

In the swoop on Sardinia Lightnings raided the docks and military dumps at Porto Ponte Romano, in the south-west of the island. Bombs hit buildings and supplies in the docks, causing a large explosion and fires. The railway was also hit.

To-day's Italian communiqué stated that Allied planes had raided San Antioco, a small island off the south-west coast of Sardinia, and Cagliari, on the south-east coast of Sardinia.

Leghorn Damage

Photographs taken during the raid on Leghorn by 100 Flying Fortresses on Friday show that four more ships were hit in the harbour, in addition to the three announced in the first report, and additional damage was done to the port and railway installations.

One of Italy's biggest oil refineries was shown to be burning fiercely.—Reuter and A.P.

PANTELLARIA FIRST

ITALIANS' BELIEF

STOCKHOLM, Sunday.

Italians to-day believe that the first Allied landings on Italian soil will be made at Pantellaria, states a despatch from the Rome correspondent of the Swedish newspaper Dagens Nyheter.

"Nobody in Italy," he writes, "doubts that the Allies intend to pul... ... Everybody wonders how long these attacks will go on before something else happens."

The Italians now argue that Italy...

ONE OF FIVE COASTAL COMMAND VICTIMS IN THE ATLANTIC

Depth-charges from a Sunderland "P" straddling one of the five Nazi U-boats recently destroyed in the Atlantic during a period of 10 days. Already partially disabled by another Sunderland "F," the U-boat is seen trying to evade further punishment. Her wake shows her still capable of considerable surface speed, but, a few seconds later, she had begun to sink. Pictures of the end of another U-boat are on Page 3.

DE GAULLE IN ALGIERS, MET BY GIRAUD

"WE WANT UNITY OF EMPIRE"

ALGIERS, Sunday.

Gen. de Gaulle arrived at a small, sun-baked airfield near Algiers at noon to-day and found Gen. Giraud waiting to meet him.

The two leaders are to begin formal conversations to-morrow morning.

FRENCH SHIPS AT ALEXANDRIA FOR ALLIES

CREWS JOINING UP

The French squadron commanded by Adml. Godefroy, which has been lying immobilised at Alexandria since the 1940 Franco-German armistice, has gone over to the French forces fighting with the Allies.

Vichy radio announcing this last night, said that the ships had been surrendered to the Allies "after several months of virtual starvation."

The German News Agency said that "according to a telegram from British sources the crews have announced that they are joining up."

The warships include the battleship Lorraine, of 22,000 tons...

Nazi paratroops free

Mussolini from prison — September, 1943

MUSSOLINI RELEASED BY GERMANS. Since the overthrow of the former Italian dictator on 24 July, he had been kept a prisoner in the Gran Sasso Hotel in the Abruzzi Mountains north of Rome. On 12 September Berlin radio announced that German parachutists and armed S.S. men had "carried out an operation for the liberation of Mussolini." The pictures on these pages show: left, Mussolini leaving the hotel surrounded by the German parachutists who freed him from captivity; above, Mussolini saying good-bye to Hitler before returning to Italy

21 November–1 December, 1943 **War conferences in**

MEETINGS OF ALLIED STATESMEN

On 21 November, President Roosevelt, Generalissimo Chiang Kai-Shek and Mr. Churchill met in North Africa for the purpose of issuing a statement on Allied policy regarding the war against Japan. After leaving North Africa, Mr. Churchill and President Roosevelt travelled to Teheran, the capital of Iran, to meet Marshal Stalin. This conference lasted from 28 November to 1 December. A joint statement declared that the Allies had come to full agreement concerning the timing of all military operations. Top left, Generalissimo Chiang Kai-Shek, President Roosevelt, Mr. Churchill and Mme Chiang Kai-Shek in North Africa. Bottom left, Marshal Stalin, President Roosevelt and Mr. Churchill at Teheran. Behind are M. Molotov, Mrs. Oliver (Mr. Churchill's daughter) and Mr. Anthony Eden. Top right, the presentation of the Stalingrad sword. Marshal Voroshilov shows the sword to President Roosevelt. Bottom right, ceremony of presentation.

NEW INDUSTRIES AND HOUSES

MAYOR OUTLINES TOWN'S POST-WAR NEEDS

WHEN Alderman Louis Tolley was unanimously elected on Tuesday last to be Mayor of Kidderminster for the second year in succession the occasion was unique, for amongst those who witnessed this typically English ceremony were some of the repatriated prisoners of war, who three weeks ago were in German prison camps and hospitals. They had come at the express invitation of the Mayor, who gave them an official welcome, and congratulated them.

After accepting office, Ald. Tolley touched upon many civic matters, including problems which would face the Council in the post-war years. Among the points which he made was the fact that plans are being made to attract new industries to the town after the war.

He also referred especially to housing needs, and revealed that at present 3,000 people had their names on the waiting list for Corporation houses. Plans, he said, are already prepared for the erection of 500 houses immediately the war is over and circumstances allow. More than that, the Council have under consideration plans and details for the erection of 3,000 houses immediately opportunity presents itself for such development.

The approach to the Council Chamber presented a festive appearance with tiers of huge brightly-coloured chrysanthemums, grown by Mr. H. W. French and the Parks Dept., attractively assembled to greet one's eye as one mounted the stairs. Another vase of these beautiful blooms rested on the central table in the Council Chamber.

The chamber itself was closely packed with citizens, in addition to the ex-prisoners of war and members of voluntary services, while there was also a sprinkling of school children present to witness the ancient custom of Mayor making.

Members of the Council present, in addition to the Mayor, were: Aldermen E. O. Eddy, H. W. Cheshire, G. Anton, and A. E. Meredith; Cllrs. F. D. H. Burcher, G. S. Chadwick, P. R. Stone, J. Brown, J. Bristow, J. Dalley, G. S. Newton, F. Wilson, P. Martin, S. Goodwin, A. Smith, J. Ferguson, and G. N. Weston, with the Town Clerk (Mr. J. H. Thursfield), the Chief Constable (Mr. H. Hodgkinson) and all other officials of the Council. An apology was read from Cllr. Miss E. C. Addenbrooke.

PRIVILEGE AND HONOUR

Addressing the assembly as "Soldiers of the British Empire, Aldermen, Cllrs., ladies and gentlemen, and burgesses of Kidderminster," Ald. E. O. Eddy said it was a privilege and honour to submit the name of Ald. Louis Tolley as Mayor for the ensuing year, and he did it with the utmost sincerity, as it was due to him that he first became a member of that council eighteen years ago. The story was an interesting one. Ald. Tolley first became a Town Councillor in ... is badly needed. Certain things happened, however, and eventually the launching of the appeal was too late and great difficulty was experienced in raising the £4,000 for the Church St. memorial Houses, however, must come first, and all were very worried about present conditions, and the new hospital would have to lie in abeyance. He hoped some day to see a new hospital built outside the town, and the present buildings could be converted into flats.

He hoped the Mayor would consider launching an appeal for a Maternity Hospital as the town's memorial. He had raised large sums of money for charities during his mayoralty and there was a desperate need in Kidderminster for such a building in view of the shortage of houses in the town.

Continuing, Ald. Eddy said that interest in public affairs would broaden and he would like the council to inaugurate a scheme whereby those interested in council matters could be taught their job—ready for the time when they wished to become Town Councillors. It took a long time to learn the work, and an apprenticeship would help the town wonderfully. Ald. Tolley thoroughly knew his work, and at the present time was taking the greatest interest in the new Kidderminster, and some day they would have a town worthy of the townspeople.

RATES INCREASE

He was glad to see that spaces had been reserved in the new Civic Centre for the two statues in the town—the removal of one he had frequently advocated. The Borough Surveyor with his usual progressiveness had gone one bet- ... pointed out at the time that if that recommendation was adopted there would have to be less political selfishness and greater honesty and perhaps a greater justice in filling that office than there had been on occasions in the past. He appreciated that at that time those remarks might not have been very popular in one or two quarters. It was therefore all the more gratifying to him that day to realise that the seed scattered on the wind had not all fallen on barren ground.

In supporting Ald. Tolley once again in that honoured position he made one public request. It may be the Mayor's privilege during the coming year to announce from the balcony of that public building a royal proclamation that the victory they all desired was an accomplished fact. When peace came and come it must sooner or later and all branches of the armed forces laid down their arms he hoped they would not be taken up by politicians in a strife that would lose the peace for which so many sacrifices had been made.

"What sacrifices have been made, and are still to be made, we, of that generation who made sacrifices in the last war and have been called upon to make even greater ones in this, ask on behalf of those who have got to follow us that those sacrifices shall not have been made in vain," said Cllr. Chadwick. "In supporting you to-day, Ald. Tolley, I ask on behalf of all parties that the same unity that has been of such value to us in time of war shall be of the same value to us in time of peace in dealing with the problems that lie ahead."

The resolution was carried unanimously and with applause.

PRISONERS WELCOMED

After accepting office, Ald. Tolley referred to the uniqueness of the occasion, as repatriated prisoners of war were present.

"I want to say to you in the name of the people of Kidderminster how glad we are to see you back home again, and congratulate you and thank you for all you have done, not forgetting those lonely years you spent without relatives or friends, when you must have wondered how long it would be before freedom was restored to you again," said the Mayor. "Yet during this time with courage and fortitude you maintained all the traditions of Englishmen, and must have proved to those in charge of you that such courage and determination was bound to win and that victory would come to England and her Allies. You maintained that tradition, and I am grateful you did so.

"In the future I wish you well and all success, and trust you will be able to share in all the prosperity that will come to us as the result of the sacrifices you were called upon to make."

THE FUTURE

When he was first elected Mayor he made an appeal to all members of the Council in particular, to plan the future. He was happy to think that as a result of that appeal they were able to, and in giving details of what had happened during the past year, he hoped to prove that in fact, they had planned wisely and well.

The greatest problem any town or city would have to face immediately after the war was that of housing, and no less so they had to face it as a local authority. During the past year, sites had been ear-marked, plans prepared, and all the details put into operation for the erection of 500 houses immediately the war was over and circumstances allowed. Even more than that, they had under consideration plans and details for the erection of 3,000 houses immediately the opportunity presented itself to build.

The Mayor went on to refer to the housing difficulties in

[illegible] to do all I had to do [illegible] the day at 1.30 a.m. Our women have played a grand part in this war, and Mrs. Tolley has set a fine example of service before self." She and Ald. Tolley were good type Rotarians.

Ald. Tolley was "father" of the Council, having 19 years service to his credit, and, as he (Ald. Eddy) had 18 years service, he was pleased to serve as a "son" to such a "father." In view, therefore, of his great work he submitted the name of Ald. Louis Tolley, thanking him for his leadership and wishing him and the Mayoress good health, and may there be peace in 1944.

REPETITION

Ald. Meredith said that 12 months ago, he had the honour and privilege to second the same resolution. To-day he was instructed or commanded to give a repeat performance not that all repeat performances merited repetition, but he did suggest that the motion that Ald. Tolley should be chief citizen at least merited repetition.

Ald. Eddy, in his own inimitable way, had given many facts and figures with regard to the long and various political activities of his career. He (Ald. Meredith), too, could give interesting facts and figures and instances which resulted, in some cases, in Labour loss, and in other cases they achieved tremendous success. He did not believe, however, that that was the time or place to divulge any such information. "Who knows, we may even yet be called upon to repeat that performance," he added.

Ald. Meredith went on to say that he knew that 12 months ago there was a certain amount of diffidence upon Ald. Tolley's ability, or perhaps he should say willingness, to subdue his inherent natural propensity for lengthy discussion and debate in the conduct of the Council and whether he would be willing or able to leave sufficient time for "us lesser fry" to take part.

He ventured to suggest that not one of them could give any points to Ald. Tolley as far as debate, rules and procedure, or standing orders were concerned. It had been that very knowledge which he had put into practice during the past 12 months and which had enabled him to so worthily fill the bill, and he (Ald. Meredith) was quite sure he was voicing the sentiments of everyone in that Council when he said that Ald. Tolley had filled the bill with credit to himself, satisfaction to the Council, and in a manner worthy of the high office he held.

SPADE WORK

His year of office had not been, perhaps, too spectacular, but there had been a tremendous lot of spade work behind the scenes. His had been a year practically of raising money. He had given no end of time, energy, and work in that connection with very marked success, and it was in that connection that he, like Ald. Eddy, would like to associate the name of the Mayoress because he knew her sterling worth. She was always a tower of strength to Ald. Tolley in the old fighting days, and he knew she had been a great help to him in the many appeals he had had to make to the public and of assistance in clerical duties and other necessary work in connection with them. He knew their thanks were due to her for the very able manner in which she had carried on her job.

It was with very great pleasure that he seconded again the resolution that Ald. Tolley should be Mayor. He did it from two points of view—from the personal one because he had been associated with Ald. Tolley for a great many years, and from the point of view that he knew he would carry on the job in the same manner which he had done in the past 12 months. Ald. Meredith added the hope that the coming year would bring the greatest thing of all—peace—and that the work of reconstruction and rehabilitation may take place so that they may bring in an era of peace, prosperity, happiness and

ing, he hoped, who had been fighting for freedom, liberty, and democracy and they would have a right to expect and perhaps to demand that the whole of the resources at the Council's disposal was used to provide homes for them, and that the Council lost no time because it would be their right to demand and the Council's duty to see they got houses.

The Council was to be congratulated on the policy adopted in that direction, and he hoped that Kidderminster would be one of the first towns to say it was prepared, and that as a result of it would be in a position to put schemes into operation.

CIVIC CENTRE

Another great step forward during the year had been the unanimous decision of the Council to ear-mark a site for the new Civic Centre.

"May I say in passing," commented the Mayor, "that I hope none will endeavour to sabotage that scheme before they have given due consideration to it. In our progress as a town, it is very necessary that we should have this Civic Centre. The site we have ear-marked, when you get a bird's eye view of it, is one which has a slum area in the main, which we shall be well advised to get rid of at the earliest possible moment. So in our decision to mark this as a site for a new Civic Centre, we have planned for the future. None of us, in all probability, will see the scheme completed, but those who come after and build upon the foundation we have laid will see and say we planned wisely and well, because in that scheme every allowance has been made for future generations to build, and the cost, which some have referred to, will be borne, not by one generation, but by several generations. Nevertheless, the scheme in its entirety is the essence of wise planning, not only for the present, but also for the future."

The Mayor went on to refer to the wise decision of the Education Committee to feed school children, which had been a great success. He thought the committee was to be congratulated on that policy which, in these difficult times, was most helpful both to the mothers who had to go out to work and to preserving and protecting the health of the children. That was most essential, because those children would be the men and women of to-morrow.

NEW INDUSTRIES

In consideration of post-war reconstruction great efforts had been and were being made to attract new industries to the town after the war. It may be happy to think that as the result of the activities of the Reconstruction Committee, there would be new industries here, and the borough would be able to grow and extend as a result.

Every development calculated to be of benefit to the people had been under consideration and were still under consideration now. Although plans were not yet completed he believed that when they were completed, they would bring with them a measure of success which would mean so much in the years to come.

The Mayor went on to refer to the opening of the new sewage pumping station. Here, again, they had planned wisely and well, because those works would not only be responsible for present flow, but if the borough extended, grew and broadened its boundaries with increased industrial activity and larger population, the scheme for many years would be able to take any additional flow of sewage it would be asked to take.

He also paid a warm tribute to the generosity of the people of Kidderminster in contributing to the many objects which it had been his pleasure and privilege to launch. The sum people had given must constitute a record for the size of the town, but he was not at all satisfied they could not do more. Particularly emphasising the work of the Red Cross, the Mayor said that the re-

BOMB'S PREMATURE EXPLOSION

French Cadet Killed and Two Others Injured

An inquest was held on Wednesday on Cadet Jean [illegible] (20), a member of a Fighting French O.C.T.U., who was killed as a result of a grenade accident just over a week ago. An instructor and another cadet were injured, and the latter has had both legs amputated. Both are now progressing favourably. The inquest was conducted by the Coroner.

Evidence of identification was given by Captain Louis de [illegible] of the Fighting French, who said the deceased man was under training at an O.C.T.U. The grenade practice was a properly authorised operation, and was in the hands of capable and experienced instructors.

The Chief Medical Officer said Jean suffered from many wounds, the chief of which was one in the heart, which was fatal.

The Coroner read a statement he had taken from the officer in charge, who was injured and who is still in hospital. The officer, said the Coroner, did not remember giving the order to fire and recalled nothing but a blow in the face. On recovering he found Jean lying on the ground by the side of Cadet [illegible] who had both legs blown off.

Lieutenant Pierre [illegible], the platoon leader on the day of the accident, said that as far as he knew, proper precautions were being observed by the injured officer who was in charge of the platoon of which Jean was a member. The injured men received attention from the medical orderly immediately after the accident, and were removed to hospital.

THE CAUSE

Witness agreed that the accident might have been caused through the grenade being put into the firing cup upside down, the shear wire being faulty or the spring being missing or faulty. Either would have caused a premature discharge of the grenade.

Lieutenant Robert [illegible], through an interpreter, said he was in charge of the platoon and returned to the party of which Jean was a member just before the accident happened. He heard the discharge and agreed with the last witness as to the possible causes of the accident.

Asked by the Coroner if there was any other evidence which ought to be placed before the Court, Capt. de [illegible] said Cadet [illegible] remembered everything, but the Coroner said he saw no reason for adjourning the enquiry to hear that now. All he was concerned about was the cause of death.

Summing up, the Coroner said his function was only to ascertain the cause of death and in a case where there was an element of accident to satisfy himself that there was no negligence, in the criminal sense, which caused the accident. "I can say straight away that I am satisfied that there is no evidence of criminal negligence, or, in fact, negligence of any kind," he added. What were considered to be proper precautions were being observed, and he had had put forward three possible causes for the premature explosion of the grenade. It was not for him to say which, if any, of these caused the explosion, but he thought that the evidence clearly indicated that it was due to an accident.

"I am surprised to find that the grenades in stock from which this particular one was taken have not been withheld from use for practice, because I should have thought the rest would have been examined first, but that is nothing to do with me. It is usual in a factory when anything lethal is found defective, [illegible] all an

where the Perkins discovery in 1856 of "mauve" was almost entirely neglected in this country and the developments up till 1914 were largely in the hands of the Germans. Yet surely no one would call the German dye industry inefficient because it had not made the original discovery.

Many of the older people engaged in the carpet trade will remember the "American invasion" of 1890-1893, when the technical skill in the British carpet factories soon produced a fabric to sell at a price that the invaders were unable to compete with. I think it would be correct to say that the import of carpets to this country from America has been small since that date and that our exports to her were quite considerable up to the time of her fiscal change to a high tariff policy. Perhaps a new American "invasion" is still to come.

The years following the war will be difficult and that we shall have to work hard to regain and extend our carpet trade is well known to all of us. I would point out however that in my view the carpet plants in this country are both up to date and efficient, that considerable sums of money have been spent in recent years on these plants, that we have available a very highly skilled labour force whose skill has been proved both in peace and in the war effort. Given conditions of reasonable security I see no reason at all why the British carpet trade should not play a worthy part in the future.

RALEIGH B. ADAM

To the Editor

Sir,—The parentage of the article in your issue of November [illegible] headed "Carpet Trade Training" has been repudiated by the Worcestershire Education Authority, and this point may be dealt with by some other correspondent.

An extract from Burton's "History of Kidderminster" may correct one inaccuracy. "The power Chenille Axminster setting loom was invented by Mr. William Adam, and in 1880 the firm of Tomkinson and Adam licensed James Templeton and Co. and [illegible] Lyle and Co. of Glasgow and [illegible] Smith and Sons of Kidderminster to use the patent. The first looms were erected at "The Sling" in the shed formerly used as a tapestry weaving shed by Messrs. Pardoe, Hoomans and Pardoe. The American patent was disposed of to the Alex. Smith and Sons Carpet Company, Yonkers, New York."

I [illegible] Templeton [illegible] Chenille was a [illegible] the [illegible] caterpillar. Messrs. Templeton certainly [illegible] Carpets and Rugs [illegible] firm of Tomkinson and Adam [illegible] patent for setting [illegible] power loom was taken [illegible] in 188[illegible] and licences [illegible] as recorded by Burton.

[illegible] TOMKINSON

FOLKLORE & HOMECRAFTS

[illegible]

Sir,—Worcestershire and the neighbouring counties contain such a mass of delightful customs, legends and traditions that the Folklore Fellowship—evacuated "for the duration" to Cemaes Bay, Anglesey—is glad to note that more and more are taking an interest in the stimulation of home crafts as well as in the possibilities of "brightening the black-out" with the fascinations obtainable through folklore.

It cannot be gainsaid that it is vitally essential in these days to encourage the peaceful study of folklore, to say nothing of the fostering of the design and making of novelties out of waste materials, and so greatly do the Folklore Fellowship view these matters as being of real national importance that pending the possible arrangement of conferences and lectures in Worcestershire, we should be happy to furnish all those who care to send a stamped envelope with the various ways in which these attractive pursuits may best be

too late. She
ox Green Road
some men shout
e said the state-
made to P.C.
true. He (wit-
accused's coat
on which there

INTERVIEW

on November 25
again saw the
Bradbury. She
ost sorry I have
also that I have
much trouble. The
told you lies was
at happened the
y." She said she
oldier she met at
He took advan-
against her will,
afraid of the
and made up the
men.
magistrate (Mr.
ald Knight would
for trial at the
dshire Quarter

aid his client did
ive evidence that
ed for bail, which
erself in £10, and
£10.

ENSIBLE'S
LUMN

MEETING

Martin's husband
rmy she decided
tribution to the
would be to run
She did not know
manufacturing, but
secret of creating

workers planned a
workroom, benches
lly converted into
ly decorated with
utumn leaves. In
of good humour
ss, both workers
sat down to

Mrs. Martin spoke
ees. She thanked
r faithfulness and
d referred to the
hat had produced
his same spirit of
she said, "has
the management
hich has enabled
ept new types of
ease production by
The aim of the
serve the markets
pturing them. This
by serving each
means creating the
in which each
the best job."
ns next day were
A new worker
an examiner for
did not realise
he high standard
intend to do
re.
came to the fore-
stained work. Her
that it had got
the tea interval in
Later on, however,
shamefacedly and
told you was a
is afternoon when
tea on the sly; the
shed."
ke this," says Mrs.
that industry can
character that
od citizenship, and
we shall need after
ll as now."

Stubbs, 54, Cobden St, Kidderminster, took place at St. John's Church Kidderminster, on Wednesday, December 4, by special licence. The service was conducted by the Rev. W. E. Witts. classical gown of white taffeta designed with a train and full-length embroidered veil arranged with a gold halo. She wore gold shoes, and carried a sheaf of gold chrysanthemums. The gold and bronze chrysanthemums. The duties of best man were carried out by Telegraphist W. Ashcroft (friend of the bridegroom). A reception, attended by 30 guests, was held.

FOR FIGHTING FRENCH

"Bring and Buy" Sale Realises £150

A banner bearing the blue, white and red badge of the Association des Amis des Volontaires Francais occupied a prominent position in the Town Hall on Tuesday, when members of the association held a bring-and-buy sale to raise funds for the Fighting French. The sale was opened by Ald. E. O. Eddy, O.B.E., J.P., C.C., who was accompanied by Mrs. Eddy.

The organisers and members, with the assistance of friends and well-wishers, had been successful in collecting an astonishing assortment of saleable goods, many of them particularly suitable for Christmas gifts. There were some delightful pieces of hand-worked linen of special interest because of the fine needlework and the quality of the material; treasures from trinket boxes included a choice old pendant of carved ivory, a basket brooch set with brilliants, a string of agates, necklaces of beads from all parts of the world, and a quantity of odd buckles and unusual clips; a lovely little Dresden figure and another of carved ivory attracted attention; a book stall and a produce stall were busy centres, and there was a ready sale for a collection of cosmetics. Competitions, including a novel rabbit dinner, complete with vegetables, a cake, eggs, lemons, honey, and a basket of onions, were well supported.

Introducing Ald. E. O. Eddy, Mrs. C. Beakbane, President of the association, expressed gratitude for the sympathy and understanding which had been shown to the French nation since June, 1940. She said open-heartedness and kindliness were outstanding traits of the British character, and the help given had been deeply appreciated.

Ald. E. O. Eddy, declaring the sale open, said France, the most intellectual of all nations, was sick, not dead, and she would eventually emerge stronger than ever, and again become a great power. She had recovered magnificently from the war of 1870 and formed her great Colonial Empire. The great Marshal Foch saved Europe in 1918. Her navy was the fourth largest in the world. In the world crisis of 1930 France stood firm as a rock. Her stock of gold at that period was greater than anywhere in the world, and her percentage of unemployment less than any other nation. France had stood as a buffer between England and Germany, and the Allies owed her a tremendous debt of gratitude. When he (Mr. Eddy) was in France in 1938, the French were beginning to realise that war was coming and they were ill prepared. It was only when the British had to evacuate Dunkirk that this country realised the seriousness of the position. It was then that the greatness of Britain manifested itself. Over £300,000,000 worth of equipment was left behind but 300,000 brave men were evacuated and are once more fighting for liberty.

Hitler had said he would destroy France, but that great nation would never be destroyed. Speaking of the Association of Friends of the Fighting French which was formed in 1940, the speaker said there were over 60 branches, and over 28,000 men had been helped during the past four years. They were concerned that day with the living, but they would never forget those who had paid the supreme sacrifice. He expressed his pleasure in being associated with the effort, and thanked Mrs. Beakbane and Mrs. Brinton for their leadership on so many occasions, and wished the sale every success.

Proposing a vote of thanks, Mr. H. H. Whitehouse (hon. treasurer) said Ald. Eddy was unfailing in his support of any worthy cause. The association had as its object the welfare of the Fighting French Forces, and it was through the enthusiasm of Mrs. Beakbane and Mrs. Nairac that the branch had been established in Kidderminster. A total of £1,100 had already been raised, £619 of which was the proceeds of efforts during the last 14 months. £800 sent to headquarters recently had been acknowledged. Mr. Whitehouse expressed thanks to Mr. Eddy and to all who had helped with the sale.

Helpers who "brought and bought" will be interested to learn that in the single day the sale was conducted, the sum of £150 was raised.

Competition winners: Whiskey, Mrs. Owen, The Grange, Stourport; pheasant, Mrs. Beaufort Clayton, Trimpley House, Trimpley; pheasant, Mr. David Frenay; Chinese carved ivory card case, Mrs. McAdam, Lachetts, Chaddesley Corbett; cigarettes, Miss Moody, Norton Close, Stourbridge; cigarettes, Miss J. ... Road North.

SALES AND MARKETS

PROPERTY SALE

Mr. O. Herbert Banks conducted a successful sale of freehold property at the Swan Hotel, Stourport, on Monday last. There was a good attendance and competition was keen for all lots. The semi-detached villa residence "Glyndale," Hartlebury Rd., sold with the benefit of vacant possession, realised £950. An adjacent plot of building land, area 468 square yards, sold for £80, and the semi-detached villa residence, "Silverdale," let at £36 per annum, realised £780.

CATTLE MARKET

Mr. O. Herbert Banks held his usual sale on Tuesday when an entry of 135 store cattle met a sharp trade and a complete clearance. Bunches of bullocks from Mr. S. White, £31 5s.; Messrs. Kirk and Neville, £25; heifers from Mr. W. Bornston, £28; from the exors. Mr. J. Broomer, £24 15s.; Mr. D. Thomas, £24 5s.; Mr. H. Weaver, £23 5s.; Mr. H. Bishop, £21 15s.; bulling heifer from Mr. T. Cadwood to £20 2s. 6d.; 25 incalvers to £29 10s.; bulls, £31. The sheep included a capital lot of strong lambs, over 400 being penned: 40 from Mr. R. Brookshaw, 86s.; 85 Mr. E. J. Guest, Meaton, 84s. 6d.; 40 Mr. L. V. Neath, 75s.; 85 Mr. R. Colwill, 73s.; 61 Mr. H. C. Spilsbury, 68s. ... Ewes ... 64s. A smaller entry of pigs were sold very dear, strong stores to £20 2s. 6d.; sows and pigs ... £12 5s. ... rearing calves ... horses to 64 gns. ... car £100 ... sheep racks to ...

WHAT A LIFE!

E WEAVER

e R.A., India
nand

ars "Walter the the imagination s, and his car- esented without y touched high- icularly affecting All kinds of eated with skill ig and many of ere exceedingly have been framed ementoes of his effort showing es with his pet whimsically at t as a soldier, good and will be y

colleagues at the have received a ter in which in ein, he describes riences. We can- than quote the

is a letter full all from the it the Middle I had better um East and be e. Sorry I have store.

I'm ative most to I writ- t in abola? doubt my still od

came out here here so long that I am eligible the local Town

interested to work I'm doing a lot of draw- I am keeping nd in. And I n the midst of y of beautiful)'s (I n d i a's Which fact cause a great mongst my num- friends in Kid- ter and the ding districts. Still, I am out all the s, and hope ly to return enough highly to last me the time.

er the British sonably comfort- Even the com- n as ative on the of a early and beds all uties eaco-

had nce of a heavy year, the mon- altogether, but p for it in full, wn continuously kan curtain for s. There were bridges were huts dissolved, and lengths

LOCAL WEDDINGS

WEDDING AT HOLY INNOCENTS', Dec. 4th: Pte. E. Anderson (U.S.A.)—Miss [illegible] Taylor.

The marriage of Pte. Eugene Anderson (U.S Army), eldest son of Mr. and Mrs J. C. Anderson, of Dudley, North Carolina, U.S.A., and Miss Patricia Joan Taylor, only daughter of Cfn. and Mrs. O. R. Taylor, 38 Tomkinson Drive, Kidderminster, was solemnised at Holy Innocent's Church, Foley Park, on Saturday, December 4. The service was conducted by the Rev. E. A. Barratt.

The bride, who was given in marriage by her father, wore a dark blue frock and beige jigger coat with navy hat, shoes and gloves. Her bouquet was of gold chrysanthemums. The bridesmaids, the Misses Aldonia and Ruth Taylor, cousins of the bride, were cornflower blue dresses embroidered with diamante flowers with accessories in a matching shade of blue. Both carried shower bouquets of gold chrysanthemums. The duties of best man were carried [illegible] C. Taylor (uncle [illegible] As the bridal [illegible] church the [illegible] with a silver [illegible] friend.

Later a recept[illegible] Holy Innocent's [illegible] attended by [illegible]

WEDDING AT HOLY INNOCENTS'

Mr. T. J. Oliver—Miss A. M. Wilkins

Holy Innocents' Church, Foley Park, was the scene of an attractive wedding on Saturday, December 18, when Mr. Thomas James Oliver, eldest son of Mr. and Mrs. A. Oliver, 16, Victoria Place, Kidderminster, married Miss Agnes May Wilkins, daughter of Mr. and Mrs. A. Wilkins, 76, Tomkinson Drive, the Rev. E. A. Barrett performing the ceremony.

The bride, who was given in [...] Juliet cap, and Miss Doreen was dressed in a frock of mauve taffeta with matching veil and Juliet cap. Both wore silver shoes and carried shower bouquets of pink chrysanthemums. The attendants, Miss Jean Wilkins and Miss Irene Oliver, were prettily dressed in powder blue taffeta with halos to match, silver shoes, and carried shower bouquets of lemon chrysanthemums. Mrs. A. Wilkins (the bride's mother) wore a floral pale green frock under a green coat with hat to match, and Mrs. A. Oliver (the bridegroom's mother) wore a brown costume with matching hat and accessories. A/B. Albert George Wilkins (eldest brother of the bride) who

WEDDING AT HOLY INNOCENTS'

Mr. H. Jasper—Miss H. Harris

The marriage of Mr. Herbert Jasper, of Kidderminster, to Miss Hilda Harris, only daughter of Mrs. Harris, 33, Greatfield Rd., and the late Mr. Harris, took place at Holy Innocents Church, Foley Park, on Wednesday, the ceremony being performed by the Rev. E. A. Barrett. Mr. Jasper is a retired butcher who conducted business in Sutton Rd.

The bride, who was given in marriage by Mr. Woodward, The Larches, wore a delphinium blue costume with hat and accessories to tone. Her shower bouquet was of multi-coloured chrysanthe-

Quarterly Council Meeting 27th day of April, 1943.

Report of the A.R.P. Committee

Your Committee beg to report on their proceedings during the past quarter as follows:

Wholetime Personnel - On the instructions of the Regional Commissioner further reductions have been made to the strength of the wholetime personnel in the Bewdley Civil Defence Services. In order to carry out the Minister's policy for releasing wholetime civil defence workers for employment in industry, the following have been released since the last meeting of the Town Council:

Wardens Service - Mr. E.E. Bradley.,
Transport Officer - Mr. R.E. Hoare.,
Equipment Officer - Mr. W.C. Bradley.

Mr. W.C. Bradley who is Head Warden for the Borough was requested by your Committee to transfer to the Wardens Service as a wholetime employee when the post of Equipment Officer was discontinued, but Mr. Bradley asked to be released entirely from paid Civil Defence work.

Transport Officer - Your Committee have appointed Mr. R.T. Hall as part-time Transport Officer for the Borough in the place of Mr. R.E. Hoare.

Emergency Mortuary Arrangements - Your Committee have had under review the Emergency Mortuary arrangements, and Mr. Eric Bache who is in charge of this service has had a meeting of volunteers and inspected the premises that have been earmarked for use as an Emergency Mortuary. Various additional requirements are being carried out, but there is still a shortage of volunteers in this service.

Fireguard Service - Your Committee have had under consideration instructions issued by the Ministry of Home Security relating to the organisation and administration of the Fireguard as a separate service. After considering the recommendations of the Head Warden your Committee have resolved to set up a separate Fireguard Service within the Borough, apart from the existing Wardens Service, and have appointed Mr. W.J. Purcell as Fireguard Officer. Application has been made to the Regional Commissioner for approval of these arrangements.

Training Exercises - The Bewdley Civil Defence Services have taken part in two large scale exercises since the last Quarterly Meeting of the Council. One of these exercises was held in combination with adjoining areas only, and the other was a large scale exercise covering a considerable area. There were no local incidents, but calls for mutual aid were received and answered in each exercise, and the services generally gained useful experience through taking part.

Messenger Service - There is still a serious shortage of Messengers in the Borough, and although your Committee are aware that there are many youths and girls in the Borough who will turn out in the event of emergency and offer their services it is most important that these willing helpers should be formally enrolled in the Messenger Service, otherwise compensation may not be payable under the Personal Injuries (Civilians) Scheme in the event of the Messenger sustaining war service injury. None of these volunteers will be called upon to report for training or exercises each week if they are already doing national service in the A.T.C., G.T.C., Boy Scouts or any other organised body.

Chairman.

27th April, 1943.

BOROUGH OF BEWDLEY

Quarterly Council Meeting 26th day of July, 1943.

Report of the Air Raid Precautions Committee

Your Committee beg to report on their proceedings during the past quarter as follows:-

New Rescue Service - On the instructions of the Regional Commissioner the amalgamation of Rescue Parties and First Aid Parties into the new Civil Defence Rescue Service was brought into operation within the Borough on the 1st June, 1943.

The Borough Surveyor (Mr. S.J. Rowe) has been appointed as the Head of the new service, and Councillor P.W. Palmer as Staff Officer.

Mr. J. Anson has been appointed as leader of the first of the new parties, and Mr. A. Morris leader of the second party, and the day party.

The organisation of the new combined service has been rapidly completed, and the new parties are now ready to answer a call at any time of the night or day.

First Aid Post - A very satisfactory report has been received from the County Medical Officer of Health on an inspection he carried out recently at the Bewdley First Aid Post.

Your Committee are pleased to report that satisfactory arrangements have now been made for the setting up of an alternative post as a temporary measure in the event of air raid damage to the First Aid Post in Wribbenhall.

Head Warden - Mr. W.C. Bradley, the Head Warden, has handed in his resignation to your Committee as he has recently been appointed as A.R.P. Officer to his firm in Kidderminster, and his duties in connection with this new appointment make it impossible for him to carry on as Head Warden in Bewdley. Your Committee have accepted his resignation with regret, and a letter of appreciation has been sent to Mr. Bradley referring to the excellent work he has done in the past, not only as Head Warden but as Training Officer and Equipment Supervisor.

Mr. S.A. Farr, the Deputy Head Warden, was asked to take over the duties of Head Warden, but Mr. Farr decided that his hours of employment at the Bewdley G.W.R. Station would not allow him to carry out the work to his satisfaction, Mr. Farr stated that he was willing to continue to act as Deputy and give any help within his power to the person appointed as Mr. Bradley's successor.

A general meeting of members of the Wardens Service was held in the Town Hall on Sunday last at 11 a.m., when the appointment of a successor to Mr. Bradley was discussed. The meeting resolved to recommend the appointment of Mr. Lake, now employed as baker to Councillor Godwin at Catchem's End, as Head Warden for the Borough, and your Committee have duly appointed Mr. Lake in accordance with this recommendation at a meeting held prior to the Quarterly Council meeting today. Mr. Lake has had considerable experience of actual blitz conditions in Birmingham where he served for some time as a Head Warden prior to taking up employment in Bewdley.

BOROUGH OF BEWDLEY

REPORT OF FINANCE COMMITTEE

Estimates - Financial Year 1943/44

Your Committee, in conjunction with the Chairmen of the Committees submitting estimates, have had before them and given careful consideration to the estimates of the probable receipts and expenditure of the various Committees of the Council for the year 1943/1944. In this connection they have also considered the requirements of the County Council for the year 1943/1944.

Yours Committee recommend that the Estimates as now submitted be approved and thereon that a General Rate of Fourteen shillings in the £ be made for the year ending 31st March 1944.

General Rate Estimates
Year ending 31st March, 1944.
Services administered by the Borough Council

Waterworks..............................	£ 456			
Housing..................................	£ 376			
Health Services..........................	£4397			
Public Lighting..........................	£ 114			
Highways.................................	£ 909			
Other Services and expenses..............	£2293	£8545		
Deduct General Exchequer Contribution	£2615			
Adjustment of Balances........	£1551	£4166	£4379	£4379
General Cunty Expenses...................	£4997			
Higher Education.........................	£ 864	£5861		
Special County Purposes				
Police:..................................	£ 936			
Elementary Education.....................	£2880			
Maternity and Child Welfare..............	£ 216			
Midwives.................................	£ 72			
Library..................................	£ 144			
Civil Defence............................	£ 72	£4320		
Leviable in addition to Poundage Rate:				
Small Pox Hospital.......................	£ 12	£ 12	£10193	
Deduct Exchequer Grant L.T. Licences			£ 2405	£7788
North West Worcestershire Assessment Committee				13
				£12180

A penny Rate is estimated to produce £72. 10.,
A 14/-., Rate is estimated to produce £12180.

Chapter Six

1944
BEFORE AND AFTER 'D' DAY

D Day - 6 June 1944 - the Invasion of France by the Allies moves the war in favour of British and Americans in Europe whilst in Russia the Germans are pushed ever west away from Moscow, Leningrad and Stalingrad. The fighting in the Far East is equally bloody, but the Allies are closing down on the Japanese in Burma, the Phillipines and China.

De Gaulle returned to Paris with the Allies, but the Germans launched flying bombs against England. In November, Churchill, Eden and De Gaulle took part in Armistice Day celebrations in Paris.

In Kidderminster, between 3 and 18 March, and exhibition took place at the Art Gallery in the library building entitled, "The Evil We Fight," depicting the philosophy of Nazi teachings and its application in Germany and the occupied countries.

Severn Valley Railway

SHIRE CANAL

STOURPORT CIRCULAR

Photograph kindly supplied by Mr. J. Harper

STOURPORT-ON-SEVERN, WHAT'S IN A NAME?

Discover the hidden delights of Stourport and its surrounding countryside

NORTH WORCESTERSHIRE
COUNTRYSIDE
Action
PROJECT
IN BROMSGROVE AND WYRE FOREST

D-DAY

6 JUNE, 1944

A little before midnight on 5 June Allied bombers made a heavy attack on the Normandy coast. These assaults in very great strength lasted until shortly before dawn. Early next morning two naval task forces under Rear-Admiral Sir Philip Vian and Rear-Admiral Alan Kirke successfully landed on the enemy beaches. These forces were under the supreme command of Admiral Sir Bertram Ramsay and were joined by the bombarding forces in the course of the night. Landing operations were successfully completed shortly before dawn. Enemy torpedo boats which attempted to interfere were successfully driven off, and one of their number was sunk and another severely damaged. Assault troops were landed under heavy fire from destroyers while battleships engaged enemy shore batteries. Further troops were landed by gliders and troop-carrying machines. The beaches were covered by intensive cross-fire from German pillboxes, but although the casualties were not light, they were not nearly so heavy as had been expected. Underwater obstacles were encountered neck deep by commandos who came first ashore, but in spite of these difficulties, they succeeded in landing and silencing the pillboxes. Meanwhile Allied fighter bombers continued to attack the beaches in very great strength, attacking gun emplacements, defensive works and communications. Continuous fighter cover was also given over the naval operations, the beaches and even some miles inland. Night fighters protected the transports. On the first day, penetrations of several miles inland were made. The enemy was completely taken by surprise and important bridges were seized before the Germans had time to demolish them. The picture, reproduced by permission of the Netherlands Government Information Bureau, shows Dutch troops of the "Princess Irene" Brigade landing on the beaches of Normandy.

June, 1944

General de Gaulle

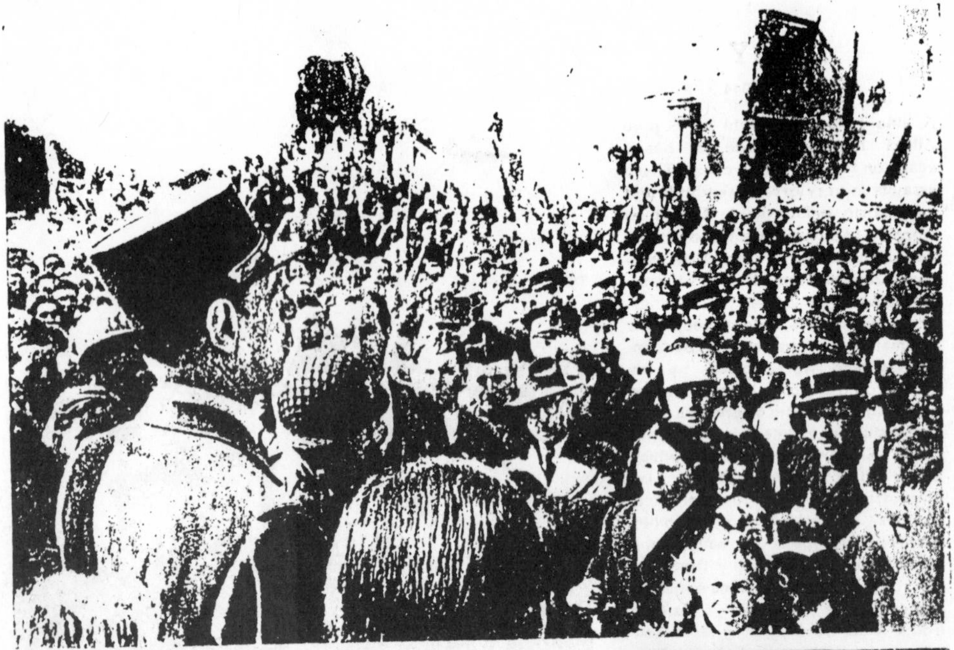

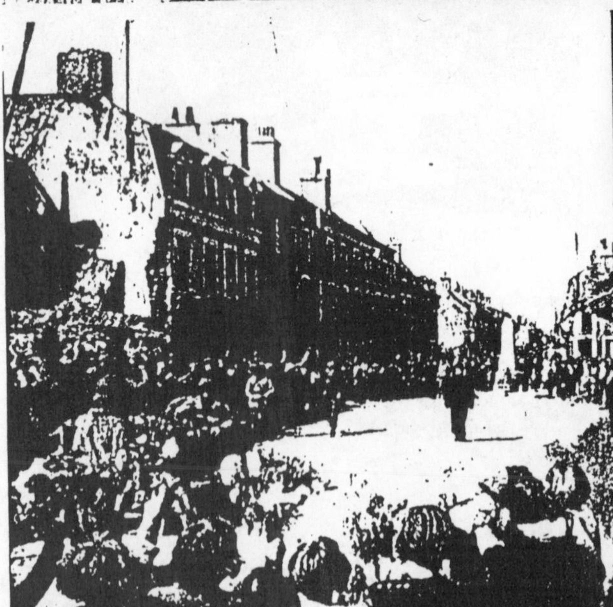

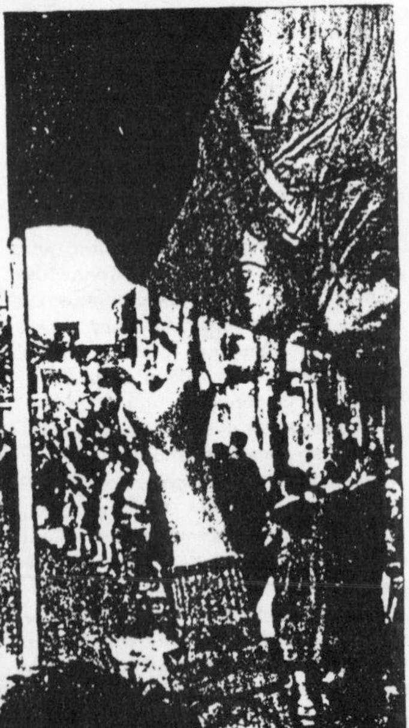

FRENCH LEADER IN BAYEUX. On 20 June, the Americans made a rapid advance towards Cherbourg without meeting serious opposition and by the evening were in St. Martin in the outer defences and only four miles from the port. A few days earlier General de Gaulle had arrived in Normandy to visit a number of places which had been liberated by the Anglo-American forces. Top left, General de Gaulle addresses a crowd. Bottom left, the people of Bayeux await his arrival. Above, General de Gaulle walks through the streets of Bayeux.

GENERAL DE GAULLE IN PARIS. After the capitulation of the German garrison, General de Gaulle arrived in Paris to celebrate its liberation from Nazi control

Anglo-Americans cross France

June—August, 1944

GENERAL DE GAULLE RETURNS TO PARIS. On the day following the liberation of Paris, the acknowledged leader of France headed a great procession from the Arc de Triomphe through the main streets of the capital to the Cathedral of Notre Dame. Here a solemn thanksgiving service was held. As the General arrived at the cathedral an attempt was made on his life by snipers hidden in an adjoining building, but their bullets fortunately missed him. The picture above shows General de Gaulle leaving Notre Dame after the service of thanksgiving.

While the British were advancing in the region of Caen and southwards to Caumont and Tilly, where there was heavy and prolonged fighting, the Americans swept across the Cotentin peninsula to the Gulf of St. Malo. Their object, of course, was to isolate Cherbourg and capture the port from the rear. On 29 June Cherbourg fell and the whole peninsula was firmly in Allied hands. Thus the bridgehead in Normandy was made quite secure and the first stage in the liberation of France was completed.

The next stage of the fighting in Normandy was one of slow progress all along the line as the Germans launched their expected counter-attacks. Such advances as there were, were achieved only by close and bitter fighting. The capture of Caen on 8 July, however, marked an important gain on the British-Canadian sector of the front for it gave us solid bridgeheads over the rivers Odon and Orne. Fighting was extremely severe here because the enemy had concentrated picked infantry and armoured forces—some of them switched from the Russian front to stem the Allied advance into the open country. Once an Allied break-through was achieved, as the Germans knew well, it would have consequences that would be far-reaching.

By the beginning of August this break-through was achieved. The battle became one of movement with the Allies holding the initiative everywhere. The Americans advanced rapidly to St. Malo and southwards to the Loire cutting off the whole of the Brittany peninsula and the Germans contained there. Driving westwards they liberated great areas of Western France, reaching Chartres and Orleans by the middle of the month. A determined enemy counter-attack from the region of Mortain, which attempted to split the Allied armies in two, was successfully held. Meanwhile, by the Canadian and British thrust southwards from Caen towards Falaise and by the turn of the columns from the south to Argentan, a large part of the German forces was trapped in the Falaise " pocket." The enemy was

MR. CHURCHILL IN PARIS. On 11 November the British Prime Minister, accompanied by Mr. Eden, took part in the Armistice Day celebrations in Paris at the invitation of General de Gaulle. After laying a wreath on the Unknown Soldier's tomb at the Arc de Triomphe, Mr. Churchill and General de Gaulle, followed by Mr. Eden, M. Bidault and other British and French leaders, walked down the famous Champs-Elysées to the thunderous cheers of "Vive Churchill!" and "Vive de Gaulle!" In the photograph Mr. Churchill is seen acknowledging crowds.

Kidderminster Shuttle

STOURPORT COURIER AND WORCESTERSHIRE MERCURY ESTA[illegible]

"THE EVIL WE FIGHT"

AN EXHIBITION

[illegible]

ART GALLERY

Kidderminster

3rd to 18th MARCH

Open Daily, 10 to 7

Sundays, 2 to 7

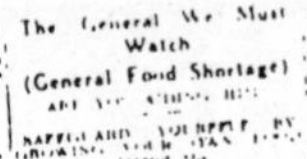

The General We Must Watch

(General Food Shortage)

[illegible]

FREE FILM SHOW

PUBLIC LIBRARY

Wednesday, March 8th

[illegible]

GARDEN & CURRENT TOPICAL FILMS

(Presented by Ministry of Information)

Join the ever increasing crowd of attenders at these interesting, educative, and instructional film shows.

ALLOTMENTS AVAILABLE IN THE TOWN

R. W. FRENCH

Parks Superintendent and Allotments Superintendent

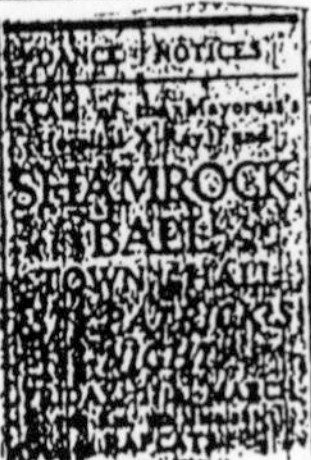

Registered for the Unit[illegible]

PUBLIC NOTICES

TRANSFER OF FOOD REGISTRATIONS

In consequence of a change of ownership persons registered with SMITHS [illegible] LTD., 1[illegible], [illegible] Road, Kidderminster, for Rationed Foods will have their REGISTRATIONS automatically TRANSFERRED to the new proprietor, MR. ALBERT FRANCIS DAVIS, unless application for transfer to another trader is made at the Food Office before 18th March, 1944.

[illegible]

SATURDAY JANUARY 15, 1944

Entertaining Americans. — Two groups of local entertainers put on performances for the patients at the American Hospital on Wednesday evening, January 12th. Children of Miss Fawcett's School of Dancing gave a dance revue in the post theatre for the ambulatory patients who have little opportunity to see children. Two wards in which most of the patients are either in casts or are confined to bed were covered by the lyrics group, who put on a show of song and comedy. The patients indicated their appreciation of the talent of both groups, and also the expression of interest in their welfare on the part of the community. Contact between the above groups and the American Hospital was made through Mr. William A. Price, 113, Mill Street, Kidderminster, chairman of the Community Hospital Council, who will be pleased to accept further offers of help.

2t Feb 1944

PARCELS FROM AMERICA

Local Distribution to Evacuees

A number of the parcels sent by school children, members of the American Junior Red Cross, to evacuated children in this country was distributed at an informal gathering at the Billeting Office on February 12th. The recipients were Smethwick evacuees living in Kidderminster. These children have some good friends among the members of the Smethwick W.V.S., and it was through the influence and interest of these ladies that the distribution of the parcels was made possible.

A similar distribution took place last year, and letters of thanks written by evacuees were dispatched to "American cousins" expressing gratitude for their kindness. These letters were the beginning of a series, and have been the means of making pleasant contact with children of the Junior Red Cross in U.S.A.

The ceremony on Saturday afternoon was arranged by Miss M. Sheward (Smethwick Party Leader), and over 60 Smethwick evacuees and their foster-parents were present. The parcels were distributed by Mr. G. F. Bennett (Chief Education Officer, Smethwick). Others attending included Mrs. Bennett, Mrs. Pickering and other representatives of the Smethwick W.V.S., Miss Billingsley, Mrs. Felton, Mrs. Dodd, Mrs. Sheward and Mrs. Pugh. The Chief Billeting Officer (Mr. W. Geo. Carter) was unable to attend as he was conducting the Old Time Ball at the Baths.

Welcoming the visitors, foster-parents and children, Miss Sheward expressed thanks to the American Junior Red Cross for the parcels. She referred to the many letters which had started a mutual correspondence between [illegible] in Great Britain and children in America, and read an interesting letter from Junior Red Cross members attending a school at No. 9 Moorestown, N.J., U.S.A. Miss Sheward reminded evacuees present to write letters of thanks to the children who had kindly sent the parcels being distributed that afternoon.

A vote of thanks was proposed by Michael Jourhis, who called for cheers. During the afternoon Mr. Bennett, on behalf of the Smethwick Education Committee, thanked foster-parents in Kidderminster for their care and kindness to the evacuees. The parcels contained varied and useful gifts such as soap, facecloths, handkerchiefs, toys, necklaces, toothbrushes, etc., and gave a great deal of pleasure to the young recipients.

COMMUNITY COUNCIL

Friends of the American Hospital

The Community Hospital Council's second meeting, held in the Mayor's Parlour, Kidderminster on Tuesday evening, was proof of the fine spirit of friendliness and co-operation that exists between the American Hospital and the surrounding community.

Early in December the group was organised into a general council to promote the welfare of the staff and patients of the hospital. Since that time the hospital has enjoyed visits from the Royal Army Pay Corps, the Boys' Choir of the Harry Cheshire School, the Kidderminster Carpet Trades, the Lyrics, Miss Fawcett's Dancing School, and lectures by Mrs. A. [illegible] and Miss Mona Matthews, and the American Red Cross has been aided in its recreation and welfare work by volunteers from the community.

The hospital [illegible] put on exhibition basket ball games, a very fast and exciting American sport, and has extended an invitation to all the community friends to attend all their games at the Baths. The hospital [illegible] against other American teams every Thursday evening and plays intramural games on Tuesday and Sunday evenings. The match scheduled for Thursday, the 24th, is expected to be a particularly exciting one. Plans are being made for [illegible] parties, darts tournaments, concert parties and lectures about the history and sites of interest in the immediate vicinity, and sightseeing tours.

Present at the meeting were the Mayor and Mrs. [illegible], [illegible] William [illegible], Mr. [illegible] Chadwick, Mrs. [illegible], Mr. [illegible] Knight, Mr. [illegible] Clifford, [illegible]

[illegible]

INSTER SHUTTLE

AMERICANS ADOPT BRITISH CHILDREN

The 52nd Hospital Entertains

Four small radiant children, their arms full of blue and white parcels tied up with red string, trooped out of warm quarters at the American 52nd hospital on Tuesday afternoon and entered waiting cars. They had been guests of the hospital personnel for a special reason, and they'd had a few hours of unforgettable happiness. American service men and nurses crowded about the cars to tuck the small visitors up warmly in rugs and wave them on their way back to their homes. As a nurse said as she looked after the departing cars, "It's done our hearts and eyes good to have these kids. They're sure grand."

The four children—two boys and two girls—are war orphans who have been adopted by the 52nd Hospital. Sandy-haired Ian and dark-eyed Audrey belong to the enlisted men; [illegible] Ronald is the nurses' responsibility and bunny little Margaret will be the special care of the officers. The children are all eight years old.

The adoptions are part of a scheme inaugurated during the last war under the Stars and Stripes War Orphans Fund which is administered under the American Red Cross. American units stationed throughout this country have during the present war, adopted 436 British children whose fathers were killed in service to their country. The vast majority of them are orphans and all are the children of people in poor circumstances. The scheme involves a cost of £100 for each adoption, and the money provides those extra comforts and opportunities which might otherwise be denied a child deprived of parental care. The children are placed in the care of foster parents (those who have mothers are, of course, permitted to remain in their charge) and the American units undertake to educate, clothe, and find these children positions in the future. In fact, they are playing the role of fairy godfathers and godmothers and to carry out the purpose of the scheme have raised a fund of £47,000. There are few things dearer to the heart of the average adult than seeing a child made happy and the security of its future assured. The generosity of our American visitors will find genuine response in this country and do much to fan the flame of friendship between the two nations.

Like the other 430 children who will benefit under the scheme, Ian, Audrey, Ronald and Margaret were chosen by the personnel of the hospital from submitted lists. Cases were investigated, and last November the adoptions were arranged and effected. Ian, Audrey, and Margaret live in London, and Ronald is residing at Dinnington.

A GREAT DAY

Men and women at the hospital naturally wished to make the acquaintance of the children they have adopted, and, after permission had been obtained for the little ones to visit their benefactors, Tuesday, February 22, was set aside for the event. The three London children did quite an amount of travelling since they had to make the journey from their homes and back in a single day. All had American Women Welfare Officers as escorts.

Great preparations had been made to give the children a good time. "Eats," naturally, figured prominently in the programme. No celebrities could have been subject to more clicking of cameras and requests for "a big smile, please," and it is safe to say that many pictures of the four excited youngsters will find their way across the Atlantic to American homes. Four large cakes decorated with white icing and pink roses had been prepared by the chefs, and one of the high spots of the outing was the cutting of these by the young guests, who were promptly given large slices to sample. The specially prepared meal, which was eaten in the company of the colonel, the officers, and men, included generous helpings of ice cream—a luxury few British children have tasted during the last three or four years.

After dinner the children stood with the colonel to watch the review and take the salute. Later, to their delight, they were wrapped up warmly and taken for a ride [illegible]

[illegible]

[illegible] the public of Kidder[illegible] recognise the necessity [illegible] continue to play their part [illegible]nancing not only this war [illegible] also the peace that is to [illegible]w.

LOCAL NEWS

[illegible]avings Committee.—A meet[illegible] of Kidderminster National [illegible]ings Executive Committee [illegible] be held in the Council [illegible]mber next Monday, at [illegible], when reports on the [illegible]lute the Soldier" campaign [illegible] be submitted.

[illegible]An Hour With John Wesley," [illegible]ext Wednesday at Birmin[illegible] Road Methodist Church [illegible] 206th anniversary of [illegible]sley's conversion) there will [illegible] an unusual service, when [illegible] speakers will deal with [illegible]pshots of Wesley's life, [illegible]rspersed with community [illegible]ging at 7.30.

[illegible]ntertainment. — Pupils of [illegible] Elsie Dyer, M.R.A.D., [illegible].T.D. (S.B.) had an [illegible]husiastic reception when [illegible]y entertained patients at the [illegible]d American Hospital on [illegible]sday, May 29th, with some [illegible] their popular song and dance [illegible]. Pupils taking part [illegible]: Daisy Rooke, A.Inst.T.D., [illegible] Vale, [illegible] Wester, [illegible] Langford, Marian [illegible], Doreen Cassler, Jean [illegible]don, Edna Oliver, Joyce [illegible] and Josephine Roberts. [illegible]companist was: Mr. Ronald [illegible]illams, L.R.A.M. [illegible]

Wardens' Entertain. — An [illegible]oyable evening was spent at [illegible] Village Hall on Mon[illegible] last, when [illegible] wardens [illegible] [illegible]

tee, which has done such great work for the Movement.

Anglo-America Ball.—Kidderminster dancers had the opportunity to dance to the music of both America and England at the Anglo-American Ball held at the Gilderdrome on Thursday, May 4th. Organised by the Kidderminster National Savings Committee for "Salute the Soldier" week, the dance was a great success. Excellent music was supplied by an American Army dance band and the Rascals Dance Orchestra, and a fully-licensed bar and buffet was in operation. During the evening the Mayor (Alderman J. Tolley) announced that Kidderminster's target of £300,000 had been reached, and that the total reached was £500,000. "Remember what we owe to our fighting men," he said. "We are all waiting for the second front to open; let us see that Kidderminster plays a part in it."

Dancing Success.—Friends of Miss Bernadette Molloy, late of Marlpool Lane, Kidderminster, now of Blackpool, will be interested to hear of her success in passing the Royal Academy of Dancing Examination (6th grade, Higher Division), with honours. At present Bernadette is appearing at the Palace Theatre, Blackpool, and also rehearsing for her third successive season with the Tower Circus. During the pantomime season she played the part of [illegible] in Tom Arnold's production of "Aladdin," at the Grand Theatre, Leeds. She has also danced in such well-known productions as [illegible] [illegible]

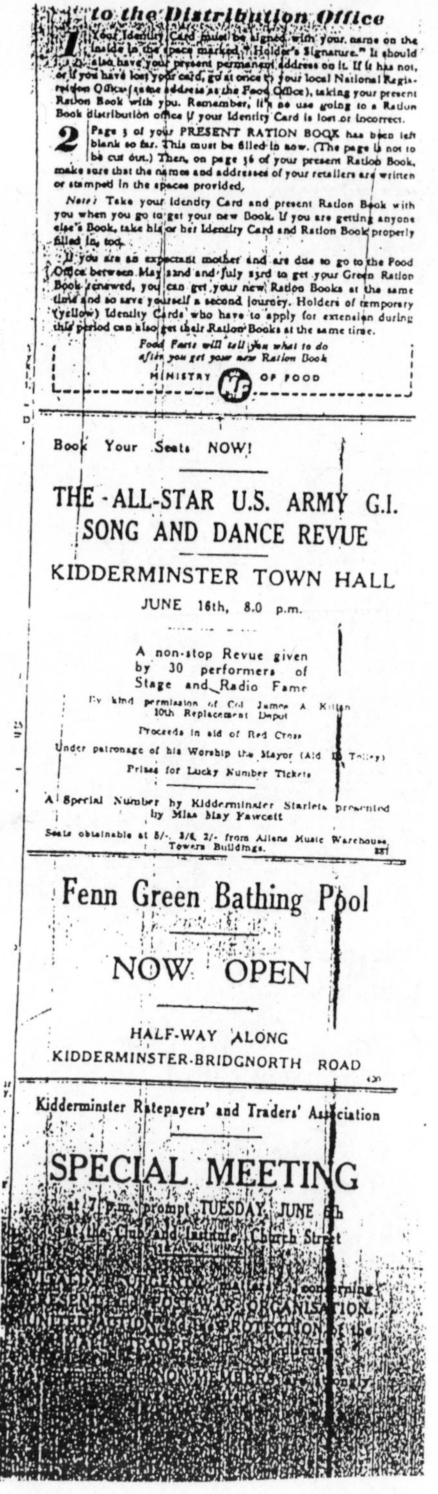

to the Distribution Office

1 Your Identity Card must be signed with your name on the inside in the space marked "Holder's Signature." It should also have your present permanent address on it. If it has not, or if you have lost your card, go at once to your local National Registration Office (same address as the Food Office), taking your present Ration Book with you. Remember, it's no use going to a Ration Book distribution office if your Identity Card is lost or incorrect.

2 Page 3 of your PRESENT RATION BOOK has been left blank so far. This must be filled in now. (The page is not to be cut out.) Then, on page 36 of your present Ration Book, make sure that the names and addresses of your retailers are written or stamped in the spaces provided.

Note: Take your Identity Card and present Ration Book with you when you go to get your new Book. If you are getting anyone else's Book, take his or her Identity Card and Ration Book properly filled in, too.

If you are an expectant mother and are due to go to the Food Office between May 22nd and July 23rd to get your Green Ration Book renewed, you can get your new Ration Books at the same time and so save yourself a second journey. Holders of temporary (yellow) Identity Cards who have to apply for extension during this period can also get their Ration Books at the same time.

Food Facts will tell you what to do after you get your new Ration Book

MINISTRY OF FOOD

Book Your Seats NOW!

THE ALL-STAR U.S. ARMY G.I. SONG AND DANCE REVUE

KIDDERMINSTER TOWN HALL

JUNE 16th, 8.0 p.m.

A non-stop Revue given by 30 performers of Stage and Radio Fame

By kind permission of Col. James A. Killian 10th Replacement Depot

Proceeds in aid of Red Cross

Under patronage of his Worship the Mayor (Ald. J. Tolley)

Prizes for Lucky Number Tickets

A Special Number by Kidderminster Starlets presented by Miss May Fawcett

Seats obtainable at 5/-, 3/6, 2/- from Allens Music Warehouse, Towers Buildings.

Fenn Green Bathing Pool

NOW OPEN

HALF-WAY ALONG KIDDERMINSTER-BRIDGNORTH ROAD

Kidderminster Ratepayers' and Traders' Association

SPECIAL MEETING

at 7 p.m. prompt TUESDAY, JUNE 6th

at the Club and Institute, Church Street

[illegible] VITALLY IMPORTANT matters concerning PRESENT and POST-WAR ORGANISATION, UNITED ACTION and PROTECTION of the SMALL TRADERS [illegible]

NON-MEMBERS are [illegible] [illegible]

[S]TALINGRAD BEDS

[£1,0]15 Effort for Russian Hospital

[It] was stated at a meeting of [Kidd]erminster Anglo-Soviet Friend[ship] Committee and donors, on [Wedn]esday, that the recent appeal [to] raise funds for endowing [K]idderminster Beds" in the new [Stali]ngrad Hospital realised £1,015 [..] 8d. Total expenses amounted [to £..] 10s. 1d. A sum of £900 had [been] sent to the General Com[mitte]e for the endowment of six [beds] which left a balance of £75 [..] 1d. for disposal. Two [of] the [beds] are to be named after the [Borough] of Kidderminster and one after the Hartlebury Rafmen... [Benev]olent Fund, Kidderminster [Indu]strial Co-operative Society, [Kidd]erminster Darts Club and [Kidd]erminster Trades and Labour [illegible]

[Th]e Mayor, Ald. L. Tolley, pre[sided] over the meeting in the [Mayo]r's Parlour and in moving [the a]doption of the financial state[ment] said people had responded generously. He [illegible] [opp]ortunity of expressing [illegible] [illegible] to everybody [illegible] a result that reflected credit on British [illegible] [enth]usiasm to recognise Russia as [a g]reat and mighty nation and a [gal]lant ally. That form of tribute was most noble.

[M]r. F. G. Bayliss, hon. treasurer, [gave] the statement which had been [meti]culously audited by Messrs. [..]natone, Moulder and Tyre[..]. Items of income were flag [days] and kindred sources of dona[tions] £246 7s. 11d., Kidderminster [Co-o]perative Society (£150), Darts [..] £92, collecting cards (£..) [..] 9d., per Mr. J. Areader (£..), [Kid]derminster Football League [..] 1s. 8d.

[R]eplying to Mr. Ernest Pearsall [who] asked what was to become of [the] balance in hand, the Mayor [st]ated that as the public appeal [was] for a definite object, the [proc]eeds must not be used for any [othe]r cause, not even to the new [fund] which was being opened for [relie]f in the liberated areas of [Rus]sia.

[T]he treasurer stated that when [the] national fund closed actually [mor]e than the amount of the target [figu]re had been raised.

[Th]e Mayor advised that the [Kid]derminster surplus should be [us]ed for additional equipment [for] the Stalingrad Hospital as the [nati]onal committee proposed. A [reso]lution to this effect was moved [by] Mr. E. W. Walters, J.P., and [seco]nded by Mr. W. Davis, chair[man] of the local Anglo-Soviet [Frie]ndship Committee, who pointed [out] that one bed at £150 was [nam]ed in the initial appeal.

[Th]e Mayor was enthusiastically [than]ked for his personal interest [and] help, on the proposition of [Mr.] E. W. Walters, who said Ald. [Toll]ey was keenly interested in [good] causes and worked hard [thro]ughout such undertakings.

[R]eplying, the Mayor said this [had] been a real labour of love to [him], for his regard for Russia was [not] newly found.

[T]he Secretary, Mr. J. E. Cooper, [stat]ed that so far it had not been [poss]ible to fix a date when the [Dea]n of Canterbury, Dr. Hewlett [Johns]on, could address a Kidder[minst]er meeting on Anglo-Soviet [Frien]dship.

[illegible]

ENGAGEMENTS

LEADING SEAMAN A. [illegible] AND MISS PAMELA [illegible]

[illegible]

MARRIAGES

[illegible]—On June 1 at [illegible] Church, Kidderminster, [illegible] son of Mr. and Mrs. [illegible], Lebanon, Kentucky, U.S.A., to Joy, daughter of Mrs. [illegible] Howard, 33, [illegible] Rd., Kidderminster, and the late Mr. S. Howard.

EVANS—SMITH.—On Thursday, June 1, 1944, at the [illegible] Church, by the Rev. [illegible], [illegible] Frank, younger son of Mrs. E. Evans, [illegible], to Miss Doris Irene Smith, of 133, [illegible] Rd.

SILVER WEDDINGS

[illegible]—Hearty congratulations, mum and dad, on the anniversary of your silver wedding, June 7. That you may enjoy good health and every happiness is the sincere wish [illegible]

GROOMS—ROWE.—On June 7, 1919, at Mill St. Methodist Church, Kidderminster, by the Rev. [illegible], William H. Grooms to Lucy Rowe. Present address: 5, Park Butts, Kidderminster.

KILLED IN ACTION

WOODWARD.—On May 19, 1944, killed on active service in Burma, Jack, the well beloved son of the late C. A. Woodward and Mrs. Woodward, The [illegible], Oldnall Rd., Kidderminster, aged 24 years.

MISSING

BRYAN-SMITH.—Missing from air operations on the night of June 5-6, 1944, Squadron Leader Martin Bryan-Smith, D.F.C., R.A.F.V.R. (Pathfinder Force), adored husband of Anne (nee Tomkinson), [illegible] Road, Wolverley, Kidderminster, and beloved youngest son of Mr. and Mrs. P. H. Bryan-Smith, of Trees, Springhill Lane, Penn, Wolverhampton.

DEATHS

BENNETT.—On May [..], at the [illegible] Hospital, Bromsgrove, Mary Anne Bennett, beloved wife of W. A. Bennett, [illegible] Hill St., Kidderminster, passed peacefully away after a short but painful [illegible] patiently borne.

DARKS.—On Sunday, June 4, 1944, at the General Hospital, Kidderminster, Julia [illegible], late of [illegible], passed peacefully away after a short illness, aged [..] years.

SOUTHALL.—On Thursday, May 25, William Henry Southall, of 39, [illegible] Rd., Kidderminster, aged 75.

THORNELOE.—On June 2, 1944, Harry Thorneloe, [illegible] Road, in his [..] year.

IN MEMORIAM

[illegible]

Mrs. SOUTHALL and Mrs. WOOD (daughters) of [illegible] Rd., Kidderminster, wish to thank relatives, friends and neighbours for sympathy shown in their recent bereavement, and the doctor for his kindness and splendid attention, also for [illegible] sent.

Mrs. F. [illegible] and family, [illegible] Rd., [illegible], wish to thank relatives, neighbours and friends for their kindness and letters of sympathy in their sad loss of [illegible] killed in action.

The Kidderminster Shuttle

SATURDAY, JUNE 10, 1944

D Day

Although for months and months we have been anxiously awaiting the day when Allied forces should set foot once again on French soil—the day for which we and patriots in all occupied countries have prayed — there was almost something of dramatic surprise when, on Tuesday morning, we learned from B.B.C. broadcasts that the great D Day had arrived. Realisation of this fact took some little time to assert itself, but as the day wore on and fresh bulletins became available the true significance of the great operation became apparent. What has been loosely termed "The Second Front" is indeed a reality, the stern battle is on, and during the next few weeks and months there will be ever-increasing activity and maybe anxieties and some disappointments. Over-riding all, however, is the fact that Britain and her Allies have launched the biggest crusade which history has ever known to rid the world of its greatest oppressor and to free from their shackles those unfortunate victims who for the past four years have been under the Nazi yoke. By the grace of God that crusade will continue to be successful until the evil that is in Europe is finally overcome and expurgated. It is with this knowledge and with the certainty that our cause is a righteous one that we go forth to battle. We know, too, of the vast might of our armour and the dauntless courage of our men and our Allies, and we who are left at home can take pride that we, too, have played our part in this great campaign against evil. But in our elation it would be wrong to feel that now we can relax. The Prime Minister has reminded us that there are stern days ahead. It is but right, therefore, that all our energies should be maintained to ensure that the men fighting our battles shall continue to receive all the arms, ammunition and equipment they need. Any slackening now might have a serious effect on the final issue. It is for that reason that we [illegible]

Appreciation. — It is not generally known that the local Y.M.C.A. numbers among its many services the repair and pressing of uniforms for men of H.M. Forces. This is a service the men deeply appreciate as the voluntary workers who undertake the job well know. Recently the hon. supervisor (Mrs. Clifford) received a grateful letter from Pte. Walter F. Barham, which expresses the gratitude of those who avail themselves of this and other services at the Orchard Street premises. "May I take the opportunity," he writes, "to thank you very much indeed for the kind action in doing the much needed job of mending the rather well-worn khaki trousers for me. It is indeed a real pleasure to find someone to do these jobs when we are far away from home and cannot get things done so easily. Thanks also for the hours of hard work you all put in for us, that we might have tea and cakes, etc., at almost a moment's notice. We should miss you all very much if you were not there at the Y.M.C.A., and be far less content than at present. Kind regards, and thanks again and again."

Savings Movement. — It is very often said that our resources enable us to spend £14,000,000 on war. They "enable" nothing of the sort. The position is that we are being held as a nation at ransom. We are forking out at the pointing of a pistol—by Hitler—every ounce of wealth that can be turned into currency. We are staking our savings and our scrapings; our capital, the life of our machinery, engines, furnaces, soil itself, and the proceeds of a mortgage on all our future; on being able to survive Hitler's pistol threat. Is it not misleading to describe the £15,000,000 a day which the war is costing us as being purely for destructive purposes? Considering that it is our lives and liberties which are at stake it would appear that it would be difficult to imagine a more constructive purpose. Money must, therefore, continue to be saved. If, by great sacrifices, the results of a sound financial policy have been hardly won, they might, by some slight relaxation, be very easily lost. It is, therefore, assumed that there will be no falling off in the magnificent voluntary effort which the country has made in response to the War Savings campaign. One Member of Parliament has suggested that campaign figures are "rigged," and the Chancellor of the Exchequer, referring to this, has said: "The honorable gentleman is indebted to his memory for his facts, and to his imagination for his facts." Since the "Salute the Soldier" campaign in Kidderminster savings have increased—the last three weeks have resulted in two weeks of over £10,000, and last week £14,[..] (R.A.F. £1,300, Carpet Trades £312, Savings Shop £[..], Royal [..] £[..]), and the grand total is now £1,[..].

SATURDAY, JUNE 10, 1944

National Cinematograph [Bene]volent Fund [illegible]

American Red Cross. — On Wednesday, local members of the Women's League of Health and Beauty under their leader, Miss Mary Hall, gave an enjoyable physical show to patients at the [..]nd General Hospital, opening with a comedy number and dressed in [illegible] [illegible] girls showed the [illegible] exercises [illegible] [illegible] display [illegible] national dances [illegible] and [illegible] Mary [illegible] were Mary [illegible] Margaret [illegible] Wright [illegible] The [illegible] Meredith [illegible] girls left with [illegible]

A [illegible]

OUR PREMIER VISITS FRANCE

On Tuesday morning it was announced that on the previous day Mr. Churchill spent several hours ashore in France. We were told that our Service men could hardly believe the evidence of their own eyes when they saw him. But when they did realise that their visitor was really Mr. Churchill their joy was unbounded. We can imagine the welcome he received. Do we, at the same time, realise the full significance of his visit? What does it mean for France and the whole world?

It was only a week after the invasion forces landed in Normandy, and Mr. Churchill walked through French villages giving the "V" sign and smoking his cigar! The imagination will supply what it means to our own men and the inhabitants of Normandy who often crowded around his car to cheer him. There is another and greater significance. It is suggested if we ask ourselves "How would Hitler be received?" That we shall never know, because Hitler would never dare to trust himself even to walk freely among his own people, much less among the people of any other European nation.

Hitler's life would not be safe, and he would not be wanted because in the words of Shakespeare, men feel regarding him, "There's neither honesty, manhood, nor good fellowship in thee." While of Mr. Churchill men feel and would say again in Shakespeare's words:

"His words are bonds, his oaths are oracles;
His love sincere, his thoughts immaculate;
His heart as far from fraud as heaven from earth."

The state of a man's conscience accounts not only for his hopes and fears; it also determines his outward conduct, evidenced in his trust, or distrust of his fellows. Conscience warns men what to expect from their fellows, and so teaches men what courses to shun and what to pursue.

GIRLS IN BLUE

W.A.A.F. Will Help To Liberate Europe

The Women's Auxiliary Air Force has a vital part to play in the Royal Air Force's contribution to the liberation of Europe. Men and women are working side by side in preparation for the great assault, and the women on the ground will have their share in whatever successes are achieved in the air.

Since the beginning of the war the two sections of the Service have worked hard together. As the war has progressed and the strength of the W.A.A.F. has grown, women have been able to release greater numbers of men for more active and strenuous work, and year by year the list of jobs which they have been able to perform has lengthened.

Take a day in the life of an R.A.F. fighter pilot of the Allied Expeditionary Force who may be concerned in the defence of liberated territory but who at present operates from Britain. It well illustrates the reliance that is placed in the W.A.A.F. A W.A.A.F. driver will drive him to the control tower where he will visit the meteorological office for the day's weather forecast. Up-to-the-minute information is supplied by R.A.F. officers and their W.A.A.F. assistants. The girls plot frequent weather charts from information supplied from all parts of the country and from their own [illegible] [illegible] the girl who can read [illegible]

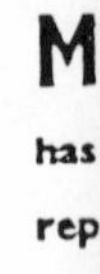

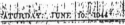

[illegible] AMERICAN VIEWS [illegible] BRITAIN

A Striking Tribute

An American soldier's views on [Brit]ain are strikingly revealed in [a] letter he has sent to the local [pa]per and a cutting of which Mr. [an]d Mrs. A. E. Pardoe, The Elms, [Bro]adbrook, Kidderminster, have [rec]eived from Mrs. Pardoe's [illegible] Mr. [illegible] Russell, [illegible] Order of Tacoma, Washing[ton]. The soldier is a Pte. Thad [illegible] and his father is [illegible] of the Tacoma Chamber [of] Commerce. The letter runs: [illegible] think you should hear in [illegible] always the tremendous [debt] you owe to England. Oh, [I] know they owe us money [but] we owe them tens of thou[sands of] American lives. They [st]ood alone under the blitz, that [mu]ch you know, but you don't [kn]ow what carrying on under a [blit]z is.

"You can't know the tight [kno]t in your belly when the [bom]bs blow and you have to fight [the] urge to run and cower in a [she]lter. It's no pleasant sensa[tio]n. Then come the bombs [sha]king the ground under you [and yo]ur only defence is your small [tin] hat, and your luck.

"These people stood under that [for] many months. Since they [bor]e the brunt, you at home [live] in peace and safety. You [sho]uld remember they are still [figh]ting. They still drop the [illegible] bombs over Germany. The [Brit]ish fleet is still patrolling the [Atl]antic, and the coastal com[mand] has sunk many a submar[ine].

"England asks nothing of [Am]erica. They hold out their [han]d as a friend. I know they [ha]ve an empire and their auto[cra]cy is condemned in the far [east]. Even here at home they [ha]ve their autocratic customs [and] they do have faults, many [of] them. They admit it, and [in] their own fashion will correct [the]m. We, however, do not come [with] little Eves, so let him who [has] no fault cast the first stone.

"I ask that you people at home [thi]nk hard about this island of [Eng]land. With them as partners [we] will have peace. Neither of [the] nations desires the goods of [their] neighbours, so together we [will] be able to see that no [illegible] party tries to take the [goo]ds they covet by force. A full [illegible] alliance covering the [worl]d may be called by some an [entan]gling alliance, and I think [it] is so, an alliance that will [entan]gle us with the web of [pea]ce. To have peace at home, [the] states became entangled with [one] another and became one of [the] greatest nations on the face [of] the earth. Think about it! [It] is well worth your while."

The right use of leisure may [illegible] in the end as urgent and [illegible] as the right use of [mac]hinery." — Sir Noel Curtis-[Be]nnett, Chairman, National Play[ing] Field Association.

3 MAY 44

The New Alderman.—To the [ge]neral regret of the members [of] the Guardians Committee [Al]derman H. N. Frost's new [ho]nour as alderman of the [Co]unty Council carries with it [the] forfeiture of the chairman[shi]p of the Guardians. For ten [ye]ars Alderman Frost has been [an] ideal chairman, and has kept [in] constant touch with all the [act]ivities of the local institu[tio]n.

Entertainment.—An enjoyable [ent]ertainment was provided by [Mr.] and Mrs. Jack Sneader with [the] "Sneaderminster" Variety [Co]ncert Party at the 82nd [Am]erican Hospital on Wednes[day] evening. The show was [abl]y compered by Arthur [Ho]wley. Artists were, Rae [Sne]ader, Dinks Johnson, Mar[ie] Baker, Stella Tyler, Eve [illegible], Irene Griffiths, Jack [Sne]ader, Arthur Howley, John [illegible], Bill Rose, Ivor Lowe: [pian]ist, Marcia Taylor.

ENTERTAINED BY THE MAYOR

Tribute to Our American Allies

It was a particularly happy feature on the part of the Mayor and Mayoress of Kidderminster (Ald. and Mrs. [illegible]) to arrange an official "get together" for members of the American forces, and both at the dance for officers on Tuesday night and at the concert for other ranks on Thursday night, one heard on every hand expressions of thanks for the cordiality of the welcome given them. Not only did the two events serve to bring together the men and women of the American units, but they also enabled them to meet in the friendliest of atmospheres local townspeople and members of British service units, and the general effect was one of mutual enjoyment.

The dance, which was held at the Gliderdrome on Tuesday, with the co-operation of Mr. E. Phipps, was a particularly happy affair. Some 350, including some Fighting French officers, had accepted the invitation of the Mayor and Mayoress, and from beginning to end the evening went with a swing. The Mayor and Mayoress, accompanied by their daughter, made it their business to meet all the guests [illegible] and [illegible] of the Town Council, Col. R. W. A. Painter (Sector Commander), Lt.-Col. C. Thatcher (C.O. 6th Bn. Worcs. Home Guard), Col. H. J. Hollingsworth (Officer Commanding R.A.P.C.), Capt. [illegible] (one of Kidderminster's repatriated prisoners of war who is now liaison officer with the American forces), and many others with local associations to extend the "glad hand" to the guests from the other side side of the Atlantic.

The Gliderdrome Orchestra was in good form, and, with Mr. E. C. Richards as M.C., a wide variety of dances was provided. Although the Americans "jived" and "jitter-bugged" with carefree abandon and obvious enjoyment, the "Palais Glide" proved the real hit of the evening. This dance was apparently new to the visitors, and they approached it with some diffidence, but before long they had mastered the steps and formed lines of happy, laughing dancers who demanded encore after encore for this novelty number.

Supper was served in the Florence Cafe where Miss Southall and her staff had arranged a tasty repast which was much appreciated, while liquid refreshment, like the supper, was also provided gratis by the Mayor's kindness.

During a brief interval the Mayor thanked all the guests for accepting the invitation to be present. He had had in mind, he said, that some of them had come many miles to take part in the conflict in the hope that ultimate victory would be ours and that they would have played some part in it.

"I felt some of you were lonely and it would be a good idea to get you together and make friendships which I hope will be lasting, and get to know each other," said the Mayor. "I am delighted to see so many accepted my invitation. May it be that you will soon be returning home. One thing I treasure most is the happy association I have had with some of you, and I wish you God-speed and good luck, and that when you go back home you will carry with you many happy memories of Kiddermin[ster]."

The dance concluded with the singing of Auld Lang Syne, with the whole company joining hands, and the American and British National Anthems.

On Thursday night the Town Hall was packed with American soldiers for a concert by the [illegible] Concert Party [illegible]. This again was by the kind invitation of the Mayor and Mayoress, whose hospitality was once again highly appreciated. A fuller report of [illegible] appears [illegible].

BIGGEST [illegible]

[illegible]

RESISTANCE AGAINST NAZIS

Sabotage Supplements Work of Air Bomb[ers]

The mass precision bombing raids on railway centres in occupied Europe such as the recent raids on Noisy-le-Sec and Juvisy in France are being supplemented by the work of patriots on the ground. The combination of air bombs and saboteurs' dynamite is throwing enemy transport into chaos. Aircraft concentrate on destroying marshalling yards, viaducts, main junctions. The underground resisters attack smaller targets such as standing locomotives, turntables, breakdown cranes, repair plants and signals.

In one month alone, December 1943, French patriots carried out 250 acts of sabotage. The bill for one day included: Repair shops at Oullins blown up; German leave-train derailed at Montelimar; [illegible] at Portes-les-Valence exploded; munition train from Clermont Ferrand derailed and Germans attempting to escape shot by patriots.

The scale of transport sabotage increases throughout Europe—a valuable invasion preparation. In Hainault, Belgium, 12 locomotives were recently derailed. As a reprisal for sabotage at the Ath station on the Brussels-Tournai line, the Germans arrested 87 officers of the reserve. In the Meuse and Oberland regions, damage to canal locks has paralysed many industrial concerns. All Ramot roads to the docks are closed to the public after black-out to prevent sabotage.

In Greece, units of Elas attacked trains in Thessaly. A goods train between [illegible] and [illegible] was derailed. On the same day another derailment cut rail communications between Salonica and Larissa for 36 hours. The Volos-[illegible] line was blown up and a crane at Piraeus seriously damaged.

In Russia, Byelorussian guerrillas operating in the Baranovichi area derailed 13 German troop trains in seven days, thereby destroying 15 locomotives, 7 petrol tankers, 80 carriages and 18 trucks. In another district Soviet patriots blew up 700 rails and cut 22 kilometres of telegraph lines.

13 MAY 44

An Urgent Appeal

Elsewhere in this issue of the "Shuttle" will be found an urgent appeal which has been made on behalf of Kidderminster Emergency Hospital. The appeal, officially launched by the Ministry of Labour, calls for volunteers to undertake domestic duties at the hospital and stresses the fact that no full-time labour of this kind is available. Girls who normally would have taken up hospital work have gone into the Forces or into the factories, and the result is that hospital staffs are faced with a problem which is becoming more and more acute day by day. In many cases nurses have had to be diverted from their duties of attending to the sick and injured in order to carry out domestic work which, we think, is very undesirable in itself, as unfair to both the nurses and the patients. Anyone who has [illegible] in hospital [illegible]

[illegible]

Penny-a-week Fund. The collectors from house-to-house did well in April. They brought in £252 2s. 3d. Next counting day, Thursday, May 25th, at the W.V.S. Rooms, Vicar Street, [illegible]

Bombs on Cologne.—A short time ago Carpet Trades Ltd. made a special Savings effort to provide bombs to be dropped on Germany. A target of £1,600 was set, but actually the response totalled £8,000. The firm have now been notified officially that their "load" was dropped on Cologne on April 19th.

H.G.'s £135 for Charity.—A cheque for £135 11s. 3d. has been forwarded to the Worcestershire Regiment Prisoners of War Fund by the 6th Bn. Worcs. Home Guard. This grand sum represents the proceeds of various social functions organised by the companies and officers of the Battalion.

Nursing Association Dance.—The Kidderminster Nursing Association held a successful dance at the Black Horse on Saturday last. Fred Reynolds and his dance orchestra were in attendance, and Mr. and Mrs. [illegible] Price, the old time dancing champions, led the dancers in several of the old time dances.

Poppy Day.—Amount collected in the appeal last November was £915,000. Kidderminster's contribution was £1,151 16s. 1d. This report has been received from London this week.

Nursing Association. — The annual meeting of Kidderminster Nursing Association will be held in the Council Chamber on Monday, May 22nd, at 3 p.m. The special speaker will be 2nd-Lieut. Ada D. McConnell, A.N.C., of the American Red Cross Department, and her subject will be "Public Health Nursing in New England States."

Young Wives' Campaign.—St. George's Branch of the Young Wives Campaign met on Wednesday, in the Parish Room, when Mrs. Joy gave a helpful reading on introducing children to Christ, and first lessons in prayer which was taken from a book of letters written to a young mother during the present war. The next meeting is on June 14, but those present were reminded of the Corporate Communion to be held in St. George's Church next Wednesday (17th), at 10 a.m.

13 MAY 44

[illegible] Mayor [illegible] the happenings in 1940 he could more than endorse what the Mayor had said about the crisis and that of to-day. We had got to gird in and sacrifice yet more than in the last 4 years. It was a tremendous and terrible responsibility, and the [illegible] foundation stone rested on one word—confidence! In that [illegible] were eminent representatives of the American Army and of the Worcestershire Regiment and the Yeomanry. Their presence meant a great deal in 1940 and not less in 1944, when we had the most magnificent co-operation of the American Army who, in the true Eisenhower spirit, represented the greatest democracy in the world. In the "Salute the Soldier" campaign he wished to put things in their proper perspective and stress the co-operation between the various services or forces which go to the making of totalitarian war.

Capt. H. Spencer Cooper, R.N., represented the Navy, which had done so much to defeat the submarine menace, and Group Capt. H. K. Tansley, of the R.A.F., and himself formed a trinity of the fighting services whose members had rendered magnificent services in hammering the Boche and the Japanese. Others present represented services who had done much to keep the fighting forces supplied. Canada was another partner in this fight.

It was surprising to behold, as he had done a few days earlier, the integration, team spirit and work amongst the American and Imperial Forces. They tried to realise the implications of the difficulties they were up against and at a time when members of the Navy, Army, and Air Force of our own and the other Allied countries were on the brink of making the sacrifices so eloquently described by the Mayor. All were watching the difficulties that might occur not only in launching the offensive on the second front, but also of maintaining it. All was vitally necessary before we could reap the fruits of victory and what might be yet more difficult—winning the peace after the war. We must also win on the financial side for that was important. Internal reconstruction and reorganisation of the future life of the people of England required confidence. They had friends [illegible] French people, Norwegians, Dutch, Belgians and others [illegible]

[illegible]

[illegible]

THE AMERICANS

The naval detachment was fo[llowed] past the saluting base [by] detachments of the R.E., R.A.S.[C.], R.A.O.C., R.A.P.C. and A.T.S. [A] special cheer was given for t[he] A.T.S. women, who stepped o[ut] on parade as smartly as any [of] the men.

There was some slight pau[se] before Vicar St. again rang [to] the strains of martial music, a[nd] this time it was United Stat[es] Army approaching. They we[re] some 150 strong, and we[re] headed by their band of [illegible] instrumentalists. This huge ban[d] thrilled the crowd immense[ly] especially when the dru[m] major hurled his baton h[igh] above the roof ou[r] [illegible] again knee high and clever[ly] swing it back around his nec[k]. It was grand to have these gre[at] Allies amongst us and their con[tribution] to the parade was ve[ry] much appreciated, both by th[e] organisers and the public.

Next came the band of the 11t[h] Worcs. Home Guard followed b[y] a detachment of the Fightin[g] French—grim determined lookin[g] men who breathed the very spir[it] of liberation for their countr[y]. At their head was their fla[g] bearing the Cross of Lorraine.

The R.A.F. and W.A.A.F. fol[lowed], both sections having thei[r] own bands, and it was partic[u]larly pleasing to notice that th[e] R.A.F. detachment and most o[f] their band consisted of men wh[o] have volunteered for flying duties. Fine and smartly drilled, they were worthy representatives o[f] that great fighting force to whom we owe so much, while the W.A.A.F. section served as a reminder of the work which women are doing to keep our bombers and fighters in the air hammering the enemy.

Cheers were renewed for the men of Kidderminster's own Battalion, the 6th Bn. Worcs. Home Guard, who were led by the band of the 22nd Bn. South Staffs. Home Guard. In marching and march discipline these "part-time" soldiers showed how well they have been trained and the crowd seemed to sense that there were many of whom have four years' service to their credit, represented the stalwarts who stood by Britain especially at that time when invasion seemed imminent and our chances of survival slight. Behind them came the youthful members of the Army Cadet Force, headed by the Stourbridge A.C.F. Band and here again one saw evidence of the smartness which army training and discipline create.

OTHER SERVICES

Another youth organisation fol[lowed]—the Air Training Corps. With the Dudley A.T.C. Band at their head they made a grand [illegible]

[illegible]

GLIDERS' PART IN MODERN WAR

Troops Who "Drop In" Where Wanted

With the introduction to modern warefare of the towed engineless aircraft and the extension of the use of the transport aircraft and the parachute, ground forces have been given a mobility and speed of movement that would have been ridiculed less than a decade ago. By using navigational aids modern aircraft are able to find their way to targets that would have been closed to them less than two years ago. Once over that target, the so-called glider and the low-level parachute enable them to place troops within a few yards of their pin-pointed objective armed with light or heavy equipment as the situation demands.

That is a large contribution to scientific planning of a modern battle, and those tacticians who are thoroughly aware of the potentialities of the new weapon are thoroughly appreciative. A great disservice is done regularly to both the Royal Air Force and the Army components of Airborne by the Jules Verne claims that are made for it. Gliders are fancifully pictured as being towed in long trains at tremendous distance from their objective, on which they swoop in utter silence and then disgorge anything from a battalion of the Guards to a Mountain Brigade.

The facts are less exotic, more compelling. In the first place, the [illegible]

STOURPORT

P.O.W.R.A.—The next meeting of the Association will be held on Saturday at Woodgreen by the kind invitation of Mrs P. Pratt (treasurer) at 3.30.

Town Comforts' Fund. — The hon secretary, Mr F. O. Rowley, acknowledges donations from Mrs. W. Mathieson and lady friends £10 10s., Mr F. Tunkiss and customers £4 3s. and Mrs R. Mann 2s 6d.

Alexandra Rose Day. — The recent house-to-house and street collections on Alexandra Rose Day conducted by Stourport W.V.S. realised £34 18s 4d. That figure does not include any amounts from factories whose collections were organised elsewhere.

Air Training Corps — Readers will note that the Ceremonial presentation of colours to the 1190 Squadron takes place at County Senior School Stourport, Saturday, June 24, at 3.30 by Air Marshal Sir Leslie Gossage, K.C.B., C.V.O., D.S.O., M.C.

Death. — The funeral took place at Mitton Churchyard on Thursday of Miss Ellen Harris (79), 21 Manor Rd., who died on Monday, seven months after the death of a sister at the same address. A member of the Plymouth Brethren officiated at the graveside.

Hospital Sunday.—At most local churches Hospital Sunday was observed on Sunday and collections taken for the Kidderminster and District General Hospital. Loose cash for this object at St. Michael and All Angels' Parish Church amounted to £8 5s. 8d.

Aid to China.—A whist drive organised by Mrs. Eric Coombs and Mrs. Tom Dorrell, in aid of the above fund, was held on Friday, June 9, at The Sturt, Dunley, and as a result a cheque for £9 2s. has been forwarded to Lady Cripps' Aid to China Fund. The following were prize-winners: Mrs. Shrimpton, Miss Sheila Dorrell, Miss Axford, Mr. Len Dorrell, Miss Bond, and Miss Hodges. The organisers thank all who provided prizes and refreshments or in any way helped.

Haven Cinema. — An amusing story of a maid who wrote an anonymous book on the lives of her employers, is told in "Once upon a Thursday," starring Marsha Hunt, Richard Carlson, Virginia Weidler and Marjorie Main, showing for the first three days of the week. It has as a supporting film "Gals Incorporated," featuring Leon Errol and Harriet Hilward. For the last three days Harry Korris and Robbie Vincent (Enoch) are featured in "Somewhere on [illegible] ... from Dunkirk.—On Sunday [illegible] Church

BEWDLEY'S RED CROSS EFFORT

Visit of Earl and Countess Baldwin

Scarcely a person seen in Bewdley streets last Saturday failed to wear a Red Cross emblem. From early morning members of the Ladies Committee and a large number of collectors and helpers were busy selling for Bewdley's Red Cross flag day, and the borough responded with customary readiness and generosity. During the afternoon workers for the Red Cross were invited to a reception at the Town Hall to meet the Earl and Countess Baldwin of Bewdley, who visited the town specially for the occasion. Guests were received by the Mayoress (Mrs. R. B. Jackson) and her daughter, Miss Hilda Jackson, and later the Mayor (Ald. R. B. Jackson) escorted Lord and Lady Baldwin to the reception where they shook hands with everyone present. Miss Jackson presented Lady Baldwin with a bouquet of roses.

Introducing the distinguished guests, the Mayor spoke of their long association with the borough and the affection in which they were held in Bewdley. Drawing attention to a medallion on the mayoral chain of office he wore, Ald. Jackson said it had been presented to the town by Lord Baldwin's father when M.P. for Bewdley. Recalling the many services rendered by Lord Baldwin's mother, special emphasis was placed on her interest in welfare work—a characteristic Lord Baldwin inherited, and an interest which was shared by his wife. Lady Baldwin's work, specially in connection with the maternity home at Stourport, which bore her name, was unfailing. They had done the town an honour by attending the reception that afternoon.

Lady Baldwin said she was touched by the welcome she had received. The Mayor had outlined to her the work done by the women of Bewdley for the Red Cross and she felt proud of them. Indicating a brooch she wore on her costume Lady Baldwin said, "It was given to me at the first election of our two selves in Bewdley. I felt I wanted to wear it to-day when I was visiting you."

At this juncture the Mayor asked for the amount collected for Bewdley's Red Cross flag day, and, though incomplete, the figure then stood at £255 15s. 2d.

Thanking Ald. Jackson for his references his mother, Earl Baldwin said his associations with Bewdley were unbreakable. It was a joy for him to shake hands with those who knew him in those early years of which he had little clear-cut recognition. Bewdley with its many charms had not been blessed with a super-abundance of this world's goods, but in no community was there greater liberality, generosity and support for good causes. The Red Cross needed full support in its great work and that help would be forthcoming. He hoped the flag day would prove a happy and successful one, and that it would not be long before peace came to the world again.

Proposing thanks to Lord and Lady Baldwin, Ald. H. W. Frost said he could substantiate Lord Baldwin's remarks concerning the generosity of the people of the borough. It would be interesting to know how much Bewdley had raised during the war. The town numbered among its achievements the winning of the Eddy Cup for savings, and the "Salute the Soldier" week had been highly successful. The women of Bewdley had done wonderful work. Ald. Frost also referred to Lady Baldwin's part in maternity work in the district and the great interest [illegible] displayed in the Lucy Baldwin [illegible] Stourport.

STOURPORT SALUTES THE SOLDIER

Aiming at £85,000 Target

With a target of £85,000, the cost of moving one division with medical unit to accompany it to Berlin, Stourport opened its "Salute the Soldier" campaign on Saturday, the big feature being a grand ceremonial parade through the town followed by a series of fete attractions. So far Street Savings and a few other groups have responded admirably; what is eagerly awaited is the "bump up" savings from the chief industries so well represented at the inaugural luncheon last week-end. On three previous occasions Stourport comfortably passed its target figure, reaching six figures for the first time in the "Wings for Victory" Week last year. This week the latest figure announced is £67,688.

THE PARADE

The grand ceremonial parade on Saturday assembled in the Memorial Park under the general direction of Police Supt. F. Malley (Stourport Division). Units taking part in the procession were the Royal Navy, W.R.N.S., Royal Army Pay Corps, A.T.S., R.A.F., W.A.A.F., U.S.A. Army, U.S.A. Army Medical Corps, Home Guard, Army Cadet Force, 7th Worcestershire Detachment Red Cross, Air Training Corps, National Fire Service, Girls' Training Corps, A.R.P. and Civil Defence, Women's Voluntary Service, Women's Land Army, British Legion, Boys' Brigade, Boy Scouts, Sea Scouts and other branches of the movement, Girl Guides, followed by a number of American Army field guns. Four bands distributed at judicious intervals in the procession were those of the 10th and 11th Worcestershire Home Guard, Royal Air Force Bugle Band, and the Boys Brigade.

Admirably timed, the procession passed the saluting base near the British Restaurant in Vale Road punctually. A guard of honour, provided by "B" Coy., 11th Batt. Worcestershire Home Guard, flanked the beflagged platform on which stood Col. W. H. Wiggin, C.B., D.S.O., T.D. (Worcestershire Regiment), who took the salute. With him were Lieut.-Col. J. A. Dyson-Perrins, M.C. (Home Guard), Group Captain H. E. Tinsley, M.C., R.A.F., and two U.S.A. Army officers, Mr. R. P. Vale, C.C. (chairman of Stourport U.D.C.), and Cllr. H. G. Southall (chairman of Stourport National Savings Committee).

A big crowd lined both sides of Vale Road and another in High Street cheered the colourful procession as it swung along the streets with admirable precision. The route of nearly two miles extended from the Memorial Park along Park Avenue, Bewdley Road, Worcester Street, Vale Road, across Mitton Street into Lion Hill, York Street and High Street, splitting up into sections at the Swan crossing for the processionists to return to their most convenient bases. Local residents and shopkeepers decorated premises in the central thoroughfare and Police control of traffic won special praise for at

JOHNSTON—TAYLOR.—On June 10, 1944 (by special licence) at St. Mary's Parish Church, Kidderminster, by the Rev. T. B. Littlewood,— Francis (L.A.C. R.A.F.), of Armadale Road, Whitburn, West Lothian, only son of Mr. Andrew Johnson, Eighth Street, Newton Grange, Midlothian, and the late Mrs. Minnie Johnston, to Beatrice Elsie, second daughter of Mr. Samuel Taylor, 47, Hurcott Rd., Kidderminster, and the late Mrs. Elizabeth May Taylor.

MIDDLETON — GARDNER — On Saturday, June 10, 1944, at St. John's Church, Kidderminster, by the Rev. H. G. I. Roberts, Bernard, eldest son of Mrs. Powell, 15, Coalfield Row, Kidderminster, to Evelyn, second daughter of Mrs. C. Gardner, Vicarage Farm, Foley Park, Kidderminster.

RUTHOWSKI — CHAMBERS — On Saturday, June 17, 1944, at St. Ambrose's Roman Catholic Church, by the Rev. Father Faulconer [illegible], William Edward [illegible] U.S. Army, only son of Mr. John Ruthowski and the late Mrs. Ruthowski, 1302 W. Thomas St., Chicago, Illinois, to Margaret Constance, second daughter of Mrs. Florence Chambers and the late Mr. Ennis Chambers, 5, East St., Kidderminster.

DEATHS

BADLAND.—On Tuesday, June 20, at her home, 116, [illegible] Avenue, Mary, widow of Mr. T. R. Badland and mother of Mary and Margaret Badland, aged 60 years.

BRITTON.—On June 12, 1944, at the Kidderminster General Hospital, Frank, beloved husband of Florence Britton, Tiptoes, Neville Avenue, Kidderminster, aged 62 years.

DAVIES.—On June 18, 1944, suddenly, at the residence of her daughter, Mrs. W. H. Nield, 19, Watkinson Road, Illingworth, Halifax, Emma, beloved widow of the late Capt. W. R. Davies (late of Kidderminster), aged 88 years.

HAWKES.—On Saturday, June 17, at her home, "Byrn-Crug," 6, Birchfield Road, Kidderminster, Mrs. Charlotte Hawkes, beloved wife of Mr. Charles Edward Hawkes, aged 73 years.—Rest at last.

KILLED IN ACTION

GALBRAITH.—Killed in action, on June 6, 1944, during the Normandy invasion, Sapper Thomas Galbraith, beloved brother of Mrs. T. Martin, 3, Prospect Terrace, aged 28 years.

IN MEMORIAM

ADAMS.—Treasured memories of my dear husband Jesse, who passed away June 28, 1942. Always remembered by his loving wife and Iris. In silence we remember.

DARKES.—In ever loving memory of my dear brother Edwin Roger (Dick), called to rest, June 19, 1938. Always remembered by sister Edna.

Though tears in my eyes do not glisten,
My face is not always sad;
For every night and morning
I think of the dear brother I had.

HAWKESWOOD.—In loving memory of my dear wife Lizzie, who passed away June 21, 1942. Ever remembered by her husband and Alice.

The blow was great, the shock severe,
No one thought her death so near;
Only those that have lost can [illegible]
The pain of parting without [illegible]

[illegible] In loving memory of James Mills, who passed away [illegible] forgotten by his wife and children, also Harry, son of the above, who died [illegible] Always remembered [illegible] sisters and brothers [illegible]

[illegible]

SATURDAY, JUNE 24, 1944

Our American Friends

We are grateful to Lord Dudley for so aptly expressing the admiration which this country feels for the American soldiers who have come over here to take part in the Battle of Europe. He referred to them as "Our American Friends," and by doing so he could not have expressed more clearly just what we feel about them. These boys certainly are our friends, and have won the affection of the people with whom they have come into contact. Many of the friendships thus created will endure long after the present conflict has ceased, and there can be no doubt that the good seeds being sown now will flourish and will go a long way to cementing Anglo-American relations in the years to come. "This I can tell them," said Lord Dudley, "there is no English man, woman or child of this generation who will ever forget the pride they feel in fighting shoulder to shoulder with the American nation in the darkest hour and the greatest moment of danger of our two great nations." Those sentiments will be readily endorsed by everyone, for not only did America help us in the days when all seemed lost, but her sons are now fighting side by side with our own men in the final struggle to overthrow Nazi oppression in Europe. They are fighting with courage and tenacity, and merit the fullest admiration. Lord Dudley's words, therefore, are particularly apt. The occasion on which he spoke is just another example of the way in which our great allies co-operate—the visit of their own G.I. Revue to Kidderminster to swell the funds of the Red Cross. Long may this spirit of co-operation exist between the two great English-speaking nations — a co-operation which will go a long way to ensure the future peace of the world.

Elections and Peace

Alderman Norman Tiptaft, of Birmingham, who is one of the most outspoken of public men, gave Rotary Club members something to think about when he addressed them last Tuesday. The subject of his talk was "Reconstruction," and during it he touched on many topics which may or may not have some bearing on affairs of the future. One thing which he emphasised, however, is well worth bearing in mind. Permanent world peace, he said, depended in a large measure on [illegible] between [illegible] and [illegible]

[illegible]

Alderman's Birthday.—Alderman E. G. Eddy, O.B.E., J.P., celebrated his 66th birthday on Thursday, and received many telegrams and letters of congratulation.

Music in the Park.—Commencing next Wednesday amplified recorded music will be heard in Brinton Park each Wednesday and Sunday from 7 to 9 p.m. The latter part of the Wednesday evening transmissions will consist of dance music.

S.J.A.B. Dance. — Another popular S.J.A.B. dance was held at the Town Hall on Saturday, when Fred Reynolds and his orchestra played for dancing. A novelty feature was the competition for spotting the deliberate mistakes made by the M.C. A prize of 10s. 6d. was given to the "spotter" of each mistake.

Gift Sunday.—July 2nd will be Gift Sunday at St. George's Church, when envelopes bearing the words: "Our Church needs £200," will be distributed among parishioners and friends. The preachers for that day will be the Rev. H. H. Williams (Rector of Oldswinford), at 11 a.m., and the Rev. J. T. Davies (Rector of Halesowen) at 6.30 p.m.

Sladen School Concert. — So successful were the scenes from "A Midsummer Night's Dream" and instrumental items by the school orchestra presented by pupils of Sladen School on Open Day last Wednesday that, at the request of many, it has been decided to hold a repeat performance. A concert will be held at the School Hall on Wednesday evening, June 28th, at 7.30 p.m.

Salvage of Bones.—A bone weighing about two ounces will yield enough grease to make the cordite to fire two shots from a Spitfire's gun, and the "degreased" bone will provide bone meal to feed a hen for half a day, glue to stick a square foot of airplane fabric, and fertiliser for a square yard of land, producing 4 lbs. of potatoes. So the Ministry of Supply urge the housewives of Britain to send to salvage the 50,000 tons of bones still being thrown away.

New Church Anniversary.—Sunday school anniversary services were held at the New Church, Comberton Hill, Kidderminster, on Sunday last, when the preacher was the Rev. E. J. Jarmin. Scripture readings were given by Dorothy Twigg, Sheila Ryder, Norman Ryder, and Ann Trehearne. Special hymns were sung by the children, and offertories were received by Maureen Brown, Jane Jarmin, and Cynthia and Eileen Burford. During the evening service attendance awards consisting of books and savings stamps were distributed by the minister. The church was decorated with flowers collected by the children during an excursion to Habberley Valley the previous afternoon. [illegible]

[illegible]

No Convictions.—There were no R.S.P.C.A. convictions for Worcestershire in the month of May, but one Bronze Humanity Medal was awarded to the county for bravery in rescuing animals.

Christadelphian Service.—An address on the subject, "Does God Care?" will be given on Sunday next by Mr. J. A. Woodall (Wolverhampton), at the Christadelphian Hall, George Street. Service at 6 o'clock.

Good Work.—The result of the "Salute the Soldier" dances organised by Mr. Russell, showed a nett profit of £150. An audited balance sheet has been forwarded to these charities with the proceeds, and it is of interest to note that these results are from admission only, and not supplemented by any competitions or raffles, etc.

The Fair.—Last week the Cattle Market was given over to the annual pleasure fair and, as on previous occasions, a wide selection of amusements was available. Very brisk trade was done during the evenings, especially on the various roundabouts and bumper cars, while the shooting gallery was also very popular with members of the services, many of whom vied with each other in testing their skill. The fair moved out on Sunday, and by Monday morning there was hardly a sign of its presence having been there.

Looking After Wounded.—A supply of special notification cards for relatives is held by each Red Cross and St. John joint county committee in whose area wounded men from Normandy have arrived or are expected to arrive. These cards, which are sent on the patients' behalf by Red Cross liaison officers at the hospitals, bring news of a man's condition and his address, and add an advisory line stating that relatives should not try to visit the patient unless they are specifically told that they can do so by the hospital. The Red Cross guide scheme is in operation, and some patients have been accompanied to auxiliary hospitals.

G.I. Revue.—Mr. A. J. Ednow has received the following letter of thanks from Mr. R. G. Boardman, chairman of the Birmingham Hospitality Committee, in connection with the recent visit to Kidderminster of the American G.I. Song and Dance Revue. "May I thank you for the hospitality Kidderminster extended to the American Concert Party. The people really did them well. I trust everything went to their satisfaction, and in conclusion would like to congratulate you on the organisation and very hard work put into this effort." Mr. Ednow expressed thanks to the Mayor (Alderman L. Tolley), Messrs. Leon Jacobs, A. A. Knight (Allens Music Warehouse), Charles Grimd, Mr. Oakes, Mr. Knight (lighting), Mr. Davis (microphone), Misses [illegible]

[illegible]

organiser throughout the proceedings.

GARDEN PARTY

British Legion Effort at Oakfield

Members and friends of the British Legion once more enjoyed their annual party in the beautiful gardens of Oakfield, Bewdley Hill, the home of Col. and Mrs. R. W. A. Painter, on Wednesday evening. National flags and bunting added a festive touch to the tree-fringed lawns as visitors moved to and fro between the various competitions and games, or walked in the gardens admiring the colourful display of flowers.

The party was organised by members of the British Legion Women's Section, of which Mrs. Painter is vice-chairman. Mrs. W. Adam is president, Mrs. G. M. Fletcher, J.P., chairman, and Miss B. Caswell, secretary. A point of interest was a stall displaying leather goods and toys made by disabled men of the last war. Miss Cooke and Mrs. C. Pagett were in charge of the stall, which attracted many interested buyers. Several competitions and games excited great enthusiasm and amusement. Mr., Mrs. and Miss Mills were in charge of the hoop-la and treasure hunt, Mrs. Dutfield and Mrs. John Andrews darts, Mrs. Rowley, bagatelle, Mrs. Thatcher, bowls, and Mrs. Pickering, guessing the beans. Miss Brookes conducted the game of "Housey-housey" which caused much amusement among players and onlookers alike.

Notable among the evening's entertainments was a display given by members of the Women's League of Health and Beauty. Wearing black trunks and white satin blouses, they opened their display with a demonstration of various exercises set to music, throughout which their movements were perfectly controlled. Then followed an exhibition of club-swinging, the girls, dressed in small satin tunics of different colours, moving gracefully against the green background of lawns and trees. They next demonstrated the Highland Reel, and Irish Jig, the dancers being dressed in appropriate national costume. The display concluded with a French Peasant dance which was delightful and beautifully costumed. The girls were vivaciously French in long, full, red and green skirts and peasant blouses with red rosettes in their hair, while those representing men were dressed in bright colours with pirate handkerchiefs and large gold earings. There was much applause at the end of this charming exhibition, and Mrs. G. M. Fletcher, J.P., thanked the girls for their display.

The members of the Women's League of Health and Beauty who took part were Mary Merritt, Jean Evans, Nell Wright, Marion Morris, Margaret [illegible] [illegible] Roberts, Betty [illegible] [illegible] Legg. The pianist was Miss Gwen Meredith.

The children were not forgotten, and found outlet for their spirits in a potato race, won by Phillip Saunders.

Lieutenant Winifred Johnson, an American nurse, who attended the party with several other nurses, was asked to distribute the prizes, which were won by the following: Treasure hunt, Miss Meredith; bowls, 1 Mrs. Picking, 2 Mrs. Milner; darts, 1 Mrs. Merritt, 2 Mrs. Johnston; bagatelle, Mrs. James; guessing the beans, Mrs. Authur Smith and Miss Osborne; potato race, Phillip Saunders. All prizes were kindly given by members of the Committee.

Mrs. Authur Smith proposed thanks to Col. and Mrs. Painter. In response, Mrs. Painter said "If you have all enjoyed the party that has amply rewarded us."

Before the visitors dispersed, much amusement was caused by the auctioning of two eggs which went to Mrs. Moor, an American nurse, for 6s. 3d. A 1 lb. jar of jam raised 7s. 6d. and, after sharp bidding, eventually went to a second American, Miss Robinson. Several other household commodities were auctioned, and the total of £1 11s. 6d., was quickly realised in aid of the British Legion Fund. [illegible]

LIFE IN OCCUPIED FRANCE

Lecture by Fighting French Adjutant

What happened to the French people after the fall of France, and what they are now doing to resist their Nazi oppressors was told in an interesting lecture given at Kidderminster Library on Friday, June 7. The speaker was Adjutant Monteux, who escaped from his native land of France in January, 1942. He is at present attached to the Ministry of Information in London.

Introducing the speaker, Miss M. C. Oldnall, M.A., J.P. (chairman), said that she was sure that all friends of the French people would value hearing about France, and that the general public were equally anxious to know more about the country figured so prominently in the news at the present time. "We have all read accounts in the Press of the courage and daring of the men of the Maquis," she said, "and many of us hear the nightly war reports direct from Normandy, but even so we do not know much about the life in present day France. To-night the curtain will be raised and we shall be privileged to have some glimpses of that life."

"In the early stages of the occupation," said Adjutant Monteux, "Germany was very clever. For a time the Germans behaved. There was terrible confusion throughout the country, and it was in the interest of the Germans to restore order. They said that they were friends who had come to protect the French from the wicked English, but the French people soon realised that this was not so. Food became scarce, labourers were deported to Germany and hostages were taken, but the French population remained cheerful and resistance movements were soon set up all over the country.

"The food conditions in France at the present time are tragic," the Adjutant continued. "After the last war in 1919, the Germans were practically starving; to-day in France it is three times as bad. A friend of mine, who escaped from France 18 months ago, told me that the workmen were so underfed that they had to knock off work at 10 a.m. because they were too exhausted to continue. There are hardly any cats left in France because there is no milk to feed them with, and the dogs are almost starving.

"Many of you will be thinking," he added, "that these food facts do not coincide with the reports you have recently heard about those in Normandy. That is because Normandy is the biggest food producing place in France, and is renowned for its butter and milk. Bread, which is the staple food of the French worker, is now black and very scarce. There is no milk available for the adult population and only an inadequate supply for children. Two results of the food shortage are a 90 per cent. increase in tuberculosis, and a [illegible] per cent. increase in infant [illegible]

[illegible] which [illegible] and resistance, sabotage, and the underground movement is of [illegible] importance to the Allies, especially since the opening of the Second Front. Eighty different newspapers are published in the underground to-day. In the early days many of them were written [illegible] but [illegible] machines have been set up [illegible] with the [illegible] [illegible] and [illegible] valuable [illegible] munition factories [illegible]

BOROUGH BENCH

Friday, July 7. — Before the Mayor, Ald. L. Tolley (chairman), Mrs. M. A. Anton, Miss E. C. Audenbrooke, Messrs. C. L. Porter and J. E. Grosvenor.

SCHOOL ABSENCES

Three mothers appeared on warrant to answer summonses for not sending their children regularly to school, and were fined £1 each.

The first defendant was Lilian Smith, 18, Northumberland Avenue. Mr. Robert H. Warnock, school attendance officer, said defendant's one child was absent 23 times, and the other child was absent 53 times, both out of a possible 70 attendances.

Sarah Price, 8 house 4 court, Hall Street, was summoned in respect of two of her four children. Both defendants were in wage-earning employment. Truancy was the alleged explanation of the negligence.

Of Lilian Brant, 20, Goldthorn Road, Mr. Warnock said her one child was absent 44 times and the other absent 58 times, both out of a possible 120 attendances.

FATHER FINED

William Barrie, 47, Park Lane, was summoned for failing to cause his child to be vaccinated. Pleading guilty defendant said the child had teeth trouble and ill-health. He was not a conscientious objector.

The Clerk pointed out that defendant had delayed the matter for 15 months in spite of repeated warnings from Mr. F. C. King, vaccination officer.

A fine of 5s. was imposed.

"JOLLIFICATION"

Thomas Oldnall, Snell Grove, Cookley, was fined 5s. for carrying a passenger on a bicycle not constructed for that purpose, and the passenger, Edith Morris, 32, Silver Street, was also fined 5s.

P.C. Gough said defendant's explanation was "We were having a little jollification."

UNSCREENED LIGHTS

For failing to screen lights in roofed buildings, the following were fined: Helen Deakin, 74, Stourbridge Road, £1; Louise Welding, 8, Hall Street, 10s.; Rosana Middleton, 464, Chester Road North, 10s.; Arthur and Henry Jones, 7, Villiers Street, (Worcester Street premises), 10s.

INSECURE LOAD

Frank Saunders, 1, Dick Shepherd Avenue, was fined 10s. for having a load insecure on a motor lorry he was driving along Stourbridge Road on June 7.

P.C. Davies said some sheets slipped off the lorry on to the roadway as the vehicle was passing Broadwaters garage.

NO LIGHTS

George Henry Gibson Harris, 11, Lorne Street, Kidderminster, was fined 10s. for driving a motor lorry without lights.

War Res. Gamson said the lorry was parked in the street, but defendant had forgotten to switch on the lights.

SIGNALS OFFENCE

Joseph Page, [illegible], Hawbush Road, Brierley Hill, was fined [illegible] for not obeying traffic signals when driving a motor [illegible] at the junction of Bewdley Road and Burton Road.

BOROUGH JUVENILE COURT

Friday, July [illegible] Grosvenor (chairman), Mrs. M. A. Anton, Miss E. C. Audenbrooke [illegible]

COUNTY GRAMMAR SCHOOL PLEA

Sebright Speech Day and Prizegiving

A plea to leave the public school, and the old county grammar school as undisturbed as possible in the post-war regime was made at the annual prize-giving and speech day of the Sebright School, Wolverley, on Saturday by speakers who contended that the county grammar school was the most valuable experiment in our educational history. The Bishop of Worcester, who distributed the prizes, made his first official visit to the handsome School Hall in which the pleasant ceremony took place, and gave the boys sound advice on the personal contribution they might make towards solving international problems in the post-war world.

In the absence of the chairman of governors, Major E. A. Knight, D.L., the vice-chairman, Mr. W. Cabern Grazebrook, J.P., presided, and others with him were Messrs. Gerald Tomkinson, J. Christopher Wilson and J. S. Preece, with the clerk, Mr. C. C. Amphlett-Morton, the headmaster, Mr. R. A. Henniker-Gotley, M.A., and the Bishop of Worcester, Dr. W. Wilson Cash, D.S.O., who distributed the war token prizes and awards.

Mr. Grazebrook said they much regretted that Major Knight was unable to attend. That was the first meeting of the kind from which he had been absent. "We are all extremely sorry that he is not here. He has given many years of devoted service to the affairs of the Sebright School; in fact, it is not an exaggeration to say that in a large measure it is due to the work of Major Knight, that we have these fine school buildings."

In his report, Mr. Henniker-Gotley said, "I am able to report that our numbers have reached a new high record. I am particularly glad to be able to tell you that no less than 104 of the present boys live in the county of Worcestershire. This means that the school, in spite of its change of name in 1930, has retained its character of an ancient county grammar school. Personally, I regard the county grammar school as the most valuable experiment in our educational history. It was at the opening of this very building, that Lord Baldwin said: 'I like to think of grammar schools not only as the homes of piety and true learning at their best, but a link between all classes.'" The headmaster continued: "That seems to me something worth preserving."

GOOD RESULTS

In the external examinations the good results of last year were maintained. All three candidates for the higher school certificate were successful; two others who were not candidates for the full certificate passed in all the subjects for which they were entered. G. A. F. H. Purshouse was awarded a State Bursary. Fourteen of the 18 candidates for the school certificate gained the certificate. J. H. Ireland, an old boy, was placed in the first class in the Bosch School of Engineering, Birmingham University. [illegible] review of the school year would be incomplete without reference to the ever-increasing number of old boys serving with the Forces. Inevitably the school [illegible] of those who have laid down their lives for their friends [illegible] their example and sacrifice [illegible] [illegible] old boys have been awarded the Distinguished Flying Cross, Capt. [illegible] Boucher-Giles [illegible] Army Air Corps [illegible] Old Wolverleian and a [illegible]

... period ... has now fully recovered from his illness. He mentioned that he had visited a Kidderminster friend in hospital, Albert Hatton, and said he was progressing splendidly. The two brothers are the sons of Mr. and Mrs. T. Waldron, 25, Sutton Rd. Both are old boys of Bennett St. School and keen football enthusiasts. They were choir boys at Holy Innocents' Church, and later Frederick became a server there.

The accompanying photograph is that of Musician John Rogers (20), Royal Marine Band, serving abroad in one of His Majesty's major ships. His parents, Mr. and Mrs. E. (C.) Rogers, live at Walcombe House, Vicarage Crescent, his father being conductor of the Kidderminster Military Prize Band. Musician Rogers was educated at St. George's School and before joining the Senior Service was employed in the Axminster Dept. Messrs. Brinton's, Ltd. He was a trumpet player in the Olliderdrome Orchestra and also a member of the Kidderminster Military Prize Band. He volunteered for service on reaching the age of 18 years and passed the test at the Royal Naval College of Music, afterwards being posted to a band for a short time, before being drafted to one of His Majesty's County class cruisers, with which he sailed abroad. In a recent letter to his parents he states he is fit, and has now seen much of the world. The ship in which he serves was recently in action in the Pacific. He sends greetings to all his musical friends in Kidderminster.

P/O E. L. ("Ted") Lawley, younger son of Mr. and Mrs. L. Lawley, 9, James Road, serving with the R.A.F. somewhere in Algeria write: "After a brief spell in Egypt I was suddenly whisked away by air to somewhere in Algeria, though not before I had spent much time and money in sampling the bright lights of Cairo. My present 'home' is somewhat different, being situated on the edge of the Sahara desert, very much an outpost of the Empire—or something! 'Tis extremely hot with shade temperatures running up to 120 and on occasions 126 throughout the summer months, and with frequent visits of the much detested sirocco to complete our discomfort—the sirocco being a fierce, hot wind comparable to the blast from furnaces at times. The long arm of coincidence seems even longer in war-time, for on numerous occasions I have run across old friends and acquaintances. Quite recently a chappie stepped out of a plane here, spotted me, and soon we were chatting of old times—it was George Parton, with whom I was at school. It is amazing how entertainment values change according to circumstances, for here our amusement depends very much on our own initiative. Above 'apenny and Ludo seem to be first choice in the Mess and it would amaze the onlooker to see us get into such a state of feverish excitement over the fluctuations of our own special brand of Ludo! During the winter a number of French people live in a nearby small town, but in the summer months they journey northwards to cooler climes near the coast, leaving the Arabs as sole occupants—they can have it, all of it!"

"Many thanks for the 'Shuttle.' It keeps me in close touch with home," writes L. Whitehouse from somewhere in Italy. He has been serving with a famous South African Squadron for the last three years and says in all his ...

... operations in Normandy. A.B. Brown married Miss Nellie Vaux in 1940. There are two small sons of the marriage, Billy (3) and Robert (2). A son of Mr. and Mrs. B. Brown, 88, Upton Road, and an old boy of Coventry St. School, A.B. Brown had been in the Senior Service since 1941. He served in three convoys to Russia, had been torpedoed and rescued after several hours in the water, and took part in the bombardment of Oran during the North African campaign. He was 26 years of age, and in civilian life was employed at Messrs. Baldwin's, Ltd. Much sympathy will be felt for his young wife, his children and parents. A younger brother, L.A.C. Frederick Brown, is serving with the R.A.F. in England. Mrs. Nellie Brown has three brothers in the Services. One is with the R.A.F., another is in the Army, and the third, Pte. William Vaux, is a prisoner of war in Germany.

AWARDED D.F.C.

Readers will be interested to hear that a former Kidderminster Rugby Club player, S/Ldr. Ronnie Wallens (seen at the controls of his aircraft in the accompanying photograph), son of Mrs. H. F. Wallens and the late Mr. H. P. Wallens, of Stourbridge and Colley Gate, has been awarded the Distinguished Flying Cross for saving a number of airmen from the sea. S/Ldr. Wallens was commissioned in the R.A.F. in 1937. He flew in a Spitfire squadron from the outbreak of war and through Dunkirk and the Battle of Britain until he was shot down in September, 1940, suffering a cannon shell wound in the leg which kept him in hospital for 9½ months. He has shot down "4½" enemy aircraft (confirmed) and two probables, and is still on active flying operations. His father was killed in the last war and he has a brother serving in Italy. He was formerly articled to Messrs. Phipps and Pritchard, auctioneers, Kidderminster.

News has reached Mr. and Mrs. F. Woodyatt, 172, Chester Road, from their eldest son, Pte. Frederick Hartley Woodyatt (30), to say he has arrived on the North European battlefront. Pte. Ronald Leslie Woodyatt (22), their youngest son, is at present in hospital in India. They have received a message of sympathy from the King and Queen in the sad loss of their second son, Tpr. Arthur Woodyatt, whose death from shell wounds in Italy on June 24 was reported in our columns some weeks ago.

Gnr. Henry Robert ("Bob") Masters, only son of Mr. and Mrs. H. Masters, Austcliffe Road, Cookley, who has been serving on the North European battlefront since a week after D-Day, is now in hospital in Scotland suffering from a thigh wound. He has written cheerfully to his parents telling them that he is making an excellent recovery after a second operation. Gnr. Masters, who is 24 years of age, was educated at Balsall Heath, Birmingham, and with his parents came to reside in Cookley about seven years ago. Prior to joining the Services in June, 1940, he was employed as clerk with the W.T.A., King Edward St., ...

Writing from the North European battlefront, where he has been serving since a fortnight after D-Day, Gnr. William ("Pez") Hall, says that he is receiving a copy of the "Shuttle" weekly, and is passing it on to his friends. Gnr. Hall, who is the second son of Mr. and Mrs. W. Hall, 65, Woodfield Street, joined the Royal Artillery in May 1940. He was educated at the Bennett Street School and was employed at Messrs. Brintons, Ltd., before joining up. He is 28 years of age.

HELPING AMERICAN HOSPITAL

Work of Local Community Council

Marking its one year anniversary since its inception, the Community Hospital Council held a meeting at the 52nd American hospital. Present were the Mayor and Mrs. Louis Tolley and the new Commanding Officer of the hospital. Mr. William A. Price, president of the Council, presided.

The Council has proved its usefulness and value to the hospital in numerous ways and offers one channel through which are routed all inquiries regarding the camp and community. In addition, it has strengthened the existing bonds of friendship and kindred spirit among allied nations. Mr. Price reported that the Ministry of Information is much interested in the manner in which the Council operates, as Kidderminster is the only community with an organisation of this kind. For the benefit of other communities, the Birmingham representative of the Ministry of Information is making a study and report of the local society.

From the Community talent the American Red Cross has been able to schedule every week one big show for ambulatory patients and entertainment for bed patients in approximately 30 wards. Among the recent groups who have been helpful and gracious in making these programmes possible are the following: Miss Elsie Dyer and the Craigmore School of Dancing, the Lyrics, the Kidderminster Carpet Trades, Miss Joyce Austin and her puppet show, the Royal Army Pay Corps, led by Lt. Ronald Davis, the Harry Cheshire Boys' School, the Sneaderminster Variety Show, the Women's League of Health and Beauty, George Lenth and Company, the Thatcher girls, piano duets, the Baldwin Variety Show, Miss Doris Crisp and the Munitions Factory, who arranged an outdoor picnic, the Baxter Church Choir, Mr. Horton of Blakeshall Hostel, Mr. Harold Lloyd, ventriloquist, Dr. J. Stainton Price and Dr. Earl Heighway, pianist and guitarist respectively, The Merrymakers, and Mr. J. F. Parker, Mr. Beeston, and Mr. J. H. Smith, lecturers. Many of the above have returned to the hospital repeatedly, so well received are their shows.

On behalf of the entire staff, the hospital representatives expressed its appreciation for the many contributions of flowers for the patients. During the spring and summer months enough flowers have been delivered to the hospital or left with Mr. Price at 113, Hill St., to keep all the wards supplied with fresh cut flowers.

At this meeting members of the present Executive Committee were unanimously re-elected. They include Mr. Price, Rev. S. J. Hooper, Mr. G. A. North, Mrs. J. H. Thursfield, Mrs. J. Stainton Price and members of the hospital staff. Mr. Price was also re-elected as chairman. The Council is composed of the following community members: Mrs. Barrington-Ward, Mr. C. D. Chadwick, Mrs. Gerald Chadwick, Mrs. M. Clifford, Mr. W. E. Daly, Mr. P. Davis, Mr. E. A. K. Forrest, Rev. Hooper, Major A. A. Knight, Miss Elizabeth Lea, Mrs. Elsie Mountford, Mr. North, Mrs. J. S. Price, Mr. William A. Price, Mrs. Charles Prowse, Mrs. K. R. Spooner, Mrs. Thursfield, the Mayor and Mrs. Tolley, Mrs. Christopher Wilson, and Mrs. H. L. Winwood.

COUNTY REGIMENT IN FRANCE

Where the Worcesters Have Been Fighting

A unit of the Worcestershire Regiment landed in France a fortnight after D-day. Elements of its division were in action near Cheux on June 27.

In July the Worcesters were in the line in the salient north of Esquay. They attacked south east on July 10, their brigade meeting heavy opposition on the left of the line. After bitter fighting among the rolling, well-wooded hills round Eterville, the Worcesters assisted in the capture of Point 112, a commanding hill from which it was possible to deny the enemy the opportunity to escape by several second-class roads. Later, north of Maltot, astride the road from Caen to Aunay, the Worcesters were engaged in heavy fighting in the course of which they advanced to play their part in the capture of Maltot on July 23, successfully resisting counter attacks pressed home with German armour.

During August the Worcesters' formation was constantly and heavily engaged. An advance was made on the first day of the month to a line from Canteloup to St. Pierre Fresne. The advance continued. Point 361, Point 301 and villages of Brenoy Les Maisons and Le Mesnil Azduf were taken and many counter attacks repulsed. All these successes were gained by August 6, and by the night of August 6 the Worcesters were among the troops who were established on Mont Pinçon, the great slope of a hill overlooking the two roads running south from Aunay to Vire and Condé.

The Worcesters took part in heavy fighting during August. On the 14th they helped to clear Caumettes and made contact with other British troops on the Orne. Two days later they held a firm bridgehead over the Noireau and led the attack upon Berjou where hard fighting developed. On August 17 Berjou was taken, and the bridgehead was held while another formation passed through to capture Hommarine de Chardonne.

MIDLAND SALVAGE LEAGUE

Herefordshire further increased its lead over the other Counties in the new Midland Salvage League as a result of the collective efforts of the local authorities during July. They recorded full points for their month's effort and have a progressive total of 20 points out of a possible 25. Warwick is the next best county with [illegible] points, Worcester and Salop have [illegible] points each and Stafford 12. There was a sharp fall in the total salvage [illegible] for all the five counties for July and whilst the [illegible] ...

[illegible] the address was given by the Rev. Canon W. H. Cory (vicar of Wilden) who spoke of his pleasure in revisiting Hoobrook for a harvest festival after a lapse of over 40 years. Canon Cory said that the harvest spoke to us of the unchanging goodness of God even in time of war. There was a large congregation, including members of St. George's Wolf Cub Pack. After the service tea was served and the offerings sold for the benefit of the Hoobrook Church Hall Fund. A total of £5 12s. 6d. (including £1 8s. from the offertory at the service) was raised for this object.

Welcome Club.—The presence of so many wounded men of the Allied Forces emphasises the need for the proposed Welcome Club. Members of the Forces have always received a warm welcome from the Y.M.C.A. and our American visitors have their own organisation in the Donut Dugout. The Welcome Club seeks to augment the excellent work being done in these flourishing concerns by providing opportunities for more individual contacts between the members of the various Forces and between our visitors and the people of the town. It will not seek chiefly to provide another canteen, but primarily a place of meeting and forming friendships—its promoters want to create a club with a home spirit and a British welcome. A great deal has been done by way of preparation and the club will be opened to-day (Saturday) at Baxter Hall, Bull Ring, by the Lord Bishop of Worcester at [illegible]0 p.m., with the Mayor (Ald. [illegible] Tolley) in the chair. As accommodation is limited, the opening ceremony will be an invitation gathering, but the club premises will be available to members and visitors at [illegible] p.m., and it is hoped that many Kidderminster people will look in then and during the following week. The committee is urgently in need of the loan of furniture, particularly a few easy chairs. Anyone who can help, either by loan or selling at a low price, is asked to get into touch with the W.V.S., 16, Vicar St., or with Mr. W. A. Price, 113, Mill St. (Phone 2476).

Street Groups.—The Mayoress (Mrs. L. Tolley) presided over the monthly meeting of the Street Groups Committee. The secretary (Mrs. S. George) gave a report on the Baby Stamp scheme. Future whist drives

Church [illegible]

Land Army Flag Day.—Kidderminster residents will have an opportunity next Saturday, October 21, of paying a tribute to the Women's Land Army, for on that day a flag day will be held in the town in aid of the W.L.A. Benevolent Fund. Mrs. R. A. Dalley is in charge of local arrangements, and makes an urgent appeal for collectors. The Lower Committee Room at the Town Hall will be open for the distribution of collecting tins next Friday from 2.30 to 6 p.m., and all day Saturday. The W.V.S. have also kindly placed a room at the disposal of the organisers, who hope that a very generous response will be forthcoming.

Old Pals Birthday.—On Thursday, October 5, the members of St. George's Old Pals met to celebrate the 86th birthday anniversary of one of their members, Mr. George Millington, Offmore Rd. There was a good number present; Mr. E. Foster presided and both he and the Rev. P. J. Martin made eulogistic references to Mr. Millington, whom they described as a real good member, always cheerful and a real Old Pal. Other speakers who paid tribute to Mr. Millington were Messrs. W. Mountford, W. Cox, C. Lincoln Porter and Mr. Potts (Stourbridge), and all wished "Good old George" a very happy birthday and every good wish. Members of the family were present. Tea was provided, and a most enjoyable time was spent.

For Airborne Forces. — The "Shuttle" is informed that all seats for the great G.I. Song and Dance Revues to be held in the Town Hall on Friday next, October 20, in aid of the Airborne Forces Security Fund, have been sold. Mr. John Brinton, has kindly donated a hand-sewn Axminster carpet, 12ft. x 9ft., for the fund, and this will be on show in the S.W.S. show room window during the coming week to give people an opportunity of looking at it as the organisers propose accepting bids for it. There will also be gifts from Coty, etc. on sale at the show, and winners of prizes will be announced by Lady Dudley. The organisers are so pleased with the response that it is their intention to present another show on November 17, when it is hoped to bring a famous concert party, the Arden Singers, to the Town Hall.

FRANCE AND HER FREEDOM

Striking Lecture at Grammar School

On Friday last a lively and attractive lecture, full of interest, pathos and humour, was given by Mrs. P. Langhorne at the Grammar School. Mrs. Langhorne herself had escaped from France at an earlier stage of the war.

"You English boys," she said, "have a stiff job ahead in the recovery of your country after the war, but for the young people of France the task is even greater, for they have lived through so many more dark and humiliating days. Nature has been very good to France and the best way to see her goodness and the great diversity of the gifts bestowed upon her was to travel by pedal cycle. The North they would pass through quickly, for it was just a continuation of the South of England, and they would come to the great fertile plains of Aquitaine in their golden, august glory through which they could cycle two or three days on end, with the landscape broken now and then by the spire of a church or occasionally by cathedral tower. They would then slip back to Brittany. The Bretons were not Latins, but belonged to the same stock as the men of Cornwall and Wales. They did much fishing, they were steeped in tradition, and deeply religious. Like the inhabitants of Alsace they kept vividly alive their traditional customs.

South of [illegible] journey they would come to the Vosges, "the land of Christmas trees," with all the melancholy of its dark greenness and the sadness of its lakes. The Germans might be near or they might be far, but the people of Alsace-Lorraine were jolly and high-spirited; they loved their food and the good things of life. Next they would meet the wall of the Alps, with its snows and glaciers, but they would not necessarily find it colder than the North because of its nearness to the Mediterranean, and it might even be so hot as to induce them to sun-bathe amid the snows. They would move down the Rhone valley into Provence and the Riviera, and they would enjoy the climatic influence of Africa and delight in the white grit-covered houses, in the lizards on the walls, and all the loveliness and the laziness. They would have seen beet being pulled in the North and oranges in the South. After such a sweep, they would agree with the saying of a German: "France is the sample-box of the Maker."

FREE FRANCE

On June 17, 1940, France lost the ownership of this varied and age-long heritage. The country was bewildered and puzzled. Someone had spoken the word "Defeat," and France did not realise its meaning. On June 18 recovery began. The voice of de Gaulle was heard: "France has lost a battle but France has not lost a war."

Another Free France was born which, with its fighting spirit, soon earned the title of Fighting France. The spirit of re-birth was shown in innumerable ways. R.A.F. pilots who had been compelled to bale out were whisked away, hidden, and secretly passed from one family to another and were back again in England within 10 to 13 days. By D-Day it was calculated that 92 per cent of the population was engaged in some form or other of active warfare against the Germans. Half-a-million [illegible] were taking orders from London, for [illegible] the French [illegible] London [illegible] "God" the Father [illegible] they referred to [illegible] as their [illegible] and were named [illegible] a description suggested by the region in Corsica where [illegible]. When [illegible] began on D-Day they became known as F.F.I. [illegible] French Forces of the Interior [illegible] there were [illegible]

EISTEDDFOD AND RALLY

Juvenile Missionary Display at Mill Street

Organised under the auspices of the Methodist Juvenile Missionary Association, the rally and eisteddfod held at Mill St. Methodist Church last Saturday was indicative of the fellowship, enthusiasm, and interest existing among the churches in the circuit. Saturday's celebrations marked the third J.M.A. Rally, but this was the first occasion an eisteddfod had been incorporated in the proceedings. It was a highly successful venture, and has undoubtedly done much not only to focus attention on the good work of the association, but also to encourage co-operation among members. The organisation was under the leadership of the Rev. T. W. Harrison (Mill St.), who had the able assistance of Mr. Jack Preston (J.M.A. Circuit hon. secretary), and many helpers who took part both in the preparations and the conducting of the rally and eisteddfod. A wide field of activities for competition was arranged, and all except six churches in the circuit were represented. Great interest was manifested throughout and the church was well filled for the evening rally, when prizes and certificates were presented to successful competitors by Mrs. Macadie.

Missionary work from all aspects was emphasised and the church was decorated with palms, a rubber plant and an acacia tree (all kindly lent by Mr. Gregory, Sutton Rd.). Most of the sections were very well supported, the fancy dress competition leading with 65 entrants. There were [illegible] junior choir entries. Lickhill Rd. Methodist Church, Stourport, headed the list as prize-winning church with Mill St. Methodist Church a close second. Miss Margaret Greenway acted as pianist throughout all vocal sections. Special mention must be made of an interesting model of a South Indian Mission made by Mr. W. Barker. It was not entered for competition, but attracted much attention because of its clever construction and excellent detail.

Miss Jean Caldwell (Broadwaters) presided at the opening ceremony. With her were Rev. Aaron Smith (chairman, Wolverhampton and Shrewsbury District), Mr. H. A. Bishop (Lickhill Rd.), Rev. L. L. Price (George St.), and Rev. T. W. Harrison (Mill St.). Wishing the venture every success, the Rev. Smith said he was much impressed by the interest being shown in a work which was of the greatest importance.

The evening rally was conducted by Master Gordon Tipper (George St.). After presenting the prizes Mrs. Macadie expressed her pleasure in the duty she performed. The success of the eisteddfod was a happy indication of what could be expected in the future. She was delighted to see so much co-operation, and felt the effort was specially helpful because it gave members of the churches a great opportunity of getting together.

Mr. Molloy gave a short talk on missionary work in India. Thanks were expressed by Mr. L. L. Price to Mrs. Macadie, those who had assisted with the rally, and the adjudicators. He added a special word of thanks to Mr. Harrison for his part in organising and conducting the rally and eisteddfod, and to all who had contributed to the success of the venture. In reply, Mr. Harrison said he had enjoyed his share in the proceedings, and had been given great support. He thanked one and all for their ready and valuable help.

PRIZE WINNERS

WOUNDED MEN IN HOSPITAL

They are Doing Fine at the General

The first battle casualties to be directed to the Kidderminster General Hospital arrived in early August. The patients, who were brought by ambulance from a railway station in the county in the care of our local Volunteer Stretcher Bearers Company, were placed in Hope Ward, and since then this section of the hospital has been given over to the wounded men arriving from European battle zones. We understand that no very serious cases have been directed to Kidderminster, though some of the men still in the ward were among the first wounded to arrive. All are recovering from their injuries, and in consequence of this and the excellent attention and care they are receiving, there is an infectious air of cheerfulness in the ward that even the most casual visitor cannot fail to sense.

The men have made many friends despite the fact that they are confined to hospital. These friends include a number of the employees of a well-known Green St. firm who have helped to make the lot of the wounded a great deal happier by their kindly gifts of cigarettes, stationery, books, etc. There are three Polish men in the ward and visitors are assisting them to learn English. They are eager pupils and making good progress. Mr. Griffin, an employee of the Green St. firm, told a "Shuttle" reporter who visited the wounded men recently that gifts were provided from the firm's war fund.

At present there are no local men in the ward, though Captain Frederick Smith, a native of Liverpool, has a wife and daughter living in Avill Grove, Kidderminster. Captain Smith, who recently returned from Italy on well-earned leave, contracted pneumonia while taking a course of instruction in this country, and was admitted to hospital.

A Czech soldier, Pte. John Beer, who resided in Kidderminster with Mrs. Preece, of 7, Neville Ave., until he joined the Services early this year, is suffering from a wound in the leg. Pte. Beer, who is 30 years old, came to this country at the beginning of the war and lived for some time at Cleobury Mortimer before he took up residence at the home of Mrs. Preece. Before he joined the Services seven months ago he was employed at Messrs. J. P. Harvey and Co., and later by the British Sugar Corporation. Pte. Beer went overseas with the B.L.A. six weeks ago and it was while serving with the Invasion Forces in Holland that he received his wound. Mrs. Preece has visited Pte. Beer on two occasions.

In a talk with Fusilier Frank Hodgkinson, of Stoke-on-Trent, who was wounded in the legs and arm during the fighting in Holland, it was learned that this is his second experience of battle wounds. Though he only arrived at the hospital on Tuesday week his wife and sister-in-law have already been to see him, a fact which makes this young soldier say that things are "fine" with him. Guardsman George Coates, of Grimsby, is "waiting to get back and have another crack at Jerry." He was serving with an armoured division just inside the border of Germany when he was injured in the left ankle and the neck. "It was a great moment when our men actually crossed the border into enemy territory," he said, "and they were in the highest possible spirits." A tribute to the kindness and friendliness of the Belgians was paid by Trooper Arthur Sheldon, son of Mr. and Mrs. Sheldon, 20, Queen's Square, Manchester. He received an injury to his left arm while fighting on the Dutch frontier.

POST-WAR PROBLEMS

Study Course for Adult Workers

Kidderminster branch, Workers' Educational Association, has decided to form an additional tutorial class for the study of "Post-war Problems of Reconstruction." The first lecture will be given at the Women War Workers' Club, Worcester Cross, on Friday, Oct. 27, at 7.30 p.m., and is to be followed by twenty others. At least a half-hour of the evening will be devoted to general discussion by the class before the lecturer's summing-up. This decision was reached at a meeting in the Hall of King Charles I Grammar School on Friday, addressed by Mr. T. Evans, the Worcestershire area resident tutor.

Mr. J. P. Hayes, local secretary, who presided, stated that Kidderminster branch hoped to celebrate its Silver Jubilee within the next few months.

Mr. Evans told the meeting that two excellent classes were felt that in an industrial town, under the auspices of the W.E.A., one on drama, the other on musical appreciation. But he felt that in an industrial town whose population exceeded 10,000 they ought to get a more balanced programme of educational activities amongst adults. He would be pleased to do all he possibly could in setting up a class for the study of some branch of Social Science that would be of vital interest to people in Kidderminster. Total membership of class students was 40—41 and in view of the transitional times we were approaching democracy would be called upon to face up to the most difficult, complicated and baffling problems mankind had ever been called upon to deal with. They must make preparation for improvement of intellectual outlook and perspective generally. A weekly meeting for the discussion of post-war problems of reconstruction ought not to be beyond their resources. They should be able to cultivate fairly clear ideas on what those problems would mean here in Great Britain and other countries of the world. We would be concerned about the maintenance of peace in Europe in particular, so must have more information on the different national characteristics involved. Talk about security inevitably led to contrasting 1938 conditions with the prospective post-war changes, and should result in taking a more cosmic view of the situation.

The W.E.A. worked in close co-operation with the nearest University, the L.E.A., Ministry of Education and public authorities who in one form or another gave financial help to the movement which otherwise would find it difficult to exist on voluntary support alone. "However, that doesn't cramp our style in any way," continued Mr. Evans. "We are free to seek light in the best way we are capable of, and have complete and absolute intellectual freedom." On that basis students were encouraged to express themselves frankly and to remember the moral obligation of speaking circumspectly in the presence of many-sided opinions. Two questions for that meeting to answer were, first the type of class required in a town so predominantly industrial like Kidderminster and secondly whether it was desirable to have one that would give them more balanced ideas of reasonable progress in their own locality, and grasp of better perspective for the happier days that lay ahead.

Mr. L. G. French, speaking for the Ministry of Labour and National Service inquired whether only wage-earning and salaried workers were welcomed at W.E.A. classes or were employers equally welcomed? In some quarters there was a tendency to assume that the W.E.A. was a party political movement.

Mr. Evans replied that the W.E.A. was not associated with any political party or organisation—it was purely a voluntary educational organisation. The late Sir Oliver Lodge, when Principal of the University of Birmingham, favoured the retention of the word worker in the title of the organisation, on the ground that we must associate with our fellows if we were to get anything done. The broadcast definition the movement gave to a worker was, "Anybody who earns a livelihood." Everybody in the country over the age of 18 had a legal right to join W.E.A. classes because those classes received financial aid from the Board of Education.

Dr. A. D'Arcy Chapman inquired how students were recruited.

Mr. A. Turner, a founder member of the local branch, said the initial tutorial class studied Industrial History and Economics attracted students not only from the trade unions but also members of the N.U.T., from one man business concerns and a few from the professional classes. Apart from that, weekly class, [illegible]

HOME GUARD STAND-DOWN

TRIBUTES TO SERVICES OF LOCAL BATTALIONS

On Sunday last the official stand-down order of the Home Guard became effective, and for the last time battalions in all parts of the country held parades.

The local battalions—the 6th (Kidderminster), 10th (Stourbridge) and 11th (Stourport)—were no exception, and the populace lined the streets to give a final farewell to these civilian soldiers who had banded themselves together to fight against the invader who never came.

Warm tributes were paid to their services and when the final dismissal was given the men dispersed—the majority of them not a little sorrowful that this fine war-time organisation, which had created so much good comradeship, had come to an end.

At Kidderminster there was a splendid muster of the 6th Battalion of the Worcestershire Home Guard for the stand-down parade, which was witnessed by crowds of spectators who lined the route in farewell tribute. Accompanying the Battalion were the personnel of [illegible] Sector headquarters and the local Post Office company of the Warwickshire Home Guard.

The route taken was from Green St., where the battalion assembled, into Worcester Cross, Oxford St., Vicar St., Bull Ring, Mill St., Park Butts, Bewdley St., to the playing field of King Charles I Grammar School. The saluting base was the Rowland Hill statue and Col. R. W. A. Painter, M.C. (Sector Commander) took the salute. He was accompanied by the Mayor (Cllr. J. S. Chadwick), Col. J. O. Woods, R.A.P.C., Major A. P. R. Godfrey, Town Clerk, (Col. J. H. Thursfield, M.C.), Deputy Mayor (Ald. L. Tolley), Aldermen E. Geo. Eddy, H. W. Cheshire, Miss [illegible] C. Addenbrooke; Cllrs. J. Bristow and J. Brown, and Chief Cons. Harry Hodgkinson. Traffic arrangements were directed by Police-Inspector B. Powell. Part of the route on either side of the saluting base was lined by the R.A.P.C. who acted as guard of honour.

Just before 10.45 three military cyclists rode past and then the Kidderminster Military Band began to play the "Royal Windsor," the Regimental march of the Worcestershire Regiment. Eight minutes elapsed for the parade to pass. At the Grammar School grounds entrance a contingent of Army Cadets Force, under Major A. E. Rollings, M.C., formed a guard of honour. After marching round the field the parade halted facing Woodfield House, and the Mayor, still wearing chain and robes of office, addressed the assembly. Himself an ex-service officer, he said: "It is my privilege to-day, on behalf of Kidderminster, to pay you a slight token of appreciation for the wonderful service you have rendered. You came forward in that spirit of service when the call of our country came and at a time when this country stood alone in the darkest hours of its history. The call came to defend our shores from the prospect of invasion, and you responded in that wonderful spirit that brought into existence the cheapest and most efficient army of its kind that the world has ever seen.

"Fortunately you have not had to fight on the beaches, in the ditches and hedgerows, or the villages and towns, but you showed the world that this country [illegible] stand-down [illegible]

[illegible] stand down. They would have come there, he expected, with rather mixed feelings. On the one hand they would be extraordinarily glad that the course of the war had ensured that they would never see any of the horrors of war breaking up our own homes; on the other they would probably be to some degree sorry to see the Home Guard passing into reserve. They were an old comrade now. They had been together for a good many years. They had built up a tradition of their own and had earned the right by their service to share in the glorious military traditions of the British Empire. If the Germans had come here it was quite certain that the Home Guard, in the words of an old Spanish chronicler, would have proved themselves "redoubtable in battle" and would have "fought silently" in grim determination to the very end.

Earl Baldwin said few things had given him greater pleasure than the intimation that it was their desire that he should say a few words to them on the day when they were going to stand down. He remembered hearing Mr. Eden broadcast, and the echoes had hardly died away before Stourport was humming about the new L.D.V. Worcestershire as usual, was to the fore in good time, and there were on the platform many who helped at that time and who, he was thankful to think, were with them still. The British Legion, true to its best traditions, played an important part in helping with the organisation.

"Why is it we all feel a small lump in the throat now this day of farewell has come?" asked Lord Baldwin. "It is because we are, as it were, one family together from this most delectable corner of the delectable county of Worcestershire, we know each other, most of us were born and bred in this county. We have taken pride in our county regiment, and we take pride together now in our Home Guard. And why do we take pride in you? We know that the Home Guard voluntarily gave up all they had to give as men. They gave their leisure, they gave up many a little holiday, many a week-end, and owing to the circumstances of the case nearly all of those who volunteered were working full time and some of them perhaps more. They knew, although they never said so, what they might have to undergo. Invasion, or the possibility of invasion, at the time you were formed was far more than a threat—it was a very real thing. Having chosen your duty [illegible] you followed up that action of free will with another [illegible] to make yourselves efficient soldiers and that was done. There was much [illegible] the soldiers of the [illegible]

BOROUGH OF BEWDLEY

Quarterly Council Meeting 31st day of January, 1944.

Report of the Evacuation Committee

Your Committee beg to report on their proceedings during the past quarter as follows:-

Rookery Cottage - Mrs. Travis, Mrs. Clarke and her child, a homeless family accommodated at Rookery Cottage, have now returned to Birmingham.

Your Committee have been in communication with the Regional Office of the Ministry of Health and also The City of Birmingham Estates Department with regard to the provision of accommodation for Mrs. Milligan and her son, the only remaining evacuees at Rookery Cottage.

Billeting Allowances - Your Committee have given further consideration to the question of billeting allowances payable to evacuees within the Borough which have to be reviewed periodically on the instructions of the Ministry of Health.

Your Committee have resolved to withdraw the allowance payable in one additional case.

Hern's Nest Hostel - Additional Members - Your Committee have co-opted Mrs. S.J. Rowe and Mrs. Mortimer Smith to serve as additional members of the Committee.

Christmas Party - A very successful Christmas party was given for the children on Wednesday, December 29th at 3.30 p.m. Each child was allowed to bring one friend, and the parents of the children residing at the Hostel were invited to attend the party.

Gifts of presents for the children were received both from the American Red Cross and also from Mr. Bishop of the Wool Shop, Bewdley. Subscriptions towards the cost of running the party were also received from His Worship the Mayor (Alderman R.B. Jackson), the Deputy Mayor (Alderman H.N. Frost), the Chairman (Alderman F.E. Mountford), Councillor Mortimer Smith, Mrs. H.G. Southall and Mrs. J.H. Thursfield.

Assistant Matron - Mrs. Morris resigned her position as Assistant Matron at the Hostel and Miss G. Edwards of Kingswinford, Staffordshire, has been appointed as Assistant Matron in the place of Mrs. Morris and took up her duties on Monday, 15th November, 1943.

Accounts - All accounts have been scrutinized and passed by your Committee each month for submission to the Accounts Committee of the Bewdley Corporation for payment.

Appointment of Chairman - Alderman F.E. Mountford has been appointed to act as Chairman of your Committee for the ensuing year.

F.E. Mountford.
Chairman.

31st January, 1944.

BOROUGH OF BEWDLEY

Water & Health Committee Report (Contd:)   31st day of January, 1944.

Salvage - At the request of the Director of Salvage and Recovery a further salvage drive is to be held in the County of Worcestershire during the month of March.

The period fixed for this salvage drive within the Borough of Bewdley is during the fortnight commencing Saturday, March 18th and ending Saturday, April 1st.

Special emphasis is to be made on the need for books, but bones, paper and rags will also be included in the drive.

Appointment of Chairman - His Worship the Mayor (Alderman R.B. Jackson) has been appointed to act as Chairman of your Committee for the ensuing year.

R.B. Jackson

Chairman.

31st January, 1944.

BOROUGH OF BEWDLEY

Quarterly Council Meeting 31st day of July, 1944.

Report of the A.R.P. Committee

Your Committee beg to report on their proceedings during the past quarter as follows:-

General Training - A special incident officers' course was held during the month of June on every Monday evening at the Town Hall for members of the Bewdley Civil Defence Services.

Arrangements have also been made for several other items of special training on individual nights, including new films recently issued.

The Training Officer reported to your Committee that the general arrangements for training under Heads of Services was working very satisfactorily and no further action is to be taken at the moment to arrange another General Civil Defence Exercise within the Borough.

A Rescue Party from Bewdley took part in a First Aid competition at Kidderminster on Sunday, June 11th, and this party was placed second to the Kidderminster No: 1 Party.

The Bewdley Rescue Party also gave a demonstration at Cotheridge on Sunday, June 18th, and earned very high praise from the Chairman of the County War Emergency Committee and the County A.R.P. Officer.

Your Committee gave instructions for a letter of congratulations to be sent on behalf of the Town Council, intimating that the excellent standard achieved by the Bewdley Rescue Party did great credit to the Borough, and this letter was sent to each member of the Rescue Party who took part in the competition and demonstration.

R. B. Jackson

Chairman.

31st day of July, 1944.

BOROUGH OF BEWDLEY

Quarterly Council Meeting 30th day of October 1944

Report of the Evacuation Committee

Your Committee beg to report on their proceedings during the past quarter as follows:-

Government Evacuation Scheme - The billeting arrangements for all evacuees other than those from London and the South of England have now been terminated by the Government, and billeting notices have accordingly been withdrawn by the Evacuation Officer within the Borough wherever necessary.

A number of evacuees coming within the official billeting categories from London and the South of England still remain in the Borough, including a few unaccompanied children and some of the evacuees from other parts of England are staying in the Borough under their own arrangements after the billeting notices have been withdrawn.

Hern's Nest Hostel

Annual Holidays - Miss Mansworth agreed to undertake the duties of Matron for a short time so that the Matron at Hern's Nest Hostel could take her annual holiday. During the Matron's absence Miss Mansworth discharged her duties as Acting Matron most efficiently and the Hern's Nest Hostel Committee have expressed their appreciation to Miss Mansworth for the services she rendered, and also asked her to act as relief for the Assistant Matron so that Miss Edwards could also take her annual holiday.

Re-billeting of Children - A communication has been received from the Ministry of Health with regard to four children that are now considered to be suitable for re-billeting with private householders, and this matter is receiving the attention of the Management Committee.

Two small girls aged 4½ and 5½ have been admitted to the Hostel during the confinement of their Mother at the Lucy Baldwin Maternity Hospital, Stourport-on-Severn.

H.E. Mountford.
Chairman.

30th October, 1944.

BOROUGH OF BEWDLEY

Quarterly Council Meeting — 9th day of November 1944.

QUARTERLY MEETINGS

It was RESOLVED and ORDERED that the Quarterly Meetings of the Council for the ensuing year be and the same are hereby appointed to be held on the last Mondays in January, April, and July at 5 o'clock p.m., and on the 9th November at 12 o'clock noon.

COMMITTEES

It was RESOLVED and ORDERED as follows:-

That the several Committees be appointed and that instructions be given to such Committees and their powers be confirmed.

That the Mayor be an ex officio Member of all Committees.

That the several Committees be constituted with powers and instructions, as follows:

GENERAL PURPOSES - To consist of the whole of the Members of the Council to whom (so far as there is power to delegate the same) be assigned all powers and duties of the Council under the Statutes or otherwise including during the continuance of hostilities all matters which are assigned to the other Committees appointed at this Meeting.

EMERGENCY - To consist of the following members of the Council that is to say - the respective Chairmen of the various Committees appointed by the Council to whom be delegated full powers to act on behalf of the Town Council in all matters of immediate urgency.

FINANCE - To consist of the whole of the Members of the Council to whom be delegated the consideration of all matters relating to the Finance of the Borough.

WATER AND HEALTH - To consist of the whole of the Members of the Council to whom be delegated all matters relating to the water supply for the Borough, the management of the Waterworks, and the carrying into execution within the Borough, of the Public Health Acts, and matters relating to public health.

HIGHWAYS - To consist of the whole of the Members of the Council to whom be delegated all matters relating to Highways within the Borough.

HOUSING - To consist of the whole of the Members of the Council to whom be delegated all matters appertaining to Housing within the Borough.

LIGHTING AND FIRE BRIGADE - To consist of the whole of the Members of the Council to whom be delegated all matters relating to the lighting of the Borough and to the provision and maintenance of the Fire Brigade and Engine.

RATING AND VALUATION - To consist of the whole of the Members of the Council with the exception of those Members who are representatives of the Council on the North West Worcestershire Assessment Committee to whom (so far as there is power to delegate the same) be delegated the consideration of all matters relating to Rating and Valuation within the Borough.

AIR RAID PRECAUTIONS - To consist of the following members of the Council, that is to say - Aldermen Frost, Jackson, and Mountford, Councillors Bates, Godwin, Mountford, Pritchard, Palmer, Webb and Windsor, to whom be delegated the consideration of all matters relating to Air Raid Precautions within the Borough.

BOROUGH OF BEWDLEY

Quarterly Council Meeting 9th day of November 1944.

EVACUATION - To consist of the following members of the Council, that is to say - Aldermen Frost, Jackson and Mountford, Councillors Gazely, Godwin, Windsor and Mountford with power to co-opt, to whom be delegated the consideration of all matters relating to Evacuation within the Borough whether by Government Schemes or individual arrangements.

TOWN PLANNING - To consist of the whole of the Members of the Council to whom be delegated all matters appertaining to the Town and Country Planning Acts 1932 and 1943.

That each of the Committees now appointed by this Council and hereinafter mentioned, viz:

General Purposes
Emergency
Finance
Water and Health
Highways
Housing
Lighting and Fire Brigade
Rating and Valuation
Air Raid Precautions
Evacuation
Town Planning

shall continue in office until the 31st day of October 1945, unless this Council shall at any time otherwise order, and shall have power to engage the services of such officers, clerks, collectors, servants, workmen and others, as may be necessary to help them to carry out the various matters entrusted to their care by this Council and shall also have power to transact any business which has been heretofore committed by this Council to any Committee in the like behalf and is not yet completed, and that the said Committees respectively may, for and on behalf of the Council, do and direct all such acts, matters and things as may be necessary or incident to the execution of the powers, authorities, and directions given or committed to them respectively and this Council doth hereby delegate to the said Committees its powers and duties in relation to the matters aforesaid.

DEVELOPMENT COMMITTEE - To consist of the whole of the Members of the Council, Messrs. A.T. Marlow, H.C. Styles, T. Williams, Mesdames S. Bache, E.R. Batchelor, and G.A. Darkes, to whom be delegated all matters relating to the Development of the Borough.

LIBRARY - To consist of the following members of the Council, that is to say - Alderman Frost, Councillors Bates, Godwin, Mountford, Palmer and Pritchard, the Secretary for the time being of the Bewdley Institute and Mr. J.A. Dixon.

HERN'S NEST MANAGEMENT COMMITTEE - To consist of the following members, that is to say - Aldermen Frost, Jackson and Mountford, with two representatives from the Kidderminster Borough Council, Stourport-on- Severn Urban District Council, and the Kidderminster Rural District Council, and two representatives from the Women's Voluntary Services with power to co-opt, to whom be delegated the consideration of all matters relating to Hern's Nest Hostel.

And that the Meetings of the General Purposes Committee be held on such days and at such times as the Mayor may decide and that the other Committees do meet on such days and at such hour as they respectively may appoint.

GUARDIANS COMMITTEE -

Proposed by Alderman Jackson seconded by Councillor Godwin and RESOLVED that Alderman Henry Neal Frost be and he is hereby nominated for membership of the Guardians Committee in accordance with Clause 6 (4) of the Administrative Scheme for the County under the Local Government Act 1929, for the ensuing year.

Chapter Seven
1945
ALLIED VICTORY - WINNING THE PEACE

Roosevelt was gravely ill even as he met Churchill and Stalin at the Crimea Conference on 3 February. Roosevelt and Churchill had their own pre-meeting at Malta the day before. Unconditional surrender would be demanded of the Axis Powers.

Mussolini and his mistress were shot and their bodies hung in a Milan City square on 28 April.

With Hitler dead, the Russians in Berlin and the Allies meeting them in Germany, war in Europe was over on 8 May, but Japan was not defeated until August. On 6 August, the Americans dropped the atomic bomb on Hiroshima. The Japanese surrendered on 2 September, signing the document onboard the US battleship, "Missouri."

In France, Laval and Petain were quickly put on trial. On 23 July the 89 year old Petain was sentenced to death, though this was later commuted. Laval was executed. De Gaulle had won a famous victory, as did the Labour Party at the General Election in Britain.

And now to win the Peace!

Ribbesford House could return to civil and domestic mode, as could Bewdley, Kidderminster and Stourport.

Civilian production was returned, but Britain faced many years of restoration in agriculture, industry and the re-establishment of its democratic institutions. The division of Europe between West and East and the Iron Curtain between the democracies and so-called Communist Bloc, divided the World politically until 1989 with the fall of the Berlin Wall. Economically and politically Russia is in relative chaos. Unless democracy becomes a reality, the victory over Nazism by the Allies will not be complete.

Chapter Seven
1945
ALLIED VICTORY - WINNING THE PEACE

Roosevelt was gravely ill even as he met Churchill and Stalin at the Crimea Conference on 3 February. Roosevelt and Churchill had their own pre-meeting at Malta the day before. Unconditional surrender would be demanded of the Axis Powers.

Mussolini and his mistress were shot and their bodies hung in a Milan City square on 28 April.

With Hitler dead, the Russians in Berlin and the Allies meeting them in Germany, war in Europe was over on 8 May, but Japan was not defeated until August. On 6 August, the Americans dropped the atomic bomb on Hiroshima. The Japanese surrendered on 2 September, signing the document onboard the US battleship, "Missouri."

In France, Laval and Petain were quickly put on trial. On 23 July the 89 year old Petain was sentenced to death, though this was later commuted. Laval was executed. De Gaulle had won a famous victory, as did the Labour Party at the General Election in Britain.

And now to win the Peace!

Ribbesford House could return to civil and domestic mode, as could Bewdley, Kidderminster and Stourport.

Civilian production was returned, but Britain faced many years of restoration in agriculture, industry and the re-establishment of its democratic institutions. The division of Europe between West and East and the Iron Curtain between the democracies and so-called Communist Bloc, divided the World politically until 1989 with the fall of the Berlin Wall. Economically and politically Russia is in relative chaos. Unless democracy becomes a reality, the victory over Nazism by the Allies will not be complete.

One can not help being overwhelmed by the enormity of the Second World War, as one is by World War One. The people of Bewdley, Kidderminster and Stourport played their full part in our victory over Nazism. Ribbesford House has a special place in our history.

3-10 February, 1945

Churchill, Roosevelt and Stalin

meeting at Yalta

3-10 February, 1945

CRIMEA CONFERENCE

On 3 February began the historic meetings between Mr. Churchill, President Roosevelt and Marshal Stalin in the Livadia Palace at Yalta, in the Crimea. On the previous day Mr. Churchill and President Roosevelt met in Malta and, after conferences, flew thence by air to a Soviet airport in the Crimea, where they were met by Marshal Stalin and M. Molotov. All three leaders were accompanied at the Yalta meetings, which lasted for eight days, by their respective Foreign Secretaries, Chiefs of Staff and other advisers. Most important of the many subjects under discussion at this, the most momentous of all the "Big Three" meetings that had so far taken place, were the military plans for the final defeat of Germany. The conference agreed on the enforcement of the "unconditional surrender" terms for the aggressors in Europe and plans for the occupation of a separate zone of Germany by forces of each of the three powers. Many of the problems involved in establishing a secure peace were also discussed by the great war leaders in a spirit of mutual accord. The results of the Crimea Conference were made known to the world on 12 February in simultaneous broadcasts from London, Washington and Moscow. In every land the news was greeted with whole-hearted approval, for it was felt that the meetings had paved the way for the creation of a long and satisfactory peace. The photograph of the three world leaders reproduced here was taken in the grounds of the Livadia Palace during the Conference. Left to right, Mr. Churchill (wearing a Cossack cap), President Roosevelt and Marshal Stalin.

End of a Dictator

28 April, 1945

MUSSOLINI PAYS THE PENALTY. On 28 April Mussolini; together with his mistress, Clara Petacci, was captured by a group of Italian partisans in a village beside Lake Como, in Northern Italy. Only a few hours after his arrest the former arrogant dictator was tried, sentenced to death, and shot by his captors. Twelve members of his Fascist cabinet were shot at the same time. Soon after the sentence had been carried out the bodies of Mussolini and Clara Petacci were taken to Milan where they were hung upside down in one of the city's squares.

Daily Mail

No. 15.311 ONE PENNY FOR KING AND EMPIRE SATURDAY,

Levant crisis shifts to Paris: storm in French Ca

DE GAULLE CRITICIS HIS MINISTERS

'Not fully informed of the serious situation'

From HENRY McNULTY. PARIS, Friday.

THE Levant crisis has shifted to Paris. A few hours after order had been restored throughout Syria and the Lebanon a new French political dispute flared up to-day over General de Gaulle's handling of the Near East situation.

Members of the French Government are reported to have been strongly critical of de Gaulle's policy at a long and very stormy meeting, and now it is uncertain whether he will send any reply to Mr. Churchill's Note.

General de Gaulle will hold a Press conference to-morrow, and he may broadcast to the French nation to-morrow night.

Members of the French Cabinet at to-day's meeting are reliably reported to have criticised General de Gaulle and to have expressed resentment at the alleged failure to keep members of the

Damascus surveys the debris

City quiet again

From HAIG NICHOLSON
DAMASCUS, Thursday.

. . . —

His V Sign gave hope to Europe

'Col. Britton' is off secret list

THE B.B.C. last night disclosed the identity of "Colonel Britton," mystery radio man and the "Voice of SHAEF," who played an important part in building up the resistance movements in Europe in the dark days of the war and popularised the V sign.

He is Mr. Douglas E. Ritchie, Director of the European News Department, of the B.B.C.

Mr. Ritchie joined the B.B.C.'s European section in March 1939. Towards the end of 1940 many suggestions were put forward for the co-ordination of resistance by means of London broadcasts.

A committee was formed of which Mr. Ritchie was chairman, and special broadcasts were begun.

A speaker was needed to give messages in English which could afterwards be translated into the appropriate foreign languages, and it was arranged for Colonel Britton to broadcast them.

PETAIN ON TRIAL. On 23 July the eighty-nine-year-old Marshal of France, Philippe Petain, head of the former Vichy Government, appeared at the Palais de Justice in Paris on a charge of treason. During the three-week trial evidence for the prosecution was given by famous French political leaders, including two former premiers, M. Daladier and M. Reynaud. The traitor Pierre Laval appeared for the defence and is seen above giving evidence while Petain listens. Petain was sentenced to death, but the death penalty was commuted by General de Gaulle to imprisonment for life. Top right, Petain in court; bottom right, listening to the evidence of M. Reynaud.

opens in Paris

23 July, 1945

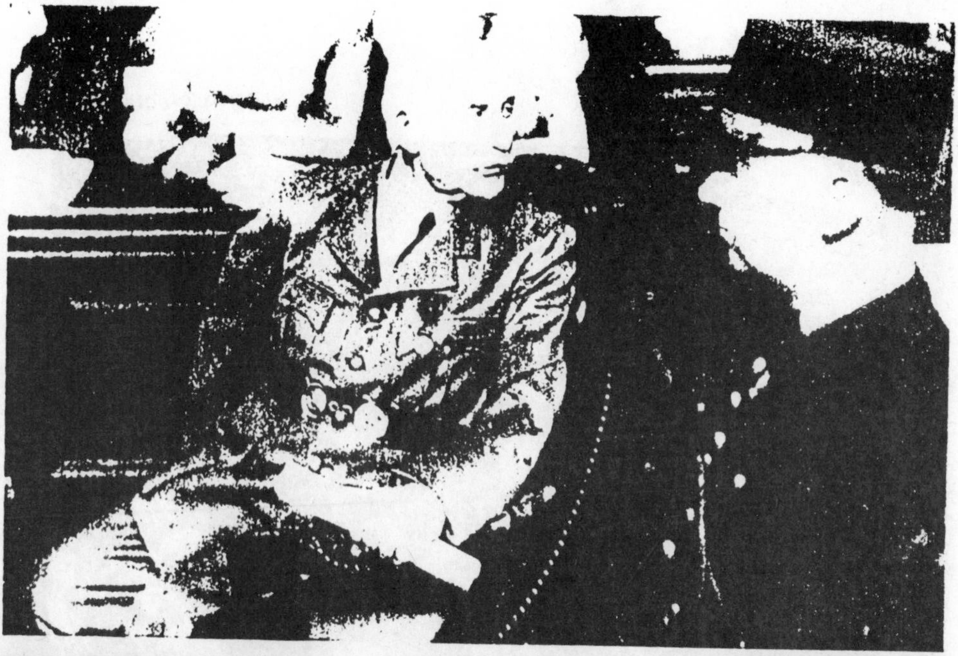

26 July, 1945

Britain elects new

Socialist Government

26 July, 1945

LABOUR WINS POWER IN BRITAIN

The result of Britain's general election, the first for ten years, was declared on 26 July, three weeks after polling day. For the first time in the history of the country the Socialist Party was returned to power with a large working majority, gaining nearly 400 seats in the House of Commons. Mr. Churchill, therefore, resigned the Premiership, and his place was taken by Mr. Attlee. Here is the new Labour Government photographed in the garden of No. 10 Downing Street, London. Back row (left to right): Mr. William Whiteley; Sir E. Bridges, Chief Whip; Sir F. Soskice, Solicitor-General; Mr. J. B. Hynd, Chancellor of the Duchy of Lancaster; the Earl of Listowel, Postmaster-General; Mr. E. J. Williams, Minister of Information; Mr. Lewis Silkin, Minister of Town and Country Planning; Mr. James Griffiths, Minister of National Insurance; Lord Winster, Minister of Civil Aviation; Mr. P. J Noel-Baker, Minister of State; Mr. Wilfred Paling, Minister of Pensions; Sir Hartley Shawcross, Attorney-General; and Mr. Norman Brook. Centre row (left to right): Sir Ben Smith, Minister of Food; Mr. John Wilmot, Minister of Supply; Mr. Aneurin Bevan, Minister of Health; Mr. George Isaacs, Minister of Labour; Viscount Stansgate, Secretary of State for Air; Mr. G. Hall, Secretary for the Colonies; Lord Pethick-Lawrence, Secretary for India; Mr. J. Lawson, Secretary of State for War; Mr. J. Westwood, Secretary of State for Scotland; Mr. Emanuel Shinwell, Minister of Fuel and Power; Mr. T. Williams, Minister of Agriculture; Mr. G. Tomlinson, Minister of Works; Sir Alfred Barnes, Minister of Transport. Front row (left to right): Viscount Addison, Secretary for the Dominions; Lord Jowitt, Lord Chancellor; Sir Stafford Cripps, President of the Board of Trade; Mr. A. Greenwood, Lord Privy Seal; Mr. Ernest Bevin, Foreign Secretary; Mr. C. R. Attlee, Prime Minister; Mr. Herbert Morrison, Lord President of the Council; Mr. Hugh Dalton, Chancellor of the Exchequer; Mr. A. V. Alexander, First Lord of the Admiralty; Mr. Chuter Ede, Home Secretary; Miss Ellen Wilkinson, Education.

245

leaders in Potsdam talks

July—August, 1945

POTSDAM CONFERENCE. On 17 July the historic Three-Power Conference opened at the Cecilienhof Palace at Potsdam, outside Berlin, with Mr. Churchill, President Truman and Marshal Stalin heading the respective delegations. On 26 July a proclamation was issued to the Japanese people and signed by Mr. Churchill and President Truman, and approved by radio by Generalissimo Chiang Kai-shek. This offered Japan the choice of unconditional surrender or annihilation; and stated plainly the terms on which surrender would be accepted. As a result of the victory of the Labour Party in the British General Election, declared on 26 July, Mr. Churchill's place at Potsdam was taken by Mr. Attlee, the new Prime Minister, who had participated in the Conference from the beginning. Mr. Ernest Bevin, who succeeded Mr. Eden as Foreign Secretary, flew to Berlin with Mr. Attlee on 28 July. Early on 2 August the Potsdam Conference ended, and a long communique on the decisions taken there was issued simultaneously in London, Washington and Moscow. On the Allied attitude to Germany it was declared that "German militarism and Nazism will be extirpated and the Allies will take in agreement together, now and in the future, the other measures necessary to assure that Germany will never again threaten her neighbours or the peace of the world." Principles were established by the Three Powers governing the treatment of Germany during the initial period of Allied control, and the Potsdam declaration insisted on "the complete disarmament and demilitarization of Germany and the elimination or control of all German industry that could be used for military production." On the question of reparations: "that Germany be compelled to compensate to the greatest possible extent for the loss and suffering she has caused to the United Nations, and for which the German people cannot escape responsibility." It was also agreed at Potsdam that all the war criminals were to be brought to swift and sure justice. On the left the Conference is seen in session with Mr. Churchill, Mr. Eden, Mr. Attlee, President Truman and Marshal Stalin seated around the table. Above, Mr. Attlee, President Truman, Marshal Stalin with Admiral Leahy, Mr. Ernest Bevin, Mr. J. Byrnes and M. Molotov.

Historic meeting off Plymouth

2 August, 1945

THE KING MEETS PRESIDENT TRUMAN. On his way home from the Potsdam Conference, President Truman broke his journey at Plymouth to exchange greetings with H.M. the King. This historic meeting took place on board the British battle-cruiser H.M.S. "Renown," anchored in Plymouth Sound about a mile from the American cruiser "Augusta" which was to take the President back to the United States. Just after midday the President left the "Augusta" to go aboard the "Renown" where, as pictured above, he was met at the head of the gangway by the King and entertained to luncheon. After lunch President Truman inspected a guard of honour of Royal Marines on board the battle-cruiser, and later His Majesty paid a short visit to the President on board the "Augusta" before the cruiser left for America. As the U.S. ship passed the "Renown" the King stood at the salute.

First atom bomb raids

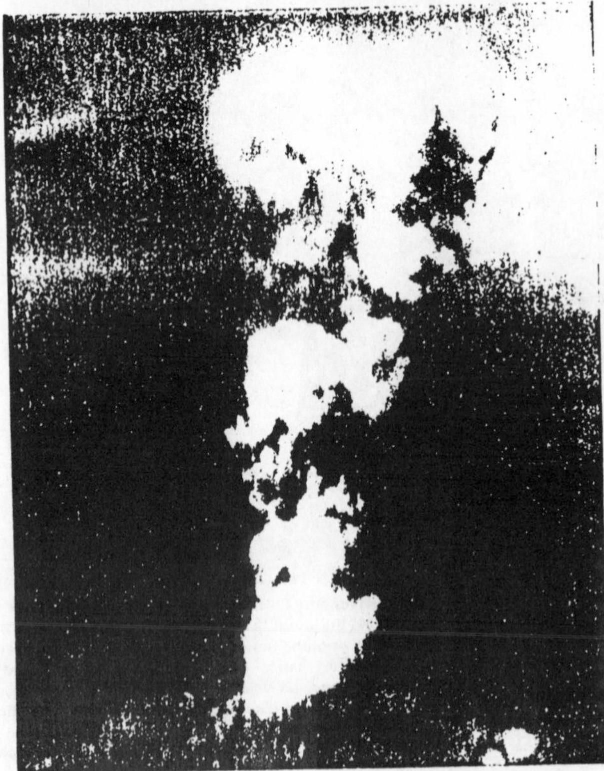

ATOM BOMBS HIT JAPAN

In the late evening of 6 August the following dramatic announcement was made by President Truman: "Sixteen hours ago an American aeroplane dropped one bomb on Hiroshima, Japan. That bomb had more power than 20,000 tons of T.N.T., and more than 2,000 times the blast power of the British 'grand slam,' which is the largest bomb (22,000 lb.) yet used in the history of warfare." Thus the world heard of the first use of the atomic bomb, the result of the epoch-making discovery by the Allies of the splitting of the atom. Hiroshima, a great Japanese naval and army base with a population of about 340,000, was virtually disintegrated by the effect of the colossal explosion, and more than a third of its inhabitants were instantly killed or burned to death. The second atomic bomb was dropped on Nagasaki, another great city of Japan, on 9 August where the results were even more appalling. The vast cloud of smoke and flame following the explosion could be seen over 250 miles away. Above, the devastated city of Nagasaki after the atomic bomb raid. Rescue workers pick their way amid the rubble. Left, smoke, 20,000 ft. high, covers Hiroshima.

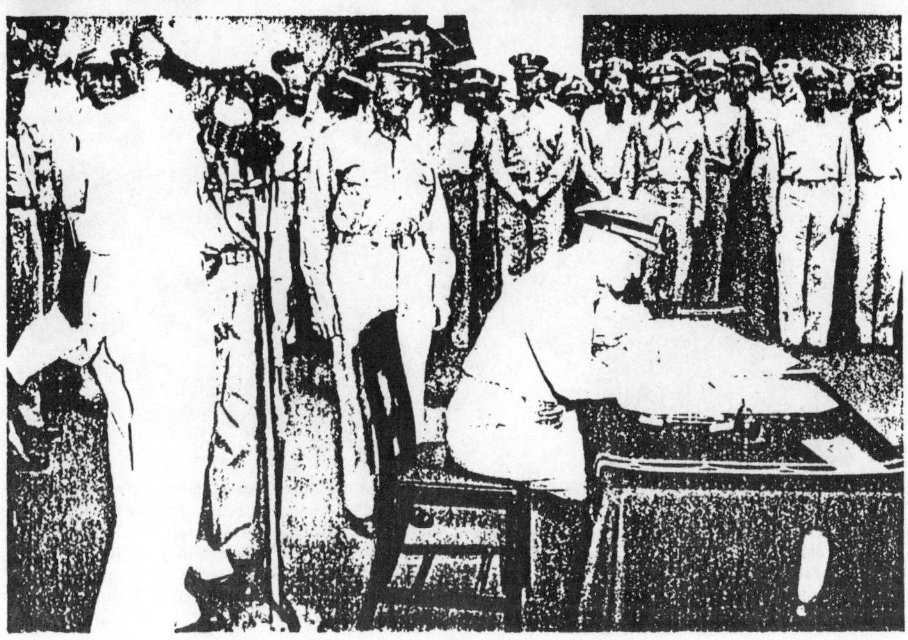

JAPANESE SIGN FINAL SURRENDER. On Sunday, 2 September, Japan signed the document of final surrender, accepting the authority of General MacArthur, on board the American battleship "Missouri" anchored in Tokyo Bay. Eleven Japanese emissaries, including four diplomats in frock coats and top hats, were present at the ceremony, and the act of signing was carried out before General MacArthur, Supreme Allied Commander in the Far East. These radio pictures were taken aboard the "Missouri". Above, arrival of Shigemitsu, Jap Foreign Secretary; top left, General MacArthur (extreme left) watches Gen. Umaza sign; below, Admiral C. Nimitz signs.

URSDAY, OCTOBER 4, 1945

FINAL NIGHT EXTRA

Evening Standard

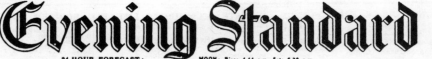

37,769 | 24-HOUR FORECAST: Mainly fair; warm. | MOON: Rises 4.44 a.m. Sets 6.30 p.m. LIGHTING-UP TIME: 7.32 p.m. | ONE PENNY

Lawyers cry 'It is blackmail': Shouts from the public gallery

LAVAL TRIAL UPROAR

Judge threatens to throw him out -AND MAKES HIM APOLOGISE

From JEROME WILLIS: Paris, Thursday

The trial of Pierre Laval opened at 1.29 this afternoon in the Palais de Justice of Paris and adjourned at 2.10 after heated scene in which Laval insulted the judge.

Immediately after the trial opened Judge ongibeaux had read a statement from MM. aud and Barraduc, Laval's lawyers, announcing eir refusal to appear because they had inifficient time to prepare a case.

The defence lawyers said in their letter that the haste the trial was "due to political reasons," and referred Judge Mongibeaux's methods as "blackmail."

M. Mornet, the Public Prosecutor, rose to protest ainst what he called an "insult to the law" in accusans by Laval that the law was being mixed with politics.

There was then an angry exchange of words. The judge silenced Laval, saying, "That's enough. You can speak later when I ask you."

The judge also threatened to eject Laval from the court for using insulting language.

Looks of hatred

Laval sat down defiant, muttering disagreement and casting looks of hatred at M. Mornet. Interrupting the public prosecutor, Laval shouted: "You can condemn me, but you have no right to insult

'XETER 'URVIVORS N BATAVIA

Evening Standard Reporter

'irst news for three years has

They are leaving 'Eisenhower platz'

Evening Standard Reporter

By January all the buildings in Grosvenor - square (Little America), occupied by the United States Army, with the exception of Nos. 20 and 47, will have been vacated and handed back to their pre-war occupants.

The U.S. Army have already moved out of 263 buildings which they held in the centre of London as billets, warehouses, parking stations, garages and storage

Bevin to speak next week

Evening Standard Diplomatic Correspondent

Mr. Ernest Bevin, Foreign Secretary, will make his first statement on the British view of the breakdown of the Foreign Secretaries Conference in the House of Commons next week.

This decision was taken when the Foreign Secretary made a full report to the Cabinet to-day.

Ministers felt that by making the statement in Parliament it would have added prestige abroad.

Mr. Bevin is convinced it is possible to save something from the three weeks' work of the conference and he will say nothing to make this more difficult. But he will be perfectly frank about the difficulties with which the conference was faced and about the manner of its breakdown.

He believes there is nothing to be gained by hiding the difficulties and deprecates a tendency to fix the blame in any one quarter.

Ministers to-day are hopeful that the U.S. Government's suggestion for an all-United Nations' peace conference will be acceptable as a means of by-passing the deadlock in the Big Five Council.

Fog covers Britain

Express 40 mph too fast over the crossing

—Inquiry evidence

Mr. J. W. Watkins, Divisional Superintendent of Operations at Crewe, told the Watford inquiry into the Bourne End railway crash today, that:

The train had too great a speed over the crossing. It is difficult to know why. Something must have happened.

"It is difficult to give an explanation as to why the driver did not reduce speed in view of the good weather and good signal. He was a good man."

There was no evidence that Sidney Swaby, the driver, had given a whistle at Bourne End, nor had the signalman observed either driver or fireman on the footplate.

74 in hospital

Mr. Watkins added that the engine of the train became derailed when travelling from the fast to the slow line at Bourne End. Twelve coaches left the rails, and eight were severely damaged.

Of the 74 passengers still in hospital 16 were seriously ill, and two were very seriously ill. The rest were going on very well.

Mr. Watkins also said that Swaby was most reliable and experienced and regularly worked over the road. Sixty-five years of age, he had been in the company's

THE DUKE HERE TO-MORROW

Evening Standard Reporter

The Duke of Windsor will arrive in Britain from France by air, to-morrow afternoon, it was stated in London to-day.

The Duke is paying a short visit to Queen Mary and will stay at Marlborough House.

It will be the first time the Duke has seen his mother for about nine years—before his abdication—and five years since he saw the King.

The Duchess will not be accom-

pressing them
! out here—
on with those
Savings on
Home Front."

FRANCE UNDER THE GERMANS

Terrors of Life in A Concentration Camp

The little, dark French woman was typical of the women of her country; she spoke with heroic stoicism of the sufferings of her people under German rule, confident that they will rise above the oppressor and become a great nation once more. In her features was indelibly traced the agony of France, but there was also something else—a culture, a resigned belief in her country's future, which made her absorbing to listen to, as she told simply, and without elaboration the story of her arrest, her life, and that of many others, in a prison camp, and the eventual and longed-for journey to England. This talk at the Welcome Club last week, was one of a series of lectures aiming to give some indication of what is happening in those parts of Europe dominated by the Germans.

Introduced by Mr. Mayne (British Council) to a large gathering of Service men and women as Madame A. Lewin, the French-born wife of an Englishman, who left France last August, the speaker began: "When in June, 1940, the Germans marched on our country there followed four years of isolation when very little was known of France to the outside world, and all the French people could do was to wait and hope. The Germans terrified the French with propaganda," she continued. "I was in Brittany at the time and kept a child, found alone on the roads by the police, hoping he would be reclaimed. But no-one owned him—that is only one of the many instancess of that time. Our soldiers were embittered, dejected. Their uniform was meaningless to them. They were all yearning for an ideal and their only thought was 'France will overcome,' how, they knew not.

"During the months following the armistice the Germans carried out, not a military occupation, but a systematic infiltration into the occupied zone by getting possession of the Press, cinemas, banks, factories, etc. The people began to suffer from humiliation, they resented and resisted, and their resistance could not be stopped by the clumsy restrictions of the Germans. Activity was somehow silent. Everyday men tried to leave the country to join the free army by extraordinary means, while there was also a group of men who stayed to face everything—to face the Gestapo—and learnt that the least mistake was repaid by torture. In the free zone the months following the armistice were bewildering for the simple citizens who never thought of doubting the authorities. Ghastly

PUBLIC v. PRIVATE ENTERPRISE

Address to Co-operators

A most instructive address was given on the subject of "Public v. Private Enterprise" at the Co-operative Hall on Friday under the auspices of Kidderminster Co-operative Society Education Committee.

Mr. E. W. Walters, J.P., who presided, said the speaker, Mrs. E. A. Wills, J.P., was a member of Birmingham City Council and a Parliamentary candidate for one of the Birmingham Divisions.

Mrs. Wills pointed out that we had reached a stage when most things they used were subject to controlled prices, whether purchased at the Co-operative store or a private enterprise shop. One advantage to Co-operators was the additional dividend they received. The Government, under war conditions, had to lay down standard quality and maximum price. "How were we going to win the peace?" she asked. Not by private enterprise, for under the stress of national emergency the Government had been forced to control most things in this country and had brought capitalists and work-people together in a system of control. Whatever their personal inclinations and beliefs might be, all had been required to practice Co-operative principles. One significant result of that regime was that we had become a nation with the largest output per operative in the world, not excluding America.

The ramp in land and building, property values went on merrily and we had the strange spectacle of the House of Lords, so often described as the millstone round the neck of democracy, having to insist on a vital amendment to the Town and Country Planning Bill in order to stave off an impossible position created by a Tory-ridden House of Commons as to deviation from the 1939 standard of land values. Sir William Beveridge, who declared himself a Radical, not a Socialist, stood for a policy of full employment administered by the State after the war.

The whole field of industry had to be surveyed satisfactorily. She saw a time coming for nationalising the banks to make them servants of the

COMMUNITY LIFE IN RUSSIA

Rotarians Hear A Visitor's Impressions

In his second address to a well-attended meeting of Kidderminster Rotary Club last week, Mr. H. M. Cashmore, Birmingham City Librarian, gave a graphic account of community life and the aptitude of the Russian people in self-government and practical study of art and science.

Mr. Cashmore said what struck him about the Russians was that they put first things first. The way they treated children was marvellous. As a general rule Russian mothers went out to work. He had observed how they put their toddlers in the creches on their way to the factories, and the care taken of the children during the mothers' absence.

Describing a "pioneer camp" which he visited, Mr. Cashmore said it was a kind of park in the centre of which was a wonderful palatial building containing a museum showing insects, birds, etc.; in another wing was the internal combustion room, and there were other departments for astronomy, wireless communications, art room, etc. In the latter he saw boys and girls copying some of the finest pictures in Russia, which had been collected from the finest art galleries for that purpose. He saw enormous numbers of printers' catalogues, enabling the seeker of information to be told what the library contained and what it lacked and could be consulted elsewhere.

Commenting on features of Russian community life, Mr. Cashmore described the Free Club for scholars, their families and friends. It appeared to him work was found for everybody in Russia, where they had the vote at the age of 18. A long holiday with pay, and one or two months for women before and after childbirth, struck him as State provisions. Everybody was entitled to pensions—men at 65, women at 60. He found enthusiasm for literature and science. As regards transport accommodation, nobody stood up in railway carriages, the only limitation on the trains being the sleeping accommodation. It was different on the 'buses, on which he saw terrific crowds. The lady conductor was the only person seated, and the passengers passed their fares on to her.

Answering the false statements of Russian children being punished by imprisonment if caught reading passages from the Bible, Mr. Cashmore said more people went to church in Russia than in Birmingham, where not more than one per cent of the population attended church. In North Russia, church-goers represented two per cent, and in Southern Russia five per cent.

BOROUGH BENCH

Friday, January 19th.—Before the Mayor, Mr. G. S. Chadwick (chairman), the vice-chairman Mr. C. C. Brinton, Miss E. C. Addenbrooke, Messrs. J. Ferguson and J. E. Grosvenor.

TRAFFIC OFFENCES.

Denis Jeffs, 113, Tomkinson Drive, was fined 5s. for riding a bicycle without a front light.

Alfred Thomas Poole, 195, Birmingham Road, was fined £1 for not conforming to a "Keep Left" sign when driving a motor car.

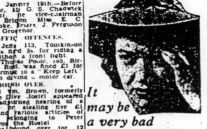

BOUND OVER.

Leonard Wm. Brown, formerly of Jubilee Drive Hostel appeared for the adjourned hearing of a summons for stealing five £1 notes, and various articles of clothing, belonging to Peter Morris from the Hostel.

He was bound over for 12 months in his own recognisances.

R.A.F. MAN CHARGED.

James McMeekin, R.A.F., appeared on remand charged with stealing a lady's dress and chromium plated dress stand, total value £2 8s 6d., the property of Philip Cohen, on January 16. Pleading guilty he added "I didn't know what I was doing at the time."

P.C. Thomas said at 11.15 p.m. he went down Blackwell Street from the Horsefair and on approaching Messrs. Fosbrook's shop he saw McMeekin with the articles in his hand. Asked for an explanation, accused replied, "I've just picked them up." Further investigation revealed that a section of the window was smashed. Whilst in custody he made a voluntary statement of having come home from abroad and of having had too much to drink. He added that he didn't remember breaking the shop window and he suffered from loss of memory at times.

Chief Constable Hodgkinson stated that McMeekin, a Glasgow-man, aged 28, joined the R.A.F. in 1939 and served in Africa for three-and-a-half years. He now awaited discharge on medical grounds.

The Mayor gave decision to hand accused over to the Military authorities.

ALLEGED BIGAMY.

Ellen Bloomfield (27), c/o. Besford Court, near Pershore, was summoned for bigamously marrying a man on April 12th, 1941.

Detective-Sergt. Powell said as a result of information on November 26th last a warrant was issued for the arrest of Bloomfield which he carried out that (Friday) morning. When charged she replied, "Yes, that is correct; I am sorry I did it now."

Accused was remanded for a week and released on bail.

Monday.—Before the Mayor, Mr. G. S. Chadwick (chairman), and Mrs. M. A. Anton.

PRISON FOR BEGGAR

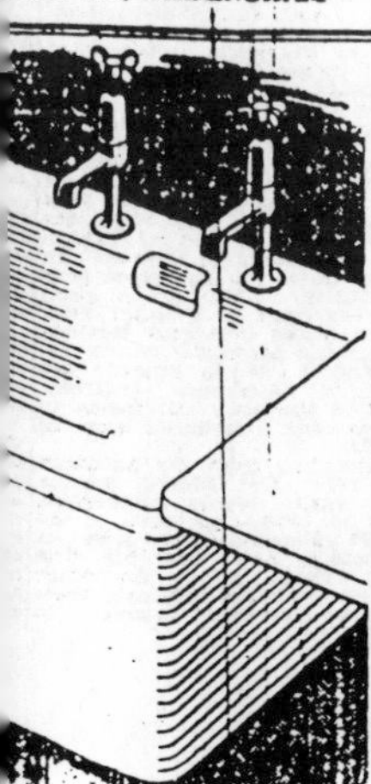

A NEW LOOM

Big Advantage to Carpet Industry

Mr William Felton, sales manager of Crabtrees Ltd., the well-known loom makers, addressed a combined meeting of the Kidderminster and District Production Discussion Group and the Three Arts Guild, at the Staff canteen of Carpet Trades Ltd., on Tuesday evening of this week. His subject was "The Spool-Gripper Loom."

Mr. Felton had the happy thought of describing the invention, of which he was the designer, as a marriage of two existing ideas in loom construction, resulting in an offspring whose future career will be of general local interest. Fundamentally the parents are the Brinton Patent Gripper-loom and what is known in the trade as the Spool Axminster loom. There are two main features in these looms which the designer sought to combine in one, to enable manufacturers to produce a fabric, structurally the best medium-priced floor covering produced with the range and choice of colours offered by the alternative process.

The combination will be known as the Spool-gripper loom, a name which goes far to explain its special features, since it is the spool-facilities of design and colour applied to the weave of the Gripper, that has been achieved. In effecting the union the inventor has had special problems to solve and at the same time has increased the production per loom and eliminated the waste factor to an appreciable extent. These last-mentioned are advances on present practice. One of the objectionable features of the Spool-loom method is wastefulness of material, whilst its chief virtue, compared with the Gripper, is its scope in colour. For the Gripper, it may be said to produce a desirable quality of fabric, which does not require sizing when it comes off the loom in contrast to spool fabric, which is very limp; and the ability to weave single carpets of any particular design, without involving prohibitive costs; against it must be laid the restriction in colouring the designs and the lesser appeal not argued artistically—but in view of public demand at home and abroad.

What has been accomplished in the new loom is a combination of the virtues of the two in—as the inventor described it—the son (the loom) is the gripper type with the addition of the spool which replaces creels and jacquard. The loom's speed has been advanced 19 per cent over normal gripper-loom production. Well-wishers will hope to see a large family of the new looms in the local factories after the war.

Mr Felton was careful to announce that in his view this is not the last word in loom construction, and invites young inventors to collaborate in making the British make of loom the

COUNTY RATE INCREASE

Effect of Education Costs

Owing mainly to the increased cost of education, Worcestershire County Council on Monday agreed to increase the county rate by 2s. in the £. The rate approved was 11s., but figures showed that the estimated rate-borne expenditure was £1,034,738, which was equivalent to 11s. 8d. in the £. The rate figure, however, was reduced by an appropriation from the surplus of £54,164.

The County Treasurer (Mr. E. T. Nicholas) stated that the year marked only the beginning of the period of steeply rising expenditure, and that during the next two or three years very little increase in rateable value could be expected. There was a net overspending during the current year of £14,272. The principal increases in the estimates were those of the Public Assistance and Elementary Education Committees. The current year opened with a record balance of £494,679, and closed with a balance of £487,000.

The main cause of the increase in the education rate, viz., 1s. 6d., was the provision made for the new salary scales recommended by the Burnham Committee. Those increases were estimatd to cost in the year 1945-46 a sum of £192,000, by the Ministry, leaving £86,000 of which £106,000 would be borne to be met out of rate. The abolition of fees in secondary schools represented a gross loss of some £38,000 and a net loss to rates of £17,000.

The combined grant for all forms of education as from April 1 next would, for Worcestershire, be equal to 55.3 per cent of the approved expenditure. This percentage was to be increased by one each year until the year 1948-49. The new grant meant a larger contribution—both actual and relative—by the State a fact on which some emphasis was laid by the Ministry. Local authorities would, however, be more impressed, at the moment, with the immediate effects of the Act on local rates than by the munificence of the central authority.

The Vice-chairman (Ald. G. W. Kenrick), presenting the budget, said the question of what was an appropriate rate for the coming year was more difficult than it had ever been, or would be again, because of three factors over which the Council had no control—the end of the war, whether local authorities would be given a high priority in respect of labour, and, thirdly, how much assistance local authorities would get from the Treasurey. The Committee realised there would be increased expenditure in the future over a number of services. The size of school classes must, of necessity, be reduced to manageable proportions, and this would put approximately 1s. on the rates.

Mr. H. N. Frost seconded, and Mr. E. G. Eddy expressed perturbation at the raiding of the Council's balances—this time to the extent of £64,000—equal to an 8d. rate. They were giving bonus shares without knowing what their position would be in post-war days. Their balances on paper were approximately half a million and with the decreased purchasing power of the £, which was not worth about 7s., the balances were

POLICE RAID ON A BROTHEL

Charges Against Two Women

A police raid on a Kidderminster house was described at the Borough Police Court on Friday, February 16, during the hearing of summonses for keeping a brothel and assisting in its management at 92 Park Butts, Kidderminster. Ivy Aslenis, 92, Park Butts—the British born wife of a Greek seaman, was summoned for keeping or managing a brothel between January 7—24 Gladys Harriet Baker, of the same address, was summoned for assisting in the management.

The case against Aslinis, who pleaded "Not Guilty," was taken first.

The case against Aslenis, who Gough, P.C. Worrall and P.C. Hilltop, all gave evidence of keeping the premises under observation at night-time and seeing both American soldiers and civilian men there. A sergeant and a private in the U.S. Army, who were on the premises when the police carried out the raid, under Police Inspector Lowe, also gave evidence, the sergeant saying that they were sitting around the fire with two women on their knees when the police entered.

Describing the raid on the house, P.C. Gough said that when Aslenis was asked to account for the presence of the American soldiers she replied that they had come up for supper. There were two sandwiches on the table. When told the matter would be reported, she said, "We have done nothing wrong." The other woman was making a statement when Aslenis interrupted her and told her to keep her tongue between her teeth.

Police Inspector H. Lowe said the premises were kept under systematic observation from January 7 onwards. He directed the raid, and the men and women on the premises were fully dressed.

Defendant on oath said there were only three American soldiers she had had anything to do with at her place.

The Mayor (Cllr. G. S. Chadwick) said the Bench found defendant guilty.

Chief Constable Harry Hodgkinson giving her record said defendant was born at Blackheath in 1920, and removed to Kidderminster when a child. She ran away from home to Manchester when 16. She returned and next went off to Shepton Mallet, Somerset, with the intention of marrying a man. She was next at Brighton. She returned to Kidderminster in February, 1942, and subsequently married a Greek seaman and went to live at Liverpool. She was subsequently charged with managing a brothel and sentenced to two months' imprisonment. In 1944, she was fined for traffic in illegal intoxicating liquor.

Defendant told the Court that after her husband left her she had no income, and as an alien was not allowed to earn more than £1 a week.

The Mayor passed sentence of three months' hard labour. On hearing it Askenis collapsed and was carried out of Court.

SECOND DEFENDANT

Gladys Harriet Baker, was then charged with assisting in the management of the brothel. She pleaded "Not Guilty," and was defended by Mr. E. W. Waldron (Brierley Hill).

Witnesses who had given evidence in the first case were recalled.

Mr. Waldron said defendant

Augu

1.—Over
mans still
Allied bom
clear the
advance i
co-operation
enough W
around Ger
Allied actio
the compa
Big Three
simultaneo
enemy fron
South and
solid motiv

2.—This
Marshal S
The Russia
Already th
now being
be a detai
plan The
for the El
armies lin
plain betw
mountains
They plan
its whole
Bohemian
reaches w
But the El
Sea, and
the area o
bility Whe
the enemy
Lower Elb
Norway.
territory in
Kiel Cana
and the N

3.—At
Russians
Dresden on
then to
Berlin fro
outflanks t
Czecho-Slov
Prague mu
Benes fo
already on
homeward

4.—Buda
hands at
Czecho-Slov
is open.
direction
Skoda, t
works, the
the Germ
They also
wonder th
in Italy of
by the G
to be defe
hope is
Nazis of
last stron
Alps.

5.—The
West cont
coming
military
armies m
pressure.
large rese
menace.
in in dri
Still the
its fatal
would pre
line of th
so any
For the
and the A
will be
crossing t
him.

6. Mea
State mac
The auth
have cease
country.
phones an
function
another, t
has broke
people ha
are too w
without
But the G
mood of
nation th

REMOVED UTILITY MARK

Court Story of Excessive Charge

Total fines of £30 with £11 costs were imposed on a Kidderminster trader at the Borough police Court on Friday, March 16th, for removing utility marks from a costume and selling it at an excessive price.

Defendant was Annie Nagler (formerly Mrs Annie Leigh, who had married again since the date), trading as Leighs, at 68, Worcester St., Kidderminster, and the charges against her were: (1) Of removing the utility mark from a utility garment on or about August 26st, 1944, and (2) Selling a utility costsume at excess price on the same date. She pleaded not guilty and was defended by Mr. Harry Faber (Birmingham).

Mr. Geo. Erskine Barrow, prosecuting for the Board of Trade, said on the Thursday, about August 26th, a Mrs. Phoebe Hart, of Springfields Lane, Kidderminster, accompanied by her husband, went into defendant's shop and saw a black costume (coat and skirt) for which she was quoted £5 5s. Some alterations had to be done to the skirt at a cost of 2s. 6d extra. Mrs. Hart was asked to pay a deposit of £1, which she did there and then and obtained a receipt for £1. Two days later Mr and Mrs Hart returned to the shop, were asked to produce the receipt for £1, which she did, and she was handed the coat and skirt—to which the alteration had been completed. She paid the balance of £4 7s. 6d. and was handed the appropriate receipt for it, but did not again receive that for the deposit. She handed in her coupon book from which the appropriate coupons were taken by the shop assistant. Upon arriving home Mrs. Hart discovered a mark was on the dress which had the appearance of a utility mark having been tampered with and cut off the article. On August 29th she wrote to the Board of Trade Price Regulation Committee in Birmingham, and complained about the matter. Investigations were set afoot. Defendant called at the Board office in Birmingham on Sept. 16th and asked to see the dress. On Sept. 28th a woman office came over to Kidderminster and saw defendant, who emphatically denied the overcharge. The allegation of cutting out the utility mark was investigated by another department of the Board of Trade. An official came down and defendant gave a flat denial. In the meantime the manufacturer identified the coat and costume for which the maximum sale price was £4 2s. 3d.

In October, it was alleged, complainant met defendant in the street and defendant offered to refund the money on return of the coat and skirt to the shop. On the same day Mrs Hart returned to the shop and her husband waited outside. Mrs. Hart, on that occasion—so she alleged—was told by defendant's shop assistant that they made a practice of cutting out the utility

WOMEN'S CLUB

Hospital Administration Described

At the fortnightly meeting of the Kidderminster Women's Club on Monday evening, Mr. C. M. Smith, House Governor of the Kidderminster General Hospital, gave an enlightening talk on Hospital administration. He was introduced by Miss E. C. Addenbrooke, J.P., who presided.

Remarking that a House Governor's position was one which required years of training so that a full knowledge of everything connected with a hospital may be learned Mr. Smith said that he himself had spent about 12 years at smaller hospitals before taking up the position of House Governor at our local hospital. "Among the many jobs which fall to a House Governor" said Mr. Smith, "are the maintenance of an efficient enquiry department a good filing system, income and expenditure, an annual report has to be made out and the Hospital's equipment must be kept up to date."

"In wartime of course," he continued, "the task of a house Governor is a much larger one. Fire watching food rationing, air raid shelters, and a hundred other jobs are added to the list." The speaker went on to give details of the numerous difficulties which are to be found at a hospital in war-time. "Our most acute problem at present," he said, "is the lack of space, both in the hospital and outside it. With the increased staff we are forced to have in war-time," he added "the lack of housing space presents a difficult problem."

Concluding Mr Smith remarked that all the work that is done at the Hospital could not be continued without an adequate supply of money. It is to the public that we look to provide this," he said. "The Hospital was built for the use of the public and it is up to you to supply the money necessary to uphold it."

A vote of thanks to Mr. Smith was proposed by Mrs. Evans and seconded by Mrs Bosward.

The next meeting will take place on April 16, and will take the form of a bridge drive. Proceeds will be in aid of the Waifs and Strays Society.

SHRAWLEY WOMAN'S DEATH

Fatal Sequel to a Fall

Evidence of a fall which terminated fatally was given at a Kidderminster inquest on Tuesday on Rose Hannah Barker (73), 6, Council Houses, Rector Lane, Shrawley, who died in Kidderminster Hospital on March 16.

Mrs. Evelyn May Oakey, Seys Cross, Shrawley said that deceased was her mother. She was the widow of William Parker, a farm labourer. She had had been in very poor health for the past 17 years, and could get about only with the aid of two sticks. She looked after a blind

BRITAIN AND U.S.

Service Men Discuss "What's Wrong?"

Among the familiar khaki-clad figures of the R.A.P.C., A.T.S. and U.S. Army who attend the Welcome Club weekly on Monday evenings, was a bright splash of colour this week, supplied by boys in hospital blue from a local convalescent hospital, accompanied by the Commandant, Miss E. Bradley, and nurses. The subject for discussion was "What's wrong with the U.K.? What's wrong with the U.S.?"

Staff/Sergt. W. Patteson, R.A.P.C., speaking for the U.K., said we must first remember a nation cannot be judged by her soldiers. One of America's main faults, he thought, was her inability, as a nation, to accept world responsibility. By her repudiation of the Treaty of Versailles 1919 she had grossly betrayed mankind and made the treaty worthless to England and France. Before the war she had only one ocean fleet—which was kept in Pacific waters.

The speaker's second point was the self-satisfaction and superiority with which America regards herself and her way of life. All her modern devices, streamlined cars, slick kitchens, etc., were not so important to us here—or had not been in the past—but now that the domestic labour shortage had become so acute, great improvements would be seen in the near future. Staff/Sergt. Patteson considered America as a nation, culturally sterile. Eire, he pointed out, with a population of only 3,000,000 had produced a band of writers who had influenced world thought, but America, though 40 times larger, was less known and appreciated and understood.

Twenty British writers to every one American are translated into the native tongues of the world," he emphasised. "Your musical appreciation is perhaps greater," he continued, "but your composers are not. I think you are suffering from acute adolescence—due partly to your educational system which I still think is one of the worst in the world. Education is not judged by the number of text books you have, your school leaving age or even the quality of your masters, but by the product of the system—the adult of the country. This failing is reflected in your newspapers, your sensational head-lines, and your comic strips, your radio entertainment and your love of exhibition—your desire to impress. In foreign travel you also prove your immaturity. You are a giant with the brain of a child! Your realism mixed with your idealism make you a paradoxial nation understand. We in England are tired of American criticism. Twisting the lion's tail seems to be becoming a favourite sport in the U.S."

Responding from the American view point, Cpl. Rosario Scibilia (U.S. Army), briefly enumerated what he considered faults of the United Kingdom—our lack of mechanical aids was his first point, about which Americans feel very strongly. He said there was no popular interest in music, the theatre and ...

KIDDERMINSTER, SHUTTLE AND STOURPORT ...

VICTORY

TORY!

... Statesmen, Commanders, men ... Services, Civil Defence Forces, ... workers in munition factories, ... workers, and all whose efforts ... of victory possible.

... fortunate to have been ... small contribution to this vital ... Seeds, Seed Grain, and ... have seeded many thousands ... Our fertilisers have enabled ... of their best. We have ... Foods under a complicated ... We have collected from farms ... thousands of tons of wheat ... and other grain for priority ... important work our transport ... distance equal to twelve times ...

... Seeds will be at the service ... during the happier days of peace.

... ALLEY & CO., LTD.
... DERMINSTER

MAYOR'S MESSAGE

"Prepare for the Future"

Yours faithfully,
G. S. CHADWICK
(Mayor).

MEMBERS' MESSAGE

Sir John Wardlaw-Milne and the Victory

STRETCHER BEARERS

Volunteers did Exacting Job of Work

CIVIL DEFENCE

Many Duties Well Done

GOD HAS GIVEN US THE VICTORY

By K. Babington Macaulay

WOMEN WAR WORKERS

A Club of Social Service

THE HOME GUARD

Ready If Enemy had Come

No record of voluntary services rendered during the war would be complete without reference to the Home Guard—that great civilian army, which stood by for more than four years in readiness for the invader, who never came.

In May, 1940, after the tragedy of Dunkirk, the call went out for volunteers for what was then known as the Local Defence Volunteers. The response was immediate and overwhelming, and within a matter of days the nucleus of what was to become the Home Guard was established on a sound basis.

Colonel R. W. A. Painter, M.C., took charge in Kidderminster, and when the title was changed to Home Guard he became the commanding officer of the 8th Worcestershire Battalion, whose headquarters were in the borough. The 11th Battalion headquarters was at Stourport under Lieut.-Colonel ... and the 10th Battalion, at Churchill, was commanded by Lieut.-Colonel ...

GIRLS' TRAINING CORPS

A Pre-Service Unit

P.O.W.R.A.

Work of the Local Association

H. ATTWOOD LTD

We congratulate our Patrons on their magnificent contribution to Victory over Germany and take pleasure in continued Service in the more Peaceful Days ahead

REGENT HOUSE
KIDDERMINSTER

THE BOROUGH RESTAURANT

An Excellent Innovation

AIR TRAINING CORPS

The Keenness of Youth

EVACUEES

War Victims Welcomed

Y IN EUROPE

... steady return to ... but it will of ... be a slow transition. ... welcome the days ... can supply each ... with first quality ... eggs and sugar ... lib.

..., we continue to ... quality rationed ... the lowest price, ... additional ... give variety to ... menu.

... & ADAMS
... GROCERS
... VENTRY STREET
... ERMINSTER

... ADWAY
... OWNS

... war brought us here, ... strangers, having attended ... Cattle Market for several ... years ... still at your service, ... smile and the usual ... civility

... L STREET
... RMINSTER

... e . . .

... AUSTIN will ... the road again. ... ERVICE ... in

Home Entertain...

THIS has been our slogan ... trying war years. In spite ... shortage, ill-health, Home G... Civil Defence duties, etc., we ... our utmost to help provide ... Entertainment" for factory ... Service men on leave, etc., b... up our stocks of Gramophone... Pianos, Sheet Music and the li... as far as our supply of valves ... parts have allowed, to mai... Radio Service Department, and ... any type of Radio Set on ... premises, with the minimum ... moderate cost. Now that host... ceased in Europe, we shall be in ... to supply new Radio Sets, etc., ... makers, at an early date.

GEORGE WHITFORD, ...
NEW ROAD, KIDDERMI...

What we have done at
BELL'S GARA...
during the War:

Stored many thousa... FOOD at our B... Machined over 3,0... for AIRCRAFT, ... and MINES

What we want to do at
BELL'S GARA...
during the Peace:

Supply you with yo... and give you the ... obtainable.

BELL'S GAR...
BEWDLEY ST., KIDDER...
Long Lane, BLACKHEATH, and ...
Deritend, BIRMINGHA...

THE KIDDERMINST...
CO-OPERATIVE SOCIET...

Wishes to express thanks to all those ... who have won this great and ...

VICTOR...

We extend thanks, too, to all our ... have been so loyal to the Society.

Yes, in the early and disturbing day... when supplies were short, transport ... our patience tried, our grumblers w... tively few.

The Sacrifice has been great. The Vic...

Co-operat...

Age shall not weary them,
Nor the years condemn;
At the going down of the sun,
And in the morning we will remember her.

CRUMPTON. — In affectionate remembrance of my dear wife Emma, who fell asleep May 12, 1944. Always in the thoughts of her husband Bill.

It is lonely here without you,
Sad is the weary way,
Life and home are different,
Since you went away.

CRUMPTON, (Emma).—In loving memory of dear mother Emma, who fell asleep May 12 1944. Ever in the thoughts of loving son Bill and daughter-in-law Irene.

CRUMPTON. — In affectionate remembrance of mother, who fell asleep May 12, 1944. Always in the thoughts of her daughter and son-in-law Flo and Ellis, 1, Oakhill Avenue.

We often look at your photo,
You are smiling and seem to say
Don't grieve I am only sleeping,
We will meet again some day

CRUMPTON.—In loving memory of gran who died May 12 1944. Not forgotten by her grand-daughter Beryl, 1, Oakhill Avenue.

May the sunshine she missed on life's journey,
Be found in God's haven of rest.

DUDLEY.—In ever loving memory of our dear father, John Edward, who passed away May 8, 1944. For ever in the thoughts of his children.

Those who knew him loved him,
He was so lovely and sweet,
May he rest in his Master's garden,
Until in heaven we meet.

KELLY.—In loving memory of my dear wife, Edna Kelly, who passed away May 9 1943.

One of the best in every way,
Loved and missed more every day.

Lovingly remembered by her husband and children, Brian Maureen and Patrick

KELLY.—In loving memory of my dear daughter-in-law Edna who fell asleep on May 9, 1943. Ever in the thoughts of mam, sisters and brothers-in-law

Many a sigh many a tear,
We that have missed you can only explain;
A beautiful memory is all we have left,
Of one we loved and can never forget.

MOSELEY.—In ever loving memory of our dear son Pte Leonard Ernest Moseley, Worcestershire Regiment. Killed in action May 12, 1941. Ever in the thoughts of mum, dad, brother Bert, sisters Edith, Emily Hilda. "For ever in our thoughts."

MOSELEY. — Loving memories of my dear husband Pte. Leonard Ernest Moseley 1st Worcs. Regt., died from wounds May 12 1941 Ever remembered by his wife Iris and son Roy.

We miss him more than words can explain
Memories of him will always remain.

PITT.—Fond memories of a dear brother who fell asleep May 7, 1942 Sadly missed by his sister Edith, Walter Ken and John.

The passing years can never change,
Our thoughts of him so dear,
Fond memories linger every day,
Remembrance keeps him near.

PITT.—In loving memory of our dear brother Sidney, called to rest May 7, 1942 Always remembered by his sister Gladys and Frank, now serving in S.E.A.C.

It is not framed in rarest gold
Nor hung where all can see,
But treasured in our hearts,
'Tis our dear brother's memory.

PLEVEY.—Treasured memories of Philip who died of wounds received in action, in Belgium May, 1940. Remembered always by mother dad brothers and sisters, 103, Baxter Avenue.

It may be a soldier's honour to die at his country's call

...thank the staff, and the nurses.

SATURDAY, MAY 12, 1945

VE DAY

Nearly six years of struggle—the "toil, sweat, blood and tears" Mr. Churchill promised us—has ended in the glorious victory in Europe. Right has once again triumphed over Might, and the Nazi reign of terror in Europe has met an inglorious end. No words of eloquence could adequately express the thankfulness of the people of this country—a people who suffered many privations, restrictions, hardships and who, at times, were in the "front line" themselves when the enemy rained down death and destruction from the skies. Now, at the end of it, we can see how justified has been our faith, and how worthily this great little island has played its part in the most stupendous war in history. To the men of all our fighting services, to the men and women who have shared the common struggle in other spheres of service, to our factory workers, and toilers on the sea and land, and to our glorious Allies whose loyalty never wavered, we give the fullest praise. In their hands rested the fate of the world; they have triumphed, and with pride can look back on the dark years that have passed. The cost has been heavy; many valuable lives have been lost, and in solemn meditation we remember them and are grateful in our hearts for their unswerving devotion in which they counted not the cost to themselves. It will be for the generation that is left to ensure that the phrase, "they did not die in vain," is no idle platitude. They gave their all that mankind should survive; we are in honour bound to see that the peace for which they so nobly strove is maintained, and that never again shall the world be thrown into the cauldron of greed, avarice hatred, suspicion and mistrust—the ingredients which breed wars. In making this solemn declaration let us not forget that we still have one enemy to defeat—Japan. No effort must be spared to knock out this last branch of the Axis; our energies must not be relaxed but rather intensified to ensure a final and speedy end to hostilities. And while we remember all our fighting men who helped to bring to an end war in Europe, do not let us forget our gallant men who are still battling in the war that has yet to end. Their ultimate triumph shall be just as great and decisive as that of their comrades in arms in Europe, and anything that we can do to expedite that day should receive the whole-hearted and ungrudging support of all of us. On then, to the Day of Final Victory!

LOCAL NEWS

M.P.'s Birthday.—Sir John Wardlaw Milne, who has represented the Kidderminster ...

... Advice office; and it is hoped that the majority will be open by the end of May. The offices are mainly for ex-Service personnel, but they will be available to all civilians. The aim is to have a central office in the district which can tell people here to go in any problem connected with re-settlement.

Musical.—At the Birmingham Road Church last Sunday evening the choir rendered a varied programme that was greatly enjoyed. Bunnett's "Magnificat," Tozer's "Deus Misereatur," Bach's ever-welcome, "Jesu, joy of man's desiring," Mendelssohn's "How lovely are the messengers," and Varley Roberts' choice anthem, "Jesu, priceless treasure" (duet by Mrs. and Miss Margaret Greenway), completed the choral selections. Mr. Harold A. Frampton, F.R.C.O., finely played as organ solos, Bach's "Allegro, Third Movement Trio Sonata No. 5," and Borowski's "Andante, from Sonata No. 1." Mr. D. Samuel conducted the service and gave a short address on the responsibilities of victory.

Savings Movement. — Before the war ends its cost to Britain will be over £30,000 millions. If the effort which has been put into the war had been directed, instead, into house building, then every adult and child in our land would have a fine four-roomed modern bungalow for himself or herself. We shall be faced with heavy income-tax for years to come as all monies borrowed for this war must have the interest paid thereon. After the war money will still be required for the building of houses, and sensible people continue to save and lend so as to make it easy for the men returning. Last week savings were excellent (R.A.F. £1,229, S.D.F. £77), the total being £16,838. The grand total is now £5,395,204.

Mombasa Wedding.—A wedding of interest to local readers took place on Saturday, April 7th, at Mombasa Memorial Cathedral, when Lieut. Edward Stewart Langford, R.A.S.C., at present attached to a unit of the E.A.A.S.C., and Madeline Lowe, Q.A.I.M.N.S., I.R., were married. Lieut. Langford is the only son of the late Mr. E. T. Langford and of Mrs. A. E. Mrs. V. Lowe, of Walthamstow, Langford, Bracebridge House, Kidderminster, and his bride is the younger daughter of the late Mr. A. E. Lowe and of London. Lieut. Langford was well-known in Bewdley in his capacities of captain of the Bewdley Tennis Club and secretary of Wribbenhall Badminton Club. He was also a member of the Bewdley Rowing Club, and of Kidderminster H.Q. Company, Home Guard, until he joined the services. A reception was held in the Sisters' Mess of the General Hospital in which the bride was working. The bridegroom's cousin, L/Cpl. T. Stanley Lambourne, R.A.P.C., of Edgbaston, obtained leave from Nairobi to be present.

Gardens Council.—The question of holding the annual show was debated for a considerable time by the Allotments and Garden Council at a meeting in the Council Chamber. Owing to difficulties over which the Council

SUNDAY SCHOOL ANNIVERSARY

SUNDAY, MAY 13, 1945

Preacher, 11 a.m. and 6.30 p.m.

Rev. JOHN KINNISH

(Former Minister at George St.)

SCHOLARS' SERVICE

at 2.45 p.m.

CHRISTADELPHIAN HALL OF TESTIMONY

GEORGE STREET

Sunday, May 13th, at 6 o'clock

Speaker: Mr. R. J. OODALL (Wolverhampton).

Subject: "If a Man Die: Shall He Live Again?"

PREACHERS FOR SUNDAY

BAXTER CHURCH. — Sunday Special Services of Thanksgiving and Dedication, 10.45 and 6.30, Rev. S. J. Hooper. Monday 2.45 Women's Fellowship. Wednesday 7, B.B. and Social Club.

BAPTIST CHURCH, Church St.—Sunday 11 and 6.30. Women's League Anniversary. Mrs F. Hearn (Astwood Bank) Monday 7.30. Girls' Guild. Tuesday Women's League Rally, 4.30, Tea Meeting 5.45, Speaker Mrs. D. Watkins (Selly Oak College). 7.30 Girls' Welcome Club. Thursday 7.30. C.E. Society. Friday 6.30 Girls' Life Brigade.

MILTON HALL BAPTIST CHURCH.—Sunday 11 and 6.30 Rev. T. J. Rowlands. Monday B.B. Tuesday 3, Women's League Wednesday 7, B.B. Thursday B.B.

METHODIST CHURCH, Mill St.—Sunday 11, George St., 6.30 Rev. T. W. Harrison.

METHODIST CHURCH, George St.—Sunday 11 and 6.30, Rev. Kinnish. Tuesday 7.45, Rev. L. Price, B.D.

NEW MEETING HOUSE (Unitarian).—Sunday 11 and 6.30 Thanksgiving Services for Peace Rev. L. Chandler, B.A. Collection for G.A. Appeal Fund.

NEW CHURCH, Comberton Hill—Sunday 11 and 6.30, Rev. E. J. Jarmin.

GOSPEL MISSION CHURCH Worcester Cross.—Sunday 11 and 6.30, Rev. Finch (Birmingham) Wednesday 7.30, Service. Saturday 7.30, Prayer Meeting.

LATTER-DAY SAINTS, Park St.—Sunday 10.30, Sunday School 6, Sacrament Service. Tuesday 7.30, Women's Relief Society Thursday 7.45 Young Women's and Young Men's Mutual Improvement Association.

CHRISTIAN SPIRITUALIST SANCTUARY, 3, Worcester St.—Sunday 6 Thanksgiving Service Address and Clairvoyance. Thursday 7.45, Healing Service.

GOSPEL HALL, Coventry St.—Sunday 11, Breaking of Bread, 3 Sunday School 6.30 Gospel Service. Wednesday 7.15, Prayer Meeting and Bible Reading

SALVATION ARMY, Dudley St—Saturday, 8, Praise Meeting Sunday 11, 3 and 6.45, Adjutant Gordon Gratton Monday 8 Devotional, Wednesday 8, Y.P.F.

REPORTED MISSING

Mr. and Mrs. J. Lowe, 25 Orchard St., have received the tragic news from the War Office that their youngest son, Gnr Sydney Lowe is reported missing at sea following the sinking of a Japanese ship which was transporting prisoners of war from Thailand to Japan. No date of the casualty was given by the Japanese authorities, but it is possible it occurred after Gnr. Lowe had written the latest card his parents received last December. Gnr Lowe who is 24, went overseas in 1941 and was taken prisoner when serving in Malaya, when the garrison at Singapore capitulated

VE DAY

JUBILANT CELEBRATIONS IN LOCAL TOWNS

AFTER nearly six years of war against Nazi Germany peace in Europe was declared by Mr. Winston Churchill at 3 p.m. on Tuesday last, May 8th. The public had already known of the pending announcement, and both Tuesday and Wednesday were celebrated as a public holiday.

Although no set programme of jubilation had been arranged in Kidderminster, everyone threw themselves whole-heartedly into the spirit of the occasion. Thanksgiving services at the various places of worship were well attended, flags and coloured streamers appeared on most buildings, people danced and sang in the streets, Church bells rang, here and there bonfires were lit, and children were given teas in some of the streets.

One of the most satisfactory features of the celebrations is that there was not a single instance reported of bad behaviour. Kidderminster celebrated joyously, and, to use a trite phrase, "a good time was had by all."

On Monday evening the B.B.C. announced that the Prime Minister would make his historic announcement of VE Day on Tuesday at 3 p.m. The response was immediate. As if by magic literally hundreds of flags and coloured bunting and streamers appeared everywhere, and some folk started their celebrations on Monday night. The centre of the town became crowded with happy people who jostled their way to the cinemas and dance halls. It was just a prologue to VE Day itself.

Rain was falling steadily on Tuesday morning and threatened to damp the spirits generally, but by the afternoon the sun was struggling to find a gap in the clouds and the rest of the day was fine. Most people were at home to hear the Prime Minister's famous speech broadcast and later at night to hear the King address his people, but here and there loud-speakers had been erected—at the Town Hall and in New Road for instance—so that people passing could hear the historic orations.

As the day wore on the crowds thronging Vicar St., and outside the Town Hall, became so dense that traffic had to be diverted. Later in the evening spirits rose higher and higher. One man, for instance, shinned up the Rowland Hill statue and implanted a resounding kiss on the cheek of the famous founder of penny postage! People sang and danced and danced and sang all along the street to music from the Town Hall loud-speakers. More and more people joined in the fun and it was not until well after 1 a.m. on Wednesday that the last reveller made his or her tired but happy way home.

It was certainly a day to remember, but that was not the end of it, for the celebrations on somewhat similar lines continued on Wednesday and when the factories and shops re-opened on Thursday morning there were many reporting for work who were tired but thoroughly content that a day to be remembered had been well and truly celebrated.

Reference has already been made to the street decorations, but one feels that a special word of praise is due for Wood St. and Dudley St., which were quite the best decorated thoroughfares. Flags and streamers hung right across the roads and the houses were a mass of flags and coloured bunting, most of which had been carefully preserved since the Coronation. The other outstanding decorative features were a carpet, bearing the full face of Mr. Churchill complete with cigar in the Carpet Trades window and the Union Jack and streamers which fluttered on the top of the gasometer towering high above the the ministry of kindness and understanding which had been entrusted to the world.

The first in a series of Peace Thanksgiving Services was the Sung Eucharist at Kidderminster Parish Church on Wednesday morning. Canon L. B. Sladen was the celebrant and the choir consisted of clergy from other churches in the Rural Deanery, with the Rev. E. A. Barrett, Vicar of Holy Innocents, Foley Park, as organist and director of music. There was a large congregation. On the following days a similar service has been held in other parish churches.

A large congregation attended the Thanksgiving Service at the New Meeting Club on Wednesday morning. The Communion Table was draped with a Union Jack and decorated with red tulips, white lilac and blue irises, while from either end hung the Stars and Stripes and the Hammer and Sickle. Prayers and hymns of Thanksgiving and praise having been offered up, the minister, the Rev. L. Chandler, B.A., delivered an appropriate address; after which the Choir, under the direction of the organist and choirmaster, Mr. W. E. Roberts, gave a very effective rendering of Blake's "Jerusalem." A collection was taken for Kidderminster's Welcome Home Fund, and the service closed with the singing of Kipling's "Recessional".

A highly successful Victory Social was held in the Vestry on Wednesday evening by the Kidderminster branch of the Unitarian Women's League. Further Thanksgiving Services will be held on Sunday at 11 and 6.30., when the collections will be for a fund for rebuilding bombed Unitarian and Free Christian Churches.

There were two well-attended Services of Thanksgiving at St. George's on V.E. Day at 3.30 and 8 p.m. These were followed by celebrations of Holy Communion at 7 a.m. and 8 a.m. on the following morning, while the School Service on the morning of Ascension Day (May 10) was observed as a Children's Service of Thanksgiving for victory. It was attended by a large congregation of children from St. George's Infant and Junior Schools, and from the Sladen Modern School, together with the head teachers and staffs. Mr R. Ferguson played the hymns for this Service.

A thanksgiving service was conducted by the Rev. W. L. Dicker on VE Day for the Old Pals at the Brinton Park Shelter. On Wednesday Mr W. Fisher, of the Kidderminster Brewery, and Mr. Hardiman, of Station Hill, entertained the Old Pals and on Thursday they were entertained to afternoon tea by the Ray Bros. of Wood St.

The Y.M.C.A. Canteen in Orchard St. was open from 8.30

resource ingenuity and dynamic energy with which all classes have met the demands of war will be no less necessary to ensure a prosperous peace. Fellow Rotarians we are called to action stations—the brave man's part."

Rotarian W. A. Price voiced the club's thanks to the speaker and touching upon his remarks respecting Anglo-American unity mentioned the work of local ladies at adjoining American military hospitals. One lady said Rotarian Price had given 1,500 hours of voluntary hospital work.

AT BEWDLEY

Bewdley received the joyful news with restrained thankfulness and although the town was gaily bedecked with lavish trappings of red, white and blue, erected in anticipation of the previous day the people did not give vent to their feelings until after the Premier's stirring speech had been heard resounding from the loud speakers in Load St. and the bells of St. Anne's peeled out the long awaited proclamation. The first impulse was to go to God's House and offer thanks for the accorded victory and although next Sunday is officially Thanksgiving Day, every church in the borough held special services.

By nightfall the bewildered sobriety noticeable earlier in the day had altogether vanished and Bewdley rejoiced amid a carnival atmosphere of decorative illumination. The bridge, bandstand and Riverside, bejewelled with fairy lights, made a festive sight as did many of the hotels and private residences in the main streets; a giant electric "V" sign, with "God bless the King and Queen" inscribed beneath, made the Guildhall a suitable centre for the town. Predominant over all was the floodlit war memorial at the top of Load St., with its stark white cross standing out in symbolic beauty, which could be seen for several miles around.

The Mayor and Mayoress (Cllr. and Mrs. O. Mortimer Smith) together with Aldermen, Cllrs. and prominent burgesses of the borough gathered in the Guildhall at 9 p.m. to hear the King address his people, and then proceeded, accompanied by a torchlight procession led by Youth organisations, to Crundles Farm where Cllr. Smith lit a mammoth bonfire which consumed a giant swastika with its flames. Several other fires could be seen in the surrounding district including a large one in the grounds of Ald. Jackson, specially for the children of Lax Lane and Riverside. Victory night festivities concluded with a dance at St. George's Hall where the largest attendance was seen there since before the war.

Celebrations continued throughout the week with dancing in the halls and, when weather permitted, even in the main streets of the town. On Friday a Solemn Eucharist was offered at St. Anne's Church and tomorrow (Sunday) the Mayor purposes to attend a Thanksgiving Service there in the morning when there will also be a parade of the various civic and youth organisations led by the Stourport A.T.C. Band.

AT STOURPORT.

Rejoicings were comparatively quiet by the time the official announcement of V.E. Day was made on Tuesday. The main streets had been crowded and the best use made of flags, streamers and other decorations. Loud speakers kept everybody well informed of the momentous news. In the evening a short service of thanksgiving in the Parish Church conducted by the Vicar drew a large congregation. Similar services were held in other churches.

A Victory parade from the Memorial Park through the town and back to the Park, was the chief feature on Wednesday afternoon. The procession consisted of Army contingents and those of the U.S.A. Army, Police, Civil Defence Services, N.F.S., Boy Scouts, Girl Guides, Cadets and various other uniformed bodies with members of the Urban District Council. Upon returning to the Park, the U.D.C. Chairman (Mr. R. P. Vale, C.C.) read an address from the Home Secretary, Mr Herbert Morrison, M.P., and in a brief speech warmly thanked all in-

THE JUVENILE SONGSTERS

Concert for Waifs and Strays Society

Visiting Kidderminster on Friday May 4, to take part in a concert organised by Mr. Fred A. Kettle in aid of the Waifs and Strays' Society, the Juvenile Songsters, pupils of Miss Mavis Bennett, of Redditch, made a highly favourable impression.

This talented group of children, numbering about 40, have broadcast several times in the Children's Hour session of the B.B.C. There was nothing forced or unnatural about their work, their diction was excellent, and their clear young voices were a delight to hear. All are under 18 years of age. The Juvenile Songsters gave part-songs, trios, duets and solos, and were under the direction of their teacher, Miss Bennett, who acted as compere. Special mention must be made of the beautiful voice of a little girl, who sang the solo part of the Lord's Prayer, an operatic offering by a gifted young singer, who appeared in a gorgeous period costume of red velvet and gold lace, and a tiny tot who charmed the audience with her song and dance number performed with a toy dog.

The guest artist, Miss Joan Butler (pupil of Miss Bennett), is shortly joining the Carl Rosa Opera Co. She has a soprano voice of exceptional range and flexibility and her singing was expressive and appealing. Miss Butler's items included the aria, "Ah, is it he" ("La Traviata"), "The Waltz Song" ("Romeo and Juliet"), "One Kiss" ("New Moon"), and a pretty trifle, "Little Polly Flinders." Len May, the popular xylophonist, who was heard the previous night in "Navy Mixture" broadcast, also contributed to the programme. Deft manipulation and sense of rhythm characterised his performance, and his items ranged from "Trees" and "Smiling Through" (sensitively and delicately played on the vibrophone) to such popular numbers as "Black Eyes," "On the Track" and "Tiger Rag."

Thanking the visitors for a most enjoyable concert, Miss E. C. Addenbrooke (chairman of the committee formed to raise £250 for the Waifs' and Strays' Society Emergency Fund) said the society was doing great work in its care of unfortunate children, and training them to become useful citizens. Money was urgently needed for the maintenance of the homes founded by the society, which had 6,400 children at present.

DISTRICT NURSES

The beneficent work of district nurses and the scope for local authorities to encourage more voluntary effort in meeting special needs in the post-war era were stressed at the annual meeting of Kidderminster Nursing Association on Monday. Ald. E. G. Eddy presided.

The 33rd annual report was presented by the hon. sec. Miss M. Hepworth, and stated that during the year the Association had received a legacy of £1,202 6s. 4d., left by the late Mrs Janet Hamilton. Nine years ago the Penny-a-week scheme was inaugurated and put into operation by the ward secretaries. It required many voluntary collectors. This year's collection amounted to £797 12s. 4d. The report made sympathetic reference to the absence of Miss Lowe, Supt. nurse, through illness. The nurses had experienced an arduous year owing to temporary shortages in staff but in spite of that hindrance they had carried

Report of the Housing Committee

Your Committee beg to report on their proceedings as follows:-

Post War Housing

Your Committee have given further consideration to the question of the purchase of additional land at Bark Hill adjoining the existing Corporation housing estate to provide a site for the additional houses that are to be erected by the Corporation as part of the first post war programme.

The Minister of Health has repeatedly urged Local Authorities to make all possible progress with the advance preparation of housing sites for the first post war year by making the necessary roads and laying the necessary sewers, water mains, and other essential services so that work can commence on the erection of the houses immediately the necessary materials and labour are available. Your Committee therefore realise that the purchase of the site for the first post war scheme must be regarded as a matter of urgency.

Negotiations have been opened with various owners of the land adjoining the present housing estate at Bark Hill with a view to the purchase of additional ground for incorporation in the first post war scheme but it has not been found possible to bring these negotiations to a satisfactory conclusion.

The District Valuer has advised your Committee to proceed to make a compulsory purchase order in order to avoid any delay on the understanding that notice to treat will then be served and the price to be paid for the ground settled in due course in accordance with the prescribed procedure. Your Committee therefore recommend that a compulsory purchase order be made for the purposes of Part V of the Housing Act 1936, relating to 2.743 acres of land at Bark Hill as follows:-

Mr. W.J. Beeman, Kidderminster.	1.78 acres
Thomas Jones, 26 Bark Hill, Bewdley.	.17 "
Alfred Price of 37 Lax Lane, Bewdley, T. Smith of 3 Oak Lane, West Bromwich, and Christopher William Pountney of 32 Bark Hill, Bewdley (jointly)	.41 "
Ernest Philip Shepherd, 33 Bark Hill, Bewdley.	.23 "
Roland Ernest Legge, Bark Hill House, Bewdley.	.086 "
Mr. A.W. Ryder, 139 Sutton Park Road, Kidderminster.	.028 "
Francis Thomas Clarke, Bark Hill Stores, Bewdley.	.039 "

F.E. Mountford

Chairman.

9th April, 1945.

BEWDLEY

14th April 1945.

To the members of the Town Council of Bewdley.

Gentlemen,

During the quarter ending March 31st 1945 there were 11 deaths registered in the Borough giving a rate of 2.4. per 1,000 of the population for the quarter or 9.6. per annum.

Of these there were 2 between 25 and 65 years of age and the rest were over 65.

There were notified during the quarter 29 cases of Measles 2 of Whooping Cough and 4 of Pneumonia.

There were no deaths from any of the diseases.

I remain Gentlemen,

Your obedient Servant,

U.W.N.Miles.

Medical Officer of Health.

BOROUGH OF BEWDLEY

MINUTES OF THE PROCEEDINGS AT A QUARTERLY MEETING OF THE COUNCIL FOR THE BOROUGH DULY CONVENED AND HELD AT THE GUILDHALL ON MONDAY, THE 30TH DAY OF APRIL 1945 AT FIVE O'CLOCK IN THE AFTERNOON.

PRESENT

Councillor	G. Mortimer-Smith (Mayor)
"	W. Harcourt Webb (Deputy Mayor)
Alderman	H.B. Jackson
"	[illegible].K. Frost
"	[illegible].E. Mountford
Councillor	J. Bates
"	P.W. Palmer
"	C.R. Pritchard
"	H.G. Gazely
"	W.J. Godwin
"	H.W. Windsor
"	H.R. Mountford

Alderman Jackson referred to the death of Mr. [illegible].G. Gibson, the Resident Engineer at Oldington Sewerage Works, and the Town Clerk was instructed to convey to Mrs. Gibson the sympathy of the Town Council in her bereavement.

MINUTES

The Minutes of the last meeting were read and ordered to be signed by the Mayor.

RIBBESFORD CHURCH

Alderman Jackson referred to the fact that there was considerable apprehension among the local inhabitants owing to the fact that a number of Italian prisoners were stationed at Ribbesford House with only a small guard, and the Town Clerk was instructed to make further enquiries into this matter and take whatever action might be necessary.

GENERAL PURPOSES COMMITTEE

The Report of the General Purposes Committee for the past quarter was read of which a copy is attached to these Minutes.

It was proposed by the Mayor seconded by Councillor Pritchard and RESOLVED that the report of the General Purposes Committee just read be and the same is hereby approved and adopted.

FINANCE COMMITTEE

The Report of the Finance Committee for the past quarter was read of which a copy is attached to these Minutes.

It was proposed by Alderman Frost seconded by Councillor Gazely and RESOLVED that the report of the Finance Committee just read be and the same is hereby approved and adopted.

WATER AND HEALTH COMMITTEE

The Report of the Water and Health Committee for the past quarter was read of which a copy is attached to these Minutes.

It was proposed by Alderman Jackson seconded by Councillor Godwin and RESOLVED that the report of the Water and Health Committee just read be and the same is hereby approved and adopted.

BOROUGH OF BEWDLEY

Quarterly Council Meeting 30th day of April, 1945.

Report of the Water & Health Committee

Your Committee beg to report on their proceedings as follows:

Water Supply, Stourport-on-Severn - The amount of water taken by Stourport-on-Severn for the quarter ending 31st March 1945 was 51,908,000 gallons, an increase over the previous quarter of 4,045,000 gallons, and an increase of 8,280,000 gallons over the corresponding quarter for last year.

Water Main, Long Bank. - The Kidderminster Rural District Council have agreed to allow the Corporation to connect up the Long Bank main at the Borough boundary with the Rural District Council main, which receives a supply from the Birmingham water mains. This arrangement has been made as a standby for use in emergency only.

Private Street Works Act, 1892 - The Borough Surveyor has completed the levelling and is preparing the specification, estimate, and provisional apportionment for the approval of your Committee.

Collection of Night Soil - Your Committee have had before them a detailed report prepared by the Sanitary Inspector stating the number of premises in the Borough from which night soil is still collected by the Corporation workmen and indicating which of these properties can reasonably be connected to the new main sewers.

Your Committee are determined to take the strongest possible action to see that the necessary connections are made wherever possible, and the Corporation workmen will not be sent to collect night soil in the future from any properties where the owners refuse to have this work carried out.

Trimpley Lane Sewer - Your Committee have given further consideration to the question of laying a new main sewer in Trimpley Lane and have had before them an up to date estimate of the cost of carrying out this work.

The Borough Surveyor has been instructed to discuss this matter with the owners of the adjoining properties and then report back to the next meeting of your Committee.

British Restaurant - Your Committee have received a communication from the Divisional Food Officer drawing attention to the fact that the charges made at the British Restaurant, Bewdley, are below the average. As all current repairs and expenditure on the replacement of equipment now have to be met out of Revenue Account, your Committee have resolved to increase the charges for food supplied at the British Restaurant as from Monday, 30th April 1945, to the following amounts:

Main Course	9d
Pudding	3d
Tea	2d

R. B. Jackson

Chairman

Chapter Eight

1945 - 1999

The following photographs, press reports and copies of artifacts portray some of the events after the War until the present day. The photograph of Columb, Merryn and myself was taken in 1998. I wanted to reproduce the obituary of Colonel Pierre Fourcaud and recall the passing of the "last cavalier" Jean Ballarin.

At the time of writing I await the return of my photographs taken at the Free French visit of 26 June. I do hope they are OK.

PS They look good!

Items

Ecole Miliaire - (St Cyr) 1958; Traversée de la Manche; Utah Beach; Ils S'instruisent pour Vaincre; 1961 - Returning to Bewdley - for a day; 1994 plaque at Ribbesford with other brass plate and 3 photos; press release 25 May 1994 and 3 photos; last cavalier; Ceremonial Sword 26 June 1999; invitation; 26 June Agenda; photograph Nigel, Jeannette and Paul; Chronicle 2 July; photograph and description of Free French Ceremony 26 June 1999; Photographs of Ribbesford House (4) and of the George Hotel, Bewdley, of the France Libre Cross of Lorraine. The Cross was made by the Free French cadets and stays "secret" to this day because a decorated door closes over it. I thank David Hugh Morgan for his information on this issue and Mr and Mrs Jones, owners of the "The George" for letting me photograph the Cross.

I then have, 1950 picture of Bewdley and 3 of concrete "tank stoppers" still positioned at the foot of Bark Hill, to be rolled out onto the road in case of invasion (Military Planning at its best).

Colonel Pirre Fourcaud

Daredevil Free French agent who was twice captured and escaped from prison and Klaus Barbie

COLONEL PIERRE FOURCAUD, who has died aged 100, was a gallant and dangerously attractive French officer with a penchant for fomenting trouble; during the Second World War he played a key part in setting up communications between the Free French in London and the Resistance in France.

Fourcaud arrived in London in July 1940, soon after the French surrender, and within two months had made his first return to France, travelling via Portugal. In London he was attached to de Gaulle's secret service, commanded by André Dewavrin, alias Colonel Passy. Fourcaud's relations with Passy, as with most people, were explosive.

He carried out several further missions to occupied France, under such pseudonyms as Lucas, Capitaine Barbès and Sphère. His most notable achievement was to link up with the Resistance at Marseilles to create the radio networks Brutus and Lucienne, and to instal the broadcasting centre Romeo.

This activity brought him into contact with leading French socialists, who were anxious that the Communists should not monopolise the entire credit of the Resistance — an aim with which Fourcaud would have been wholly in sympathy. Discussions with the socialists led to the formation of the National Council of the Resistance, led by Jean Moulin.

Fourcaud also followed de Gaulle's instructions to look for possible supporters in the Vichy Regime. To this end he boldly turned up in Vichy in 1940 — though de Gaulle seems to have felt he had gone rather too far in returning to London with the help of an exit visa provided by Paul Badouin, Pétain's foreign minister.

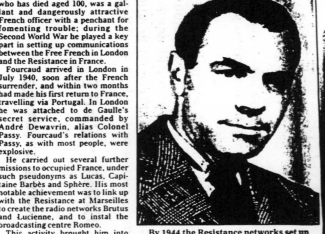

By 1944 the Resistance networks set up by Fourcaud, above, were staging daytime parachute drops in the South of France

Fourcaud managed to escape from prison at Clermont-Ferrand and cycle more than 700 miles across France to the Riviera. There he was picked up by *Sea Wolf*, a sailing felucca used by Special Operations Executive and crewed by piratical Poles whom General Wladyslaw Sikorski described as "too rough even for the Polish navy". Transferred to the destroyer *Middleton* at Gibraltar, Fourcaud reached London on September 20, 1942.

Characteristically, he was soon involved in the internal struggles of the Free French in London, as a result of which he replaced Roger

Albertville, [illegible] re he came under the scrutiny [illegible] laus Barbie.

Fourcaud [illegible] twice shot in the head by an [illegible] eutenant, who left him for dea[illegible] he regained consciousness, [illegible] was taken to a Red Cross hospit[illegible] with wounds in his skull and [illegible] Transferred to another pris[illegible] in Lyon, he managed to esc[illegible] August 1944, and returned to [illegible] ondon via Spain.

At the end [illegible] the war Fourcaud went t[illegible] ermany to try and locate F E [illegible] o-Thomas ("The White Rabbit"), who had fallen into the hands [illegible] f the Gestapo, and was thought t[illegible] be in Buchenwald.

was a doctor and his mother Russian) returned to France. Pierre was educated at a lycée in Nice.

In 1916, the moment he was 18, Fourcaud volunteered for the army and joined the 116th Battalion of the Chasseurs Alpins in the front line at Verdun. By the end of the war he had been commissioned and wounded three times.

Back in civilian life, Fourcaud worked for the Standard Oil Company, but maintained a close association with the army as a reserve captain specialising in intelligence. It seems that he might also have been associated with the Right-

Bliesbruck in Alsace. It was while lying in hospital that he heard the broadcast in which de Gaulle pledged to carry on the struggle. Escaping via Spain, he reached London in July 1940.

After the war Fourcaud, by now a colonel, continued to work in counter-espionage, and continued to have difficulties with his colleagues — one of whom was Wybot, against whom he had plotted successfully in 1943.

In 1950 Fourcaud was dismissed when a report by his friend General Georges Revers on the situation in Indo-China reached the public

THE TIMES MONDAY FEBRUARY 8 1999

France loses last cavalier

Paris: Lieutenant-Colonel Jean Ballarin, who in January 1941 led the last charge on horseback in the history of the French cavalry, against the Italians at Umberga in Eritrea, died aged 85, friends said. *(Reuters)*

SOUVENIR du 2S - 138

THE HEADQUARTERS CLUB, 4 ST. JAMES'S SQUARE, LONDON, S.W.1.

The Chairman of Wyre Forest District Council
has pleasure in inviting

Councillor D. Knowles and
Mrs. Jennifer Knowles.

to a Presentation by Monsieur Pierre Lefranc
President de L'Amicale des Cadets de la France Libre
of a ceremonial sword, in recognition of the association between
The Ecole Militaire des Cadets, the town of Bewdley and Ribbesford House

at Bewdley Museum, Load Street, Bewdley
on Saturday 26th June 1999 at 12noon

A Buffet Lunch will be served
(Please present invitation on arrival at Bewdley Museum - Thank You)

R.S.V.P. by 26th May 1999 to Heather Jones, Leisure Secretary, Leisure Services,
99 Coventry Street, Kidderminster, Worcestershire DY10 2BL.
Tel: (01562) 732654 Fax: (01562) 732667

Free French Cadets Presentation Ceremony

Saturday 26th June 1999 At Bewdley Museum

Order of Ceremony

11.45 am - 12 Noon Guests arrive and register at the Museum entrance and are shown through to the marquee where soft drinks will be served.

Les Invités arrivent et s'inscrivent à l'entrée de Musée.

12 Noon The Civic Party and V.I.P.s process from the Guildhall through the Museum with the Ceremonial Sword to the marquee.

Le Groupe Civique et les Personnages de Marque se rendent au Musée.

12.10 pm Introduction of Guests and welcome by the Head of Leisure Services, speech and presentation of the Ceremonial Sword by Monsieur Pierre Lefranc, President de L'Amicale des Cadets de la France Libre.

La présentation d'Invités et accueille par le Chef de Loisir avec le discours et sa présentation.

The Chairman of Wyre Forest District Council will receive the Sword on behalf of Bewdley Museum.
Monsieur Pierre Lefranc will then call for a toast.
The Chairman will then lead the Civic Party and V.I.P.s from the marquee through the Museum to the permanent display case, where the Ceremonial Sword will be placed in situ and the display declared officially opened.

Le Président de Wyre Forest District Council recevra l'épéé. Monsieur Pierre Lefranc portera un toast. L'Epéé sera apportée au Musée et l'exposition sera ouverte.

1.00 pm The Guests will re-assemble in the marquee for light refreshments.

Les Invités rassembleront dedans la grande tente pour des rafraïchissements léger.

3.00 pm Proceedings conclude.

Fin de la réunion.

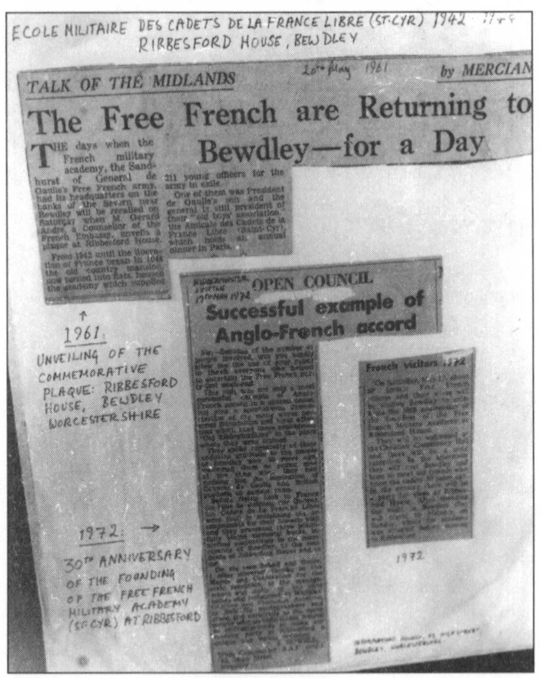

Un exemple d'exploit de Résistants

Traversée de la Manche en canoé canadien

16-18 Septembre 1941

Au moment de la déclaration de guerre, en septembre 1939 — j'ai alors 15 ans — je me trouve avec ma famille en vacances à Fort Mahon, une petite station balnéaire située à une dizaine de kilomètres au nord de l'embouchure de la Somme.

Mon père, ingénieur civil de l'aéronautique, travaille pour le compte de l'O.N.E.R.A. Comme sa présence à Paris n'est pas nécessaire, il décide, suivant en cela les conseils du Gouvernement de rester à Fort Mahon. Un certain nombre d'estivants ayant fait de même, l'Université de Lille y ouvre, pour la rentrée d'octobre, un cours secondaire.

J'y fais la connaissance de Pierre Lavoix, fils d'un avoué près la Cour d'Appel de Douai, qui prépare comme moi la première partie du baccalauréat et dont le frère Jean-Paul se trouve en quatrième avec le mien, Guy.

Au moment de la débâcle, en mai 1940, les Lavoix récupèrent un canoë canadien, en fort bon état, rejeté par la mer.

Le cours secondaire ayant été fermé en juillet 1940, juste après les examens, je prépare math. élém. sous la direction de mon père, les Lavoix prenant de leur côté des leçons particulières. De temps en temps, nous nous retrouvons pour faire du canoë ; les Allemands ne s'y opposent d'ailleurs pas.

A la fin du mois de juillet 1941, je rencontre un garçon de 16 ans venu de Saint-Denis, où son père est directeur d'école, dans l'espoir de trouver à Fort Mahon une organisation clandestine de passage en Angleterre dont il a entendu parler, mais qui en fait n'existe pas.

Nullement découragé, il envisage alors de faire la traversée en canoë canadien. Pour cela, il achète à un pêcheur un canoë que celui-ci a trouvé échoué sur la côte. Comme ce bateau est très endommagé, il l'amène chez mes amis Lavoix où nous entreprenons de le réparer.

Lefebvre a trouvé un équipier pour faire la traversée, mais lorsque tout est prêt, celui-ci renonce. Mon frère qui n'a pourtant que 15 ans 1/2 se propose de le remplacer. Informé de son projet, il me vient à l'idée que, si les Lavoix décidaient également de gagner l'Angleterre, nous pourrions effectuer la traversée avec les deux canoës, ce qui réduirait sensiblement les risques, une embarcation pouvant toujours aider l'autre. Je prends donc contact avec eux : ils me donnent sans tarder leur accord.

Nous rassemblons le matériel nécessaire : des pagaies simples, des sièges, une toute petite voile taillée dans un rideau, deux casseroles pour écoper, une chambre à air d'auto car trois d'entre nous ne savent pas ou peu nager, deux boussoles, une lampe de poche, un réveil, un drapeau français, un fusil de guerre et 40 cartouches que Lefebvre tient à avoir pour le cas où nous rencontrerions une patrouille allemande. Comme vivres, nous disposons de sucre prélevé sur nos maigres rations, de 10 kg de pain, de quelques biscuits de soldat, d'un peu de rillettes et de 14 litres d'eau. Nous décidons d'emporter, en outre, quelques objets personnels, dont certains des plus inattendus : c'est ainsi que mon frère emmène une bible et moi, mes livres de Math Elem.

Le mauvais temps retarde notre départ. Finalement, dans l'après-midi du 16 septembre, l'état de la mer s'améliore très nettement et le vent tourne à l'est. Le départ tant attendu est fixé pour le soir même.

A 20 h. 30, nous quittons notre villa en compagnie de Lefebvre qui y a vécu avec nous pendant près d'un mois à l'insu de notre père que nous avons préféré ne pas tenir au courant de nos projets et nous nous rendons

ECOLE MILITAIRE
des CADETS de la
FRANCE-LIBRE

SAINT-CYR

ANNUAIRE

Publié par l'Amicale des Cadets
de la France Libre (Saint-Cyr)

Deuxième édition

1958

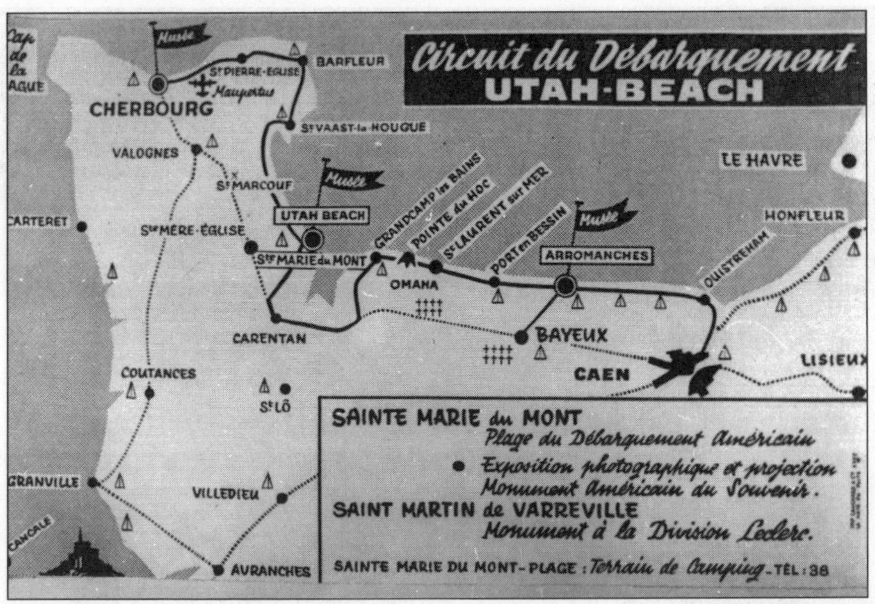

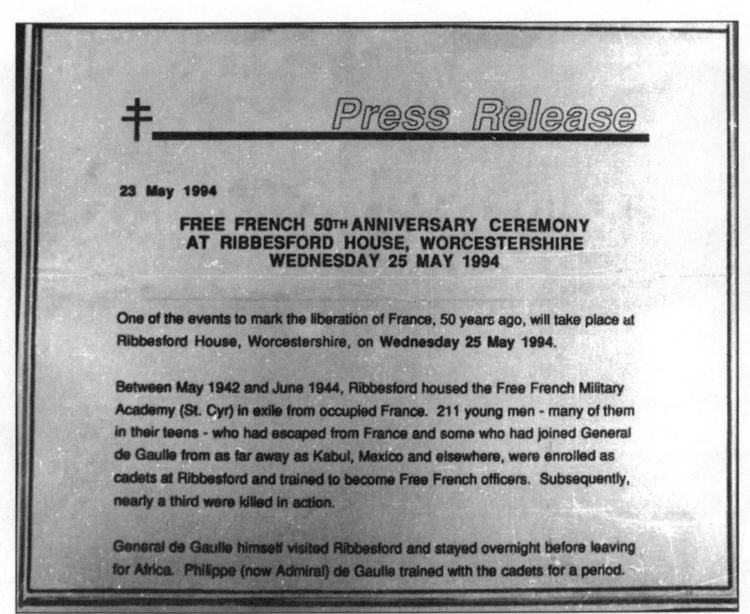

Press Release

23 May 1994

FREE FRENCH 50TH ANNIVERSARY CEREMONY AT RIBBESFORD HOUSE, WORCESTERSHIRE WEDNESDAY 25 MAY 1994

One of the events to mark the liberation of France, 50 years ago, will take place at Ribbesford House, Worcestershire, on **Wednesday 25 May 1994.**

Between May 1942 and June 1944, Ribbesford housed the Free French Military Academy (St. Cyr) in exile from occupied France. 211 young men - many of them in their teens - who had escaped from France and some who had joined General de Gaulle from as far away as Kabul, Mexico and elsewhere, were enrolled as cadets at Ribbesford and trained to become Free French officers. Subsequently, nearly a third were killed in action.

General de Gaulle himself visited Ribbesford and stayed overnight before leaving for Africa. Philippe (now Admiral) de Gaulle trained with the cadets for a period.

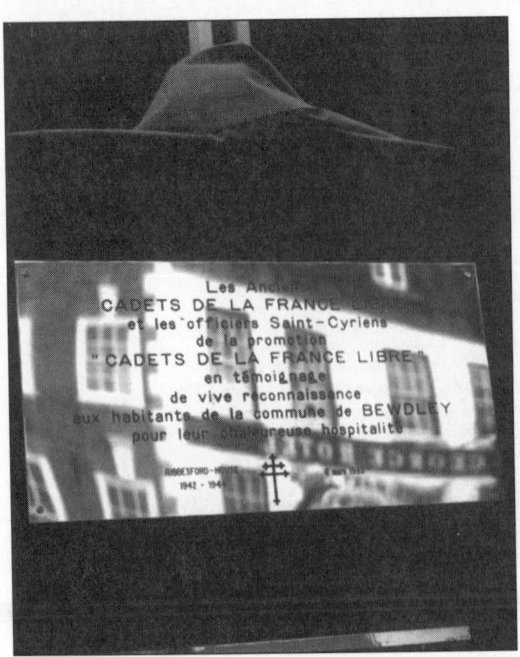
CADETS DE LA FRANCE
et les officiers Saint-Cyriens
de la promotion
"CADETS DE LA FRANCE LIBRE"
en témoignage
de vive reconnaissance
aux habitants de la commune de BEWDLEY
pour leur chaleureuse hospitalité

ES CADETS
DE LA FRANCE LIBRE
EN FRATERNEL HOMMAGE
A L'HOSPITALITE DE LEURS
ALLIÉS BRITANNIQUES
DANS CETTE DEMEURE
DE MAI 1942 A JUIN 1944
L'ECOLE MILITAIRE DES CADETS
DE LA FRANCE LIBRE
CONTINUANT SAINT-CYR
A FORMÉ
CINQ PROMOTIONS D'OFFICIERS
POUR LA LIBERATION
DE LA FRANCE
THE FREE FRENCH CADETS
IN GRATEFUL MEMORY
OF BRITISH HOSPITALITY

L·E·I·S·U·R·E

Bewdley at War
FREE FRENCH CADETS
AT RIBBESFORD
THE SWORD

Jennifer Knowles ***Jean-Paul Lavoix***

Veteran freedom fighters present sword to museum

A GROUP of French second world war veterans visited Bewdley last Saturday to present the museum with a ceremonial sword commemorating the town's wartime connection with freedom fighters.

Monsieur Pierre Lefranc, president of the Free French Veterans Association, handed the sword to the museum in recognition of the strong links formed by the Free French cadets' use of nearby Ribbesford House as a military academy from 1942 to 1944.

General Charles de Gaulle chose the house as a training base for members of the French military forces who had escaped to these shores following the Nazi invasion.

The young cadets spent a lot of time in the town, forging friendships with the community which have lasted until the present day.

More than 100 guests attended the ceremony, including military officials from both Sandhurst Military College in Hampshire and its French equivalent, Saint Cyr.

The sword will now form the centrepiece of an exhibition focusing on the relationships that developed between the Ecole Militaire des Cadets, Ribbesford House and Bewdley during the war.

Other items on display at the exhibition include a kasoar, the traditional ceremonial head dress of the academy, and a cavalry instructor's kepi.

The sword was received by Councillor Mike Oborski, Wyre Forest Council's vice chairman, who was particularly pleased to be involved as his father had met and entertained General Charles de Gaulle in Poland in 1920.

■ Pierre Lefranc, president of the Free French Veterans Association, presents the ceremonial sword to Councillor Mike Oborski, deputy chairman of Wyre Forest District Council.

NEWS BRIEFS

THERE will be bingo at the Wribbenhall Community Centre on Monday July 5 from 7pm. There are plenty of prizes available and lots of fun is promised for all. For more information ring 01299 402670.

WRIBBENHALL Womens' Institute are presenting a talk about the life and work of Noel Coward on Monday July 12.

The talk will be given by Mr C J Russell and takes place at Wribbenhall Community Centre at 7.15pm.

Non-members will be charged £1.50.

A MUSIC fan is appealing for instrumentalists to join her scratch symphony orchestra in a public rehearsal and performance of Schubert's *Unfinished Symphony*.

Rachel Greenwood is looking for grade 5 string players, plus players of the following instruments; flutes, oboes, clarinets, bassoons, trumpets, horns, trombones and the timpani.

The performance which will take place at Wribbenhall Parish Room on Sunday July 18 from 4-6pm. Contact Rachel on 01299 402513.

THERE is a blood donor session at Bewdley High School, Stourport Road, on Sunday 4 July from 10am to noon and 2-3pm. For information about being a donor call 0345 711 711.

THERE will be an art display at the public library from Saturday 3 July till 29 July.

The display, entitled *Pastel and Paint*, is the creation of Beryl Percival and June Lapworth, two members of Kidderminster Art Society, and will feature paintings, ceramics, sculptures and silk paintings, based on flowers and local scenes.

A BIBLICAL musical, called *Rock on Simon Peter*, will be performed at the St Anne's Church Centre on Friday 2 July and Sunday 4 July.

The show follows the life of Christ through the eyes of his disciple, St Peter, and is a rock musical in the tradition of Jesus Christ Superstar.

There are hopes to tour the show around the Midlands after the show in Bewdley, which starts at 8.15pm.

Tickets cost £3 and £2 for concessions. For further information ring 01299 402275.

Private

LOAD STREET, BEWDLEY

Further Items - 12 September 1999

Jennifer and I first met members of the Peplow family at the Centenary dinner of Worcestershire Cricket Club on 3rd September - Richard and his wife Rosalind, their son Francis and Richard's sister Sarah Reilly. The Peplow family are a long established Worcestershire jewellers. I noticed that Sarah was wearing a silver Free French charm bracelet. They explained that Richard's late father Augustus and aunt Gladys indeed had association with the Free French. Richard remembers wearing a Free French badge as a child. Indeed, two certificates of thanks were given to the Peplow family for helping the Free French, dated 18th June 1948 and 15th January 1946, signed by de Gaulle himself. I thank them dearly for allowing me to photograph and reproduce the documents and silver charm bracelet.

I must formally record that Phillippe de Gaulle, son of the General, stayed at Ribbesford House for a short while to attend a military training course. Alas, Phillippe is not on the photograph of the contingent of officers at the house.

Finally I record with gratitude, respect and pleasure the lists of the Free French at Ribbesford House - Promotion, Liberation; Morts Pour La France. My thanks again to Columb and Merryn, who also generously lent the interesting map of Ribbesford House dated 1938, showing the distance to Bewdley to be $1\frac{1}{2}$ miles and to Worcester 14.

I wish to sincerely thank the staff at Stargold for their excellent work. Any mistakes are mine.

ASSOCIATION DES FRANÇAIS LIBRES

Président d'Honneur : Général de Gaulle

Président : Général de Corps d'Armée de Larminat

12, Rond-Point des Champs-Élysées
PARIS-VIII°

Téléphone : Élysées 90-85 77-14
Adr. Télégraphique. Freefrench-Paris

LE PRÉSIDENT

Paris, le 18 Juin 1948

Le Président de l'Association des Français Libres a l'honneur de vous remettre le Diplôme de remerciements accordé par le Général de GAULLE aux étrangers qui ont activement aidé la France aux heures difficiles et vous témoigne à cette occasion ses sentiments de bien cordiale sympathie.

Le Général de Corps d'Armée de LARMINAT
Président de l'A.F.L.

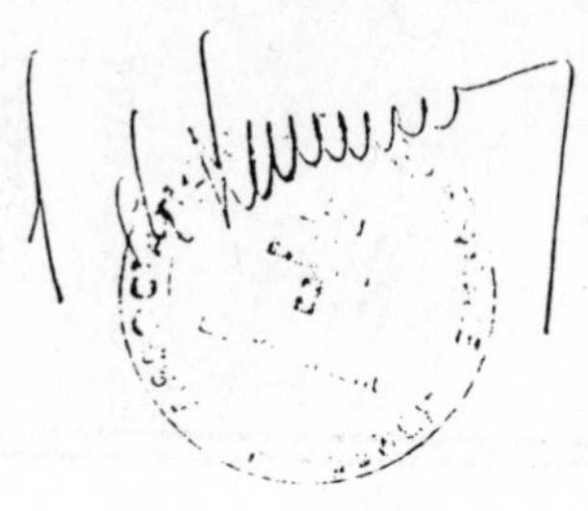

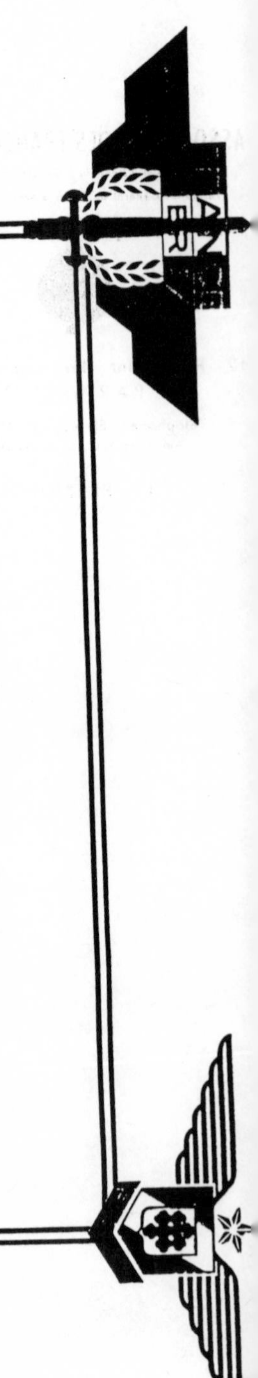

LE GÉNÉRAL DE GAULLE

REMERCIE M. W.A. Peplow Esq.

de l'aide généreuse qu'il n'a cessé de prodiguer aux **VOLONTAIRES DES FORCES FRANÇAISES LIBRES.**

La France libérée n'oublie pas ses amis des temps difficiles.

15 Janvier 1946

C. de Gaulle

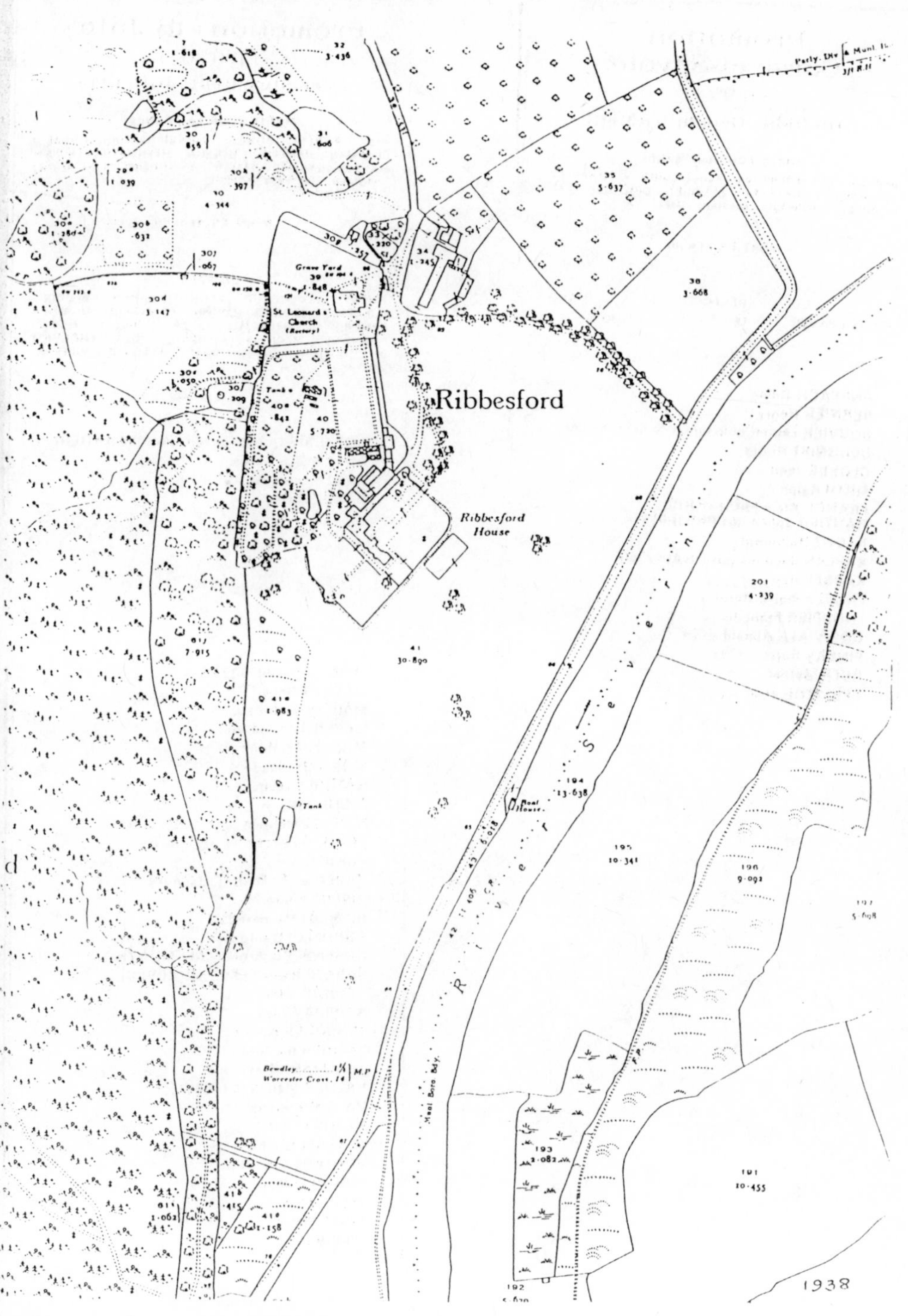

Ribbesford
Ribbesford House
St. Leonard's Church (Rectory)
Grave Yard
Tank
Boat House
River Severn
1938

Promotion « Corse-et-Savoie »

129e/4

Juin 1943 - Décembre 1943

MORTS POUR LA FRANCE

BARRÈS - BEAUFRÈRE (dit Charles DUROC et STAEHLE) - BOULANGER - CHATENAY - CHUQUET - DIGO Guy - FAFA (dit BUSSY) - HERBOUT - MARIANI - METZ

MORT EN SERVICE

BACUEZ

DÉCÉDÉS

CURTIS - HARDRE - POOLE - SCHERDLIN - TUROVER

ANSPACH Gilles
BERNIER Henry
BOUVIER Léon (Compagnon de la Libération)
CEUGNIET Roger
CLOSSE Jean
FIRTH Ralph
FRANCK Alain (dit HARRIS)
GAUTIER Julien (dit PHILIPPE)
ILLOUZ Raymond
KAPLAN Jacques (dit CHAPLAIN)
KASSEL Harry
LAGÈZE Pierre-Henri
LOCUFIER François
ODE-VIALA Ronald
PINSKY Boris
RUFF Marcel
SERVIERE Jean

Promotion « 18 Juin »

129e/5

Décembre 1943 - Juin 1944

MORTS POUR LA FRANCE

ALIX - BANZET - BOSCQ - BUISSIÈRE - BURGUIÈRE - CHAPMAN - DARRIEUX - GEILLON - HEYNES - LEGENDRE - MARX (dit HEBRARD) - MAYER - SAINT-DENIS (dit DUCHESNE) - VIGUIER - WEYL (dit BARRERE)

MORT EN SERVICE

EDME M.

DÉCÉDÉS

ALIFAT - ARMENGAUD - ARON (dit CARON) - BLOUIN - BONNEVAL - BOUZOLS - CHOPIN - DELALANDE - DUPOUY - EDME R. - KATZ (dit CASTEL) - LAZAR - L'HUILLIER - PERES - RANVILLE - RICCI (de) (dit DENIS) - SICÉ - THOUVIOT de CONINCK - TREBUCQ - VITTE - WEMAERE - WEYL (dit WALLON)

AGSTERIBBE Patrick (dit Georges ASTIER)
ARVENGAS Serge
BAILLY Louis
BARBIER Paul

LYON Gilles (dit GILLES)
MARBOT René
MARTIN Jean-Paul
MEYER Jean-Gabriel
MORAND Gabriel
MORTIER Claude
NATUREL Jacques
NICOL Joël
NIDELET Maurice
PAOLI Louis
PHILIP Olivier
RABEC-LE GLOAHEC Jacques
RIBERT André
RICHERT Raymond
ROCHELLE Georges
ROSENBERG Armand (dit MONTROSE)
SABATIER Jean (dit DARCHIVES)
SAVIGNY Marc
SCHILTZ Aloïse
TENSORER André
TERRIER Bernard
THALMANN Raymond
VALLIER Claude (dit WEYL)
VAUTRIN Michel
VERGES Paul
VOELKEL Charles
VOILLERY Claude
WAGNER Jean
WAHL Jean
WAHL Pierre
WEISS Louis

166

Promotion « Fezzan-Tunisie »

129e/3

Décembre 1942 - Juin 1943

MORTS POUR LA FRANCE

DIAMANT-BERGER - HERLAUT - HULOT - JÉANNE - LANDAIS - LEFEBVRE - LEMARINEL (Compagnon de la Libération) - LYON-CAEN - WITT

DÉCÉDÉS

BERTHON - BOUGUEN - FOLLIOT - GALLIÉ (dit BRAULT) - LEFEVRE - LEHRMANN - NOUVEAU (Compagnon de la Libération) - VASCHALDE - VOURC'H

BEADLE Roy
CACHERA Jules
DEMOREST Jean-Jacques
DUNO Maurice
HENRY Charles
LEJEUNE Marcel
MARTIN d'ESCRIENNE Jean
MIDDLETON Georges
SCHLOESING Olivier.

Promotion « Bir-Hakeim »

129e/2

Juin 1942 - Décembre 1942

MORTS POUR LA FRANCE

BLANCHARD - CAMORS (Compagnon de la Libération) - LIGAVANT - PIERREPONT - TABURET - TAYLOR (Compagnon de la Libération)

MORT EN SERVICE

WRENACRE

DÉCÉDÉS

BLOCH - BOUFFARTIGUE - LOEILLET

ALLIOT Louis
BILLARD Georges
COUTANT Henry (dit CORTA)
DREYFUS Daniel (dit PLOWRIGHT)
LANCIEN Yves
XOUAL Guy

Promotion « Libération »

129e/1

Décembre 1941 — Juin 1942

MORTS POUR LA FRANCE

BRIAND - DUCHÊNE - FÉVRE (Compagnon de la Libération) - GAULTIER de CARVILLE - LE ROUX - LESPAGNOL - SEITÉ (Compagnon de la Libération) - TARAVEL

DÉCÉDÉ

MECHIN

ARNAULT de LA MÉNARDIÈRE Hervé
CASALIS André
DULUAT Michel
LAURENT Étienne
MULSANT Robert
PELLÉ Jean

CADETS
MORTS AU CHAMP D'HONNEUR

ALIX (J.L.)
BACUEZ (A.)
BANZET (R.)
BARRÈS (C.)
BEAUFRÈRE (P.)
BLANCHARD (J.)
BOSQ (J.)
BOUCLET (J.)
BOULANGER (C.)
BOURGEOIS (Q.)
BRIAND (J.)
BUISSIÈRE (J.)
BURGUIÈRE (A.)
CAMORS (J.-C.)
CHAPMAN (F.)
CHATENAY (J.)
CHUQUET (P.)
COLCANAP (R.)
DARRIEUX (B.)
DIAMANT-BERGER (J.-C.)
DIGO (G.)
DIGO (J.)
DUCHÈNE (J.)
FAFA (M.)
FÈVRE (J.)
GAULTIER DE CARVILLE (G.)
GEILLON (A.)
HAINAUT (R.)

HERBOUT (M.)
HERLAUT (J.)
HEYNE (L.)
HULOT (L.)
JEANNE (J.)
LANDAIS (P.)
LEFEBVRE (R.)
LEGENDRE (G.)
LEMARINEL (J.)
LE ROUX (L.)
LESPAGNOL (G.)
LIGAVANT (M.)
LYON-CAEN (G.)
MARIANI (F.)
MARX (J.)
MAYER (A.)
METZ (P.-A.)
PIERREPONT (G.)
SAINT-DENIS (J.)
SEÏTÉ (F.)
TABURET (A.)
TARAVEL (M.)
TAYLOR (G.)
TORRÈS (G.)
VIGUIER (G.)
WEYL (F.)
WITT (C.)
WRENACRE (R.)

BERBERIAN Jean
BERNARD Jacques
BERNHEIM André
BERTHOUMEAU François
BILLET Christian
BLANC Guy
BLIN Albert
BOISSIÈRE Jacques
BOKANOWSKI Étienne
BOYE Marc (dit BOYER)
BRAUN Jean-Pierre
BRIAULT Charles
CALONNE LE CAMUS Pierre
CANTIN Yves
CASSEL Raymond
CERA Pierre
CHAMBURE (de) Yves
CHARLES Marcel
CHEVRIER Henri (dit Henry LESLIE)
CORTADELLAS Yves-Bertrand
CRAIPIN Guy
CRÉMIEUX Claude (dit CORMIER)
DELILLE Georges (dit Arthur RICHARD)
DESMAISONS François
DESROUSSEAUX Guy
DUPREZ Bernard
ENGELS Joseph
EYMOND Jean
GAITZ Robert
GANAY (de) André
GEORGELIN Louis
GÉRARD André
GESKIS Robert
GILBERT de GOURVILLE Louis
GOLENDORF Alix
GONTHIER Marcel
GUIBERTEAU Paul
GUNZBURG (de) Alain
HANNEBICQUE Jacques
HAUSSMANN Philippe (dit NICOT)
IRIART Michel
KAUFMANN Jacques
KURK Anthony
LAGAILLARDE Jean
LEFRANC Pierre
LEMOINE René
LUCY de FOSSARIEU (de) Louis

Chapter Nine

WHAT LOCAL PEOPLE RECALLED

I now begin to put together the particular recollections of local people.

Mr and Mrs Birch say de Gaulle was at Ribbesford House in 1940. They saw him on several occasions. They lived at Winterdyne House, very near to Ribbesford House where Mr Birch's father was a chauffeur and groom for the Sturt family. Mr Birch was in the armed forces and left Bewdley after 1940. So they are certain of De Gaulle's early time here. I have not been able to find anyone else who recalls De Gaulle being at Bewdley in 1940, but if we consider that he was there on a reconnaissance, then perhaps. But de Gaulle did not arrive in England until June 1940.

David George remembers the Free French marching over Bewdley bridge, and suggests they may have been going to the Rifle Range for target training. "They carried guns and wore helmets with a bar across the top." David attended Wribbenhall School.

Judy George was extremely helpful to me. She gave me the photograph of Bewdley1950, wrote letters containing information and clues to follow up. She makes the valid point that many ordinary people "were busy getting on with their own lives." But she adds, the French were known and accepted. "Local girls were escorted out by the French men, higher rank preferred." Margaret Phelan of Kidderminster, a high school girl, recalls the older 6th form girls cycling over to dances with the young French men at Bewdley.

Bill Mason, deputy Mayor of Bewdley - remembers the Free French and Americans in Bewdley. In the area were Axis prisoners - Italian and German and many displaced persons from Estonia, Lithuania etc.Bill says Morley Hall near Cleobury Mortimer was a place where refugees stayed. He talks too of the

American Tanks at Sturt Common and tanks breaking up the pavements in Bewdley, during the black-out, presumably the same tanks and vehicles which were later used for the D - Day landings, 6 June 1944, (Bill was born 14 November 1925).

Eric Baildhan (born 18 December 1917) was stationed at Dog Lane Camp with the Royal Army Service Corps.There were two platoons. He remembers the Free French in 1942 and 1943 at Ribbesford. Eric later served in North Africa and was torpedoed on the Strathallan in 1943. Of the 1500 crew, 500 lost their lives. He also worked at the US Hospital Base at Burlish.

Eva Landon has vivid recollections of the Americans being in their Dog Lane camp, and, said David George, Canadians. It seems another camp could have been in the Sunflower fields past Bewdley High School. Eva and Judy commented upon the 52nd US Army Hospital at Wolverley. They also saw the fires of Coventry and Birmingham after bombing. I have spoken with other people who also witnessed the fires from Kidderminster, some 20 to 30 miles distance.

Eva lived in the White Cottage at Habberley Valley, which was bombed by a German aeroplane. She has more pleasant memories of the Free French coming to tea. Italian prisoners helped to make Richmond Road. They were based at Lea Castle and Columb Howell says Italians were also in the Ribbesford House area.

Mrs Helen Collins has lived in Bewdley all her life, and had ten children. She remembers a bomb going off at Ribbesford, "everybody flocked to see it, but I was too busy washing napkins."

Marge Scriven, whom I met at Mayor Making, 22 May 1998 lived in Bewdley during the War. She recalls "the Free French, the banquets, dances and the men with white rufflets on their sleeves."

In May 1998, I visited Harold Fernihough, aged 82, at Liveridge Farm, Heightington. He had known two of the Free French, Grego - a black man from Martinique, who settled in Bewdley and Johny Francois, a man recently deceased, but who also lived the rest of his life in Bewdley. Harold went to a Free French party at Ribbesford House. He recalls the Americans being, "here today, gone tomorrow - a lot of soldiers - then there weren't". There were US Military Police who drove jeeps around the three towns, they had cigarettes, dollars and pounds. Fights with English were regular, but Harold liked the Yanks. He says the US Army were very noticeable at Burlish near Stourport, Wolverley and Bewdley. Harold described War as, "the philosophy of the lunatic asylum." The British Army billeted soldiers on his farm, 20 soldiers once commandered a field and a shed and put up a searchlight. The troops came and went regularly, none stayed very long. Two German prisoners worked on the farm and stayed until 1946.

For their talks with me about the period, may I also thank Mr Terry Seal (born 1927), Mrs Josie Tongue, David Hugh Morgan, Ted and June Harrison.

Tom Webb, aged 77, said the Parachute Regiment visited The Free French at Ribbesford House 4 or 5 times before D-Day. Tom has remained in touch with Free French until the present day.

I met Mr and Mrs Richardson at the 26 June Free French sword presentation ceremony. Mr Richardson was in the crowd who saw De Gaulle outside Bewdley Town Hall in 1942.

I contacted Lord Williams, who has extensive knowledge of De Gaulle, but alas not about his time in Bewdley.

Acknowledgments and Thanks

Mr Fred Kleinbardt.
Fred was based at Burlish US Army Hospital in 1943, 44 and 45. He married Bea, a local girl and later returned to the States. We remain good friends with the Kleinbardts and Madge Wells, of Kidderminster, Bea's sister.

Mrs Judy George (nee Jordan) - for all of her help and information about 52nd Army Hospital, Wolverley and the Free French, also her many tips for sources of information and suggested contacts.

Mrs Hilda Carter who had lived in Dowles Road. Her husband Albert was in the 6th Airborne Division, and took part in D-Day landings in France. He walked out to the boats at Dunkirk in 1940. She recalls the Free French in Bewdley.

Mavis Addison - Her memories of the Free French and of Johny Francois.

Jeffrey Tolley - of Winbrook, recalls Free French and Americans in Bewdley and Burlish. The English were at Dog Lane. Jeffrey had been a miner in Highley. (born 1930)

Percival Powell of Lyttelton Road (born 1928), spoke of the Free French and Americans being based at Dog Lane (English also) and at Kinlet. After 1945, squatters settled in the camp, they were Bewdley people, including a Mr 'Trotsky' Bourne. The field belonged to Mrs Cooper of the George Hotel.

Tony Goodwin - mentioned bullet holes in the weather vane at Ribbesford Church - Free French target practice?

George Timmis, Lilian and Jim Dredge - my uncles and aunt - for their help and chats about that period and others, before and after 1942 - 1944.

Jennifer, Natasha and Keiran - for their help.

Conrad Bourne; his aunty remembered the Crown Prince of Jordan, Hussein being based at Areley Kings during the War and of course, the Americans.

Maisie Parker of Chaddesley Corbett. Worked with my mother Florence, at Carpet Trades making bullets all through the War.

Ken and Barbara Crump. Ken remembers the bomb at Harry Cheshire School being dropped.

Sheila Jones (nee Wright) explained 27 July 1999 - her infant sister Jean had died aged 18 months and was buried in Ribbesford Church. She remembers being in a family group wishing to attend her sisters grave, but on that occasion, being denied access for security reasons relating to the Free French.

May I thank especially Councillor Paul Gittins, The Mayor of Bewdley, for allowing me to photograph the signed portrait of General de Gaulle dated 8/4/43, "Au Lord Maire de Bewdley."

REFERENCES

"Charles De Gaulle." Jackson, Julian . Sphere Books 1990

"De Gaulle." Ashcroft, Edward. Odhams Press 1962

"De Gaulle." Crawley, Aiden. Collins 1969

"De Gaulle." Sheenan, Andrew. Longman 1993

"Memoirs of Hope." De Gaulle, Charles.
Weidenfield and Nicolson 1971

"The Last Great Frenchman." Williams, Charles Littlebrown 1993

"De Gaulle - the rebel 1890 - 1944." Lacoutre, Jean.
Collins Harvard 1990

"De Gaulle - the ruler 1945 - 1970." Lacoutre, Jean.
Harper Collins 1991

"Kidderminster Since 1800." Tomkinson and Hall 1975.
Published by the authors, printed by Bewdley Printing Co.

"Worcestershire within living memory."
Worcs. Federation of Womens Institutes. 1995
Countryside Books, Newbury.

"The War in Pictures" Odhams Press, London 1948

Kidderminster Shuttle

Worcestershire County Record Office

Kidderminster Borough Records

Kidderminster Library

Bewdley Library

Bewdley Town Hall and Museum, Council Records

Mayors Parlour, Bewdley

Wyre Forest Leisure Services & WFDC

Worcestershire County Council

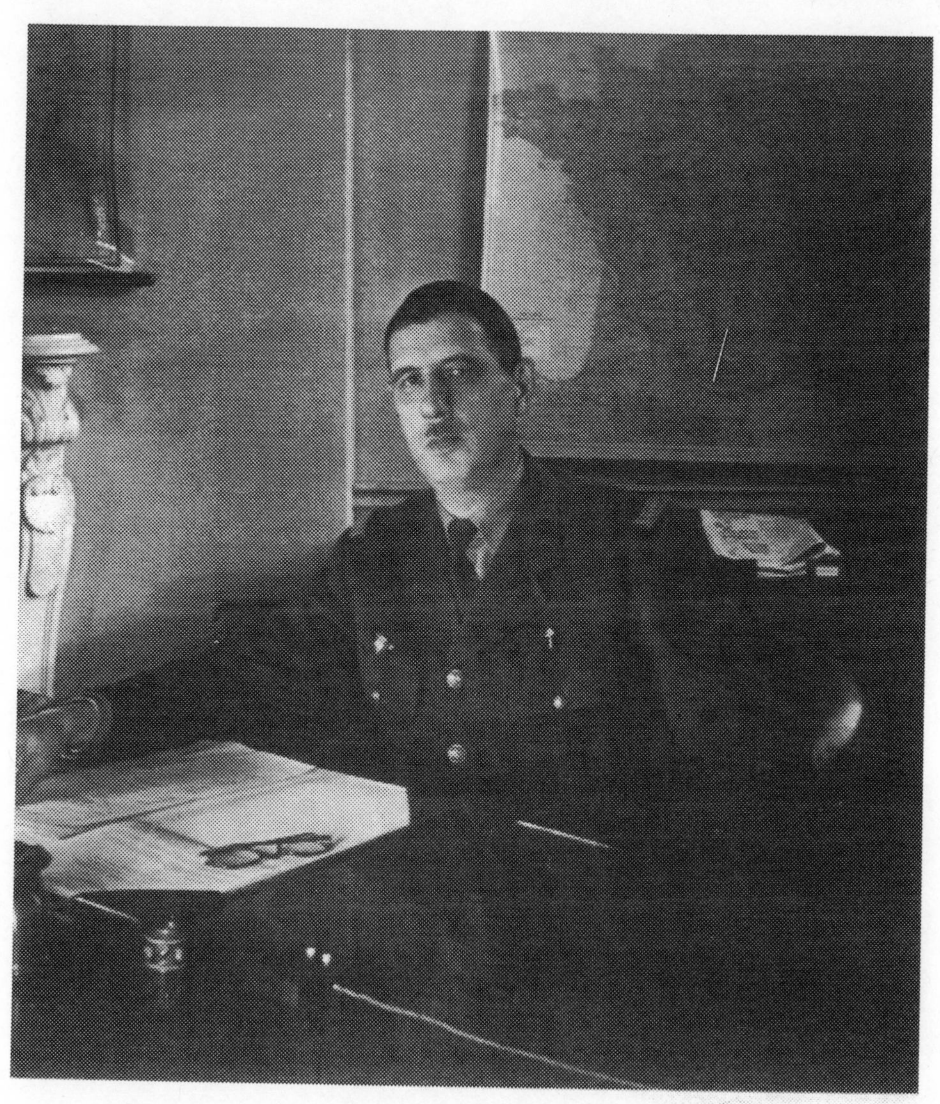